MW00512839

THE SOCIOLOGY OF SPORTS

REVISED FIRST EDITION

Edited by Brandon Lang
Bloomsburg University of Pennsylvania

cognella® | ACADEMIC PUBLISHING

Bassim Hamadeh, CEO and Publisher
Carrie Montoya, Manager, Revisions and Author Care
Kaela Martin, Project Editor
Celeste Paed, Associate Production Editor
Emely Villavicencio, Senior Graphic Designer
Alexa Lucido, Licensing Associate
Natalie Piccotti, Director of Marketing
Kassie Graves, Vice President of Editorial
Jamie Giganti, Director of Academic Publishing

Cover image copyright © by Depositphotos / mazzzur.

Printed in the United States of America.

cognella® | ACADEMIC PUBLISHING
3970 Sorrento Valley Blvd., Ste. 500, San Diego, CA 92121

Contents

SECTION 3
Technology and Sports

SECTION 6
Sports, Politics, and Business

DEDICATION

This book is dedicated to

my wonderful mother, Ariel,
who has always supported and encouraged me;
my beautiful wife, Molly,
who has always been there for me;
and my amazing children, Adam, Sarah, and Nathan,
who love me unconditionally.

Thank you.

Acknowledgments

I have always been a very big sports fan. Although I have used my socio-logical training to make sense of sports for years, I did not study or teach about the sociology of sports until after graduate school. I am grateful to my colleagues in the Sociology, Social Work, and Criminal Justice Department at Bloomsburg University for giving me the opportunity to teach the sociology of sports. I found my proverbial calling in this area and absolutely love it.

Putting together this book has been a dream come true for me. I am so appreciative of the time and energy with which John Remington and everyone else at Cognella Academic Publishing have provided me. John, Monika Dziamka, Carrie Montoya, Kaela Martin, and everyone else I worked with answered all of my questions and gave me so much guidance along the way. I would like to express my sincere thanks to all of the authors who contributed to this book. Your contributions and insights have really gone above and beyond what I could provide on my own. I would also like to thank the reviewers who took the time to offer thoughtful critiques that have really served to improve the book.

Lastly, I would like to thank my family. My mother, Ariel Lang, is especially generous and has taken me to many sporting events, bought me merchandise, and supported the athletic endeavors of my kids. Similarly, my sister-in-law, Megan Monahan, indulges my interests in sports in numerous ways. She, too, is a very generous and supportive person to me, my wife, and my children. Although my dad and father-in-law are both deceased, I bonded with each of them over sports. Together, we went to countless games, tailgated, and experienced the so-called thrill of victory and the agony of defeat. Although my wife is not a great sports fan, she has been to more baseball stadia than she can count and has always been so encouraging of me playing sports and going to sporting events. She has helped me to heal after breaking bones playing hockey and has always encouraged me to stay fit. My three kids, Adam, Sarah, and Nathan, are active children who enjoy physical fitness and being outside. I will fondly remember our days of playing wrestle basketball and dodgeball long after they grow up.

Preface

The sociology of sports is a growing area of sociology that has brought together scholars worldwide to study the social dynamics of athletics at all levels. In recent decades, sociologists have published research and other writings that have helped to generate more of an understanding concerning the social dimensions of sports. This book is a collection of writings from academic scholars who study sociological issues that apply to sports, ranging from inequality and education to gambling and crime. My goal is to prompt readers to see how vibrant and interesting the sociology of sports really is and to ultimately encourage them to look at sports more sociologically.

THE PURPOSE OF THIS BOOK

The main purpose of this book is to acquaint readers with some of the many very interesting findings that have been made by social scientists who study different aspects of sports. Articles have been chosen for this book that really make sense of a number of social issues pertaining to sports. Collectively, these articles work to communicate the idea that sports have many beneficial qualities—while also having their share of problems.

One aim of this book is to celebrate sports. Sports remain a very positive force in the lives of tens of millions of Americans who play sports, go to sporting events, and follow their favorite teams. Think of how big the Super Bowl has become. Super Sunday is as big a day in the lives of many Americans as the Fourth of July or Easter. It has become an unofficial holiday in the lives of millions of people around the world and is connected with food, alcohol, and even gambling. There is no question that sports have improved the quality of life for millions of Americans. Playing sports and attending sporting events and rooting for particular teams make up a very big part of people's identities. Some people love sports so much that they get team tattoos on their bodies, name their pets after legendary athletes, propose to their partners at sporting events, and have team-themed weddings.

Additionally, this book will introduce readers to the concerns that many people have regarding sports. Many people are concerned about the connection between inequality and sports. Numerous athletes of color have faced racial taunting in recent years. Similarly, many others are very strongly opposed to the idea of women participating in male-based leagues such as the PGA and NASCAR. For many, youth sports and amateur sports have spiraled out of control. There is great concern that many youth athletes are pushed too hard and that amateur organizations like the NCAA and the Olympics have become increasingly professionalized and even corrupt. Other concerns that people have relate to the downside of sports gambling, fan and player violence, and increased ticket prices.

THE SCOPE OF THIS BOOK

This book consists of six sections. Section 1, "Looking at Sports Sociologically," defines sports and examines the different theories used by sociologists to make sense of people's motivations for participating in sports as players, fans, coaches, executives, and so on. Section 2 is called "Inequality and Sports." In this section, the chapters identify how social class, race, gender, and religion connect with sports. The third section, "Technology and Sports," considers ways that technological innovations and the mass media have affected sports. "Amateur Sports," Section 4, considers how sports have changed over time at the youth and collegiate levels. Section 5, "Fan and Player Behavior," examines how violence and gambling connect with sports. Section 6 is titled "Sports, Politics, and Business." In this section, the chapters look at the political and economic ramifications of sports. Finally, I conclude the book by examining the current state of sports in the United States.

This is an updated edition that has more recent information concerning a host of issues including the connection between the Black Lives Matter movement and sports, sports gambling, the relocation of professional teams, and fantasy sports. Two new readings have also been added to this book. The first one considers the importance of social media in the lives of athletes, sports media personalities, team executives, and fans, alike. The second one examines the positive role that sports play in the emotional, mental, and physical development of adolescents.

I hope that you enjoy reading this book. Whether you are a huge sports fan, a nonfan, or somewhere in the middle, sports play a huge role within the social context of American life. Knowing more about the social dimensions of sports provides valuable insights into human behavior in general.

Brandon Lang
Summer 2019

SECTION 1

Looking at Sports Sociologically

A variety of academic disciplines can be used to further people's understanding of a wide range of sports-related issues. For example, physiology helps medical practitioners understand, among other things, why athletes get injured and what can be done to facilitate healing during the rehabilitation process. Similarly, psychology aids people in understanding the role that many psychological variables—such as self-confidence, determination, and a desire to win—has in sports. Even business helps people understand the financial implications of running professional teams, marketing team merchandise, and publicizing team events.

The field of sociology provides academics with a framework to understand the social dynamics of sports. Sociology produces a plethora of research that really helps to explain the social implications of athletics at the youth, amateur, and professional levels. For decades, sociologists have helped to explain numerous sports-related issues relating to the challenges that minority athletes have historically faced, concerns that exist with the growing commercialization of sports and dozens of others. At its core, sports is a human endeavor. People play sports, they attend live games, and they take their kids to games and tournaments. Because of this, sociology is the perfect discipline to develop a meaningful understanding concerning the vast array of social relations that exist within sports.

In this section, sociology is defined; the history of the discipline is outlined; and its connection to sports is established. More specifically, Chapter 1 defines the sociology of sports and examines many of the temporal and spatial changes that sports have undergone. Chapter 2 explores the theoretical traditions within sociology and applies each of them to sports. Together, these chapters identify and explain why sociology is such an important academic discipline in which to study sports.

CHAPTER ONE

What is the Sociology of Sports?

BY **BRANDON LANG**

A fascinating topic of inquiry, the sociology of sports really enhances people's understanding concerning the nexus between people and sports. Sociologists have studied everything from the challenges faced by youth athletes to the off-the-field behavior of professional athletes and recruiting strategies used by many NCAA colleges and universities. In this chapter, sociology is explained, sports are defined, and trends within the sociology of sports are discussed.

WHAT IS SOCIOLOGY?

Sociology is a relatively new academic discipline compared to more traditional ones such as history or English. Although its origins trace back to the late 19th century, most North American colleges and universities did not offer sociology classes until after World War II.

Since then, sociology has become a mainstream discipline with classes and majors being offered at most colleges and universities. Examples of some of the many classes offered around the country include the sociology of the family, inequality, environmental sociology, and sociological research methods.

In its most general form, sociology can be defined as the study of people. Sociologists study human behavior and people's corresponding motivations in a vast array of different social contexts and settings. There are two distinct branches of sociology. Quantitative sociology follows the scientific method and seeks to obtain and interpret data in an objective and empirical manner. Quantitative sociologists use closed-ended surveys with defined answer sets that look like multiple-choice exam questions. This is amenable to the creation of variables such as gender, degree of support, or opposition to any number of social issues such as divorce and abortion, political orientation, and education. These variables can be analyzed in such a manner that uncovers the strength and direction of the relationships among them. Qualitative sociology, on the other hand, uses such research methods as observation or fieldwork, interviews, and open-ended surveys. Although qualitative sociology has been criticized for being subjective, it has helped academics uncover insights relating to sensitive questions about drug use, sexual behavior, and other personal matters that most people are reluctant to answer honestly on conventional surveys.

Although sociology classes tend to be fairly specific, sociology, as a whole, is a very broad academic discipline. Because sociology relates to the study of human behavior, there is a huge number of topics that can be studied sociologically. In order to promote an in-depth understanding of social issues, sociology graduate students specialize in two or three areas of study. Similarly, sociology classes are organized around particular themes. Most schools offer classes that focus on specific topics such as religion, race, work, and even sports.

Lastly, sociology is a progressive discipline whose practitioners are oriented toward social change. Sociology faculty and students were very involved in the antiwar protests and feminist rallies that took place on dozens of American university campuses throughout the 1960s and 1970s. Most sociology classes tap into some form of inequality and seek to enhance students' understanding of how different groups of people perpetrate and experience discrimination.

DEFINING SPORTS

Sports can be defined in any number of different ways. For the purpose of this book, we define *sports* as a physical activity that is oriented toward competition between players and/or teams. Of course, there are different gradations of physical activity and competition. Sports do not just include activities like organized football and swimming that are very physically demanding and require a huge commitment. People who golf recreationally or play Wiffle Ball at the beach are also playing sports, regardless of whether or not they are keeping score. As it turns out, keeping score is a very interesting social construct because even if players or teams are not keeping score, they are still likely to have a sense for which players and teams are the best. Ultimately, this unofficial ranking of players and teams is often meaningful for people in terms of their self-confidence, interest in the sport, participation in leagues, interaction with others, and so forth.

Some physical activities are, clearly, more fitness oriented than others. Golfers who walk the course are exerting themselves more than golfers who ride in carts. Similarly, cross-country skiers are exerting themselves more than downhill ones. In some cases, the same activity may be considered to be a sport in some situations and not considered a sport in others. Consider fishing, for example. Taking two hours to reel in a 120-pound marlin is a sport. Meanwhile, sitting in a boat and drinking beer while casting a line into the water is more of a leisure activity.

WHAT IS THE SOCIOLOGY OF SPORTS?

The sociology of sports can be defined as the study of people who play, watch, support, organize, and report on sports played at the recreational, amateur, and professional levels. The sociology of sports, like sociology itself, is a very broad subdiscipline that examines sports as they unfold in myriad social contexts. For instance, sociologists of sports study everything from the unfolding of race, class, and gender in different sports to sports gambling, the business of sports, the challenges faced by amateur athletes, and politics and sports.

As mentioned above, sociologists of sports do not just study people who play sports. The sociology of sports studies fan behavior, the parents and family members of athletes, and people whose job it is to manage teams, train players, and help athletes manage their finances. In short, sports play a large role in American culture, and sociologists have studied many aspects of it.

SPORTS, TIME, AND SPACE

There is no question that sports have evolved over time. Think, for example, about how advanced the equipment used by today's athletes is. It is far superior than it was even 20 or 30 years ago. Among other things, this has prompted and coincided with a number of changes in the rules of many sports. Sports are also played differently in different parts of the world. Not only are different sports played in different parts of the world, but the same sports, like basketball and football, have different rules in different countries.

TECHNOLOGY

Technological advances have changed the face of sports over the 20th century. Technology allows players to heal faster from injuries, compete at higher-than-ever levels, and break records that have stood for decades. Consider how the Speedo LZR swimsuit revolutionized swimming or how footwear has evolved. If Wilt Chamberlain could score 100 points in Converse Chuck Taylor sneakers, imagine what he could do in Air Jordans. An obvious example of technological development is racing cars. NASCAR vehicles have improved so much that restrictor plates are used on oval tracks to keep the speeds down. In other words, if their speed was not governed, these cars would travel much faster than would be safe.

In the span of 70 years, golf clubs went from being made out of aluminum and wood to lighter-weight composite fibers, titanium, and zinc. The clubs that many golfers use today are much lighter, have a bigger sweet spot on the club head, more spin control, and have more whip/bend in the shaft than older models ever did. Today's golf clubs are so advanced (and expensive) compared to older models that recreational golfers can drive the ball much farther than older professional legends like Ben Hogan ever could. In fact, many older golf courses have become obsolete in that professional players can practically drive the ball to the green. Although many players welcome these changes, so many technological advancements have been made that the argument could be made that golf is a very different game from what it used to be.

Ice hockey is an example of another sport whose equipment has changed drastically over the years. Today's hockey equipment is much lighter and more protective than it ever was. Goalie pads are lighter, stronger, and more durable than they were even 20 years ago. Like golf clubs, the hockey stick has really changed over the years. In the 1960s, players like Gordie Howe and Frank Mahovlich used heavy wooden sticks with straight blades. In that era, players had difficulty raising the puck and shooting with the accuracy that a lot of today's players take for granted. Meanwhile, today's hockey sticks are made of composite materials that make them very light. Furthermore, the blades are curved and have a fair amount of lift to raise the puck off of the ice with ease. Of course, this comes with a cost. A top-of-the-line composite stick costs about 20 times more than a run-of-the-mill wooden stick.

Another area that has evolved over time is medical technology. Many of today's athletes use hyperbaric chambers, nutritional supplements, and other nutrients to promote healing and work to prevent some injuries. Shattered bones, torn ligaments, and other medical problems that have ended the careers of thousands of athletes over time do not have the long-term effects they once did. Tommy John surgery—named after the successful MLB pitcher whose blown out arm was surgically reconstructed using a breakthrough procedure in 1974—exemplifies the strides that have been made in modern medicine. As recently as 25 years ago, an athlete who tore his or her ulnar collateral ligament would have been forced to retire. Today, a fairly routine surgical procedure can rebuild the throwing arm of a baseball pitcher and have him or her back in the game after a year or so.

An additional development concerns the development of technology to assist game officials in making the correct call. For years, tennis tournaments have used the Cyclops and Hawk-Eye devices to ascertain if a serve is in or out. With today's players hitting the ball harder than 200 km/hour, the ball simply moves too fast for the line judges to correctly judge if a ball is in or out. More and more sports are using instant replay to see if players are in-bounds after they make catches in football, to see if pucks cross the goal line in hockey, and balls clear the fence in baseball.

The advancement of mass media represents an additional factor in explaining why sports have changed over time. Thanks to the Internet, sports fans can watch games from all over the world. With subscription packages like NHL GameCenter and NBA League Pass, fans living in one part of the world can watch games happening in another. Internet sites like myp2p.eu and atdhe.net also allow fans to watch pirated broadcasts of thousands of different sporting events for free. All of this has resulted in more interest around the world. The Yankees have a growing base of loyal fans in Japan and many other parts of Asia, while Newcastle United has fans throughout Australia, Africa, and Canada who can watch all of the games with ease.

The Internet has done more than allow fans to watch games. Blogs, newspaper articles, and websites like grantland.com allow people to follow sports very easily. We have come a long way from box scores on the sports page and baseball cards. The Internet can be used to instantly call up statistics and other information relating to injuries, salaries, and trades.

RULE CHANGES

Another way that sports have changed over time is that rules have been amended and altered to a great extent. In the NHL, for example, the two-line pass rule was eliminated in 2004. In NCAA basketball, it was not that long ago that a three-point line was created and a shot clock was introduced. Similarly, rules have been created to limit helmet-to-helmet contact in the NFL, pitchers hitting batters in Major League Baseball, and players diving in soccer.

Rules change for a variety of reasons. In some cases, they have been changed to promote scoring. The NHL expanded the offensive zone in 2004, and the NCAA created a three-point line to make it easier for players to score points. That is similar to why overtimes and shoot-outs were implemented in many levels of professional and amateur sports like football and hockey. Simply put, many fans were not that excited by the prospect of a game ending in a tie. In other cases, rules have been changed to promote player and fan safety. The NFL's current protocol is to sit players out who have experienced head trauma and only allow them back on the field once a trainer has monitored them. Leagues have passed rules that terminate alcohol sales well before games are over.

PROFESSIONALIZATION

Many observers note that youth and amateur sports are becoming increasingly professional-ized. Like most things, this carries with it some benefits and some concerns. One benefit is that young players today are able to devote themselves fully to a sport. Many youth athletes train year-round, play on high-profile travel teams, and are coached by talented and dedicated mentors. The commitment is substantial, but many youth athletes respond positively to the high expectations placed upon them. Another benefit of the professionalization of youth sports is that many young athletes are able to attend special camps and tournaments where they garner exposure from college and professional coaches and improve their chances of turning pro.

One concern that many people share is that youth sports are more expensive than ever. Having special coaches, paying for extensive travel, purchasing equipment, and establishing a brand, if you will, is very costly. Youth sports are also more time consuming than ever before. Today, elite youth athletes travel extensively, train harder than ever, and, in many cases, devote their lives to their respective sports. The biggest concern people have about youth sports is the phenomenon of burnout. So many youth athletes train so hard; they play so much and immerse themselves so fully in their sports that it becomes more like work than fun for them. Thousands of youth athletes grow so tired of parents yelling at them and coaches pushing them so hard that they decide to quit the sports they excelled in.

COMMERCIALIZATION

A central theme in the sociology of sports is that most sports have become increasingly expensive over time. Playing sports, attending sporting events, and purchasing team gear are far more expensive today than they were in times past. The rising cost of sports has greatly outpaced inflation and resulted in a situation where a growing percentage of people are priced right out of sports.

Recreational athletes of all ages are paying more money for fees and equipment than ever before. Through the late 1980s, a top-of-the-line hockey stick was made out of wood; it would last for much of the season and cost around $20. Today, a mid-range composite stick costs around $200. Now, athletes pay hundreds of dollars for footwear, baseball bats, golf clubs, swimsuits, lacrosse sticks, and other necessary pieces of equipment. Joining teams requires more money than before to pay for multiple jerseys, cover insurance costs, and pay for the use of facilities themselves. Whether we are talking about ski lift tickets, rounds of golf, or recreational hockey, the costs to use the facilities are prohibitively expensive for many people.

Numerous academic studies have noted that the costs of attending a professional sporting event have escalated in recent years. Not only have the premium tickets become more expensive, but so have the proverbial cheap seats. A standing-room-only ticket for an NHL game will cost around $50, while a seat in the highest level of the outfield of an MLB game costs around $20. If you combine these costs with those of parking and concessions, it can be easily seen that going to a sporting event is a very expensive proposition. A family of four could easily spend $500 going to a Pittsburgh Pirates, St. Louis Cardinals, or Chicago Cubs game once all of the costs are tallied.

And now, the cost of team gear is higher than ever. Most professional teams have team stores, and websites sell everything from branded baby onesies and a range of casual clothing to game-used items. Of course, all of these products are very expensive. Authentic jerseys cost $250, caps cost $40, T-shirts $25, and jackets can cost as much as $60. This is a lot of money for most people.

When talking about commercialization, we can also examine the increasing connection between advertising and sports. Teams no longer have just power plays in hockey or get to the red zone in football. Rather, they have corporate underwriting for them. For example, the Philadelphia Flyers have the PECO power play and the Pittsburgh Steelers play in the Heinz Red Zone. Of course, this happens in conjunction with stadia named after corporations; stadium entrances named after other corporations; signage everywhere in the stadium, including on the ice in hockey, on the stairs in basketball, and over the men's urinals in football. We also have dozens of consumer products that are the official deodorant of this league and the official sausage of that league. Needless to say, many sports fans and nonfans alike have concerns with this practice.

CULTURE

So far, all of the listed changes in sports are temporal changes. It is also worth noting that at the same time, the very same sport could be played differently in various parts of the world. Consider the differences, for example, between American football and Canadian football. Unlike American football that is played on a 100-yard field with four downs, Canadian football is played on a 110-yard field with three downs. Moreover, Canadian football has a wider field and deeper end zones; 12 players are used instead of 11; a different size ball is used; and receivers can be in different stages of motion before the snap. These are two very different types of games. American football is a fall sport, while Canadian football is played in the summer. The Canadian version also tends to be much higher scoring than its American counterpart.

These same kinds of differences apply to hockey and basketball, among many other sports. European hockey is played on a much bigger rink than its North American counterpart. In general, European hockey is oriented toward finesse and is not very physical, while Canadian and American hockey revolves less around the idea of puck possession and is very physical. Similarly, basketball teams in Israel and throughout Europe play on shorter courts, use slightly larger balls, have different-sized keys, and have different three-point lines from NBA teams.

The cultural differences in sports can be explained with regard to the variations between professional baseball in Japan and North America. There are, of course, some differences. Japanese baseball, for example, tends to be played on smaller fields than North American baseball. Japanese baseballs and strike zones are also bigger than their North American counterparts. There is a host of cultural differences as well. Different foods are served, and different norms are observed by fans. Japanese baseball fans are expected to return foul balls to ushers who, in turn, return them to the home team. Many Japanese fans are part of supporter clubs who chant, blow whistles, and make much more noise than typical North American baseball fans.

CONCLUSIONS

In general, the sociology of sports has helped people to understand the social bases of sports. Using sociological insights, sociologists have not only examined dozens of social issues that apply to sports, but they have also been able to explain changes in sports across time and space. Both qualitative and quantitative sociologists undertake research that develops insights into many facets of athletics. The next chapter identifies the four different theories in sociology and illustrates how they connect to sports.

CHAPTER TWO

Looking at Sports through a Theoretical Lens

BY **BRANDON LANG**

U nlike the natural sciences, which are guided by a single paradigm, sociology is a discipline with multiple paradigms. It has four distinct schools of thought. Each of these perspectives has different assumptions and explanations for social behavior. When looking at social issues such as crime or divorce, for example, sociologists recognize that there is a host of competing explanations for them rather than a single one. In this chapter, the concept of theory is explained; the four major sociological perspectives are outlined, and each of them is used to explain important elements of sports culture.

WHAT IS A THEORY?

A theory is an explanation regarding a particular phenomenon. Physicists use theories to explain how lunar cycles impact ocean tides and art historians have theories about why different design elements emerged in different historical eras. In sociology, theories are used to help make sense of human behavior. As mentioned above, theories are used to explain such issues as why some married people get divorced and others do not, or why some people go to prison while others do not.

It is important to note that all theories have assumptions. Theories are not what sociologists would call value free, as they are influenced by a wide range of political, religious, and ethical issues. Needless to say, a devout Catholic would likely be drawn to sociological conservative theories rooted in the belief that divorce is bad, and that people get divorced because they lack commitment. Meanwhile, a progressive person would probably be attracted to more liberal sociological theories that reflect the fact that people make mistakes, people grow apart, and divorce is not always that bad for families.

Just because a theory exists, it does not mean that it fully explains a social issue. Sociologists and non-sociologists alike develop theories all the time that really do not have explanatory value. Racist, sexist, and homophobic people, among others, have come up with hundreds of theories that simply are not true. In sociology, theories gain credence by being tested. Theory guides research and sociologists test theories in their academic scholarship. More specifically, research questions that relate to a new or existing theory are generated, tested, and compared with the findings in other studies.

Different sociological theories are used to explain human behavior as it applies to sports. Theories are used to explain a number of issues, including why some training methods work better than others, why some elite kids sometimes drop out of organized sports, and why high school athletes often have higher grades than high school kids who do not play school sports. In short, several sociological theories have been developed and tested to help enhance our understanding concerning the human dimensions of sports. Four of these theories are discussed below.

FUNCTIONALISM

Functionalism is a positive and optimistic sociological theory that seeks to see the best in people. The main assumptions of functionalism are that people are well-meaning, human nature is good, and that people are oriented toward cooperation. The entire theory of functionalism rests on the premise that everyone serves a function within a social system. Of course, there are varying degrees of prestige and status shared by people, but the general idea holds that they all serve a particular role. Sociologists have long used the metaphor of the human body to explain functionalism. The human body consists of different body parts, including the spleen, liver, lungs, and so forth that all serve specific functions and complement each other. In other words, they all serve a different function, yet contribute to the overall functioning of the body. We can use another metaphor—a symphony—to explain functionalism even further. In a symphony, woodwind, brass, string, and percussion instruments play different pieces of music at different tempos using different sounds, yet they work together to produce a collective sound that is greater than the sum of its parts.

FUNCTIONALISM AND SPORTS

Building on the metaphor of different parts of a system working together, a football team can be used to explain how functionalism and sports come together. On a football team, dozens of different players with various body types and skills work together as a team. The role of the lineman is very different from that of the running back. Similarly, the role of the place kicker is unlike that of the defensive back or linebacker. A football team needs a wide range of people with different skills and talents to be successful. People are needed to undertake very specific tasks such as protecting the quarterback, blocking, covering receivers, kicking extra points, etc. A team made up entirely of quarterbacks or punters would clearly lose every game.

Building on the idea that functionalism is a positive perspective, functionalists would agree that sports provide people with life lessons. Sports teach kids respect for authority, as well as humility and grace. Moreover, sports reinforces the notion that hard work pays off, that teamwork is a vital component of success, and that we should always strive for gracious winning and losing, even though this is not always easy. Many retired athletes of all levels have used experiences in sports to guide them as parents, politicians, and teachers, among others.

Functionalists also contend that there can be a strong sense of community among players on a team and even fans who root for a given team. Many players and fans alike have experienced a strong sense of togetherness with other athletes, parents, and fans over the years. This strong sense of attachment is developed among teammates who work together and collectively reach different goals. Similarly, many fans have a strong attachment to

15

other fans whom they sit close to at games, interact with at road games, and tailgate with in parking lots throughout the country. Among those fans who have rooted for their favorite team in the home venue of another team, they have likely bonded over high-fives, chanting, and other types of fan behavior.

CONFLICT THEORY

Unlike functionalism, which has an optimistic view of social life, conflict theorists assert that capitalism often brings out the worst in people. The essence of conflict theory is that within a capitalist society, people are often self-centered, competitive, and only out for themselves. The father of conflict theory is Karl Marx. One of his Marx's main assumptions is that in capitalist societies, a very small percentage of people control a very high percentage of the wealth, leading to what he termed class struggle between those without resources and those with resources. Ultimately, for Marx, wealth is associated with power, and those with resources have much more power than those who do not.

Marx wrote extensively about the class struggle between the bourgeoisie (the so-called *haves*) and the proletariat (the *have-nots*). The haves own and control what Marx terms the means of production, while the have-nots work for the haves. According to this perspective, the haves exploit the have-nots and generate wealth and profit at their expense, which serves to exacerbate their alienation, fuel the class struggle, and pave the way for class revolt.

CONFLICT THEORY AND SPORTS

Conflict theory brings to the table a number of important ideas that relate to sports. One is that sports are, by definition, competitive. Many people see sports as a battle between two individuals or teams. Moreover, contact sports like football and rugby can be seen as a form of warfare between two enemies. Just like war, sporting events produce a winner and a loser, where the winning side often rejoices in its victory, while the losing side often wallows in its loss. Sometimes, this line of thinking even carries over to fans. Think of the tension that exists among rival fans. Rivalries such as the Boston Red Sox and New York Yankees or the

Philadelphia Eagles and Dallas Cowboys, for example, carry with them tension and drama that unfolds in the stands of games.

Another connection between conflict theory and sports is the tension that exists between many professional athletes and team owners. Using conflict theory, the team owners are the haves and do everything in their power to limit the compensation provided to their players, the have-nots. Marx developed the term surplus value to describe how profits are generated. Surplus value is the difference between what it costs to produce a good and how much it can be sold for. In a capitalist setting, Marx argues that the goal of businesspeople is to make goods for as little as possible and sell them for as much as possible. The connection between this and professional sports is that the players in the NBA, NFL, NHL, and MLB are unionized. Labor disputes have become very common, and players have gone on strike in recent decades. A related connection applies to how commercialized sports have become in recent decades. Tickets, concessions, and merchandise are all so expensive that many working- and even middle-class people have been priced out of many sporting events.

SYMBOLIC INTERACTIONISM

Symbolic interactionism (SI) is a nuanced set of ideas that connect to qualitative sociology. One assertion made by symbolic interactionists is that social life is inherently subjective, and that people are always interpreting the social world around them differently. Summed up as "the definition of the situation," a central feature of SI is that different people are likely to define the same social experience in different ways. Although exaggerated, SI tells us that a person who fells trees for his or her livelihood will view a forest differently from a person who feels strongly about the environment. Similarly, an art enthusiast is likely to view a modern painting dissimilarly from someone who is either uninterested or not trained in art.

Another important and related issue among symbolic interactionists is that meaning is inherently subjective. Just because something is meaningful to one person does not imply that it will also be important to others. The same concert, shirt, trip to Hawaii, or apartment, for example, will always convey different feelings to different people. In other words, different people do not necessarily have the same emotional reaction to similar foods, music, experiences, weather, and so on.

SYMBOLIC INTERACTIONISM AND SPORTS

Symbolic interactionism can be used to explain many very interesting aspects of sports. It can help explain why some people find sports so much more meaningful than others; it explains why we feel strongly about the teams we root for and against; and it offers insight concerning the huge amounts of money that people spend buying sports memorabilia.

The very idea that people have varying degrees to which they like sports supports this wider notion that we all define social situations differently. It is not just that some people love sports while others do not. Clearly, some people love certain sports more than they love others. I am not a big NBA fan, but I love college basketball. Curiously, I am not a big college football fan, but I love the NFL.

Symbolic interactionism also helps to explain the emotional reaction that many people have regarding their favorite teams. It is not just that many people in western New York love the Buffalo Bills. Many of them are also likely to strongly dislike the New England Patriots and the other two teams in the AFC East with whom they have strong rivalries. Similarly, a Boston Red Sox fan will probably have a different emotional response to meeting a friend wearing a Yankees jersey than to someone else wearing a Nationals jersey or even a soccer jersey. Supporting a team is very meaningful for people because they likely grew up rooting for them, they probably watched games with grandparents and other family members, and they feel connected to the players and other fans. This is precisely why so many grown men cry like children when old stadia like Veterans' Stadium are razed. It is very hard for them to come to terms with and accept those changes.

As you can see, SI is really good at explaining the emotional connection that many people have with sports. Building on this, think of all the money sports fans have spent on jerseys, hats, trading cards, game-used gear, and other merchandise. They do that to represent their teams. Just like gang members represent their respective gangs by wearing different colored bandannas and hats, fans represent their teams by buying and wearing hundreds of dollars' worth of team gear. It is clearly very meaningful for many fans to show their loyalties and to feel included at games, bars, or parties where they watch games.

FEMINIST THEORY

Feminist theory is the newest of the four sociological theories. It emerged in recent decades as more and more academic attention was being devoted to the broad notion of gender inequality. Although there are different branches of feminist thought, the main ideas of feminist theory borrow from conflict theory. Inasmuch as conflict theory characterizes the tensions that exist between the haves and the have-nots as being economic, feminist theorists contend that the tension between these two groups is rooted in gender. In other words, males are the haves, and females are the have-nots. There is a struggle that exists between these two groups, as males are seen as doing whatever they can to preserve and increase their privileged status, even if it comes at the expense of females.

FEMINIST THEORY AND SPORTS

Feminist theory brings a number of important points to the table relating to the connection between sports and gender. All of these revolve around the idea that femininity is often devalued within the context of competitive sports. This is evidenced by the high percentage of men and women who assume that men are better athletes, coaches, referees, and announcers than women.

One expression of this occurs when males insult other males by telling them that they throw or hit like a girl. Clearly, this is meant to be an insult and a challenge to their masculinity. Sociologists have found that mostly male sports are covered on highlights programs like ESPN SportsCenter, and men who love sports are not that interested in leagues such as the WNBA, the LPGA, and the WTA. Women's sports are often devalued and dismissed as being too low-scoring, not physical enough, or slow paced. In short, there exists a definite double standard when it comes to men's and women's sports. In fact, many male sports fans and athletes have been outspoken against the recent practice of women participating in male-based leagues like NASCAR and the PGA. There is nothing more evident of this than the fact that many women's teams are coached by men, but very few—if any—male teams are coached by women.

CONCLUSION

Sociology is a discipline with multiple paradigms. It is comprised of four distinct schools of thought. Functionalism sees society as being a balanced collection of people who have different roles and complement each other. Meanwhile, conflict theory asserts that there is a great deal of tension and competition between those people with money and those without. Symbolic interactionism outlines that meaning is subjective, and that all of us interpret social reality differently. Lastly, feminist theory is based on the inequality that exists between males and females. Each of these theories discussed above has some important insights concerning sports. In the next section, Inequality and Sports, six different readings examine the challenges that many minority athletes regularly experience.

SECTION 2

Inequality and Sports

It has been evident for decades that inequality and sports are a package deal. Historically, American sports have been segregated, not solely based on race but also according to social class, gender, and religion. Major League Baseball was segregated until 1947; most people assume that women's sports are inferior to men's, and many non-Christian athletes feel obligated to play on high holidays such as Passover. In this section, different articles introduce the concept of inequality, connect it with sports, and identify how programs such as Title IX have been used to lessen inequality within sports.

SOCIAL CLASS AND SPORTS

The main theme of the relationship between social class and sports is that sports are often so expensive that only a limited segment of society can afford to participate in them. Lacrosse sticks, baseball bats, and soccer cleats can easily cost over $100 each. The fees that are associated with sports like golf, hockey, and skiing are steadily rising. Clearly, not everybody has the disposable income to pay for their kids to be involved with sports. In this day and age of travel teams, parents spend thousands of dollars paying for gear, hotel rooms, and private coaching. They also spend countless hours driving to tournaments, practices, and games. The general consensus among sociologists of sports is that kids of limited means grow up playing sports like basketball and football, while wealthier kids grow up playing sports like hockey, golf, and equestrian activities.

A related issue pertains to how expensive it has become to attend a professional sporting event. It was not that long ago that MLB, NHL, NBA, and even NFL games were very affordable. Through the early 1990s, many teams sold upper-level seats for a few dollars. Now, in this era of new stadia, club-level seats, corporate lounges and luxury suites, and tickets to professional sporting events are prohibitively expensive for many people. The average price of sporting tickets has soared in the last 25 years. When that is coupled with increased concession prices and the cost of parking, attending a sporting event could easily cost a few hundred dollars for a family. Events like the MLB All-Star Game, the Stanley Cup Finals, and the Super Bowl have become so corporate and expensive that regular fans either simply cannot procure or afford tickets to attend them.

In their article entitled, "Anyone for Tennis? Sport, Class, and Status in New Zealand," Mark Falcous and Christopher McLeod reaffirm this notion that rich kids often play different sports than poor kids. More specifically, they identify and illustrate that tennis is a sport that not only produces, but also reproduces, social class distinctions. In their ethnographic study of the Oakwood Tennis Club, Falcous and McLeod reveal that middle- and upper-class families are drawn to tennis precisely because of the symbolic capital that it generates. Being part of a tennis family transmits a series of meaningful and important messages relating to a player's taste, skills, education, and health. Although this study was conducted in New Zealand, the authors' contention that sports is a "classifying practice" certainly rings true in the United States as well.

RACIAL INEQUALITY AND SPORTS

Upon looking at the history of sports in the United States, it is absolutely clear that they have been segregated along racial lines for much of their existence. American professional and college sports were largely segregated until the middle of the 20th century. In the case of professional baseball, for example, there were separate baseball leagues for White and Black players. Many cities such as Philadelphia, Chicago, and Pittsburgh had two teams—a Black team and a White team—that often shared the same stadium but maintained different fan bases. Generally speaking, White fans rooted for MLB teams such as the Washington Senators and the Chicago Cubs, while Black fans cheered for Negro League teams such as the Homestead Grays and the Kansas City Monarchs.

Most people know that second baseman Jackie Robinson was the first African American to play Major League Baseball. Many are unaware, however, of the obstacles he faced on a daily basis living in Jim Crow America. When traveling with the team, he often could not eat with teammates or stay in the team hotel, as they did not serve patrons of color. Opposing players threw at his head and slid into second base spikes high while opposing fans insulted him mercilessly. Umpires called balls strikes, and even members of his own team resisted the idea of him playing. This same sort of treatment also characterizes the treatment that trailblazing African American athletes experienced in other sports.

Thankfully, the racial climate in America is not as bad today as it was 60 years ago. That is not to say, however, that race is no longer an issue in American sports. Unfortunately, it is. In recent years, a banana was thrown at Wayne Simmonds, a forward for the Philadelphia Flyers, who is Black. Fuzzy Zoeller, a golfer, made a racist remark concerning the food (fried chicken) that Tiger Woods would choose at a banquet in Augusta after he won the Masters. Similarly, fans at Atlanta Braves games do the Tomahawk Chop while chanting a Native American–sounding chorus. Some people even feel that the imposition of a dress code among NBA players was done to keep them from dressing in a manner that Whites consider to be "too Black." Simply put, when it comes to race and sports, there is certainly room for improvement.

Perhaps the most obvious expressions of racial tension relate to the recent controversy surrounding the decision of dozens of NFL players and other athletes to not stand during the singing of the National Anthem prior to games. Colin Kaepernick, a biracial quarterback playing for the San Francisco 49ers, began this trend during the 2016 NFL pre-season as a way to draw attention to the racial injustice and systematic oppression of minorities that he and many others felt was still occurring in the United States. It did not take long for dozens of other players to kneel themselves and entire teams to lock arms as an expression of solidarity during the anthem in subsequent games. This led to the NFL trying to mandate that players stand during the anthem or stay in the locker room while it was being played. It also appears to have cost Kaepernick his job who went unsigned as a free agent. Despite his talent, teams were reluctant to sign a player who was so outspoken politically.

During this period, many high-profile NBA players, including LeBron James, also offered support for the Black Lives Matter Movement through displaying messages such as "I Can't Breathe" on their shoot-around T-shirts and social media accounts. Black Lives Matter emerged in response to the deaths of Eric Garner, Freddie Gray, and other racial minorities who were, in the eyes of many people, victims of police brutality. Since the early 1980s, the champions of various high-profile professional and amateur sports leagues such as the NBA and NFL were invited to meet the president at the White House. President Trump was so against the practice of athletes using their celebrity to advance political beliefs that ran counter to his own that he went so far as to rescind the invitations of individual players (Stephen Curry in 2017) and entire teams (Philadelphia Eagles in 2017) that won championships to meet him at the White House.

In this section, two articles look at the connection between race and sports. In Chapter 4, entitled "Racism and Stereotyping on Campus: Experiences of African American Male Student-Athletes," Krystal Beamon identifies the numerous challenges that are unique to many athletes of color. More specifically, she identifies the extent to which male African American athletes attending predominantly White institutions experience racism. In the next chapter, entitled "Missing the Point: The Real Impact of Native Mascots and Team Names on American Indian and Alaska Native Youth," Erik Stegman and Victoria Phillips make clear how offensive team names like Braves, Redskins, and Indians really are. They assert that Native mascots and team names reinforce negative stereotypes and have resulted in the discriminatory treatment in particular and the reduced quality of life in general of Native youth. Although a small number of American colleges, including Miami University and Stanford, have changed their team names so as to not offend Native Americans, many professional teams with Native mascots and team names, including the Washington Redskins, have been unwilling to even consider changing their names.

GENDER INEQUALITY AND SPORTS

A third form of inequality that connects to sports is rooted in gender. Although girls and women have made numerous strides over the years, many males continue to embrace the idea that the world of sports is the domain of men. Women are still underrepresented as coaches, referees, team executives, and media personalities. Think of all the controversy surrounding Annika Sorenstam or Michelle Wie playing in the PGA, Danica Patrick racing in NASCAR, or females wrestling against males at the high school level. Many men are resistant to the idea of competing against women for a number of reasons. One is that they often assume that women are not worthy competitors. A second reason is that if they by chance lose to a woman, they will never live down the humiliation of it. A third reason is that women are much more likely to be sexualized than men. As such, many men have bought into the idea that the role of women in sports should be limited to cheerleader and dance team member.

Sociologists talk about people "doing gender." In short, this means that we have come to expect females to act in feminine ways and males to behave in a masculine manner. Men are expected to be tough, insensitive, competitive, and so forth, while women are expected to be docile, sympathetic, and cooperative. This is where the double standard of gender comes into play. When males act in feminine ways or females act in masculine ways, many people feel uncomfortable. Part and parcel of this phenomenon is that tough and athletic women are often assumed to be lesbians, whereas caring and compassionate men are often assumed to be gay. Many Americans, for example, are likely to assume that men who are cheerleaders, figure skaters, or gymnasts are gay because these activities do not fit in with their definition of masculinity. Similarly, many male athletes call opposing players names like "fag" to emasculate them, insult them, and assert their own superiority over them.

In their article, "Where are the Female Athletes in *Sports Illustrated*? A Content Analysis of Covers," Jonetta Weber and Robert Carini make clear that *Sports Illustrated* focuses mainly on male sports. Upon analyzing the content of *Sports Illustrated* covers from 2000 to 2011, the authors found that women accounted for less than 5% of cover images. Moreover, when women were on covers, they tended to share them with men and be oversexualized. Chapter 7, by Mallary Allen, is called "A Closer Look at Title IX" and looks at how federal legislation has been used to offer more sporting opportunities to women at the collegiate level. In addition to tracing the history of Title IX, Allen identifies the many positive outcomes in college sports that Title IX has brought, along with some of the concerns that many have with this controversial piece of legislation.

RELIGION AND SPORTS

Religion and sports come together in two important ways. One way occurs when religious Christian athletes and other religious athletes pray before big games, big shots, and so on. Dozens of Christian athletes make the sign of the cross and invoke God's assistance before, during, and after games. A second way occurs when religious athletes are ill-treated based on their religious beliefs. Many Jewish athletes, including Sandy Koufax, have been criticized for not playing on holidays like Yom Kippur or the first day of Passover. Similarly, the International Basketball Federation (FIBA) does not allow female players to wear headscarves during basketball games, meaning that Muslim women representing their countries have to go against their religion if they wish to play international basketball.

Erik W. Dailey is a Presbyterian minister and academic whose piece entitled "Religion and Sports" identifies and explains the similarities and differences between sports and religion. Ultimately, Dailey establishes that sports are not a religion. Rather, they represent an aesthetic activity that appeals to our senses through emotion and what he refers to as "responsive openness." Although sports and religion are different, they elicit many of the same feelings and passions in people. Both have the potential to inspire awe, bring people together, and give people the expectation that great things will happen.

CHAPTER THREE

Anyone for Tennis? Sport, Class, and Status in New Zealand

BY **MARK FALCOUS** AND **CHRISTOPHER MCLEOD**

"It's hard to think of anything quite as un-Kiwi as our British-based titular honours arrangements. For a country that has discovered its identity on the back of an egalitarian vision, deliberately and unashamedly distancing itself from class and rank, the awards seem … [inappropriate] … Nowhere has this seemed more apparent than in sport."

—Richard Boock, *Sunday Star Times*
(Auckland), 7th September 2009, p. 1

In the above attack on the knighthood 'honours' system as 'un-kiwi', journalist Richard Boock, reinforces the idea of sport as a paragon of egalitarianism and reasserts longstanding myths of Aotearoa as a land of social equality. In this paper we question the frequently aired idea of sport as the most meritocratic of institutions. We argue that sports cultures are far from level-playing-fields and in fact operate in significant ways to create and sustain class-based inequity. In the piecemeal literature on sport in New Zealand, social class has largely been overlooked with analysis instead focussing largely on gender and 'race'. We first historically contextualise the dynamics of social class in Aotearoa New Zealand. We follow with a short discussion of research surrounding social class and sport, and youth sport in particular. We also discuss the work of Pierre Bourdieu in this section. Bourdieu's work underpins the subsequent analysis, which draws upon an ethnographic study of a youth tennis club—Oakwood—to explore the intersections of social class and youth sport.

NEW ZEALAND SPORT, CLASS, AND SOCIAL-STATUS

The prevailing belief that New Zealand society is classless and egalitarian is deeply rooted in colonial circumstance and constructions of white settler—Pākehā-defined national consciousness. As Simon During (1998) notes, settler (national) identity has long sought to reconcile competing claims between British ethno-cultural roots, and the desire for national distinctiveness and legitimacy. That was, the idea of a 'better Britain' gave rise to representations of an absence of class difference, affluence and equality in contrast to a divisive British class hierarchy. These deep-rooted aspects of the national imagination have endured a host of transitions since the neo-liberal turn in the 1980s and the reformulation of the economy, and structures and patterns of employment and trade (see Kelsey 1997). Such transitions complicated the long-standing nature of the dividing lines of class stratification. Furthermore, New Zealand's economy, based on the primary sector of goods production and export (e.g. dairy industry), Bowden (2008) suggests, generates modes and concentrations of employment that are unique to the country. For example, farmers and other forms of self employed tradespeople represent major occupational groups. Thrupp (2001) highlights how these factions vary widely in terms of their resources and class background. Therefore, they do not easily reinforce any particular class stratification (Thrupp, 2001). The second difficulty arises when defining the class make up of the service industry, which has increased significantly due to the limited labour market of the production sector (Bowden, 2008). Indeed, neo

Weberian and neoMarxist theories differ vastly as to whether these workers are most accurately categorised as middle, lower or a mixture of both, classes (see Rudd & Roper, 1997).

National inequality statistics suggest that since the 1980s New Zealand has shifted further from any ideal of equity. Imbalances accelerated in the 1980s with income shares by decile group, and Gini coefficients of pre-tax and after-tax incomes from 1979 through to 1990, revealing an increase in the gap between rich and poor (Chatterjee & Birks 2001). More recently, income comparisons show there is a disparity with around 6.5 times more being earned by the top 20% of earners than the bottom 20% (Wilkinson & Picket, 2009). This places New Zealand in the bottom quarter for equality statistics in developed nations and belies myths of equity. Such transitions, the historian David Hackett Fischer (2012) notes have gone hand-in-hand with an ongoing cherishing of a "heritage of fairness" (p. 490). Fairness, he notes, is deeply entrenched in public discourse and espoused from all points of the political spectrum, despite self-evident inequity.

Achievement in sport has long been significant to the dominant construction of the New Zealand national imagination, and participation in sport is frequently asserted as a fundamental right of its citizens. Indeed, as Boock's comments above convey, sport is often revered as a particularly egalitarian institution. For no demographic are sports' apparent social benefits valued more so than amongst youth. Indeed, there is a widely held belief that all children can benefit from playing organised sport. This is demonstrated by government agencies, such as Sport New Zealand[1] which places emphasis on promoting young people's participation and the subsequent benefits of sport to national performance and well-being (e.g. SPARC, 2011). We consider youth sport to be a field of particular interest when analysing social class, opportunity and ideas of egalitarianism in New Zealand.

A breadth of international research suggests that youth sports experiences are intimately entangled with social class stratification (Sack, 1988; Collins & Buller, 2003; Daykas & Stathi, 2007; Lee et al, 2009; Swanson, 2009, Light & Kirk, 2001). Sack (1988) provides a useful description of how German children from two contrasting sports clubs and class backgrounds learn their specific class habitus through engaging in sporting situations. For example, he shows how children (and parents) from a working class football club and a middle class hockey club practice divergent gait, movement, social interaction, everyday clothing and sportswear options, and refreshment choices. These contrasting practices reflect

---

[1] Formerly known as Sport and Recreation New Zealand (SPARC) until 2012.

differing class backgrounds and also act as distinctive signs which classify the children as belonging to particular class stratifications.

Organised youth sport is inherently shaped by the involvement of adults and unlikely without the input of parents. Therefore, the role of parents is highly influential in determining what sports children engage in and the ways in which they participate. For example, Swanson's (2009) ethnographic study of 'soccer moms' from the USA demonstrates how mothers shaped their sons' sport experience "to produce cultural capital in and through their sons" (p. 412) as a means to reproduce upper-middle-class status and establish an 'appropriate' (middle class) track toward adulthood. The 'soccer moms' used their labour to encourage participation in soccer and guided their sons away from (American) football which they feared as physically harmful.

To date, however, there is no research exploring sport and social class intersection in a New Zealand context. In a fleeting reference Krishnan et al's (2002) survey research indicates there is a relationship between income and New Zealand children's 'sporting chances'. Children whose main source of income was government benefits, for example, were three times more likely than those above the poverty threshold to have 'limited' involvement in sport. Yet, while such findings reveal material barriers to youth sport participation, we are interested in the ways in which social class is implicated in particular lived practices and cultures that include and exclude in sport. Specifically, we are concerned with how class cultures are produced and reproduced in and through sport. It is in that sense that, as several sport researchers have done, we draw upon the work of Pierre Bourdieu as a means to explore sport as both a function of, and producer of, social class.

Unlike many 'mainstream' sociologists, sport was a major theme of Pierre Bourdieu's work. Bourdieu drew upon both Marx and Weber, and saw sports participation as guided by the power of both economic and cultural capital i.e. *both* the capacity and ability to 'fit-in': appropriate behaviour, clothing, competence, etiquette. For Bourdieu, the historical resonance and exclusivity of particular sporting practices to selective class groupings are entangled in a continual striving for different types of capital as a means to distinguish class fractions in the form of class-based distinction. Bourdieu's landmark text, the oft-cited *Distinction* (Bourdieu, 1984), was preceded by a 1978 article[2] in which he advocated analyzing sport within wider

---

[2]The article was a translation of a paper given at the International Congress of the History of Sports and Physical Education Association, held in March 1978 at the *Institut National des Sports et de*

conceptions of social class. The notion of class *habitus* is used by Bourdieu to refer to patterns of behaviour, thought, and taste, which link social structures to practice and action. Booth & Loy (1999) describe it as encapsulating "a system of lasting unconscious dispositions and acquired schemes of thought and action, perception, and appreciation, based on individuals' integrated social experiences under specific sets of objective social conditions (e.g., socialization into a given class)" (p. 5). These 'schema' result in a set of acquired/learned habits, bodily skills, styles, sensibilities, dispositions and tastes, and other non-discursive knowledge that might be said to "go without saying" for a specific class group.

Importantly, habitus is embodied; its schemes are firmly implanted within the body. This is recognised by Bourdieu (1984) as a bodily *hexis*, evident in 'the most automatic gestures or the apparently most insignificant techniques of the body—ways of walking or blowing one's nose, ways of eating or talking—and engage the most fundamental principles of construction and evaluation of the social world' (p. 466). Bourdieu (1984) proposes that, the logic behind a choice to engage in physical activity is influenced by a bodily disposition: 'a sport is more likely to be adopted by a social class if it does not contradict the class's relation to the body at its deepest most unconscious level, i.e., the body schema, which is the depository of a whole world view and a whole philosophy of the person and the body' (pp. 217–18). Examples of this theory in practice include the working class's instrumental relationship to the body which results in their participation in potentially physically harmful sports, whereas the middle classes tend toward an ascetic model of sobriety and control which lends itself towards keep-fit activities (see Booth & Loy, 1999).

The appeal of various sports, then, is wrapped in their symbolism as bodily demonstrations of the particular tastes and preferences of class groups in the struggle to gain social capital. Upon this basis Bourdieu mapped out a series of examples demonstrating how 'the constitution of a field of sporting practices' served a distinguishing function to enable "gains in distinction" (1978, p. 828). He noted the 'hidden' entry requirements such as family tradition and early training, markers such as clothing, 'bearing' and etiquette that connect particular sports—and provide the distinguishing boundaries—to particular class groups. Such 'social markers', Bourdieu (1978) suggests, 'close' certain sports to particular class groupings. Thus, in his analysis of France in the 1970s he notes that golf, riding, skiing

---

L'Education Physique, Paris. It was some time—at least with English speaking sports scholars, however, before his influence became manifest.

and tennis were 'closed' to the working classes. Importantly, however, Bourdieu (1978) also observed that particular sports' connections with class habitus codes can be and are contested. The very same sport, he noted, can "have a very different meaning or function" (p. 832) in varying cultural contexts, citing the widely varying meanings of rugby union for aristocratic adolescents in English public schools compared to those of the sons of peasants in south-western France. A series of studies of sport have drawn on Bourdieu's approach (e.g. White & Wilson, 1999; Schreeder et al., 2002, 2005; Stempl, 2005; Wilson, 2002; Zevenbergan, 2002). Interestingly, Noble and Watkins (2003) note that Pierre Bourdieu himself "was quite a keen tennis player" (p. 521). For Bourdieu, they suggest, this was symptomatic of a consciously sought 'acquired capital' which departed his lowly class origins to see him play what he himself described as a 'bourgeois sport' with an 'aristocratic image'. It is to tennis that we now turn.

The origins of lawn tennis can be traced to medieval court systems and the European aristocracy (see Gillmeister, 1998). In its modern form the game's social meanings were profoundly shaped by the class dynamics of late Victorian Britain. In this context, Lake (2011) notes, the game came to be defined by a specific set of behavioural norms, expectations and codes of conduct. Playing tennis, he notes, was "a means for the socially aspirant upper middle classes to enhance their social standing and to demarcate themselves from social inferiors" (p. 878). For the middle classes, tennis was an excellent means to generate 'cultural capital'[3]. The game at this time became firmly attached to the ethos and rules of amateurism, which was disdainful of playing for pecuniary gain. Under this ethos "playing style and conduct . . were of utmost importance" (Lake, 2011, p. 878). Thus, protocol, behavioural restraint, dress codes and 'fair play', both within and beyond the rules, characterised tennis.

The global diffusion of tennis saw new pressures and interpretations emerge. Subsequently, the game has undergone transitions and at the elite level professionalism superseded amateurism following the Second World War. Notably, however, in spite of major changes to the sport, in terms of the social context of how tennis is played, the amateur ethos has remained a potent legacy (Jeffreys, 2009). Indeed, Lake notes that whilst how the sport is played has changed in terms of etiquette, and an increasing focus on winning, elements of

---

[3]The upper classes, Lake (2011, p. 878) notes, "soon dropped the sport, except in their patronage of clubs and associations in light of increasing middle class participation."

the long-standing 'social character' of tennis have remained. Thus behavioural codes have continued to be influential in the everyday experiences of tennis.

In New Zealand, little has been written about tennis. The governing body Tennis New Zealand (TNZ) (formally the New Zealand Lawn Tennis Association) dates back to 1886. The NZLTA was affiliated to the Lawn Tennis Association (England) which reveals the significance of colonial linkages and suggests that class based codes of amateurism would have diffused with the game itself. There is, however, also evidence of Māori participation, with Sir Apirana Ngata a significant patron in the creation of an independent Māori tennis movement. This independence resulted from the exclusionary requirements of dress codes and subscriptions to clubs which restricted the game to "the well off members of society" (Reedy, 2006, p. 16)[4]. Such an initiative indicates the New Zealand game as enwrapped in class and colonial politics. The everyday experiences and social dynamics of tennis participation, however, are undocumented.

EXPLORING (SPORTS) FIELDS OF DISTINCTION

The field research component for this paper entailed a small-scale, ethnographic study at Oakwood Tennis Club[5] in a large New Zealand city. The study involved observation of the day-to-day lives of those who played, spectated, and worked in the youth section of the club during a summer season. This included three youth coaches, the club's head coach, the youth coordinator and the children in six youth teams and the parents of these children. The children's ages ranged from 9 to 13. Time in the field was split into two periods. In the first period the fieldworker established himself as a volunteer and immersed himself in the club and built rapport. During this time the fieldworker helped run a day long youth tournament hosted by the club, attended squad coaching and children's coaching sessions, accompanied interclub teams to games, and participated in a fundraiser.

During the second phase of fieldwork the field worker identified six interclub teams as a research focus, attending after-school squad training and accompanied them to weekly game. During this period the field worker interviewed parents and children and made

---

[4]Ngata, a champion of Māori land retention and development, politician, leader, scholar, and writer is widely credited with the creation of the New Zealand Māori Lawn Tennis Association in 1926.
[5]This name, and all those used within the paper, are pseudonyms.

observations. Interviews were semi-structured and conversational. Group interviews were also used depending on the situation. All interviews were organised informally and as the opportunity arose. During this period the coaches and the youth coordinator interviewed. The interviews were transcribed and the data categorised into themes and subthemes constructed through deduction. Ethical approval for the project was granted by the University of Otago ethics committee.

Oakwood Tennis Club is an established club being founded in 1925. The club moved to its current premises in the centre of a large (29 hectare) multipurpose sports and recreation park in the affluent suburbs in 1978. The complex boasts a well maintained club house and ten courts and is situated beside a children's playground. The local suburbs are categorised as middle to upper middle class status. The demographic of the area is largely Pākehā, however, there is also a notable south Asian population. In order to understand the relationship between social class and youth sport we categorise tennis at Oakwood as a *classified* practice (i.e. appealing to a specific taste and class habitus), and as a *classifying* practice (i.e. playing a part in constructing children's habitus and serving as a marker of position in social space). Thus, we view tennis as *both* a function of, and generator of, a middle class habitus.

TENNIS AT OAKWOOD AS A CLASSIFIED PRACTICE

> I think it's ... two hundred and sixty dollars, a season, and that's just to play, that's not um the gear or the time or anything like that, there's no way that a lot of families. I mean even we ... baulk at it really, cause that's just for summer (Stuart, 5/1/11)

As the quotation above demonstrates, parents were acutely aware of the financial cost of playing tennis at Oakwood. Despite concerns about the cost, the parents remained resolute in support for their child's participation. We suggest this is because involvement coheres with particular bodily habitus codes and is seen to offer advantages in reproducing middle class status and hence social advantage in the next generation. As Booth and Loy (1999) note, "self restraint, discipline, sobriety, frugality, and piety—the hand maidens of hard work—combined with individual competitiveness frame the ethical and aesthetic preferences of the middle classes" (p. 13). Below we endeavour to construct what practicing tennis means at Oakwood. Specifically, we will focus on how participants judged and appreciated the benefits of tennis.

Michael, the father of a 12 year old boy playing for the club, provides a view on the social benefits of tennis.

> He's ... going to have a good game of tennis and hopefully win ... and I think it's a bit of a metaphor for later in life, if you can meet someone new and interact and get something out of it um ... yea I think it's ... we all have to do that and the sooner you learn to do that, the better it is and ... an individual sport like tennis is really good for that, you know, soccer is almost, possibly a little bit against that because you can get together and mutter with your team ... and so that doesn't really teach you to deal with an issue (Michael, Parent, 5/1/11).

Here, Michael values tennis because it provides 'life-lessons' for his son, particularly, the importance of taking individual responsibility. This idea reflects the aspiring upper middle classes' preoccupation with self improvement and, particularly, social mobility. Michael alludes to specific lessons that his son is learning in tennis which will transfer into the competitive job market. This 'lesson' is specifically suited for facilitating the interpersonal interactions that are a requirement of middle class trajectories: job interviews, tertiary education, and 'making contacts' in which being able to meet and interact with new people is critical. That he may 'hopefully win' is clearly secondary. The value of tennis in this sense is alluded to explicitly by the head coach at Oakwood below:

> I see why a lot of people, parents, put their children into sport, I mean tennis is a tough sport to be good at and it teaches kids a lot of skills in terms of being extremely competitive, whether they grow up to be competitive tennis players or whether they are competing with people in the job market later on or at university (Brian, 14/1/11).

A further connection with middle class habitus codes was the view of tennis as judicious planning for the future, and in facilitating lifelong participation in sport. This is demonstrated in a series of parental quotes below:

> I think tennis is quite important, it's a sport that kids can play all their life, there's only three sports kids can do all their life ... tennis, golf and skiing (Doug, 5/1/11).

> I think the main reason people like their kids playing tennis is because it's something that they will always have and can play forever (Daniel, 5/1/11).

> You can play it through your whole life, you see seventy year olds still playing ... you can't get seventy year olds playing rugby really so ... I guess ... they are trying to think for their later life as well, it's a great sport to learn, a great skill for the rest of your life (Anita, 16/1/11).

> It's a sport that you can play throughout your lifetime (Ian, 11/12/10).

Here, parents laud tennis as providing long-standing opportunities—that is, investments of capital at an early age are judged to provide value in the long term. Interestingly, in the opening quote, Doug cites 'golf' and 'skiing' as similarly valuable—both archetypically associated with upper middle-class values, displays of style and social connections. Indeed, Bourdieu (1984) suggests that the one feature of sport that appeals to the dominant taste is 'a relatively high investment—and the earlier it is put in, the more profitable it is—of time and learning (so that they are relatively independent of the variations in bodily capital and its decline through age)' (p. 215–216). The benefits that we have discussed thus far are, essentially, deferred benefits. For example, learning skills for university or a competitive job market, gaining physical capital which will lend symbolic legitimacy or getting long-term social and health benefits. It shows that, for many parents at least, the emphasis is on the future and not so much the present, the game, or the score:

> I think playing the game in general is really important right now and just improving on his strokes so that he knows how to play [it is important] that he enjoys it enough that he will keep playing it when he gets older (Ian, parent, 11/12/10).

> ... tennis ... costs a bit of money to enter, ... [but] I look further than just the next game, you know, you look ten, fifteen years down the track and think I want my

38

> kid to have the skills so that when … a friend says lets go down and have a hit of tennis then they can hit the ball (Doug, 5/1/11).

Therefore, these parents looked into the future when judging the value of sporting participation. In relation to this, tennis at Oakwood meets the requirements of what middle class parents aspire for their children.

An additional feature of tennis that can have value for the children at Oakwood, is the specificity of the skill involved, characterised by: different grips, shots and sequences of footwork required to play at a competitive level. This idea is articulated by one father in comparison to other sports:

> It's quite a specific skill set, tennis, isn't it, compared to netball … golf is the same … If they haven't been exposed to it then they are not going to be able to hit the ball it's, it's too … it's not specialised but you've got to know, there is skill involved, whereas in rugby league, there is skill, but it's a bit easier to carry the ball and walk up the, run up the field (Doug, parent, 5/1/11).

By learning the art of tennis at a young age, at the hands of the coaching team at Oakwood, the children that persevere long enough will learn tennis in its most *legitimate* form. This legitimacy is achieved through tennis played with a natural ease and style. Competent tennis is recognisable, even more so in the eyes of other practitioners. Thus, tennis ability (a form of physical capital) lends symbolic capital to those who posses it. In turn, this symbolic capital may be higher than for someone with similar ability in other sports. This is because, as the father cited above has shown, the skills involved in other sports—specifically those not affirming middle class habitus codes (e.g. rugby league) are not valued as highly. Physical capital gained through early tennis familiarity lends symbolic legitimacy to tennis played later in a child's life. The person who learns tennis in their youth will always be distinguishable from the person who decided to learn as an adult. As Bourdieu (1978) noted "the connoisseur has schemes of perception and appreciation which enable him [sic] to see what the layman cannot see" (p. 829). This in turn may result in the distinction between the established class background of the legitimate practitioner and the upward mobility of the newly ascended (less legitimate) learner.

EMBODIED DISPOSITIONS AND FAIR PLAY

An important aspect of class habitus is that it is embodied, meaning that sporting practices appeal differently to class factions based on how they engage bodily sensibilities. As Booth and Loy (1999) note, for the middle classes corporeal concerns focus upon control (finesse, style), (long-term) health, and appearance (dress, speech, deportment).

Walter:	I like the style of it
Researcher:	the style of tennis?
Walter:	yip
Researcher:	what's the style of tennis?
Walter:	it's like … agile and yea … smooth yea (Walter, 13yrs old, 12/1/11).

> I like racquet sports in general so … and um yea there is something as well about the aesthetics, I like the courts and I like, you know, the kind of outdoor quality of it (Ian parent, 11/12/10).

Above, thirteen year old Walter struggled to tell us what he meant by the 'style' of tennis. If asked to elaborate upon his preferences, Ian—the father of twelve year old Timothy—would also provide an answer that fell short of a deep explanation. Bourdieu (1984) provides a possible answer for why Walter and Ian value these aspects of tennis, and simultaneously, why they struggle to articulate why this may be. Bourdieu notes: "A sport is more likely to be adopted by a social class if it does not contradict the class's relation to the body at its deepest most unconscious level, i.e., the body schema, which is the depository of a whole world view and a philosophy of the person and the body." (1984, p. 217–18). Thus the bodily movements, gait, and deportment that tennis emphasises are something that Oakwood players and parents struggled to articulate as they were such deeply ingrained embodied dispositions.

Tennis is a game of distance; the single point of contact between the players is via the return of the ball, mediated by the presence of a racquet. Baseline rallies consist of deep, strong strokes, the aim is not to let the opponent gain an advantage on the court. They push each other back, exerting topspin on the ball with stylish, exaggerated strokes to make it drop in with more speed and kick off at a higher angle. The drop shot has its place but must be used well, otherwise it gives your opponent a dominant position at the net. The middle class body is distanced from physical necessity in tennis. Children learn this relation to the body when practicing tennis at Oakwood, under the guidance of the coaches and their parents. In addition, the *way* legitimate tennis is played also works to distance its practitioners from necessity. A further example is 'self-reffing'—officiating by the players on court. In fact, there are guidelines that aim to keep parental influence out of the game as much as possible. As Bourdieu (1984) proposes, the 'cult of fair play' was a 'logical development of the distinctive function of sport' (p. 215). Therefore we can see how Oakwood Tennis Club provides a sporting practice reflecting middle class habitus. However, not all children 'naturally' embody this habitus or automatically play tennis in its most *legitimate* form. We will now give examples of how this exclusive class habitus is 'policed'. What happens when children offend the sensibilities we have described? How is tennis at Oakwood also a 'classifying' practice?

TENNIS AT OAKWOOD AS A CLASSIFYING PRACTICE

Sandy attends the majority of her two boys' Friday night games. We are discussing her son's tennis participation when one of the boys in their team carries on a rally in which the ball was obviously (from our view) out.

Researcher: that might have been a little bit out Jake

Sandy: I think that was well out Jake, you could have won that rally, woooa so frustrating (undertones of laughter)

Researcher: why do you think they sometimes … ?

Sandy: I think they just, sometimes when you are out there it's really hard and our boys, well we've come up against some really dishonest kids, I have to say, in the past, these boys are pretty honest, so if they were a bit uncertain it's in, so they just keep playing *although it's very devastating as a parent* (puts on a mock weeping voice) haha, when they call it the wrong way, but then you know, it's only a game of tennis isn't it …

Researcher: do you think that's maybe something to do with tennis? The willingness to keep a game going if it's a fifty-fifty call?

41

Sandy: Um I think it depends on the children, so some children, if it was a fifty-fifty call, would call it to their advantage *regardless*, but our kids ... I've pulled them up a couple of times when they were younger and said 'that's cheating', in front of everyone else, so they wouldn't just because that would be ... oh there is nothing worse, if you win if you've cheated ... that's not, well there's no point playing sport is there (28/1/11).

This conversation brings two things to light. The Oakwood children are schooled in self-restraint and discipline that underpins ideas of 'fair play'. Legitimate sport in Sandy's view is played fairly and, in turn, Sandy felt she was required to teach the boys in her sons' team what was expected of them. It is also apparent that Sandy believes some 'other' kids that they have played against are 'really dishonest', a trait of which there is 'nothing worse'. Their exclusivity is reaffirmed in the face of what are seen as the abhorrent moral attitudes of others to sport, which is, after all, 'only a game'. 'Fair play' Bourdieu (1978) notes, is utterly opposed to the plebeian (working class) pursuit of victory at all costs (p. 825), and here we see that distinction reinforced at Oakwood.

Part of playing tennis at Oakwood is learning *the* legitimate form of tennis and the embodied habitus that goes along with it. Youth tennis at Oakwood is imbued with specific codes, taking the form of a relation to the body as distanced from instrumental use, or in forms of dress. An example of this later lesson was provided in a conversation with a coach at Oakwood:

I think anytime you want to be successful then you should look the part, you should be professional from the moment you wake up, from the moment you step out the door, you know, I think having the right gear is a part of that ... for example (gestures to a boy training) he's not wearing the right shoes ... so you know, I'll have a word with him about it (Daniel, coach, 16/1/11).

Here, Daniel 'polices' the dress code. The Tennis New Zealand Code of Conduct (Tennis NZ, 2011) identifies 'unacceptable' attire, which includes gym, beach or rugby shorts, sweatshirts or T-shirts and any other attire deemed inappropriate by the referee or tournament management in consultation with the referee' (p4). This code reveals much about middle class sensibilities. It is interesting that much of the 'inappropriate' clothing is functional attire for participation. The code thus reproduces a particular image of *legitimate* tennis and

42

reinforces exclusivity by introducing a further requirement to be satisfied for participation. Oakwood requires its interclub youth teams to wear a uniform, one of the few clubs to do so. This consists of a collared polo shirt in the club's colours and embroidered with the club's name. The dress that is valued by Oakwood suggests a conservative, 'respectable' aspect to middle class taste, and is reinforced by uniform requirements and coaches who ensure that the children are 'properly' attired, which acts to 'distinguish'.

By involving their children in tennis, the parents at Oakwood ensured that their children spend time in appropriately 'character building' activities with other children that were a good influence because they shared 'respectable' values instead of 'getting in trouble'. This is a result of having a similar class background; which throws light onto issues of social homogeneity in sporting circles. For example, when talking to the '13s' boys and their mothers it became apparent that tennis was not the only sport they shared in common:

> A lot of people that you meet through tennis, their kids are associated in a lot of other sports the kids do, so you meet them in athletics, or sporting groups ... it's always the same parents that are going off to zones or centrals (Margaret, parent, 1/1/11)

Evidently, the parents of children who engage in a lot of sport become familiar with each other. These parents share a similar orientation to their children's sport which reflects a particular class habitus. As Sandy points out: 'the people we associate with seem to give their children a lot of opportunities in sport across the board' (18/1/11). For example, Allen talks about his family's tennis involvement:

> We have met a lot of people over the years through tennis that have become friends and um I think if you've got something in common with people, for adults and children, you tend to ... um socialise and gravitate towards those people ... we've got some good friends now that we wouldn't have, had the kids not played tennis (Allen, parent, 5/1/11)

Thus, social groups evolve sharing a common outlook which values particular types of sport participation. If we can assume that this ideology is representative of class-based child rearing strategies, then tennis works to reaffirm class stratification by building social connections between children, and indeed parents, of a similar habitus and class backgrounds. Therefore, at the same time as Oakwood provides practices that appeal to the middle classes, it simultaneously reproduces middle class exclusivity.

DISCUSSION: THE 'GAME' OF TENNIS

Contrary to popular myth, the apparently 'level playing field' of sport is wrought with barriers. The existence of economic barriers to sport participation is, at times, recognised both in policies and public discourse. They are combated by government funding for 'sport-for-all' programmes, yet simultaneously masked by wider beliefs that 'anyone can join in'. What these views neglect is the unseen structuring forces at play, and that one's position in 'social space' may determine the *choice* to play a sport, just as much as it determines the *ability* to be able to play. That the same game, (tennis at Oakwood) may literally be changed (tennis played at municipal courts in board shorts) to accommodate differing habitus codes, is not widely recognised. Therefore, contradicting journalist Richard Boock's proclamation with which we started this article, sport is far from egalitarian but laden with cultural capital requirements alongside economic barriers.

Our account of Oakwood tennis club is a story of the reproduction of middle class distinction. What Bourdieu's notion of habitus is powerful in highlighting is not simply the existence of structural forces in children's lives, but in *how* these forces work in the minutiae of everyday embodied (sporting) lives as an expression of cultural values. Thus, how a tennis racquet is held, deportment, how 'rules'—both constitutive (of the game) and normative (e.g. dress codes) are understood and enforced are revealing in how class-based capital is expressed. As we have also noted, the club also acts as a site of social connection and hence reproduces middle class networks. Playing tennis at Oakwood, thus, is a site at which middle class habitus codes are embodied and (re)produced in significant ways. For children playing tennis at Oakwood it is a site in which they are socialised into and through a particular class location. This involves them learning particular attitudes toward, experiences of, and relationships to their bodies and the internalisation of particular aspirations. These include norms of self-presentation, investing in the present for future physical and social benefits, and crafting their bodies for well being and ongoing acceptance.

Our study also illuminates the importance of adults in shaping 'classed' youth sport experiences. Indeed, our findings bear similarities with those of Swanson's (2009) work on 'soccer moms' in the USA who work to secure middle class aspirations and trajectories in their boys' leisure lives. That is, the 'concerted cultivation' of middle class parenting, coaches and administrators through tennis is a significant theme here. For example, it is clear from what we have presented above that parents were acutely conscious of why they promoted their children's tennis involvement, and much of this relates to the wider considerations of aspirational middle class life trajectories rather than anything inherent to tennis *per se*. Specifically, tennis was a form of capital with lifelong considerations, and was very explicitly articulated in these terms. In this way children become embodied expressions of their parent's middle class habitus codes, centred upon social presentation, advancement and status. In this sense further work exploring these aspects of youth sports experiences, and perhaps drawing on the likes of Laureau's (2003) work may be useful. Specifically, Laureau points to the classed nature of child-rearing strategies, and involvement in (a particular form of) tennis may be seen as a feature of this.

It is also worth reflecting here upon Brown's (2009) observation that "much of the research that employs the notions of habitus tends to emphasize its reproductive nature in sporting contexts" (p. 316). Indeed, much of what we have noted above reinforces how habitus is structuring, in that agents tend to work in ways that reinforce social class structure. We don't wish, however, to deny the active capacities of agents. Indeed, it was clear is our observations that there were subtly varying orientations toward tennis according to how aspirational parents appeared, their level of status 'security' and family history in the sport. That is, tennis did mean subtly differing things to differing people at the club; orientations were not always identical. Of course the very orientation toward tennis at Oakwood suggests some existing pre-dispositions. Indeed, it also worth noting how classes are fragmented and dynamic, and we do not wish to present the idea of the 'middle class' in an overly monolithic way. Thus, as Laberge and Sankoff (1988) note there are middle class fragments—an 'intellectual bourgeosie', for example—favouring an anti-ascetic ethic and who may favour the likes of artistic hobbies (photography, painting or playing musical instruments) and are disdainful of disciplined, effort-laden sports such as tennis at Oakwood.

As Brown (2009) notes, research on sport that employs Bourdieu's concept of class habitus has also been broadened to multiple axes of identity extended to incorporate gender and ethnicity (e.g. Wacquant, 1992; Mennenson, 2000; Back et al., 2001). In our own study it is worth noting the way in which the reproduction of middle class habitus codes in and through tennis is overwhelmingly a tale of Pākehā privilege. That is, the values and preferences reflected and reinforced particular expressions of middle class, white identities. Yet, as we noted above, there was also a small, yet not insignificant, south Asian presence at Oakwood which hints at sport as a site of aspirational mobility amongst 'third wave' migrants and emerging manifestations of class stratified sporting multiculturalism. Whilst we have not had the space to explore these issues in depth here, the intersections of class and ethnicity are significant and worthy of future exploration.

REFERENCES

Back, L., Crabbe, T. & Solomos, J. (2001) *The Changing Face of Football: Racism, Identity and Multiculture in the English Game.* Oxford: Berg.

Boock, R. (2009) *Say Good Night to Knighthoods.* Retrieved June, 2009, from http://www.stuff.co.nz/sunday-star-times/sport/247960/Richard-Boock-say-good-night-to-knighthoods

Booth, D. & Loy, J. (1999) Sport, status and style. *Sport History Review,* 30(1): 1–26.

Bourdieu, P. (1978) Sports and social class. *Social Science Information,* 17: 819–840.

Bourdieu, P. (1984) *Distinction: A Social Critique of the Judgement of Taste.* London: Routledge and Kegan Paul.

Bowden, J. (2008) *The Economic State of the Nation,* Kiwicap Research Ltd.

Chatterjee, S. & Birks, S. (2001) *The New Zealand Economy: Issues and Policies.* Dunmore Press, Palmerston North.

Collins, M. F. & J. R. Buller (2003) Social exclusion from high-performance sport: are all talented young sports people being given an equal opportunity of reaching the Olympic podium. *Journal of Sport & Social Issues,* 27(4): 420–442.

Daykas, J. & Stathi, A. (2007) Exploring social and environmental factors affecting adolescents participation in physical activity. *European Physical Education Review,* 13(3): 369–384.

During, S. (1998) Postcolonialism and globalisation: A dialectical relation after all? *Postcolonial Studies* 1: 31–47.

Hackett Fischer David. (2012) *Fairness and Freedom. A History of Two Open Societies: New Zealand and the United States.* London: Oxford University Press.

Gillmeister, H. (1998) *Tennis: A Cultural History.* London: Leicester University Press.

Jeffreys, K. (2009) The heyday of amateurism in modern lawn tennis. *The International Journal of the History of Sport,* 26(15): 2236–2252.

Kelsey, J. (1997) *The New Zealand Experiment: A World Model for Structural Adjustment?* Auckland: Auckland University Press.

Krishnan, V.; Jensen, J. and Rochford, M. (2002) Children in poor families: Does the source of family income change the picture? *Social Policy Journal of New Zealand,* 18: 118–147.

Laberge, S. and Sankoff, D. (1988) 'Physical Activities, Body Habitus, and Lifestyles', in J. Harvey and H. Cantelon (eds.) *Not Just a Game: Essays in Canadian Sport Sociology,* pp. 267–286. Ottawa: University of Ottawa Press.

Lake, R. (2011) Social class, etiquette and behavioural restraint in British lawn tennis, 1870–1939. *The International Journal of the History of Sport,* 28(6): 876–894.

Lareau, A. (2003) *Unequal Childhoods. Class, Race and Family Life.* University of California Press.

Lee, J.; Macdonald, D. & Wright, J. (2009) Young men's physical activity choices: The impact of capital, masculinities, and location. *Journal of Sport and Leisure Issues,* 33(1): 59–77

Light, R. & Kirk, D. (2010) Australian cultural capital—rugby's social meaning: physical assets, social advantage and independent schools, *Culture, Sport, Society* 4(3): 81–89

Mennesson, C. (2000) "Hard" women and "soft" women: The social construction of identities among female boxers. *International Review for the Sociology of Sport,* 35(1): 21–34.

Noble, G. & Watkins, M. (2003) So, how did Bourdieu learn to play tennis? Habitus, consciousness and habituation. *Cultural Studies,* 17(3/4): 520–538.

Reedy, T. (ed.) (2006) *A History of Māori Tennis: He Hitori O Te Tenehi Māori.* Aotearoa Māori Tennis Association: Auckland.

Rudd, C. & Roper, B. (1997) *The Political Economy of New Zealand.* Oxford University Press.

Sack, H-G. (1988) The relationship between sport involvement and lifestyle in youth cultures. *International Review for the Sociology of Sport,* 23: 213–232.

Shilling, C. (2003) *The Body and Social Theory,* Second Edition. London: Sage Publications

SPARC (2011) *The Economic and Social Value of Sport and Recreation to New Zealand: An Overview*. Wellington: SPARC.

Stempel, C. (2005) Adult participation sports as cultural capital: a test of Bourdieu's theory of the field of sports. *International Review for the Sociology of Sport*, 40: 411–432.

Swanson, L. (2009) Soccer fields of cultural [re]production: creating "good boys" in suburban America, *Sociology of Sport Journal*, 26: 404–424.

Tennis NZ (2011) *Tennis New Zealand player code of conduct*. Retrieved August, 2011, from http://www.tennisnz.com/Resource.aspx?ID=15716

Thrupp, M. (2001) Education policy and social class in England and New Zealand: An instructional comparison. *Journal of Education Policy*, 16(4): 297–314.

Wacquant, L. J. D. (1992) The social logic of boxing in black Chicago: Toward a sociology of pugilism. *Sociology of Sport Journal*, 9(3): 221–254.

White, P. & Wilson, B. (1999) Distinctions in the stand: An investigation of Bourdieu's habitus, socio-economic status and sport spectatorship in Canada. *International Review for the Sociology of Sport*, 35: 254–264.

Wilkinson, R. & Pickett K. (2009) *The Spirit Level: Why More Equal Societies Almost Always Do Better*. London: Penguin.

Wilson, T. (2002) The paradox of social class and sports involvement: The roles of cultural and economic capital. *International Review for the Sociology of Sport*, 37 (1): 5–16.

CHAPTER FOUR

Racism and Stereotyping on Campus

Experiences of African American Male Student-Athletes

BY **KRYSTAL BEAMON**

Reported cases of racially charged occurrences continue on college campuses. With "Blackface" party incidents and "noose" hangings making news at numerous universities all over the country, African American students at predominantly White institutions (PWIs) may face challenges beyond the academic scope of tests, papers, and projects (Costello, 2010; Strausbaugh, 2006; *Teaching Tolerance*, 2002; Van Kerckhove, 2007; Wade, 2011). Facing and coping with racism has been identified as a risk factor and an impediment of achievement for African American students at PWIs (Feagin, Heman, & Imani, 1996).

Graduation rates of college students are the most tangible measures of student outcomes and success. By this measure, African American male college students are considered one of the most at risk students on campus, having the lowest graduation rates of any other demographic group (*The Journal of Blacks in Higher Education*, 2012). Similarly, as a faction of this group, African American male student-athletes' graduation rates are also of concern (Lapchick, 2010). In a recent longitudinal study of 76 universities in major Division I-A athletic conferences, only 50.2% of African American male student-athletes graduated within six years and 55.5% of African American men overall; this is in comparison to 66.9% of all student-athletes, 72.8% of undergraduate students overall (Harper, Williams, & Blackmon, 2013).

Less than 4% of students at Division I universities are African American, while 61% of men's basketball players and 46% of football players are African American (Harper, Williams, & Blackmon, 2013; Lapchick, 2010). These statistics suggest that further study of African American male student-athletes is important because they comprise a substantial proportion of African American students on many college campuses. This study adds to the current body of literature by presenting a glimpse into experiences and possible risk factors of one of the most at-risk student groups on Division I campuses.

PURPOSE OF THE STUDY

African American male student-athletes have a unique experience on predominantly White college campuses (Anderson, 1996; Beamon, 2008). In addition to the isolation that many student-athletes often experience, African American male student-athletes must also contend with negative racial, gender, and athletic stereotypes. Due to the overrepresentation of African American males participating in collegiate and professional sports, it may appear that the athletic world is free from racial discrimination. However, racism and exploitation exist in several areas of college and professional sports. Examples are found in the lack of effort given to improve the educational success of African American student-athletes in comparison to their White counterparts, stacking African American athletes at skilled positions as opposed to thinking positions, the absence of African Americans in decision-making and leadership positions at universities and in professional leagues, labor exploitation, and even in the salaries and endorsement opportunities of professional athletes (Edwards, 2000; Eitzen, 2000; Hall, 2001; Hoberman, 1997; Kahn 1991). Student-athletes of color are said to face specific difficulties such as social and academic integration and racism (Person, Benson-Quaziena, & Rogers, 2001; Person & LeNoir, 1997).

Scholarship exploring the experience of African Americans on predominantly white campuses has been presented by several researchers (Davis, 1995; Feagin & Sikes, 1995; Marcus et al., 2003; Smith, 2007; Thompson et al., 1990). However, this study fills a gap in the literature by acknowledging the uniqueness of high-profile African American male student-athletes' experiences. For the purposes of this study, high-profile is conceptualized as Division I athletes in revenue-generating sports such as men's basketball and football. College sports and sports history in general seems to be filled with stories and images of cultural pluralism, fairness, racial harmony, and color-blindness (Hylton, 2009); but what do the student-athletes themselves think? This study qualitatively examines the perceptions of 20 African American male former Division I-A student-athletes' experiences with racism while on campus. It seeks to answer the following research questions:

- What are the experiences of high profile African American student-athletes concerning racism on predominantly White campuses?
- Does the status of "athlete" serve as a buffer to racism?

The data are presented in the form of meaningful narratives garnered through in-depth interviews. Insight was provided by the tenets of critical race theory (CRT) that helped to impart meaning to the data.

CONCEPTUAL FRAMEWORK

African Americans face a wealth of difficulties in the United States, many of which can be explained by past and present perceived and actual discrimination (Anderson, 1996). Racism is defined in many ways. In short, it can be understood as discriminatory behavior coupled with prejudicial beliefs toward an entire race that places that group in a subordinate position in society (Anderson, 1996; Feagin & Feagin, 2012; Singer, 2005). There are several forms of racial discrimination such as individual racism, which refers to face-to-face hostile acts of a person toward a racial group; and institutional racism, which refers to systemic, cumulative, and covert acts ingrained into the everyday practices of institutions that negatively affect subordinate groups (Feagin & Feagin, 2012).

51

CRT can be understood as a paradigm employed to produce a better comprehension of the contemporary racial dilemma, revealing how racial stratification is more powerful or enduring than is initially evident (Delgado & Stefancic, 2000, 2001). This theoretical perspective entered the literature during the era of civil rights litigation. It was at this time legal scholars began to recognize that racial oppression is so ingrained into the interworking of American society, that even the law, which proclaims race neutrality, works to perpetuate racial stratification rather than foster the deconstruction of oppressive conditions. "Critical Race Theorists have, for the first time, examined the entire edifice of contemporary legal thought and doctrine from the view point of the law's role in the construction and maintenance of social domination and subordination" (Crenshaw et al., 1995, p. xi).

Today, CRT is not just used by legal scholars; it has spread rather rapidly throughout disciplines. Employed by diverse scholars in sociology, education, psychology, political science, critical race feminism (CRF), Latino/a studies (LatCrit), Native American studies (TribalCrit), and the study of sports in society to better understand how "racial stratification operates on implicit, explicit, institutional, and individual levels to impact how Blacks and Whites and racialized others live and die" (Brown, 2003, p. 294). CRT has five major tenets:

1. Racism is a salient and normal experience that impacts the life chances of racial groups; "the usual way society does business, the common, everyday experience of most people of color in this country."

2. Interest convergence: Racism is addressed only when there is an interest convergence between the White majority and People of Color.

3. Race is a social construction rather than a biological or genetic difference; "races are categories that society invents, manipulates, or retires when convenient."

4. Differential racialization: refers to the manner in which dominant groups "racializes different minority groups at different times, in response to shifting needs such as the labor market."

5. Storytelling: The recipients of racism have the authoritative voice to describe the experience of racism; "voice-of-color thesis holds that because of their different histories and experiences with oppression, Black, Indian, Asian, and Latino/a writers and thinkers may be able to communicate to their White counterparts matters that the Whites are unlikely to know." (Delgado & Stefancic, 2001, pp. 7–9)

Not all CRT subscribers adhere to every tenet, and some have added additional tenets that suit the needs of their particular discipline. In the study of race and sport, CRT can help "highlight systems of oppression and negative power relations in sport" (Hylton, 2009, p. 30). Although most of the tenets of CRT are useful in understating race and college sports, this study is best served by applying the first (racism as normalcy) and fifth tenets (storytelling). Although many may perceive that overt acts of individual racism have declined in mainstream society, the athletes in this study describe this type of racism marked by stereotyping, name calling, and so forth as everyday occurrences in life and in sports. Therefore, the tenet of storytelling and counter-storytelling is very useful in the research of student-athletes on campus. Storytelling as a tenet of CRT supports the choice of methodology in this study. African American student-athletes perception of racial discrimination has been quantitatively researched (Brown et al., 2003), but the narratives presented in this study give a deeper look at their experiences.

LITERATURE REVIEW

Racism can't be overcome. It will be there for the rest of your life. You have to figure out how to deal with it. Racism is not an excuse to not do the best you can.

—Arthur Ashe (Lapchick, 1997, p. 53)

As an advocate and activist promoting equality for African American athletes and students, Arthur Ashe, similar to CRT theorists, recognized racism as a part of life for minority groups. On college campuses where African American students are largely underrepresented and African American faculty, coaches, and administrators are virtually absent, African American students at predominantly White universities face institutional racism, as well as overt acts of discrimination (Biasco, Goodwin, & Vitale, 2001; Feagin & Sikes, 1995; Lapchick, 1997). In fact, FBI data recorded 250 reported incidences of racial hate crimes on college campuses, and the number is likely under-representative of the actual level of hate on campuses (McGrew, 2000; Southern Poverty Law Center, 2000). A great deal of research exists in the literature highlighting African Americans students experiences with racism on campus. For example, Biasco and associates (2001) found that 66% of the African American students in their sample had experienced racism on campus and 85% viewed the campus as racially

53

hostile. African American students often feel alienated from Whites at PWIs (Altbach, 1991), and notice very quickly, as one student stated, "everywhere I look, everywhere I turn, right, left, is White" (Feagin & Sikes, 1995, p. 91). In a qualitative study, students discuss in vivid detail constant battles with racism, prejudiced students and professors, and culturally biased curriculums (Feagin and Sikes, 1995). Solórzano and colleagues (2000) found that African Americans experience persistent microaggressions (subtle insults) in both the academic and social spheres of college life. African American males reported stress, frustration, anger, hopelessness, and fear due to anti-Black male stereotyping, hypersurveillance, and campus and social microaggressions (Smith, 2007). The current research seeks to discover whether being a high profile student-athlete protects African American revenue-generating athletes from what is described by other African American students, particularly other African American male students.

It is difficult to discuss any area of athletics without noting the variable of race. This is illustrated in the overrepresentation of African Americans in certain sports and their absence in others. Sports, often thought of as a great equalizer, are highly segregated. Although African Americans comprise around 12% of the population, approximately 77% of the National Basketball Association, 65% of the National Football League, and 15% of all Major League players (another 25% are Hispanic, many of Afro-Hispanic descent) are African Americans (Lapchick, 2000). While the National Hockey League, Pro Golfers Association, and the professional tennis circuits are almost exclusively White.

Racism in sports reflects similar patterns of racial discrimination seen in the larger American society, meaning that it is mostly institutionalized (Washington & Karen, 2001). Racial stratification becomes more evident in the sporting world than what is initially apparent when one examines the positions of power within sports. These statistics challenge conventional beliefs about color-blindness and a level playing field in the world of athletics. While there is an overrepresentation of African American student-athletes at Division I-A universities, the decision-making occupations such as administration, leadership, coaching, and advising positions are still largely occupied by White males. Table 4.1 lists the percentages of African American administrators and coaches at NCAA Division I universities excluding HBCUs for 1995–1996 and 2009–2010.

As illustrated in Table 4.1, African Americans have not benefited from the same administrative opportunities in athletics as Whites. This also leaves few role models for Black student athletes on campus for careers related to athletics. Black coaches and administrators at PWIs

Table 4.1 Percentages of African American Administrators and Coaches at Non-HBCU Division I Universities

POSITION	PERCENT BLACK	
	1995–96	*2009–10*
Director of Athletics	2.7	3.9
Associate Director of Athletics	5.9	7.6
Assistant Director of Athletics	6.7	7.4
Academic Advisor	18	17.3
Head Coach Men's Revenue Sports (football and basketball)	8	9.4

Note. Data from National Collegiate Athletic Association. (2010). *2009–2010 Race demographics of NCAA member institutions' athletic personnel.* Overland, KS: NCAA.

are necessary due to their unique ability to understand the distinctive experiences of African American student-athletes (Sellers 2000; Singer & Armstrong, 2001). Singer's (2005) study of African American student-athletes perception of racism revealed a significant concern regarding their position in athletic opportunity structure off the field.

Eitzen (2000) presented several problems African American student-athletes face on college campuses, which are a lack of preparation for college courses, isolation, a lack of African Americans in leadership positions in athletic departments, and stereotypes that are held by professors and members of athletic departments. Educational stereotypes of Black athletes continue to persist, with some White faculty members and students having lower expectations of the academic potential of African American student-athletes (Sailes, 1993, 1998). Similar to other African American students, Adler and Adler (1991) also found that many athletes in their study felt antagonism from their professors.

Although African American student-athletes graduate at a higher rate than non-athlete African American students, the disparity between White and African American athletes' graduation rates continues to be extensive. For football players, White players graduate at a 20% higher rate and the gap in basketball is consistently widening and in 2010 was at 32% (Lapchick, 2010). In fact, African American male student-athletes at Division I-A universities have the lowest graduation rate of all race, ethnic, and gender classifications (Smith, 2004).

METHODS

Qualitative inquiry is the research method used in this study. More specifically, ethnographic interviews were conducted. These interviews allowed the research to capture meanings, common experiences, and themes that ran constant through the respondent's narratives. In-depth interviewing allowed the respondents to engage in the "storytelling," outlined in the tenets of CRT to understand and uncover racism as experienced by members of oppressed groups. Although there is quantifiable evidence of institutional discrimination in college athletics, how do student-athletes describe their experiences with racism on campus and in college athletics? What stories do they tell when given the opportunity to do so? This study presented the experiences of 20 African American men who played football or basketball at Division I universities about the racism that they faced as collegiate student-athletes. Another study applied qualitative methods to explore the racism that this particular group experiences. The study was exceptionally insightful, however, the sample size was small ($n = 4$) and it was limited to one university (Singer, 2005). The current study adds to the existing literature by presenting data from a larger sample and from Division I-A universities in every region of the country. There are recognized obstacles to gaining research access to members of Division I teams and professional athletes (Benson, 2000; Funk, 1991; Singer, 2005; Winbush, 1988). Interviewing high-profile athletes involves some of the same difficulties as studying elites in that they are rare and unlikely to participate (Neuman, 1997), so any original data concerning this group are unique and significantly adds to the literature.

SAMPLING

Both purposive and snowball sampling were used in this research. Possible respondents were recruited through a list of names provided by academic-athletic counselors at several universities. The criteria for participation were must be

- African American male
- former student-athlete from a predominantly White Division I-A university and,
- a full athletic scholarship athlete in a revenue generating sport (football or men's basketball).

The sample was restricted to African Americans because of the marked difficulties that this group faces on campus such as lower graduation rates and academic success when compared to their White counterparts (NCAA, 2010). Also, this group was of particular interest to the researcher. The study was exclusively of Division I universities because of their high media visibility. Full athletic scholarship recipients in revenue-generating sports were targeted because the researcher is most interested in exploring "high profile" athletes that may be well-known and recognized on campus and by local citizens. The twenty participants were from universities all over the country. As a former Division I athlete, this researcher used personal connections with academic-athletic advisors for many of the initial contacts. The researcher did not have personal relationships or friendships with any on the respondents, most were interviews were first-time interactions. The respondents were contacted by telephone or in person and given (or read) the description of the study. The interviews took place in comfortable social settings away from the university and by telephone. Snowballing led to the identification of additional participants. Pseudonyms were used to protect the confidentiality of the respondents. Table 4.2 provides the background and demographic data for each of the participants.

DATA COLLECTION

In-depth semi-standardized interviews were used as the data collection technique. An interview guide was employed; however, semi-standardized interviews allow for probes and elaboration to occur throughout. As a section of a larger study, this study represents narratives about a specific series of questions on collegiate experiences. Interviews ranged from one to five hours, with the average interview lasting about two and one-half hours. The questions were open-ended, non-biased, and designed to elicit candid responses. For example, respondents were asked: "Do you think that there is racism in college sports?" and "Did you experience racism as a student-athlete, on or off campus?" If the respondent answered yes, the researcher followed up with a series of probing questions to elicit elaboration such as, "What was your experience with racism in college?" These questions produced very similar responses from the majority of participants. The appendix shows the semi-standardized interview guide for the section of the research on the collegiate experience. As demonstrated in

Table 4.2 Participant Background Information

PARTICIPANT	COLLEGIATE SPORT	CURRENT AGE	CURRENT OCCUPATION	YEARS IN PROFESSIONAL SPORTS	UNDERGRADUATE DEGREE
Adam	Football	27	AFL[a]	6 in AFL	Computer Science
Brad	Football	23	NFL[b]	1 in NFL	Hotel and Restaurant
Calvin	Football	22	Unemployed	0	Hotel and Restaurant
Devin	Football	25	Unemployed	3 in NFL	Business Adm.
Eddy	Basketball	34	Business Sales Manager	0	Criminal Justice
Fred	Football	23	Agility Trainer	6 months in NFL	Business
Gavin	Football	22	Unemployed	0	Education
Hubert	Football	26	Mortgage Broker	1 NFLE[c] 1.5 in NFL	Journalism
Ivan	Football	34	Manager	1 in CFL, 1 in NFLE, 7 in AFL	Exercise and Sport Science
Jack	Basketball	31	Advertising And Sales	0	None
Kevin	Football	27	AFL	4 in NFL, 1 in AFL	None
Lenny	Football	31	Firefighter	3 in NFL, 1 in CFL[d]	Sociology
Matt	Football	27	Mortgage Loan Officer	1 in AFL	Fine Arts
Nate	Football	26	College Football Coach	2 in NFLE	Sports Administration
Oliver	Football	26	Police Officer	0	Sociology
Perry	Football	36	Firefighter	Less than 1 in NFL	Social Work
Quinton	Basketball	45	Firefighter/ Entrepreneur	Harlem Globetrotters, Europe	Missing Data
Richard	Football	47	Firefighter	2 in NFL	Sociology
Steve	Football	33	Fire Rescuer	0	Accounting
Tevin	Football	33	Firefighter	5 in NFL/NFLE	Criminal Justice

Note. [a]Arena Football League; [b]National Football League; [c]National Football League Europe; [d]Canadian Football League.

it, the questions about racism were only a portion of the overall interview schedule designed to capture the respondents' experiences as student-athletes.

DATA ANALYSIS

Data analysis in qualitative research endeavors to uncover a deep, meaningful understanding or conceptualization of a particular phenomenon, person, or group. It is a process of reviewing, synthesizing, and interpreting verbal data to give meaning to the social world from the perspective of those who are a part of that world (Fossey, McDermott, & Davidson, 2002). Qualitative research, including the current study is not meant to be generalized. However, it can be deemed trustworthy and reliable by providing a detailed, transparent account of how the data were collected and analyzed.

The interviews were transcribed by the researcher that aided in developing an intimate knowledge of the narratives provided by the respondents. The analytic procedure used in this study occurred in three stages. The first stage was coding. Coding simply refers to applying a meaning or interpretation to verbal data (Berg, 2004). The researcher initially conducted open coding. During preliminary line-by-line readings of the transcribed interviews, key points by which the data could be grouped were identified (Emerson, Fretz, & Shaw, 1995). For example, the researcher grouped together responses that indicated experiences with racism separate from responses that did not. After repeated line-by-line readings, focused coding, or "fine-grained, line-by-line analysis ... and elaborating analytically interesting themes," led to the second stage of the analytic plan, which was developing concepts (Emerson, Fretz, & Shaw 1995, p. 160). The data were hand-coded thematically as common terms, ideas, and phrases emerged. As common concepts developed, the data were grouped together accordingly. For example, discussions on stereotypes, hostile classroom environments, incidents on campus, racial elements of the teams, and fan racism emerged as themes in the on the transcribed interviews. Finally, as the third stage of analysis, categories were identified. At this stage of analysis, the responses were group together according to the overall category they elucidated. The categories that emerged through data analysis were "campus life" under which responses concerning racism in the classroom and campus environments were catalogued; and "athletics" under which responses concerning teammates, coaches, "locals," and fans were grouped.

FINDINGS

Respondents described their experiences with racism on campus, in "college towns," and in the classrooms. In line with CRT, many (18 of 20) considered racism as systematic and a part of everyday life as an African American, therefore, they expected to experience some level of discrimination while attending college. As Adam stated "It wasn't the first time that I had ever experienced racism, and it wasn't the last." Devin stated that "I attended college in one of the most racist places in America, so yeah I felt racism damn near every day."

RACISM AND CAMPUS LIFE

Although many people believe that high profile athletes in big time athletic programs receive special treatment, the respondents in this study discuss feeling mistreated and stereotyped while in college. Calvin details his experiences in the classroom, and denotes that racism "is a part of everyday life":

> ... in the classroom they made a racist statement in which I was the only African American in the classroom and they tend to forget that I was in there, and once they realized I was in there everybody face turn red and I had a whole lot of apologies. But ya know that's a part of life, you have to accept it and move on.

Most of respondents identify the classroom as a racially hostile environment. This was due in part to stereotypes that they perceived the professors employed concerning African American males and student-athletes. Additionally, these student-athletes felt isolated because there were so few African Americans on campus. Devin shares his experience with both stereotyping and racial isolation:

> Um, me personally, I was usually like the only Black person in a lot of my classes and being an athlete and the only Black person in the class, that's two strikes against you. A lot of professors see athletes as a problem. They figure you not gone come to class, you not gone do your work, you know a hassle.

60

Ivan also discussed stereotypes of African Americans on campus:

> I'm a big dude … and I'm for real Black (laughing) so I kinda stood out all of the time … people knew I was a athlete so sometimes that worked to my advantage, not with professors; it's like all they could see was a big, Black, so I must be dumb.

African American students at PWIs often discuss the overwhelming stereotype that those African Americans attending White universities must be doing so based on athletic talents (Feagin & Sikes, 1995; Hall, 2001; Harrison & Lawrence, 2004). Eddy stated that "people assume that a 6'5" Black dude walking around campus must be an athlete." This sometimes angered Eddy because students or professors would automatically assume that basketball is the only way that he could "belong" on campus. He was a bright student and felt that he had earned his spot in college with or without sports, but he did not believe that professors or other students ever saw that side of him. One of the most salient stereotypes of African American males is innate athletic superiority (Hall, 2001; Lapchick, 1996). This coupled with the "dumb jock" stereotype, creates a double jeopardy for African American athletes on campus.

Additionally, African American student-athletes struggle with isolation from other African American students on campus. Although they faced racism and many had a strong racial identity their athletic status overshadowed their racial identity. For example, two respondents attended the same university at the time that a major racial conflict occurred on campus. White fraternity members posted offensive "Black face" pictures on the Internet and the African American students on campus were protesting about the lack of action taken by the university toward the fraternity members. The respondent discussed the difficult position that being an African American student-athlete posed during that time:

> I remember (a racially charged incident) happened. Coach said that we could not get involved … I mean, man, it was hard because the Blackness in me wanted to protest with everybody else, but ya know, I'm a athlete and we have to represent in a certain way and we have to do what the coach says if we wanna play too though. I kinda felt like a sellout (laughing) but ya know, (the Black

student association) they knew we had their back we just couldn't go against the coach.

This was an extremely difficult position for this respondent, which further separated the student-athletes from the African American non-athletes on campus.

RACISM AND ATHLETICS

A majority (11 of 20) of the respondents in the study discussed the segregation among team-mates. Although there was limited racial tension between the African American athletes and the White athletes, there was indeed a racial divide. This self-segregation was seen in the locker room and among teammates on campus. The African American and White players had very little meaningful contact outside what was required as teammates. When asked if sports brings racial groups together, most (15 of 20) of the respondents did not agree that sports create racial harmony. Tevin's statement summarizes the thoughts of several of the athletes in this study:

> That's some bull! The White boys stayed to themselves and we stayed to our-selves, not that we weren't good teammates to each other and there wasn't like beef or anything between us, but it is like a divide between races, though, in the locker room and everywhere really.

Quite intriguing was the racism that the athletes experienced at the hand of fans and local residents of the college towns. "The first time I EVER got called a nigger was by a fan," stated Devin. Many (13 of 20) of the athletes discussed fans from opposing teams calling out racial epithets during and after games. Matt had even experienced this type of overt racism at the hands of his own team's fans:

> I had a fan yell out "you sorry nigger" after I missed an easy catch, they loved me when I was winning, but I was a "nigger" when I messed up.

62

When asked if he had experienced racism, Lenny discussed the irony of White fans that have racist stereotypes concerning the players that they cheer for at the games:

> I played at the (stadium) and it was right across the street from (my university) and after the games a lot of times we would have … to walk back to the campus and it was surprising that the same Caucasian uh, fans that was cheering for us about thirty minutes ago on the field, well we didn't have our uniform on so they would be grabbing their purses, locking the door, and I actually went up to one and I asked her "Miss I'm not at thief, just cuz you see I'm Black, I'm not a mugger, but I am the same individual that you was just cheering for on that field." And she was kinda hurt by it the statement because she was like 'oh I'm so sorry' I said 'oh don't be sorry, just educate yourself that not all Black people are robbers. So you do feel that racism as far as they just see you in the uniform but when they see you outside of the uniform you just another ya know minority in the population and they stereotype you … they treat you accordingly to your color.

Many of these student-athletes had not experienced name-calling and overt racism before coming to campus, mostly because they come from predominantly African American high schools and neighborhoods. Matt discussed in detail the "local" citizens in his university town:

> The first time I had ever been called a "nigger" was in good ole (college town), unless I had on something that said (University) Football, the people in the town just acted like they didn't want me there.

DISCUSSION

Critical race theory points out that racism is a salient, normal function of everyday life for racial/ethnic minorities. This study aimed to allow African American male former student-athletes to engage in storytelling concerning racism in their collegiate experience. With the troubling graduation rates, this study provides narrative data in which former athletes discussed this very important risk factor. Facing and coping with racism has been identified as an obstacle to success for African American students. This study shows that for these athletes, their status as a high-profile athlete did not protect them from experiencing racism at Division I universities. In fact, they may have an even more difficult experience with racism on campus than non-athlete African American students. As discussed in previous studies, the respondents in this research mention being forbidden to speak out against racism, which at times may detach them from their non-athlete counterparts (Lapchick, 1996). This may enhance their feelings of isolation and as one respondent stated makes one feel like a "sell out." However, similar to other African American students at PWIs, the respondents in this study faced racial isolation as one of few African American students on campus and negative academic stereotypes associated with race (Altbach, 1991; Feagin & Sikes, 1995; Smith 2007).

CONCLUSIONS AND LIMITATIONS

In Singer's (2005) qualitative study, the respondents discussed racism as associated with the opportunity structure, a more institutionalized form of racism. The respondents in this study only mentioned the lack of African American coaches and professors as exacerbating the negative stereotypes of African Americans. In fact the overwhelmingly common negative experiences that the respondents faced were associated with stereotyping. Additionally, the respondents faced a great deal of face-to-face individual level racism through name calling by fans and other students. The racism that the athletes suffered at the hands of fans was an unexpected finding. Fans seemed to feel a sense of entitlement and did not hesitate to use racial descriptions, as well as racial epithets, to insult athletes when they fell short in competition.

Additionally, the storytelling, or in this case, counter storytelling tenet of CRT was useful. The athletes in this study discussed segregation among White and African American team-mates. Popular culture clings to the 'feel-good' media image of sports bringing racial groups together, but respondents in this study described very little meaningful interaction outside of required participation between athletes of different races. CRT was also useful in seeing racism as a normal part of minority students-athletes lives. Even these high profile respondents who were revered as great athletes faced racism on several levels during their stay on campus. They were not exempt from this aspect of American life or the college experience of African American students at PWIs. However, while racism seems to be a factor in the experiences of African American athletes, 17 of the 20 athletes in this study graduated. Therefore, although these African American athletes experienced racism, there may be other variables that play a larger role in their academic outcomes.

This study is not without limitations. The respondents were recruited through personal connections that the researcher developed as a student-athlete and as a mentor/tutor to student-athletes. Although this was helpful in gaining entry to the field, establishing credibility with gatekeepers, and relating to the lifestyle the respondents, this could have biased some of the responses. Additionally, the fact that the interviews were collected, transcribed, and analyzed by the researcher could also invite bias. Another possible limitation of this research is the lack of generalizability of the findings. This study focused on twenty participants whose responses were internally consistent with one another, and consistent with the issues identified in the current body of literature. However, the findings cannot be generalized to the experiences or perceptions of all African American male athletes' experiences with racism on campus. Sampling limitations also exist. Although the sample consisted of men of various ages from universities across the nation, snowballing may have led to respondents with similar experiences. This limitation was addressed by assuring that the five initial contacts were varied by occupation, university, age, and region of the country. Another limitation of the sample is its small size ($n = 20$). However, as previously discussed, there are recognized obstacles in gaining research access to members of Division I teams and professional athletes (Benson, 2000; Funk, 1991; Winbush, 1988). For this reason, although small, any sample significantly adds to the current body of knowledge. Because this study was limited by gender, a suggestion for future research would be to examine African American females' experiences with racism coupled with sexism on campus. Finally, the research cannot be directly replicated due to the influence that the race and gender of the researcher may have had on participant's responses.

IMPLICATIONS OF THE STUDY

This study has important implications for the development of future research. Although the sample size is small, this study gives one a glimpse into the experiences of athletes from universities all over the country. Most of these respondents experienced racism on campus.

As a significant risk factor for student success, larger more generalizable data could give universities important information about the degree to which student-athletes' face racism. Additionally, these findings lead one to inquire how other racial/ethnic minorities are experiencing racism on campus. Future research is needed to compare the experiences of other racial/ethnic minority groups and female African American student-athletes. For example, how do Hispanic or Native American student-athletes experience the racial isolation that they must feel in sports and on campus? This research has implications for Division I-A institutions. As has been recognized for quite some time, universities should continue to make fervent efforts to add racial diversity to faculty, coaching staffs, athletic-academic counseling staffs, administration, and the student body of their institutions. Also, diversity training for professors would help them recognize their unconscious stereotypes of African Americans and student-athletes.

Once they are aware that student-athletes are facing racism, university athletic departments could implement programmatic thrusts to help them to develop coping mechanisms. It has been found in previous research that mentorship is vital in retaining at-risk students, particularly African American students (Himelhoch et al., 1997). In this study, student-athletes discuss feelings of racial isolation, racism, and stereotyping. Universities should provide an interconnected support network along with their current life skills programs to include mentors for student-athletes. Additionally, student-athletes should have an outlet to report racist occurrences without fear of repercussions. Finally, to combat feelings of isolation, universities could provide programs that "bridge" student-athletes, or intentionally connect them in meaningful ways to the larger student body.

REFERENCES

Adler, P. A., & Adler, P. (1991). *Backboards and blackboards: College athletes and role engulfment.* New York: Columbia University Press.

Altbach, P. G. (1991). The racial dilemma in American higher education. In P. G. Altbach & K. Lomotey (Eds.), *The racial crisis in American higher education* (pp. 3–17). Albany: State University of New York Press.

Anderson, P. M. (1996). Racism in sports: A question of ethics. *Marquette Sports Law Review, 6,* 357–408.

Beamon, K. (2008). Used goods: African American student-athletes' perception of exploitation by Division I universities. *The Journal of Negro Education, 77*, 352–364.

Benson, K. F. (2000). Constructing academic inadequacy: African American athletes' stories of schooling. *Journal of Higher Education, 71*, 223–246.

Berg, B. (2004). *Qualitative research methods* (5th ed.). Boston, MA: Pearson.

Biasco, F., Goodwin, E. A., & Vitale, K. L. (2001). College students' attitudes toward racial discrimination. *College Student Journal, 35*, 523–529.

Brown, T. N., Jackson, J. S., Brown, K. T., Sellers, R. M., Keiper, S. & Manuel, W. J. (2003). 'There's no race on the playing field': perceptions of racial discrimination among White and Black athletes. *Journal of Sport & Social Issues, 27*, 162–183.

Brown, T. N. (2003). Critical race theory speaks to the sociology of mental health: Mental health problems produced by racial stratification. *Journal of Health and Social Behavior, 44*, 292–301.

Costello, M. (2010). *Noose on campus: Teachingtolerance.org*. Retrieved from http://www. tolerance.org/blog/noose-campus.

Crenshaw, K., Gotanda, N., Peller, G., & Thomas, K. (Eds.). (1995). *Critical race theory: The key writings that formed the movement*. New York: The New Press.

Davis, D. R. (1995, April 9). *Perceptions of the college experience: African American students on a predominantly White campus or a qualitative piece of the retention puzzle*. Paper presented at the Annual Conference for Recruitment and Retention of Minorities in Education, Syracuse, NY.

Delgado, R., & Stefancic, J. (Eds.). (2000). *Critical race theory: The cutting edge* (2nd ed.). Philadelphia, PA: Temple University Press.

Delgado, R., & Stefancic, J. (2001). *Critical race theory: An introduction*. New York: New York University Press.

Edwards, H. (2000). Crisis of Black athletes on the eve of the 21st century. *Society, 37*, 9–13.

Eitzen, D. S. (2000). Racism in big-time college sport: Prospects for the year 2020 and proposal for change. In D. Brooks & R. Althouse (Eds.), *Racism in college athletics: The African American athlete's experience* (pp. 293–306). Morgantown, WV: Fitness Information Technology, Inc.

Emerson, R., Fretz, R., & Shaw, L. (1995). *Writing ethnographic field notes*. Chicago: Chicago University Press.

Feagin, J., & Feagin, C. (2012). *Racial and ethnic relations* (9th ed.). Upper Saddle River, NJ: Pearson.

Feagin, J., Heman, V., & Imani, N. (1996). *The agony of education: Black students at White colleges and universities.* New York: Routledge.

Feagin, J., & Sikes, M. (1995). How Black students cope with racism on White campuses. The *Journal of Blacks in Higher Education, 8,* 91–97.

Fossey, E., Harvey, C., McDermott, F., & Davidson, L. (2002). Understanding and evaluating qualitative research. *Australian and New Zealand Journal of Psychiatry, 36,* 717–732.

Funk, G. D. (1991). *Major violation: The unbalanced priorities in athletics and academics.* Champaign, IL: Leisure.

Hall, R. E. (2001). The ball curve: Calculated racism and the stereotype of African American men. *Journal of Black Studies, 32,* 104–119.

Harper, S., Williams, C., & Blackmon, H. W. (2013). *Black male student-athletes and racial inequalities in NCAA Division I college sports.* Philadelphia: University of Pennsylvania, Center for the Study of Race and Equity in Education.

Harrison, C., & Lawrence, S. (2004). African American student-athletes' perception of career transition in sport: A qualitative and visual elicitation. *Race, Ethnicity and Education, 6,* 373–394.

Himelhoch, C. R., Nichols, A., Ball, S. R., & Black, L. C. (1997, November). *A comparative study of the factors which predict persistence for African American students at historically Black institutions and predominantly White institutions.* Paper presented at the annual meeting of the Association for the Study of Higher Education, Albuquerque, NM.

Hoberman, J. (1997). *Darwin's athletes.* New York: Houghton Mifflin.

Hylton, K. (2009). *Race and sport: Critical race theory.* New York: Routledge.

The Journal of Blacks in Higher Education. (2012). Black student graduation rates remain low, but modest progress begins to show. Retrieved from http://www.jbhe.com/features/50_blackstudent_gradrates.html

Kahn, L. (1991). Discrimination in professional sports: A survey of the literature. *Industrial and Labor Relations Review 44,* 395–418.

Lapchick, R. (1996). Race and college sports: A long way to go. In R. E. Lapchick (Ed.), *Sport in society* (pp. 5–18). Thousand Oaks, CA: Sage.

Lapchick, R. (1997). Arthur Ashe and the next generation of student athletes. *Black Issues in Higher Education, 14,* 53.

Lapchick, R. (2000). Crime and athletes: New radical stereotypes. *Society, 37*, 14–20.

Lapchick, R. (2010). *Racial and gender report card: College sport.* Retrieved from http://www.tidesport.org/RGRC/2010/2010_College_RGRC_FINAL.pdf.

Ley, B. (1998). *Race and sports: Running in place?* Bristol, CT: ESPN.

Marcus, A., Mullins, L. C., Brackett, K., Tang, Z., Allen, A., & Pruett, D. W. (2003). Perceptions of racism on campus. *College Student Journal, 37*, 611–627.

McGrew, J. (2000, June 19). Campus hate, bias higher. *The Montgomery Advertiser*, pp. 1A, 4A.

National Collegiate Athletic Association. (2010). *2009–2010 Race demographics of NCAA member institutions' athletic personnel.* Overland Park, KS: NCAA.

Neuman, W. L. (1997). *Social research methods: Qualitative and quantitative approaches* (3rd ed.). Needham Heights, MA: Allyn and Bacon.

Person, D., Benson-Quaziena, M., & Rogers, A. (2001). Female student athletes and student athletes of color. *New Direction for Student Services, 93*, 55–64.

Person, D., & LeNoir, K. M. (1997). Retention issues and models for African-American male athletes. *New Directions for Student Services, 80*, 79–91.

Sailes, G. A. (1993). An investigation of campus stereotypes: The myth of Black athletic superiority and the dumb jock stereotype. *The Sociology of Sport Journal, 10*, 88–97.

Sailes, G. A. (1998). Betting against the odds: An overview of Black sports participation. In G. Sailes (Ed.), *African Americans in sports* (pp. 23–35). New Brunswick, NJ: Transaction.

Sellers, R. (2000). African American student-athletes: Opportunity or exploitation? In D. Brooks & R. Althouse (Eds.), *Racism in college athletics: The African American athlete's experience* (pp. 133–154). Morgantown, WV: Fitness Information Technology, Inc.

Singer, J. N. (2005). Understanding racism through the eyes of African American male student-athletes. *Race, Ethnicity, and Education, 8*, 365–386.

Singer, J. N., & Armstrong, K. L. (2001). Black coaches' roles in the holistic development of student-athletes. *Academic Athletic Journal, 15*, 114–131.

Smith, E. (2004). The African American student-athlete. In C. K. Ross (Ed.,) *Race and sport: The struggle for equality on and off the field* (pp. 121–145). Jackson: University of Mississippi Press.

Smith, W. A. (2007). Assume the position ... you fit the description: Psychosocial experiences and racial battle fatigue among African American male college students. *American Behavioral Scientist, 51*, 551–578.

Solórzano, D., Ceja, M., & Yosso, T. (2000). Critical race theory, racial microaggressions, and campus racial climate: The experiences of African American college students. *The Journal of Negro Education, 69*, 60–73.

Southern Poverty Law Center. (2000, Spring). Hate goes to school. *Intelligence Reports, 98*.

Strausbaugh, J. (2006). *Black like you: Blackface, Whiteface, insult and imitation in American popular culture.* New York: Tarcher.

Teaching Tolerance. (2002). Hate in the news. Retrieved from http://tolerance.org/news/article_hate.jsp?id=617

Thompson, C. E., Neville, H., Weathers, P. L., Poston, W. C., & Atkinson, D. R. (1990). Cultural mistrust and racism reaction among African American students, *Journal of College Student Development, 31*, 162–168.

Van Kerckhove, C. (2007). *University of Arizona students celebrate MLK day with Blackface party.* Retrieved from http://www.racialicious.com/2007/02/12/university-of-arizona-students-celebrate-mlk-day-with-Blackface-party/#disqus_thread

Wade, L. (2011). *Race themed events at colleges (trigger warning).* Retrieved from http://thesocietypages.org/socimages/2011/09/23/individual-racism-alive-and-well/

Washington, R. E., & Karen, D. (2001). Sport and society. *Annual Review of Sociology, 27*, 187–212.

Winbush, R. A. (1988). The furious passage of the African American intercollegiate athlete. *Journal of Sport and Social Issues, 11*, 97–103.

CHAPTER FIVE

Missing the Point

The Real Impact of Native Mascots and Team Names on American Indian and Alaska Native Youth

BY **ERIK STEGMAN AND VICTORIA PHILLIPS**

The debate over the racist name and mascot of the professional football team based in the nation's capital, the "Redskins," has reached a fever pitch in recent months.[1] Fifty U.S. senators signed a letter urging the National Football League, or NFL, to take action and change the name.[2] The U.S. Patent and Trademark Office recently canceled several of the team's trademarks because they were disparaging to American Indian and Alaska Native, or AI/AN, people and communities.[3] And several media outlets across the country have stopped printing and using the name, including the *San Francisco Chronicle*, Slate, and *The Seattle Times*.[4]

Much of the recent debate has centered on issues such as economics. Many fans and media commentators have debated the cost of changing the name for the team and the league. Others have focused on the "legacy" and memories that fans will lose with a new name. And perhaps the most referenced issue is the team's supposed lack of racist or derogatory intent. But too much of the debate misses the point. It is not just about a name, a logo, a business, or a matter of intent. Racist and derogatory team names have real and harmful effects on AI/AN people every day, particularly young people.

AI/AN students across the country attend K-12 and postsecondary schools that still maintain racist and derogatory mascots. Research shows that these team names and mascots can establish an unwelcome and hostile learning environment for AI/AN students.[5] It also reveals that the presence of AI/AN mascots directly results in lower self-esteem and mental health for AI/AN adolescents and young adults.[6] And just as importantly, studies show that these mascots undermine the educational experience of all students, particularly those with little or no contact with indigenous and AI/AN people.[7] In other words, these stereotypical representations are too often understood as factual representations and thus "contribute to the development of cultural biases and prejudices."[8]

These are some of the many compelling reasons why major professional organizations have already weighed in. For example, the American Psychological Association called for the "immediate retirement of all American Indian mascots, symbols, images, and personalities by schools, colleges, universities, athletic teams, and organizations" nearly a decade ago.[9] Similarly, the American Counseling Association passed a resolution in 2011 calling on their members to advocate for the elimination of these stereotypes where they are employed,[10] and the American Sociological Association called for the elimination of AI/AN names, mascots, and logos in 2007.[11]

The need to eliminate these derogatory representations and stereotypes is urgent and long past due. Racist team names and mascots provide a misrepresentation of AI/AN people that masks the very real and continuing hardships that these communities endure today. For example, AI/AN communities struggle with poverty at nearly double the national rate,[12] have some of the lowest high school graduation rates in the country,[13] and suffer from extreme health disparities.[14] Perhaps most disturbing, suicide is the second leading cause of death for AI/AN youth ages 15 to 24—a rate that is 2.5 times higher than the national average.[15]

The effects of these representations on AI/AN youth have spurred a growing nationwide movement to eliminate racist names and mascots. Although many inside the Beltway and in the national media portray the debate over the Washington football team name as something new, it is a decades-old movement that is finally getting the attention it deserves.

This report examines the current research about the impact of these mascots and team names on the mental health and self-esteem of AI/AN students, while sharing the real stories of AI/AN students in their own words.[16] It also provides an overview of the ongoing movement across the country to retire them from K-12 and postsecondary schools.

Finally, the report proposes recommendations to local, state, and federal agencies that will help school administrators, educators, and community members transform learning environments that are hostile and unwelcoming to AI/AN students and their families into ones that are supportive. These recommendations include:

- The U.S. Department of Education's Office for Civil Rights should use its full authority to enforce civil rights protections for AI/AN students and promote a safe and welcoming learning environment.
- State-level boards of education and education agencies should identify schools in their state with AI/AN representations, examine their impact, and develop recommendations to remove harmful representations.
- Nonprofit legal assistance organizations and law school clinics should develop programs to support AI/AN students who want to file complaints.
- The federal government and foundation community should identify and fund new research on the impact of derogatory AI/AN representations in schools.

Although the debate over the Washington football team may rage on until either the NFL or the team's owner, Dan Snyder, finally does the right thing and changes the name, there are many things that can be done right now to support AI/AN students in schools that perpetuate harmful stereotypes. Instead of debating merchandise economics and fan sentimentality, it is time to get to the point in this debate and to stop the harm that racist mascots and team names do to AI/AN youth.

NOTES

1. The authors of this report choose not to use the name of the Washington professional football team and will use "Washington football team" instead.
2. Nate Scott, "50 senators sign letter urging Redskins to change team name," *USA Today*, May 22, 2014, available at http://ftw.usatoday.com/2014/05/senators-washington-redskins-team-name-letter.

3. *Amanda Blackhorse, Marcus Briggs-Cloud, Philip Gover, Jillian Pappan, and Courtney Tsotigh v. Pro-Football, Inc.*, 92046185, available at http://ttabvue.uspto.gov/ttabvue/v?pno=92046185&pty=CAN&eno=199.

4. Andrew Beaujon, "Here's a list of outlets and journalists who won't use the name 'Redskins,'" Poynter, June 19, 2014, available at http://www.poynter.org/latest-news/mediawire/256258/heres-a-list-of-outlets-and-journalists-who-wont-use-the-name-redskins/.

5. American Psychological Association, "APA Resolution Recommending the Immediate Retirement of American Indian Mascots, Symbols, Images, and Personalities by Schools, Colleges, Universities, Athletic Teams, and Organizations," available at http://www.apa.org/about/policy/mascots.pdf (last accessed July 2014).

6. Stephanie A. Fryberg and others, "Of Warrior Chiefs and Indian Princesses: The Psychological Consequences of American Indian Mascots," *Basic and Applied Social Psychology* 30 (3) (2008): 215–216, available at http://sitemaker.umich.edu/daphna.oyserman/files/fryberg-markusoysermanstone2008.pdf.

7. American Psychological Association, "Summary of the APA Resolution Recommending Retirement of American Indian Mascots," available at http://www.apa.org/pi/oema/resources/indian-mascots.aspx (last accessed July 2014).

8. American Indian Cultural Support, "Society of Indian Psychologists of the Americas," available at http://www. aics.org/mascot/society.html (last accessed July 2014); American Psychological Association, "APA Resolution Recommending the Immediate Retirement of American Indian Mascots, Symbols, Images, and Personalities by Schools, Colleges, Universities, Athletic Teams, and Organizations."

9. American Psychological Association, "Summary of the APA Resolution Recommending Retirement of American Indian Mascots."

10. American Indian Sports Team Mascots, "Resolution: Opposition to Use of Stereotypical Native American Images as Sports Symbols and Mascots," available at http://aistm.org/2001aca.htm (last accessed July 2014).

11. American Sociological Association, "Statement by the Council of the American Sociological Association on Discontinuing the Use of Native American Nicknames, Logos and Mascots in Sport," Press release, March 6, 2007, available at http://www.asanet.org/about/Council_Statements/use_of_native_american_nicknames_logos_and_mascots.cfm.

12. Bureau of the Census, "Poverty Status in the Past 12 Months by Sex by Age Universe: Population for whom poverty status is determined: 2008–2010 American Community Survey 3-Year Estimates," available at http://factfinder2.census.gov/bkmk/table/1.0/en/ACS/10_3YR/B17001/0100000US%7C0100089US (last accessed July 2014).

13. Marie C. Stetser and Robert Stillwell, "Public High School Four-Year On-Time Graduation Rates and Event Dropout Rates: School Years 2010–11 and 2011–12" (Washington: National Center for Education Statistics, 2014), p. 4, available at http://nces.ed.gov/pubs2014/2014391.pdf.

14. Indian Health Service, "Disparities," available at http://www.ihs.gov/newsroom/factsheets/disparities/ (last accessed July 2014).

15. Centers for Disease Control and Prevention, "Suicide Facts at a Glance" (2012), available at http://www.cdc.gov/violenceprevention/pdf/suicide_datasheet-a.pdf.

16. These personal stories have been condensed from the original versions submitted to the authors, but the meaning and intent remain unchanged.

CHAPTER SIX

Where Are the Female Athletes in *Sports Illustrated?*

A Content Analysis of Covers

BY **JONETTA D. WEBER** AND **ROBERT M. CARINI**

The media is a powerful purveyor of messages about culture and gender ideology. This is true of the sports media, which sends mixed messages to females about sport participation. On one hand, sport is viewed as a means of achieving health and fitness, personal empowerment, and movement toward equality among the sexes. Yet females are not socialized as strongly into sport as their male counterparts, and strides they make within the sports world are often minimized, for example, considered less important than physical beauty or sexual worth. Socialization into sex roles is shaped, in part, via a lifetime of interactions with the media; thus, media portrayals are instrumental in helping females determine their place in society—and sport. Despite increased sports participation in recent decades, women occupy a marginal place in media coverage of sport (Bernstein, 2002; Bishop, 2003; Fink and Kensicki, 2002). This blatant example of symbolic annihilation (Tuchman, 1978) trivializes women's sports and devalues participants by their omission and the manner in which they are portrayed. The media sends potent messages of what it deems culturally important via what it chooses to omit and include. Through such careful regulation, the media influences how society 'perceive[s] movements about gender and gender itself' (Wood, 2010: 259). The sports media, then, can reinforce deep-rooted ideologies and stereotypes, but also has the potential to resist sex-role stereotyping by promoting female athletes as talented performers worthy of respect and emulation (Fink and Kensicki, 2002).

What role the media should play with respect to 'responsible' portrayals of females continues to be debated, but any discussion of how women are portrayed must also consider how often women are portrayed. There is emerging evidence that coverage of female athletes may be slipping from already thin levels. Televised sports coverage of females has dropped since 2004, and coverage in 2009 dipped to its lowest level in at least 20 years (Messner and Cooky, 2010). Specifically, women's sports garnered only 1.6 percent of time on the three major networks and 1.4 percent on ESPN's *SportsCenter* in 2009 (Messner and Cooky, 2010). Even when female athletes are featured, limiting and dangerous stereotypes tend to prevail, for example, the emphasis of physical beauty over performance, sexual objectification, women as more fragile and domestically oriented, and that there are 'inappropriate' sports for females to play. When females venture into gender neutral or traditionally masculine areas, the sports media often compares them against male counterparts, rather than treating females for their own performances (Jones et al., 1999). University of Connecticut women's basketball coach Geno Auriemma argued that media attention surrounding his 2010–2011 team's historic winning streak stemmed from the fact that they were chasing a *men's* basketball record, that of the UCLA team from 1971 to 1974 (*Associated Press*, 2010). Thus, the sports media continues to situate women's participation within a sports system constructed and controlled by males.

Hardin et al. (2005) found that women's sports magazines launched in the mid-to-late 1990s reflected the growth in women's sports, especially after the 1996 Olympics, a watershed achievement for women in sport. However, they often folded due to lack of interest or funding; *Women/Sport* was launched by *SI* in 1997 but ended after only four issues, and *SI for Women* was discontinued in 2002 after only 20 months. *Sports Illustrated* offers a litmus test regarding whether media coverage of female athletes has improved over time. For instance, Salwen and Wood (1994) found that 1.3 percent of a sample of covers from the 1960s and 1970s contained one or more female athletes, while 5.1 percent did so from 1987 to 1989. Looking at the percentages of articles and pages about women in *SI*, Reid and Soley (1979) found no significant change from 1956 to 1976. Bishop (2003) noted an ephemeral uptick in articles and pages devoted to female athletes in the early 1990s, but the broader pattern from 1980 to 1996 evinced a paucity of coverage similar to that reported by Reid and Soley. Bishop (2003: 192) concluded that '*SI* does not yet reflect the growing popularity of women's sports.' Likewise, Fink and Kensicki (2002) did not find greater female representation in *SI* articles and photographs for the three-year period after the 1996 Olympics.

We are not aware of published studies that have examined *SI* content after 1999, and especially with a focus on covers. We update and extend earlier analyses of *SI* to assess if women have made strides toward greater representation on covers in the 21st century. As *SI for Women* was discontinued in 2002, it would be interesting to see if *SI*'s flagship publication increased its coverage of women over the remainder of the decade.

RESEARCH QUESTIONS

1. What percentage of *SI* covers depicted females between 2000 and June 2011?
    *   How does this percentage compare to its first 12 years (1954–1965) and since the 1980s?
2. In what manner were females portrayed?
    *   What percentages were traditionally feminine, masculine, or gender-neutral sports?

METHODOLOGY

DATA SOURCE

SI is one of the most popular sports magazines, read weekly by nearly 21 million adults (*SI* Media Kit, 2011) and with a circulation of 3.2 million (Audit Bureau of Circulations, 2011). Nearly 8 in 10 (77%) subscribers are men (Echo Media, 2011). We analyzed 716 *SI* covers from January 2000 through June 2011 (available at: http://sportsillustrated.cnn.com/vault/

79

cover/home/index.htm) because they provide a spotlight on timely and central matters, are designed to entice casual readers at the newsstand, and should provide a first—and perhaps lasting—impression of their content. The annual swimsuit issue was excluded, as its focus is not on sport performance per se. We also analyzed the first 12 years of *SI* covers (1954–1965) and juxtaposed findings with those after 2000.

ANALYSIS

We totaled the number of covers depicting females and derived a percentage for each year. We used a two-way chi-square test to assess whether the frequency of women on covers changed significantly over the period. We also tallied the sports represented to gauge the diversity of the portrayals. Much has been written about the perceived appropriateness of particular sports for women and men, or sex-role typing (Koivula, 2001). Following Koivula, we categorized the sport for each female athlete into one of the following: a) feminine sport, b) masculine sport, or c) gender-neutral sport.

RESULTS

PERCENTAGE OF COVERS

From 2000 through June 2011, there were 716 opportunities to depict a figure (or figures) from the sports world on the cover of *SI*.[1] Women appeared on only 4.9 percent of covers, a representation similar to that found by Salwen and Wood (1994) from 1987 to 1989. Table 6.1 depicts how the 35 covers including women were distributed over the span. Women appeared on the highest percentage of covers in 2000 (10.2%), yet appeared on only 1.7 percent of covers the following year. Other highs of 8.9 percent occurred in 2003 and 6.9 percent in 2010, but no women appeared during the first half of 2011. The number of covers with women did not change significantly over the interval ($\chi^2 = 10.754$, d.f. = 11, $p > .05$).[2] Less than 5 percent of covers including females from 2000 to 2011 compares dismally with 12.6 percent from 1954 to 1965 (see Table 6.1; $\chi^2 = 24.968$, d.f. = 1, $p < .001$).

80

Table 6.1 Females on *SI* covers, selected years

YEAR	TOTAL COVERS	COVERS WITH FEMALE(S)	PERCENTAGE WITH FEMALE(S)
2000	59	6	10.2
2001	59	1	1.7
2002	62	2	3.2
2003	56	5	8.9
2004	61	4	6.6
2005	58	3	5.2
2006	66	2	3.0
2007	65	2	3.1
2008	68	3	4.4
2009	72	3	4.2
2010	58	4	6.9
Jan–June 2011	32	0	0.0
2000–2011	**716**	**35**	**4.9**
1954	20	3	15.0
1955	52	9	17.3
1956	56	7	12.5
1957	51	6	11.8
1958	51	8	15.7
1959	51	7	13.7
1960	52	9	17.3
1961	51	4	7.8
1962	51	8	15.7
1963	51	5	9.8
1964	51	5[a]	9.8
1965	51	3[a]	5.9
1954–1965	**588**	**74**	**12.6**

[a]One cover during this year was considered 'fashion'-related but would later become the original swimsuit issues.

81

MANNER OF PORTRAYAL

Although the limited number of depictions on *SI* covers serves to minimize women's sports, the manner in which females are portrayed may further trivialize their participation. This is done by limiting the number of covers in which they appear as the primary or sole image, placing them in comparable poses with a male so they share the 'spotlight', visually minimizing them by including an 'inset' or smaller image of the female or including them as part of a collage background, promoting more socially acceptable gender-neutral sports or feminine over masculine ones, sexually objectifying women, or using anonymous women (only connected to sports as a fan or family member of a male athlete) on the cover.

Of the 35 covers including a female, only 18 (or 2.5% of all covers) featured a female as the primary or sole image. Three covers included females but only as 'insets' (small boxed image) or as part of a collage background of both male and female athletes, and another three covers featured anonymous women only connected to sports as a fan or family member of a male athlete. An additional 11 covers featured a female in a comparable pose with a man, and nine of these represented basketball, considered a gender-neutral sport (Koivula, 2001). In fact, the most commonly represented sports were gender-neutral and appeared on 25 covers: basketball (14 covers), tennis (five), skiing (three), swimming (two) and track/field (one). Three feminine sports (cheerleading, figure skating, and softball) were featured on four covers, and masculine sports (soccer and auto racing) were featured on three covers, one with Mia Hamm and two with Danica Patrick, both of whom are considered attractive *and* feminine and likely chosen for those reasons.

Most of the covers included an athlete in sports apparel posing for the camera or actively participating in their sport, but the three covers that did not are blatant examples of sexual objectification. First is the 5 June 2000 cover of Anna Kournikova, lounging on a pillow in her street clothes, peering seductively into the camera, and clearly not prepared for any sanctioned sports activity. Even the author of the interior story suggested she was not on the cover for her athleticism: 'She won't win the French Open, but who cares? Anna Kournikova is living proof that even in this age of supposed enlightenment, a hot body can count just as much as a good backhand' (Deford, 2000: 95).

The second cover (11 July 2005) featured 2004 Olympic softball team member Jennie Finch, holding a ball and bat, but not dressed for softball. Instead, she wore a tank top and mini skirt which revealed part of her provocatively positioned hip on which her hand rested. Finally, the third cover (8 February 2010) depicted Olympic skier Lindsey Vonn in appropriate sports attire and with skiing equipment, but smiling at the camera and placed in a provocative pose, bent forward on her skis with her backside raised. While a natural position for a skier and similar to the 27 January 1992 cover of male skier, A.J. Kitt, there was one marked distinction: Kitt's cover was an action shot, taken while he was skiing, whereas Vonn's cover was clearly posed.

DISCUSSION

Are there really so few notable female figures in the sports world to feature? Our findings differ sharply from the early days of *SI* when women were featured more regularly. Much is revealed about the current social milieu if the number of covers reached its zenith almost a half century ago. Of course, it is possible that greater representation and different portrayals might have been found *between* the covers of *SI* over this current period, but we find little evidence of meaningful change on what is tantamount to the face of *SI*, that is, what it presents most prominently—its cover.

We question the practice of so few females on *SI* covers in this 'age of supposed enlightenment' (Deford, 2000: 95). It would be instructive to understand *why* certain sports media have been so unresponsive to calls for greater representation of female athletes. Our analysis suggests a continuing pattern of anemic representation of women on the cover of *SI*, a trend that was apparently unaltered by any compensatory coverage after *SI for Women* was discontinued in 2002. Increasing the number of women on covers seems straightforward to remedy, especially since so few covers feature women in the first place. Portrayals of women of color are also affected by the paucity of female athletes; only 11 covers depicted women of color.

The media enjoys a symbiotic relationship with society, influencing ideologies by its language and representations, but it is also influenced by ratings and the level of attention from its audience. Therefore, while *SI* continues to minimize women's sport participation, society reinforces this by continuing to purchase—and make both popular and profitable—a magazine such as *SI*. For *SI*, then, 'if it ain't broke, don't fix it!' However, covers were more than twice as likely to portray women during 1954–1965, an era not known for progressive gender ideologies, but a period in which *SI* featured a wider variety of professional sports, recreational sports, active leisure, and even fashion themes on its covers. In subsequent decades, *SI* covers have both reflected *and* swayed their audience's interests toward corporate sport, particularly lucrative football, basketball, baseball, and even hockey; female representation on covers dwindled over the period and has remained at low levels for decades. While *SI*'s underrepresentation of women might be said to simply reflect demand from a predominantly male readership for male-dominated sports, sports media also have the power to raise awareness of—and hone appreciation for—women in masculine sports, and sports classed as feminine or gender neutral. A similar phenomenon has occurred with upstart professional women's leagues, such as soccer and bass tournament fishing. While these organizations may struggle to capture audiences, they often are not provided sufficient—and sustained—media coverage necessary to socialize fans into the sport.

More frequent depictions are one means of promoting women in sport, but the manner of portrayal may be both more important and difficult to change. These images serve as role models for millions of females, who receive the message that athleticism and skill are not enough, but should be supplemented or even replaced by beauty and sexiness. However, following such a prescription may be a risky proposition. For instance, Harrison and Secarea (2010) found that when a woman basketball player is portrayed as 'sexually tawdry', she is judged by college students to be more feminine, more heterosexual, worthy of greater disapproval, less worthy to pay to see, and, very poignantly, *less athletic*. The sexualization of female athletes also reinforces heterosexism and indirectly suggests that lesbian athletes are less worthy of attention and emulation. Thus, more does not equate with 'better' covers.

We concur with Messner and Cooky (2010) that change is slow because it requires the enactment of simultaneous social forces, for example, greater representation of women in sports organizations and media outlets, as well as fan bases that insist on more quantitative and less sexist media treatment of female athletes. Only then is *SI* likely to fulfill its original goal of being 'not *a* sports magazine, but *the* sports magazine' (MacCambridge, 1997: 27); *the* sports magazine would include more females on its covers, show women in more diverse sports, and work diligently to avoid covers which trivialize women's participation.

NOTES

1. Enumerated by totaling *SI* publications each year, then subtracting the swimsuit edition(s) and issues for which there were multiple same-date publications differing only by regional publications.

2. Our conclusion does not change if we collapse adjacent years into either six categories or two categories (2000–2005 versus 2006–2011).

REFERENCES

Associated Press (2010) Auriemma: Gender dictating coverage, 20 December. Available at: http://msn.foxsports.com/wcbk/story/Connecticut-Huskies-coach-Geno-Auriemma-critical-of-coverage-121910 (accessed 25 December 2010).

Audit Bureau of Circulations (2011) *The top 25 U.S. consumer magazines from June 2011 FAS-FAX.* Available at: http://accessabc.wordpress.com/2011/08/09 /the-top-25-consumer-magazines-from-june-2011-fas-fax/ (accessed 22 November 2011).

Bernstein A (2002) Is it time for a victory lap? Changes in the media coverage of women in sport. *International Review for the Sociology of Sport* 37: 415–428.

Bishop R (2003) Missing in action: Feature coverage of women's sports in *Sports Illustrated. Journal of Sport and Social Issues* 27: 184–194.

Deford F (2000) Anna Kournikova. *Sports Illustrated*, 92 (5 June), pp. 94–100.

Echo Media (2011) Available at: http://echomedia.com/mediaDetail.php?ID=4489 (accessed 22 November 2011).

Fink J and Kensicki L (2002) An imperceptible difference: Visual and textual constructions of femininity in *Sports Illustrated* and *Sports Illustrated for Women. Mass Communication & Society* 5: 317–339.

Hardin M, Lynn S and Walsdorf K (2005) Challenge and conformity on 'contested terrain': Images of women in four women's sport/fitness magazines. *Sex Roles* 53: 105–117.

Harrison L and Secarea A (2010) College students' attitudes toward the sexualization of professional women athletes. *Journal of Sport Behavior* 33: 403–426.

Jones R, Murrell A and Jackson J (1999) Pretty versus powerful in the sports pages: Print media coverage of U.S. women's gold medal winning Olympic teams. *Journal of Sport & Social Issues* 23: 183–192.

Koivula N (2001) Perceived characteristics of sports categorized as gender-neutral, feminine and masculine. *Journal of Sport Behavior* 24: 377–393.

MacCambridge M (1997) *The Franchise: A History of Sports Illustrated Magazine*. New York: Hyperion.

Messner M and Cooky C (2010) *Gender in Televised Sports: News and Highlights Shows, 1989–2009*. Los Angeles: Center for Feminist Research, University of Southern California.

Reid L and Soley L (1979) *Sports Illustrated*'s coverage of women in sports. *Journalism Quarterly* 56: 861–863.

Salwen M and Wood N (1994) Depictions of female athletes on *Sports Illustrated* covers, 1957–1989. *Journal of Sport Behavior* 17: 98–107.

SI Media Kit (2011) About us. Available at: http://simediakit.com/about/ (accessed 22 November 2011).

Tuchman G (1978) Introduction: The symbolic annihilation of women by the mass media. In: Tuchman G, Daniels A and Benét J (eds) *Hearth and Home: Images of Women in the Mass Media*. New York: Oxford University Press, 3–38.

Wood J (2010) *Gendered Lives: Communication, Gender and Culture*, 9th edn. Boston, MA: Wadsworth Cengage Learning.

CHAPTER SEVEN

A Closer Look at Title IX

BY **MALLARY ALLEN**

At the time of its ratification, Title IX's supporters probably did not imagine that the law—formally an amendment to the Civil Rights Act of 1967—would become so strongly and controversially associated with sports. Its sponsors, Representatives Birch Bayh of Indiana and Patsy Mink of Hawaii (for whom Title IX was officially renamed the Patsy Mink Equal Opportunity in Education Act in 2002), championed the broader goal of equality for women and men in all areas of education, a vision with far-reaching impact. Today, like 40 years ago, Title IX requires that female and male athletes are given equal resources and opportunities to participate in sports, but it also does much more. Title IX protects students from sex-based discrimination in accessing higher education, career counseling, and course selection; it holds schools accountable for the hostile environments which are the result of sexual harassment and assault on high school and college campuses; and it ensures that pregnant and parenting students have access

THE SOCIOLOGY OF SPORTS

to education. Indeed, early work on Title IX was carried out in direct response to Senate subcommittee hearings concerned with women's experiences of sexual harassment and hiring discrimination in higher education. Soon after its passage in 1972, however, it was clear that Title IX would become best known for its controversial impact on high school and college athletics.

The law is clear. Title IX states simply, "No person in the United States shall, on the basis of sex, be excluded from participation in, be denied the benefits of, or be subjected to discrimination under any education program or activity receiving Federal financial assistance." At the time of its enactment, schools across the country were given until 1978 to demonstrate compliance. The law implicated all public schools, from elementary through college and also encompassed most private colleges and universities, as some percentage of students attending these institutions receive federal loans and grants to finance their educations.

Many schools, however, were unsure of what compliance with Title IX would look like. Where practices concerning career counseling and course offerings would simply need to accommodate whatever interest existed among female students (i.e., schools would not need to create separate classes or programs as this, in fact, would be contrary to the spirit of the law), athletics presented a different challenge. Sports, as they exist at most high schools and colleges, are sex segregated. Compliance with Title IX in athletics is therefore more easily quantified: Title IX required that schools give girls' and women's teams equal funding and equal opportunities for participation. Some schools panicked. Did this mean that athletics budgets would have to be split evenly between women and men? Did it mean that schools would have to provide female and male athletes with precisely the same number of spots on athletic teams? Did it mean schools would lose federal support if they were not in compliance by 1978?

In the 1970s in the United States, many schools resisted implementation on the grounds that women did not constitute 50 percent of students (at least on college campuses) to begin with, that their interest in sports did not approach the level of men's interest anyway, and that schools would face undue hardships if forced to achieve equality quickly. In response to dozens of complaints in the first few years of its enactment, in 1975 the Civil Rights Office added implementation guidelines to Title IX, specifically in references to sports. These three-part guidelines, commonly referred to as the three-prong test require that schools comply with just one of the following standards in order to be deemed compliant:

88

1. *Proportionality.* This prong states that schools are in compliance with Title IX if opportunities for male and female athletes mirror each sex's representation in the larger student body within 5 percent. In other words, if women constitute 55 percent of a school's student body, between 50 and 60 percent of its athletes should be women.

2. *History of progress.* This part of the test states that a school is in compliance if it demonstrates steady improvements toward including women in its sports programming. If a school has consistently added women's sports or has added spots to existing teams, it is in compliance, whether or not funding and opportunities for female athletes are proportionate to those available to males.

3. *Accommodation of interest.* This prong states that a school is in compliance when it offers sports demonstrated to be of interest to its female students. Traditionally, this has meant a school is in compliance if it offers programs like those available in the broader region from which it draws students or if female students are not actively lobbying for specific additional programs or protesting the elimination of an existing one.

As controversial as Title IX remains in reference to athletics, its impact on girls' and women's participation in sports is undeniable. R. Vivian Acosta and Linda Carpenter of Brooklyn College have been studying the influence of Title IX for more than 35 years. They note that in 1972, 16,000 women participated in intercollegiate sports, mostly in unfunded programs led by volunteer coaches (Acosta and Carpenter, 2012). Today, 200,000 women play sports in college (basketball, soccer, and volleyball are the most popular), and many of these women receive scholarships—a phenomenon virtually unheard of for female students prior to Title IX (Acosta and Carpenter, 2012). Furthermore, their teams are sponsored by their schools, and the vast majority of their coaches are paid professionals. In 1972, note Acosta and Carpenter (2012), the average college had 2.5 women's teams; today, that number is close to 9.

At the high school level, trends are even more pronounced. In 1971, 294,015 girls played sports in high school, while more than 3.6 million boys did (Acosta and Carpenter, 2012). Put another way, for each girl playing sports in high school, there were 12 boys. Now, athletic opportunities have grown for girls and boys, and the gap between the sexes has narrowed considerably; nearly 4.5 million boys and 3.2 million girls were high school athletes in 2012—a ratio of 1.4 to 1 (Acosta and Carpenter, 2012).

Support for Title IX is far from consensus, however. Since the addition of the three-prong test in 1975, Title IX has been at the center of numerous court cases, the outcomes of which have weakened the law's impact at times and strengthened it at others. In 1984, the Supreme Court significantly limited the scope of Title IX when it ruled in favor of Grove City College, a private institution seeking exemption from Title IX in its sports programs. The college argued that, while many of its students received federal grants to afford tuition at the school, public money did not directly support its athletic programs. As a result of the ruling, most private schools—and even many public schools with privately sponsored and self-supporting athletic programs—became exempt from equity requirements in sports. In 1988, however, the Civil Rights Restoration Act was passed and reinstated previous standards which require compliance in all programs within institutions receiving direct or indirect federal funding.

In ensuing years, Title IX has been the impetus of several legal cases on behalf of female athletes citing unfair treatment. In 1993, a court of appeals ruled that a school's financial constraints are not sufficient grounds for violating Title IX (*Favia v. Indiana University of Pennsylvania*), setting a precedent for future discrimination cases involving preferential treatment of higher-profile men's teams. As Title IX requires schools to devote equal budget resources to equipment, travel, recruiting, and coaching of women's and men's teams, schools must, for instance, devote the same funds to sending a women's team to tournaments as it does to sending a men's team, even if only one of those teams is likely to recoup the investment through ticket sales or receive positive media attention.

This was the case in 1996 when the Louisiana State University women's volleyball team brought suit against its school for funding tournament travel for its men's basketball team and then, citing a shortage of funds, denying its volleyball players the same support. Unique to this case is that LSU is one of very few public institutions whose athletics programs are completely privately funded and separate from the operations budget of the rest of the school. The court sided with the volleyball players in this case, arousing dissent by critics who believe that the profitability of a program should supersede standards of gender equality.

This argument, that less popular women's teams hold successful men's teams back, is among the most visible examples of opposition to Title IX, but it is not without its counterpoints. Director of the Tucker Center for Research on Girls and Women in Sports at the University of Minnesota and leading Title IX expert, Mary Jo Kane points out that the idea that football generates profit or creates revenue for other programs is simply false. In 2012, 106 out of 120 Division 1 football teams *lost money* for their schools, inaccurate phrasing if one considers that the expectation of profit does not exist for other extracurricular activities. Where football is profitable, it has perhaps become controversial for other reasons. In 2012, Buzz Bassinger, journalist and author of the best-selling book-turned-television series *Friday Night Lights*, publicly argued that college football should be banned, inspiring a wave of editorials and a televised debate between Bassinger and sportscasters Tim Green and Jason Whitlock. Football on many campuses, said Bassinger, does not contribute to the academic missions of colleges or promote the best interest of players, who are frequently injured and made to prioritize their sport over their studies (Bassinger, 2012).

Other opposition to Title IX is rooted in the belief that the law has led some schools to discontinue popular men's programs in order to bring the ratio of male-to-female athletes into proportion. Throughout the 1980s and 1990s, hundreds of schools have dropped men's programs (most frequently, wrestling and tennis) and have cited Title IX requirements in their decision making. No case argued under Title IX, however, has found that men's teams have been discriminated against unfairly to the advantage of women's teams. Cuts to women's sports, on the other hand, have inspired more legal controversy because opportunities for women are often lacking at these institutions in the first place.

Several schools in recent years, for instance, have been accused of double-counting female athletes in order to avoid creating additional opportunities. As the result of legal loopholes, some count male athletes on women's fencing and rowing teams as female. Since 1994, schools have been required to keep a public record of their compliance with Title IX, and, though these reports do not spurn formal investigations, some schools prefer to avoid unwanted attention via these controversial "roster management" tactics.

Such tactics were brought to light in 2009 when the women's volleyball team at Quinnipiac University, a private school in Connecticut, filed a lawsuit after administration moved to eliminate volleyball and replace the sport with a new cheerleading program. While the suit launched a debate about the merits of cheerleading as an athletic activity, it perhaps more importantly uncovered a years-long trend by Quinnipiac of double- and even triple-counting members of its women's track team, including athletes on the rosters of separate field and cross-country teams who had never participated in these events. In 2011, a district court sided with the volleyball players and ordered the school not to eliminate the team (*Biediger v. Quinnipiac University*).

Such underrepresentation and underfunding of women's sports is the rule and not the exception at colleges across the country, however, as studies show that men's sports consistently receive a greater share of athletic funding and boast larger rosters. Scholars like Kane (2012) are eager to point out that football is, in fact, least likely to face cuts, even though the steady expansion of football rosters over the past several years (the average team has added more than a dozen spots since 1972) often drives decisions between creating costly new women's programs or saving money by cutting existing men's. In addition, the National Women's Law Center (2015) notes that women still constitute 44 percent of athletes on college campuses, in spite of making up 57 percent of undergraduates as a whole. At Division 1A-FBS schools, 42 percent of athletic scholarship dollars go to women, 31 percent of recruiting dollars, and just 28 percent of the total athletics budget (NWLC, 2015). Furthermore, while several schools have been ordered to improve these inequalities over the past four decades, federal funds have never actually been withheld from a school as a result of noncompliance (Acosta and Carpenter, 2012).

But while supporters applaud the strides of women under Title IX and remain committed to realizing fuller equality, concerns exist beyond the participation rates of female and male athletes. In recent years, athletic injuries among high school students have skyrocketed, and girls appear to be shouldering disproportionate risks in sports popular with both sexes. Boys still bear the brunt of sports-related injuries overall (many stemming from football and other heavy contact sports), but female basketball and soccer players are more likely than their male counterparts to be seriously hurt. In basketball, tears and injuries to the anterior cruciate ligament (ACL) occur among girls at three times the rate they do among boys. In soccer, girls suffer 1.5 times as many ACL and concussion injuries as boys (Sokolove, 2009).

Serious injuries to high school and college athletes, regardless of sex, are still rare, however, and research shows that participation in sports has positive health benefits for the vast majority of women and girls who participate (NWLC, 2015). Supporters of Title IX do not interpret rates of injury as any reason to abandon the goal of gender equality, but rather point out that extreme pressure on today's young athletes has had some negative consequences across the board. At the same time, the growth of female participation in once male-dominated sports has far outpaced the development of safe and effective training techniques, especially those which would take into account typical differences in physiology by sex. Researchers are just beginning to recognize, for instance, average differences in girls' and boys' running postures, muscle use, and neck strength to head-size ratios, the latter perhaps important for understanding concussion risk (Sokolove, 2009).

Another concern for supporters of Title IX lies in ambiguous gains for women in leadership positions. Acosta and Carpenter (2012) observe that 90 percent of coaches for women's college sports teams were female in 1972—most of them physical education faculty who volunteered their time to lead unfunded and often unrecognized teams. In 2012, just 43 percent of coaches, 30 percent of trainers, and 20 percent of athletic directors for women's teams were female. Meanwhile, for men's sports, just 2 percent of coaches, mostly in non–team sports like tennis and track, are female. So while the exponential growth in women's sports today means that—in real numbers—more women are employed in coaching than ever before, the true beneficiaries of the move toward the professionalization of coaching women's teams have by and large been men.

The gains, challenges, and controversies discussed in this chapter represent just some of the important issues related to Title IX. Advocates continue to push for more complete equality for athletes in high school and college: The High School Data Transparency Acts were passed in 2013 to address inequalities at the high school level, where 1.3 million fewer athletic opportunities exist for girls nationwide. In addition, legal advocacy groups like the American Civil Liberty Union and the National Women's Law Center continue to represent individual athletes and their teams in discrimination cases. In the 21st century, Title IX's important role in protecting victims of sexual assault on college campuses is also becoming more visible as the Department of Education has released additional accountability guidelines for schools when it comes to addressing such cases in higher education (US Department of Education, 2011, 2014). A few years into its fifth decade, high school and college sports attract more interest from athletes and fans than ever before, and Title IX remains a symbol of optimism as well as controversy.

REFERENCES

Acosta, R. V., and L. J. Carpenter. (2012). "Women in intercollegiate sport. A longitudinal, national study, Thirty-five year update. 1977–2012." Unpublished manuscript. Accessed 2/23/15 at www.acostacarpenter.org

Bassinger, B. (2012). "Why college football should be banned." *Wall Street Journal*, May 8, 2012.

Kane, M. J. (2012). "Title IX at 40: Examining mysteries, myths, and misinformation sur-rounding the historic federal law." *President's Council on Fitness Sports and Nutrition Research Digest*, 13:2.

National Women's Law Center. (2015). "Athletics under Title IX." Accessed 2/23/15 at http://www.titleix.info/10-Key-Areas-of-Title-IX/Athletics.aspx

Sokolove, M. (2009). *Warrior Girls: Protecting Our Daughters against the Injury Epidemic in Women's Sports.* New York: Simon & Schuster.

US Dept. of Education. (2011). "Dear colleague letter: 2011 Title IX guidance." April 4, 2011. Accessed 2/28/15 at www2.ed.gov/about/offices/list/ocr/letters/col-league-201104.pdf

_____. (2014). "Questions and answers on Title IX and sexual violence." April 29, 2014. Accessed 2/28/15 at www2.ed.gov/about/offices/list/ocr/docs/qa-201404-title-ix.pdf

CHAPTER EIGHT

Religion and Sports

BY **ERIK W. DAILEY**

British track and field sprinter Eric Liddell was highly criticized for his refusal to compete in the 100-meter race at the 1926 Summer Olympic Games in Paris. While it was his best event, he chose not to race because the qualifying heat was held on a Sunday. Liddell, a devout Protestant Christian, would not run on the Christian Sabbath. To his credit, he went on to run the 400 meters, an event that was not his best, and win by setting a world record. His story is recorded in the classic film *Chariots of Fire*, and while he is lauded as a hero among many Christians, it should be remembered that he was chastised by the media and even the British Parliament. Honoring the Sabbath was not seen as being a valid excuse to refrain from running.

In 2011, Pakistani American weightlifter Kulsoom Abdullah was eliminated from American Open qualifications because of her clothing, a full-body covering worn in compliance with her Muslim faith. Judges said that her clothing restricted their view of her elbows, which should not be locked, in accordance with the rules of competitive weightlifting. The International Weightlifting Federation has since changed their policies to better accommodate full-body coverings.

These are just a few of the many stories where sports and religious practice have conflicted with each other and caused controversy. Which should take priority? Which is more important? As a Presbyterian minister, I can give many accounts where the youth of my church have had to make decisions between attending important church functions or competing in high-level sporting events. And their confusion and indecision were matched by their parents' own uncertainty. The level of devotion with which many people now approach sports has led some to wonder if sports have become a religion. Has practicing or watching sports now become a religion of its own? Or have sports even replaced religious devotion, unseating the once dominant force in global culture? The purpose of this selection is to tackle these questions by taking a close look at what constitutes a religion and how sport does or does not fit that description. Upon doing so, I offer a reading of sports as an aesthetic activity, valuable for human flourishing, yet in need of critical reflection.

SPORTS AS RELIGION

An observer aware of the shape and character of religious life will quickly see how sports mirror the life of faith. There are high holy days like Super Bowl Sunday or the NBA draft. There are massive celebratory festivals like the World Cup and the Olympic Games. There is rigorous ascetic devotion shown in the training regimens of elite athletes, who must closely monitor their diets, sleeping habits, and nonsporting activities, all of which might separate them from their nonathlete peers. Overall though, there is a love and zeal for sports that is matched by few other human activities.

Both religion and sports also have an established set of rituals and rites of passage that create and help to maintain strong bonds between families and their corresponding religious communities or sports fan bases. Jewish adolescents, for example, participate in bar and bat mitzvahs, Muslims observe Ramadan, and Catholics consume communion wine during mass. All of these are very significant events for devout religious people that can serve to strengthen their faith. Within the social context of sports, New York Yankees fans have the first-inning roll call, Chicago Cubs fans sitting in the outfield of Wrigley Field throw back home run balls hit by the visiting team, and Detroit Red Wings fans throw octopuses on the ice during every home game. Teams all over the country also have certain songs that they play at certain points of the game. Neil Diamond's famous song "Sweet Caroline" surely strikes an emotional chord with Boston Red Sox fans, as it is played at Fenway Park after every Red Sox victory. Because of its many symbolic and meaningful rituals, sports are likely to be as important to many people as religion is to others.

Esteemed philosopher and journalist Michael Novak (1988: 19–20) states that sports flow "from a deep natural impulse that is radically religious: an impulse of freedom, respect for ritual limits, a zest for symbolic meaning, and a longing for perfection." He continues by stating that "among the godward signs in contemporary life, sports may be the single most powerful manifestation. I don't mean that participation in sports, as athlete or fan, makes one a believer in 'God,' under whatever concept, image, experience, or drive to which one attaches the name. Rather, sports drive one in some dark and generic sense 'godward.'" (Novak, 1988: 19–20). This is a knowingly high estimation of sports, but Novak hits on what many who love sports feel: there is something great there. There is something to be cherished and treasured, cultivated and appreciated, just as there is with religious faith. Historian William J. Baker (2007: 2) states that "for all their differences, religion and sport seem to have been made in the image of each other. Both are bathed in myth and sustained by ritual; both reward faith and patience; both thrive on passion tempered with discipline." So then, is it right to call sport a religion, or even a form of religious practice? To answer this, one must look closely at what constitutes a religion.

A SOCIOLOGICAL DEFINITION OF RELIGION

Sociologist Émile Durkheim offers a classic definition of religion that, while highly critiqued, can serve as a good starting point. He states that a religion is any "unified system of beliefs and practices relative to sacred things, that is to say things set apart and forbidden, beliefs and practices which unite into one single moral community called a Church, all those who adhere to them" (Durkheim, 1965: 62). How might this definition work with sports? Take, for example, a baseball game. It could be argued that the codified rules of baseball form a unified system of beliefs, as those participating believe that those rules are the best way to play the game. Sacred things might consist of the field, where only the players may go, or

97

the dates of major games like the World Series. The single moral community might comprise all of the fans who laud, or even worship, the players and events taking place on the field. But even in Durkheim's broad definition, it is difficult to shoehorn baseball into his categories and markers for a religion. There is something bigger missing.

CAN SPORT BE A RELIGION?

Rather, I argue that even though sport and religion look and feel very similar, sport is not a religion and should not be referred to as such for one main reason: The two have different ends. Joan M. Chandler (1992: 55) asks whether or not "people who would consider themselves religious and people who are sports fans expect the object of their devotions to meet the same needs." Does the person who attends the baseball game have the same expectations there as the person who attends church on Sunday morning? It is most likely that they do not. While the baseball fan might find community, camaraderie, and even a sense of purpose at the game, he does not find what Chandler identifies as the key elements to religious life. Religions, even highly divergent religions, offer "detailed explanations of the origin and purpose of the world, clear statements about questions of ultimate concern (what many would call 'the supernatural'), and continuing attempts to explain and cope with the existence of pain" (Chandler, 1992: 56). In other words, sports do not tell us where we came from, who we are, where we are going, or how to deal with the difficulties of life. While to many people sports might be of intense concern, sports do not attempt to explore matters of ultimate meaning. Sports do not explain the biggest parts of life, even if they might *be* a big part of someone's life. It has long been the place of religion to make sense of life's biggest questions, and in that it differentiates itself from sports.[1]

Still, there is still some deep relationship between sports and religion, and here, I believe, it is helpful to look at the work of anthropologist Clifford Geertz. He proposes an understanding of culture through the metaphor of "webs of significance" (Geertz, 1977: 5). Cultural forms and products—like both sports and religion—exist in an intertwined web of meaning. Philosophers Jeffrey Scholes and Raphael Sassower (2013: 157–162) continue this line of thought, saying that:

We may think of sports and religion as two spiders on the same web. They are different spiders but when one moves on the web, the other is affected by the movement of the thread. And because, according to Geertz, the web is one of cultural significance and meanings, both sports and religion must, at times, utilize the same pathways and channels on the web to get where they are going.

So we see the kinship of sports and religion because they are made out of the same stuff, they travel on the same roads and on the same web of interconnected meanings. But even though they are made out of many of the same elements, they are not the same, primarily because of their functions. Both an airplane and a soda can are made out of aluminum, but they are obviously not the same thing, and they perform very different functions.

So why, then, if sports are not a religion of their own, might people choose sports over religion, or even chastise those who do not choose sports over religion? Why do sports hold such a deep attachment for so many people? I believe that this conversation can be approached from the realm of aesthetics. Aesthetics have long been a cornerstone of the religious life. Sacred spaces like churches, mosques, and temples are often beautiful and awe-inspiring places. Numerous religions incorporate music and particular musical styles into their religious events and services. There are also celebrations and times for festivals and remembrance, as well as large gatherings and social events. The religious life is aesthetically rich, and my few examples here only scratch the surface of the complex aesthetics of religion. Beauty and the appreciation of beauty, however that might take form, have long held a place in religion.

SPORTS AS AESTHETIC ACTIVITIES

In the summer of 2014, former NCAA gymnast Kacy Catanzaro became a feminist folk hero as she became the first woman ever to finish the qualifying round of *American Ninja Warrior*, a televised obstacle course competition that originated in Japan. *American Ninja Warrior* challenges athletes to complete four stages of grueling obstacles. No American has ever finished all four stages, and until 2014, no woman had ever finished the qualifying round. The final obstacle of that round was a series of vertical poles, which the athletes had to cross without touching the ground. The last two poles were 5 feet 1 inch apart, and

Catanzaro, at only 5 feet tall, had a reach of the same. For her, it would be impossible to simply reach out and grab the last pole as every other competitor had done.

And then, in a moment of unbelievable tenacity, she leapt between the poles, safely and elegantly, and finished the course. I have to admit that at that moment, while watching the event on television, I jumped off the couch and shouted with praise and acclamation at her accomplishment! I was almost moved to tears. For a well-composed Presbyterian and academic like myself, it was a rare and even surprising experience. This is all to say that there is no denying that sports have an aesthetic element. We want to rise and shout. We want to marvel at incredible accomplishments and feel that we have witnessed something amazing! But how is it that sports elicit such reactions? How exactly are sports engaging with our aesthetic sensibilities?

First, sports are undeniably sensuous, meaning that they appeal to our senses. Historian Donald Kyle (2007: 340) argues that the allure of sports is "visceral and elemental—more subliminal than cerebral." Jumping off the couch and shouting is not a rational activity. Granted, there is a great deal of mental work to all sports (plays in football, strategy in baseball, etc.), but the goal of the participant and the viewer is to experience those great feelings, like the joy of winning, completing a great play or record-breaking achievement, or witnessing an amazing, and arguably beautiful, accomplishment. For philosopher Hans Gumbrecht (2006: 16), sport "is a fascination in the true sense of the word—a phenomenon that manages to paralyze the eyes, something that endlessly attracts, without implying any explanation for its attraction." Sport grabs us on that basic, often unexplainable level.

Second, there is the aspect of what many call "responsive openness." Both playing and watching a sport require comportment to the world that is more responsive and aware than our everyday activities. Walking down the street requires focus out ahead, but little focus on other items in the vicinity. The soccer player, however, must have a different comportment and level of awareness. She or he needs to know where the other defenders are at all times, where the ball is, what potential avenues there are for moving toward the goal, and the ways the goalie might choose to defend the goal. The long-distance swimmer must be responsively open to the language of his body, how much energy is being expended, and how much distance remains in the race. And the engaged spectator stands in openness to the possibility of witnessing an amazing feat. She must know the rules of the game and be looking for great acts as they are accomplished within that bounded area of the game. Sport requires that type of comportment to the world, one of responsive openness. Gumbrecht (2006: 52) sums this up by stating that "athletic experience—and aesthetic experience in general—is not qualitatively different from our experience in other less marked situations. What is different is that our physical and emotional capacities are operating close to their maximum."[2]

In summary so far, I have shown how sports and religion often collide in dramatic and confusing ways. Sports themselves do not constitute a religion, as they do not deal with matters of ultimate concern. They do not tell us who we are or where we are going. But they do share a kinship with religion, a spot on the web of cultural meaning, in terms of aesthetics. Both sport and religion are aesthetic endeavors, activities that form and inform our aesthetic sensibilities. Put simply, they are both things that elicit love. One's religious devotion is ideally motivated by love, just as one's engagement with a sport is motivated by love. They both engage us in that love-based manner and because of that, they are both valuable for human flourishing.

THE RELATIONSHIP BETWEEN SPORTS AND RELIGION

Now, because of this aesthetic kinship, I believe that sports and religion have a lot to offer each other, for the betterment of both. So what might sports have to offer religion? First, there is the appreciation of that visceral sense of awe, that overwhelming feeling of having experienced something amazing. Gumbrecht (2006: 231) states that:

> Under present-day conditions, in a culture that has a sharper awareness than any culture before about the limits of human performance, and that also has more efficient ways of using this knowledge to reach those limits, watching sports is a way of waiting for that which may occasionally happen but is never guaranteed to happen, because it lies beyond the precalculated limits of human performance. To let happen and to see happen, occasionally, what we have no right to expect—this may indeed be the kind of experience toward which we fans are open when we watch sports.

Again, there is that responsive openness to the potentially amazing. Speaking as a Western Protestant Christian, I can attest there is a great need for comportment like that within the church. I believe that sports can help us recapture that sense of amazement, that expectation that great things will happen, which has been lost in an environment of reductionist appropriations of religious faith. The religiously affiliated should be encouraged to wait in anticipation for moments of awe, just like sports fans. On another level, the world of sports, which is undeniably body-centric, can help some religious traditions regain an appreciation for embodiment, for life in the physical body. Again, speaking for the Christian tradition, there is a lack of focus, especially in terms of health and wellness initiatives, that focus on the body. Sports engage the body, and by doing so, develop an appreciation for the body, one which is often lacking in religious faith.

But does religion have something to offer sports? Absolutely. Shirl J. Hoffman, who critically analyzes sports because of his deep love for them, notes that in recent decades many Christians have lifted up sports as a platform for evangelism and have lauded numerous athletes as models for righteous living. Hoffman (2010: 11) states that this is problematic though, because sport has been:

> Variously described by those inside it and outside it as narcissistic, materialistic, self-interested, violent, sensational, coarse, racist, sexist, brazen, raunchy, hedonistic, body-destroying, and militaristic, the culture of sports is light years removed from what Christians for centuries have idealized as the embodiment of the gospel message.

This is a lengthy indictment, but Hoffman homes in on some of sport's enduring problems. As I have stated already, I do believe that religious traditions should engage with sports, but that does not mean that they should do it without criticism. The time-honored ethical stances of many religions can offer a dramatic correction for the abuses that plague sports. And this should be done not from a place of resentment or jealousy, but from a desire to further refine the life-giving aspects of sports. People enjoy sports, and when critiqued from a robust ethical framework, they can become even better, even more enjoyable.

CONCLUSIONS

Sports and religion play very important roles in the lives of millions of Americans. Within the context of sports, there are many people who live and breathe sports. This group is comprised of fans who are season-ticket holders, name their pets after prominent athletes, have team-themed weddings and parties, travel extensively to support the athletic endeavors of their children, and so forth. For this group of people, sporting events like the Super Bowl, March Madness, and the Masters evoke meaning, emotion and passion. Similarly, within the context of religion, there are many people who devote themselves to their faith. This group is comprised of people who study religious texts, regularly attend religious services and, in short, live what we can term a faith-based lifestyle. Although there is also no doubt that sports and religion have often had an uneasy relationship with each other, they are both aesthetic enterprises that ignite our love and fervor. But they are not the same thing; and yet, they both offer much toward the abundant and well-lived life. There will inevitably be future encounters between the two, but one can hope that the future relationship will veer toward mutual appreciation and refinement.

NOTES

1. There are, however, arguments that have been made that sport serves not as a traditional institutional religion, but rather as a folk or civil religion. For detail on this, see Christopher H. Evans and William R. Herzog II, eds., *The Faith of 50 Million: Baseball, Religion, and American Culture*, 1st edition (Louisville, KY: Westminster John Knox Press, 2002) and Shirl J. Hoffman, ed. *Sport and Religion* (Champaign, IL: Human Kinetics Books, 1992).
2. Another worthwhile conversation stemming from these points is around whether or not sports can be considered art. That question is beyond the scope of this chapter, but it is thoroughly dealt with in Drew A. Hyland, *Philosophy of Sport*, 1st ed., Paragon Issues in Philosophy (New York: Paragon House, 1990).

REFERENCES

Baker, W. J. (2007). *Playing with God: Religion and Modern Sport*. Cambridge, MA: Harvard University Press.

Durkheim, É. (1965). *The Elementary Forms of the Religious Life*. New York: Free Press.

Evans, C. H., and W. R. Herzog II, eds. (2002). *The Faith of 50 Million: Baseball, Religion, and American Culture.* 1st edition. Louisville, KY: Westminster John Knox Press.

Geertz, C. (1977). *The Interpretation of Cultures.* New York: Basic Books.

Gumbrecht, H. U. (2006). *In Praise of Athletic Beauty.* Cambridge, MA: Belknap Press of Harvard University Press.

Hoffman, S. J., ed. (1992). *Sport and Religion.* Champaign, IL: Human Kinetics Books.

Hoffman, S. J. (2010). *Good Game: Christianity and the Culture of Sports.* Waco, TX: Baylor University Press.

Hyland, D. A. (1990). *Philosophy of Sport.* 1st edition. Paragon Issues in Philosophy. New York: Paragon House.

Kyle, D. G. (2007). *Sport and Spectacle in the Ancient World.* Malden, MA; Oxford: Blackwell Publishing.

Novak, M. (1988). *The Joy of Sports: End Zones, Bases, Baskets, Balls, and the Consecration of the American Spirit.* Lanham, MD: Hamilton Press.

Scholes, J., and R. Sassower (2013). *Religion and Sports in American Culture.* 1st edition. New York: Routledge.

SECTION 3

Technology and Sports

Technology has changed sports in hundreds of different ways. Among other things, technology has provided athletes with better equipment, allowing them to heal from injuries more quickly and improving their technique by providing video recordings of their efforts. Technology has also changed the way that fans consume sports. Of course, fans can see sporting events live, but they can also watch them on television and the computer from virtually anywhere in the world. This section explores three related themes. First, it explores how technological developments have changed sports. Second, it examines the role that performance-enhancing drugs play in modern-day sports. Third, it looks at the connection between the mass media and sports.

TECHNOLOGICAL DEVELOPMENT AND SPORTS

As articulated in Chapter 1, technological advances have really changed the face of modern sports. Players have better equipment and are able to make plays that were unthinkable 40 or 50 years ago. Prior to World War II, professional athletes traveled to road games on trains, played with what would be considered archaic equipment by today's standards, and really did not pay much attention to nutrition and fitness. The equipment and training methods that today's athletes use are very sophisticated. Most athletes use state-of-the-art equipment and work with everyone from video technicians and nutritionists to expert trainers and social media consultants.

Technology has not just changed how athletes play their respective sports. Computers have also helped referees officiate calls. Athletes today are so fast and strong that referees need help in order to decide if catches were made or a ball went out of bounds. Technology has helped people gain access to games. People routinely watch sporting events taking place halfway around the world on their computers and phones. An additional issue relates to the use of analytics in sports. Most American professional sports teams use mathematical analysis, known as analytics, to chart the play of athletes. Now, general managers have an incredible amount of information at their disposal relating to a player's performance and are able to track trends. Similarly, computers have helped streamline golf swings, free-throw shots, and the performance of bobsleds and racing cars by putting sensors on players and equipment that can be monitored and evaluated.

In his article entitled, "Cyborg and Supercrip: The Paralympics Technology and the (Dis)empowerment of Disabled Athletes," David Howe traces the development of wheelchair and prosthesis technology used by Paralympic athletes over the last 30 years. The article revolves around two major points. The first is that technological innovations have really lessened the gap between able-bodied athletes and disabled athletes. The second is that this technology is so expensive that not all athletes can afford it. In general, disabled athletes from developing countries have a much more difficult time accessing the state-of-the-art wheelchairs and prostheses that many disabled athletes from developed countries are likely to take for granted. Thus, technological innovations have increased the gaps among disabled athletes.

PERFORMANCE-ENHANCING DRUGS AND SPORTS

There is no question that performance-enhancing drugs (PEDs) have changed the face of sports. Many players feel so much pressure to play at a high level that they take PEDs for the sake of gaining a competitive edge. Broadly speaking, there are three categories of PEDs. The first of these is steroids. Athletes inject steroids, take pills, and use creams that build muscle mass and allow players to recover more quickly from workouts. The second kind of PED is testosterone. As with steroids, many athletes have taken testosterone pills and injections to help build muscle and gain strength. The third category of PED is blood doping. Many athletes have also enhanced the oxygen levels of their blood to promote healing and strength. Blood doping is similar to the dialysis treatments that people receive with ailing kidneys. Blood is removed from the body, it is oxygenated, and then ultimately returned to the body.

There is clearly a number of concerns that exist with PED usage. The first relates to the well-chronicled adverse health effects of PED usage. People who use steroids often experience changes in their moods, along with a number of other changes like hair loss and acne. A second concern with PED usage is that it is unfair to players who are not using them. For players who compete against those using an illegal substance, it makes the playing field uneven. It is not fair for a non-PED-using pitcher to face a PED-using pitcher in the same game. A third concern is that championships have been won and records have been broken by players who were essentially cheating by using PEDs. In the case of baseball, we know that the top two single-season home

run leaders were both using steroids when they broke those records. For many fans, this taints these and other records.

In response to increased patterns of PED use, sports organizations around the world have engaged in more stringent testing practices. The International Olympic Committee, the NFL, and numerous other leagues have implemented testing procedures to randomly test players for banned substances. Severe penalties have also been established in many leagues to deter athletes from using PEDs. In the case of Major League Baseball, for example, the first time a player tests positive, he is banned for 50 games; the second time being caught results in a 100-game ban.

In her article entitled, "Tour du Dopage: Confessions of Doping Professional Cyclists in a Commodified Work Environment," Charlotte Smith identifies how and why steroid usage has become a normalized practice within professional cycling. According to Smith, cycling is a rationalized work setting where athletes are under such intense pressure to win races that they do whatever they can to maximize their performance. Based on her analyses of over 100 steroid-related confessions in the media, Smith found that these athletes justified their usage of steroids in several ways. For example, they felt the need to limit the damage to their bodies, protect their careers, be loyal to their teams, and fulfill team expectations. Many of them also blame the cycling "system" itself for being so cut-throat, strenuous, and demanding.

THE MASS MEDIA AND SPORTS

The advent of mass media has absolutely changed the way that American fans follow sports. It was not that long ago that people's only coverage of a sporting event was on the radio. Through the 1940s and 1950s, families would gather around the radio to listen to boxing matches and other games. Today, people can watch sporting events from all over the world on their computers and smartphones. Most teams, and a growing number of players, also use social media to expand their brand and reach fans. Many professional athletes have hundreds of thousands of followers on sites like Instagram and Twitter and communicate with fans in ways that were historically undreamed of.

Mass media outlets choose to cover sports because of their popularity. Generally speaking, sporting events are not that expensive to produce and have a high potential for viewership. If you look at the 25 highest-rated television shows in American history, all but a small number

of them are sporting events. In the United States and around the world, events like the World Cup, March Madness, the Super Bowl, and the Olympics draw millions upon millions of viewers. Moreover, leagues like the NCAA, FIFA, and the NFL secure millions and millions of dollars in revenue that media outlets pay for the rights to broadcast these big games. Every year, the NBC, CBS, and FOX networks duke it out for the rights to broadcast the Super Bowl. Even though they are likely to pay several hundred million dollars for the rights to broadcast these games, they sell so much commercial time at such a high price that it is still a profitable endeavor for them.

In his article, "Does the Game Really Change? How Students Consume Mediated Sports in the Age of Social Media" Jan Boehmer examines the extent to which college students use Twitter to consume sports-related content. More specifically, he assesses students' use of Twitter relative to other sports-related content distribution systems. He also investigates students' consumption of sports content relative to other forms of content on Twitter. Boehmer's results show that television remains the primary distribution system for sports and that the perceived importance of Twitter in students' lives may be overstated. The one exception relates to students who see themselves as members of a community of

THE SOCIOLOGY OF SPORTS

sports media personalities. This smaller sub-group of users is actually more likely to rely on Twitter than television for sports-related content.

CHAPTER NINE

Cyborg and Supercrip

*The Paralympics Technology and the
(Dis)empowerment of Disabled Athletes*

BY **P. DAVID HOWE**

Issues concerning eligibility for elite sporting contests may have never been more debated than when South African 400m runner Oscar Pistorius decided that he was searching for a new challenge. Pistorius is a bi-lateral below the knee amputee who came to the attention of those interested in Paralympic sport following his success in the Athens 2004 Paralympic Games. In that event Pistorius destroyed the field in the 200m, setting a new world record in a race that included athletes that were uni-lateral below the knee amputee and considered to be less impaired than him. It was clear that Pistorius was a unique athlete, not only for his physical achievements but also because an absence of lower limbs required the adoption of two pros-thetic limbs that have catapulted him beyond the horizon of the Paralympic Movement to the point where he was a few strides away from eligibility in the Olympics. Athletes such as Pistorius who have amputated lower limbs often run on carbon fibre 'blades' that act as feet and as a result Pistorius has been referred to as the *Blade Runner* (Hunt-Grubbe, 2007; Morrissey, 2008; Swartz and Watermeyer, 2008). The utilizing of such technology by Paralympic athletes means that they can be conceptualized as the embodiment of Haraway's (1991) cyborg, which is a hybrid body resulting from fusion of a live organism and man-made technology. It is the Paralympian cyborg, rather than Pistorius himself, that is at the heart of the research presented here.

In the context of Paralympic sport the most successful cyborg athletes may be seen as 'supercrips'. Following Berger, supercrips 'are those individuals whose inspirational stories of courage, dedication, and hard work prove that it can be done, that one can defy the odds and accomplish the impossible' (2008: 648). It also has been argued that the label of supercrip can be negatively bestowed on impaired individuals who simply manage to live 'an ordinary' life (Kama, 2004). Specifically in the context of Paralympic sport and for the purpose of this article, the supercrip is the athlete who wins and also gains a relatively high-profile media exposure. Those athletes who win but do not receive recognition in mainstream media are not supercrip in the context of the Paralympics as they are often marginalized by the degree or nature of their impairment. This marginalization is in part determined by the classification process that sports people with impairments must undergo to determine their eligibility to compete. Also of importance in this article is whether or not athletes use mobility technologies and, by extension, the degree to which they are cyborgs. The process of making a cyborg I articulate as cyborgification as it is useful to understand that in the contemporary world all our bodies use technology in some way. Our bodies can be placed along a continuum from those that require very little technological aid to those whose lives benefit from a great deal from technology. Paralympian wheelchair racers and prosthetic-wearing athletes are the most explicit examples of cyborgification in sport today.

This article explores the interrelatedness of the process of classification of athletes within Paralympic sport and the issues of cyborgification and the supercrip that surround the mobility technologies which facilitate the participation of athletes who would be unable to practise their chosen sport without them. To begin, the article briefly highlights the central importance of classification within the practice of Paralympic sport and how this accentuates different forms of impairment that relate in very particular ways to mobility technologies. Throughout the article I refer directly to these impairment forms as this is standard practice within Paralympic culture.[1] Following this, the article considers technology and how the process of

112

continual advancement and development of two particular mobility aids (wheelchairs and prosthetic limbs) used in track and field athletics have led to the Paralympic Games becoming increasingly commercial and successful in attracting sustained levels of media coverage. As a result of the influence of technology certain impaired bodies of athletes may be seen as a product of cyborgification that ultimately leads to the successful competitors being seen as supercrips (Berger, 2004, 2008). Bodies that are the product of cyborgification, so it will be argued, are the vanguard of the sport for the disabled and as such they are celebrated far more than those competitors that do not use mobility technologies. The article concludes by asking whether the advances in technology are actually empowering disabled athletes.

CLASSIFICATION AND ITS CENTRALITY IN PARALYMPIC SPORT

The International Paralympic Committee (IPC) currently organizes and administers both the Paralympic Games and the quadrennial World Championships for individual Paralympic sports such as athletics. Using the resources of the International Organisations of Sport for the Disabled (IOSD) (Jones and Howe, 2005)[2] (including athletes, volunteer administrators, and classification systems), the IPC has made the Paralympic Games into the most recognizable and influential vehicle for the promotion of disability sport.

Classification is central to the structuring of competition in Paralympic sport, similar to the systems used in the sports of judo and boxing where competitors perform in distinctive weight categories (Howe and Jones, 2006; Jones and Howe, 2005). In the Paralympics, competitors are classified by their body's degree of function within their chosen sport. Classification takes the form of a series of functional tests that determine the appropriate category in which to place the athlete so that equitable sporting contests can be achieved (Sherrill, 1999) and as such is a fundamental component of Paralympic culture (Howe, 2007, 2008). It is a process that is conducted by a group of qualified classifiers who have between them an expertise in physical impairments and the sporting practice in which they are classifying athletes. The classification process used by the IOSDs is a form of selective classification (Tweedy and Vanlandewijck, 2009) that makes a distinction between the physical potential of athletes. The successful athletes in each class should have an equal chance of accumulating physical capital (Jones and Howe, 2005). In reality, however, there are a number of factors that impact on the accumulation of capital (both physical and cultural) in various classifications, the most salient of which for the purpose of this article is whether or not the athlete uses mobility technologies while they perform. For example, the wheelchair is the ubiquitous symbol for disability. The ever-present iconography of the wheelchair in disabled parking bays, for example, means that the public can relate easily to this mobility technology in the context of Paralympic sport. There has also been research to suggest that in Paralympic sport there is a hierarchy of 'acceptable' impairment within the community of athletes (Schell and Rodriguez, 2001; Sherrill and Williams, 1996). As a result, it reinforces the position of wheelchair athletes on the top of a hierarchy of disabilities that locates the less socially acceptable disability categories as marginal (Haller, 2000; Kama, 2004; Mastro et al., 1996). Another factor that impacts on the accumulation of capital is the number of athletes within a particular event. If a competition has six athletes and another has three times that many the winner of the latter is like to gain more capital because more individuals are beaten to secure the victory. A further important factor in terms of whether winners ultimately gain capital from their involvement in sport is the nature and degree of their impairment. The more minimally impaired a wheelchair athlete is, for example, the more likely that they will become the embodiment of the supercrip (Berger, 2004, 2008).

The original classification system that was developed by the International Wheelchair and Amputee Sport Association (IWAS) can be understood as a major reason why wheelchair athletes are celebrated ahead of athletes from other impairment groups. This system classified athletes with spinal cord injuries according to where the lesion was in their spine because back function is of great importance in sport. It was believed that athletes with a greater level of function in their spine should be in a different class from those athletes that have less. Athletes who were leg amputees could easily be fitted into the most able class in this system as they had full use of the spine. It was the IWAS system that was at the heart of the establishment of the Paralympic Movement and which all other impairment groups had to petition to join in the early days of the movement. As an increasing number of athletes with different impairments aspired to get involved in sport for the disabled IWAS established a broad class known as les autres.[3] Some les autres athletes who use wheelchairs, including those with spina bifida and polio, were able to be slotted into the IWAS system, but it was and never has been an exact science. However, many les autres were ineligible because they did not need to use a wheelchair and this ineligibility eventually led to the development of the remaining IOSDs and, ultimately, the development of the IPC. In this way, the classification system that led to the development of sport for the disabled was not political or culturally neutral.

> It is often supposed that one of the goods delivered by successful science is the right way of classifying the things in the world. Surely there is something right about this: any body of scientific knowledge will include ways of classifying, and will not serve its intended aims unless the classifications it embodies reflect real differences and similarities in the world. (Dupré, 2006: 30)

Following Dupré, a philosopher of science, we can see that a classification system can be developed to make sense of the world, in this case that of Paralympic sporting practice. Importantly, however, Dupre adds a caveat to the statement above suggesting:

> ... there is a highly questionable implication of there being some unique best classification ... Classifications are good and bad for particular purposes, and different purposes will motivate different classifications. (2006: 30)

In other words, the systems of classification developed and adopted within the cultural context of Paralympic sport are the product of the history of this practice. Since the history of the Paralympic Movement places athletes in wheelchairs at its centre in part because athletes with spinal cord injuries and amputations were the first to compete in disability sport (Howe, 2008),[4] it is likely that the classification system currently in place continues to favour these athletes who are reliant on constantly improving mobility technologies to enhance their performances. It is to the issue of mobility technology development that this article now turns.

WHEELCHAIRS IN TRACK AND FIELD ATHLETICS

In the mid-1980s, racing wheelchairs were four wheeled and cumbersome by the standards of today's state-of-the-art technology, but they were a significant improvement on the technologies of the rehabilitative sport era of the Paralympic Movement (Howe, 2008). Specially designed racing wheelchairs may be seen as the first major step toward a high performance Paralympic Games. Indeed, performances in terms of speeds of the track events at the Paralympic Games have been improving with the turning of every Paralympiad. For example, the able-bodied male 800m world record during the 1980s stood at 1:41.73 and the record at the time of writing is 1:41.11. The record for wheelchair racers from the 1980s was 1:55.67 and the record today is 1:32.17. Over this period wheelchair racers have gone from being considerably slower than their able-bodied counterparts over the same distance to significantly faster in part due to advances in wheelchair technology. The rules of wheelchair racing also allow for drafting which is an additional factor in the improved performances and, as a result, elite races on the track are similar (at least in terms of tactics) to road cycling where drafting is an advantageous way to save energy. The desire of athletes to move better and faster and also to assist in the production of technology by offering expert advice has allowed them to achieve these aims. However, developing improved technology is only half the battle, since technologies develop at different rates. Some nations might make advances in performance simply because of their access to superior technology. Medal tables at the Paralympic Games have been traditionally dominated by western nations in part because they are at the forefront of the technological advancements in mobility apparatus. Like the Cold War arms race the Paralympic Movement quite literally, in the race to produce the most efficient and advanced mobility aids, has a *leg race* on its hands.

Today's high performance racing wheelchair has three wheels and is aerodynamically built of lightweight carbon fibre so that developing more speed takes considerably less effort than it did in the heavier models of two decades ago. The frame is T-shaped which provides stability, through the long front, and a degree of rigidity, both of which are required when the chairs travel at high speeds (Yilla, 2000). Racing machines with very thin highly pressurized tires and a carbon fibre frame that year on year weigh less and less also benefit from a steering mechanism called a compensator. This is a technology that has been developed to allow wheelchair racers to 'forget' about turning their chairs through a corner. The compensator can be set to direct the chair around the bend once it has been activated by the athlete. Compensators are fixed to the front wheel axle so that the athlete hits it on entering and exiting a turn. This is all racers have to concern themselves with (that is apart from the art of racing) while on the bend. This technological advance has allowed racers to improve their performances markedly.

Within track and field athletics, throwing events (discus, javelin, shot put and club)5 wheelchairs have, since the early 1990s, been replaced by throwing frames which do not have wheels. These frames are more robust than a wheelchair and as a result they are easier to make into a solid platform for competition. The frame is tied to a series of points on the ground either in a shot put or discus circle or behind the line on the javelin 'run-up'. Each frame is specifically designed for the athlete and so enables them to get the most out of their throwing technique. The complex nature of the technique associated with throwing implements such as the shot, discus and javelin means that the rules regarding seated throws have come under close scrutiny in recent years (Frossard et al., 2006). Some classes of athletes are not allowed to let their gluteus leave the seat of the throwing frame. Breaking of this rule has been increasingly monitored by officials at top level events including the Paralympic Games and IPC World Championships. Those throwers who are able to use their legs as well as their upper body ultimately face the prospect of being reclassified into a more able class since the use of one's legs can be an obvious advantage in a sport where the longest distance thrown in six attempts establishes the winner.

There has also been concern about the use of materials in the frames that allow for a 'spring like response' to the throwing action. Athletes hold onto a pole that is part of his or her frame and recoils the body and then releases the implement. Excess energy generated by this action cannot force the body outside the throwing area. In other words if the force from the pole is so great it allows the body to break the plane of the throwing arena the resulting effort will be considered a foul. What is important with regards to discussions about technology is that there is a strong correlation between 'the interaction between the design of the athlete's throwing frame and their throwing technique' (Frossard et al., 2006: 1). In other words, the synergy between the frame and the body produces a cyborg.

For the top racers and throwers their wheelchairs and throwing frames are now an extension of their bodies. These athletes are all individuals who are accustomed to using a wheelchair for mobility, to the degree that moving in a wheelchair becomes habitual, and allows them to develop a hybrid body (Haraway, 1991: 178). While this is the case with wheelchair racers and throwers it is perhaps more self evident with users of prosthetic limbs.

FROM WOODEN LEG TO CARBON FIBRE BLADE

Perhaps the most popular imagery of the past associated with prosthetic limbs is that associated with the haggard old 'sea dog' who hobbles around on a wooden peg-leg. These wooden prostheses have a long history and are more than adequate mobility aids

(Chaloner et al., 2001; Webling and Fahrer, 1986). The term prosthesis is Greek for an addition designed to remove physical stigma.

> Prosthetic medicine is dedicated to physical normalisation and is devoted to the artificial alteration of both function and appearance, but it enters the realm of biopolitics because it uses the 'normal' body as its tribunal and blueprint for action, and treats the impaired body as a spoilt entity that must be hidden and corrected. (Hughes, 2000: 561)

There is a desire to 'create' the normal and at the same time allow individuals to be more mobile and therefore independent. In the context of sports participation as well as day-to-day mobility one of the problems associated with traditional technology is the development of pressure ulcers and painful stumps that develop where the prosthesis joins the body (DesGroseillers et al., 1978). Such dermatologic ailments are at their most painful during the process of rehabilitation where part of gaining an ability to use a prosthetic limb means the skin at the point of contact needs to 'toughened up' (Rossi, 1974). This is particularly acute for leg amputees as the act of bearing weight on a prosthesis can create pressure on the 'stump' that is the result of the amputation. Regardless of technological advances the pull of gravity means that this pressure will pose an ongoing challenge.[6]

Since 1988 there has been a marked improvement in the technology associated with leg prosthetics, particularly in western nations. The materials from which prostheses are made have changed markedly from wood to fibreglass to all manner of carbon fibre and lightweight metals used in advanced scientific design. These mobility aids have been a product of state-of-the-art technologies and, as a result, the athletes who are the vanguards of the deployment of this new technology are producing performances that would have been considered impossible 20 years ago. It can be argued that this sporting technology has advanced with three aims in mind: to produce better performances; to increase the comfort for an individual—athlete or otherwise; and to enable an improvement in efficiency of movement. Advancement is most evident on the track, but also in field events where athletes with amputations have the option of competing as standing athletes or as athletes who use throwing frames. Traditionally, a large percentage of track and field athletes with full or partial leg amputations have for reasons of comfort competed from a wheelchair. The treatment of the nexus between the prosthesis and the body has developed

118

at pace with the actual replacement limb. Today the top of the range 'flex foot' legs are built around the individual's stump and are secured in place by a vacuum seal device which often includes gel padding to greatly reduce the risk of injury from swelling and friction (Howe, 2006).

The use of flex-foot technology instead of the old-fashioned prosthesis, where flexion of the ankle was either mechanical or non-existent, is universal at the highest level of Paralympic sport. As a result there is little advantage to having this technology once you are at the Paralympic Games, but it is required to get there. Countries who are at the developmental stages of sport for the disabled programmes may find it unrealistic to train runners and throwers in leg amputee classes as the cost of up-to-date the technology can be prohibitive. This is a problem with the *leg race* for technology. With state-of-the-art racing wheelchairs costing upwards of £5000 and ergonomically designed prosthesis costing up to £20,000, athletes from across the globe can find participation as cyborgs with state-of-the-art technology prohibitive. While the technology is becoming more affordable there will likely always be nations and athletes left behind in the *leg race*. Therefore eligibility can be limited by economic factors as well as physical ones. Performance standards, however, have improved dramatically across the board within the classification of leg amputees in large part due to increased accessibility to state-of-the-art technology. As the technology becomes more affordable there are likely to be as many ambulant cyborgs competing as there are currently in wheelchairs.

The previous two sections of the article have highlighted the development of both wheelchairs and prosthetic limbs. Attention is now turned to the notion that such developments signal a 'technocratic ideology' that Shogun (1998) has suggested is becoming increasingly pervasive within the Paralympic Movement.

TECHNOCRATIC IDEOLOGY

The technological innovations discussed in the two preceding sections are important factors in helping to focus the Paralympic spotlight on athletes that are members of IWAS. It is important, however, to remember that these technologies have to be purchased and therefore the Paralympic Movement represents a developing market for the sale of technologically advanced mobility aids. Many of the most up-to-date mobility technologies highlighted in this article are inaccessible to athletes from much of the 'developing' world where the population is generally poorer. In this sense, Paralympic athletics may be seen as technologically advanced on the one hand, but isolationist and exclusionary on the other. The importance of technology in the context of Paralympic track and field athletics can best be expressed in the phrase 'technocentric ideology' (Charles, 1998: 379).

The move to hi-tech mobility devices specifically designed for sport is a response to the general push for more technological advancement in society but it also relates to the desires of the athletes to perform with greater proficiency. Today, many of the elite athletes work with leading wheelchair and prosthesis suppliers to ensure their future success is based on the technologies they use as much as it is on the training regimes they follow. As a result the top cyborg athletes also receive commercial reward for their involvement in the development and manufacture of the state-of-the-art technology that is at the heart of technocratic ideology. Technology is literally pushing the Paralympic Movement. As Charles suggests:

> Technology and kinesiology are symbiotically linked. They have a mutually beneficial relationship. As technology advances, so does the quality of scientific research and information accessible in the field. As kinesiology progresses and gains academic acceptance and credibility, technology assumes a more central role in our field. The more scientific the subdiscipline, the more we can see technology at play. (1998: 379)

Following this statement it is clear that the field of high performance sport (of which Paralympic sport is a subset) has benefited from an increase in technologies that have been developed to harness the power of the human body (Burkett, 2010; Davis and Cooper, 1998). Able-bodied high-performance athletes rely on technology in their day-to-day training (Hoberman, 1992; Shogun, 1999) yet when these athletes perform in sports like track and field athletics the technology that has allowed them to train and compete in the sporting arena may be completely obscured from view.[7] An able-bodied athlete takes technology with him or her to the start of an Olympic final as their clothing and footwear are products of advanced technology. In fact Butryn (2002, 2003) has highlighted that high performance (able-bodied) track and field athletics is surrounded by technologies that enable athletes to become cyborgs. However, specialist clothing and shoes appear less like advanced technology in comparison to racing wheelchairs and prosthetic limbs that lead to the cyborgification of bodies, as they are not explicitly aids for mobility. As Shogun suggests:

> When persons with disabilities use technologies to adjust the participation in 'normal' physical activity, the use of these technologies constructs this person as unnatural in contrast to a natural, nondisabled participant, even though both nondisabled participants and those with disabilities utilize technologies to participate. (1998: 272)

Technologies such as racing wheelchairs and flex-feet (artificial legs biomechanically designed for running) have enhanced the performances of athletes whose impairments benefit from their use and are central to the identity of the Paralympic Movement. It is these cyborg sporting bodies that are most often celebrated by the IPC (Howe, 2007). Bodies that are able to successfully adapt to technology that wherever possible normalizes their movements within society generally and on the athletics track specifically are seen as (the most) successful. According to Seymour:

> A winning wheelchair athlete is seen as the epitome of rehabilitative success. The vision of strong male bodies competing for honours on the sports field is an image that has currency in the able-bodied world. Bravery in overcoming the catastrophe of a damaged body is a quality everyone can admire. (1998: 119)

This image extends to amputee athletes who have also suffered traumatic injuries and use performance-enhancing prosthetic limbs. The use of mobility technologies provides an opportunity for the user of re-embodiment (Seymour, 1998) that is not available to individuals who are congenitally impaired. Users of both wheelchairs and prosthetic limbs that have acquired their impairment are able to establish a distinctive identity with their new *cyborg* bodies. These bodies are the hallmark of IWAS and central to the public understanding of the Paralympic Movement. One explanation for this may be the fact that these athletes more than any others expose the ability in disability sport. Elite wheelchair racers over distances longer than 800m are considerably faster than able-bodied runners and those athletes who wear hi-tech prostheses have higher visibility associated with their performances than ambulant athletes with cerebral palsy and visual impairment.

SUPERCRIPS, CYBORGS, AND LES AUTRES

The bodies that have been absent from this article thus far are those that derive benefit from advances in sport science support, such as biomechanical and physiological analysis, but do not require a mobility aid such as the use of a wheelchair or prosthesis. Visually impaired, ambulant cerebral palsy and those with intellectual impairments are able to compete in sport without the use of special technologies of mobility. This relative normality can be seen as detrimental to how these groups may be treated both inside and outside the Paralympic Movement. Athletes with visual impairment are relatively easily understood by the public. A high percentage of the world's population use either spectacles or contact lenses which are designed to help us better read the world around us. When our eyesight deteriorates as a result of spending too much time at the computer or through the passage of time and old age, we can understand and appreciate the difficulties associated with poor sight. As a result athletes with visual impairment are not treated as marginal in western society to the same extent as those who have cerebral palsy or an intellectual impairment (Sherrill and Williams, 1996).

Some impairments are more difficult to understand than others, such as the uncontrol-lable spasticity of an individual with cerebral palsy or for those where the manifestation of their condition is only evident in social environments, such as an athlete with an intellectual disability. Mobility technological intervention has a minimal role to play in managing these types of bodies to a norm that is acceptable to mainstream sporting practices. Therefore, it is often difficult for the general public to see ability in some of the performances of individuals with impairments. In referring to athletes with cerebral palsy a former president of Cerebral Palsy International Sport and Recreation Association (CP-ISRA) Colin Rains stated:

> It's tough to say but I believe people think that athletes with cerebral palsy are not totally media friendly, visually. They can be slightly uncoordinated both in their running and their visual expressions. It is possible people find this off-putting. (Mott, 2000)

122

The result of this can be stigmatization of a young person with an impairment that cannot benefit from mobility technologies and therefore is unable to actively engage with the explicit cyborgification associated with athletes who use a wheelchair or prosthesis.

Following Shogun (1998) it could be argued that the mobility technology used in sport for the disabled is unnatural because it is seen as making athletes less than human. However, in light of the 'super human' results achieved through the use of either state-of-the-art wheelchairs or prosthetic limbs, within Paralympic track and field athletics it has become an accepted currency over the last two decades. Mobility technology allows for exceptional sporting performances in the sport of athletics which, to some extent, are celebrated by the able-bodied public, but such performances are unlikely to be achieved by athletes who compete without these mobility aids. The use of what Butryn (2003) coined 'implement technology' has made the Paralympic Games into a significant sporting spectacle.

The use of these technologies has led to a litany of supercrip stories. As highlighted earlier, the supercrip can leave the observer with the sense of impossible achievement. It has been argued by Kama (2004) that the term supercrip applies either to a person with a disability that performs ordinarily in their daily life or to persons with disabilities that really excel, elevating themselves over the common person. In other words, some people with impairments receive patronizing super-status just by living a normal life and in this way the tag of the supercrip can be seen as a double-edged sword. According to Berger:

> 'Supercrips' are those individuals whose inspirational stories of courage and dedication, and hard work prove that it can be done, that one can defy the odds and accomplish the impossible. The concern is that these stories of success will foster unrealistic expectations about what people with disabilities can achieve, what they *should* be able to achieve if only they tried hard enough. Society does not need to change. It is the myth of the self-made man. (2004: 798)

By and large these narratives closely follow athletes who benefit from technological aids as it is 'easier' to see ability in a fast sprinter on blades like Pistorius or a wheelchair racer that can 'run' a mile faster than the current able-bodied world record. However, many Paralympians who are highly trained and motivated athletes but do not require these technologies can never therefore live up to these ideals, which appear imperative in the commercialized world of the 21st-century Paralympic Games.

123

More recent work by Berger highlights the role model capacity of the supercrip and clearly indicates that celebrated athletes are more than a media construction and can act as 'real' mentors (2008). While this is a useful point, Berger's research is conducted within the context of wheelchair basketball, a sport where high performance technology is also clearly evident (2004, 2008). His conclusions would probably have been different if he had researched the ambulant cerebral palsy or visually impaired athletes who do not require mobility technologies and generally received very little media coverage. Hence their role model capacity is diminished. The same tension Berger mentions between athletes and non-athletes in his study could be made between athletes who are accepted (technology users) as supercrips and those who are not (2008).

DISCUSSION

At the outset of this article I asked whether or not an increased emphasis on technology at the Paralympic Games, and the media spotlight it engenders, leads to the empowerment of the athletes with impairments. In an increasingly commercial world the technocratic ideology (Charles, 1998) that surrounds track and field athletics at the Paralympics will be hard to transform. The athletes who use wheelchairs and prostheses are at the centre of the Paralympic Movement and will be better consumers simply because they have specialist materials to purchase if they wish to compete at the highest level. The body policing (Cole, 1993, 1998) that goes on in mainstream high-performance sport between what is acceptably human and what is not has, in the Paralympic world, been paradoxically reversed. Oscar Pistorius is a case in point. When Pistorius tried to compete in the Olympic arena his cyborg body was seen as not human enough (Hunt-Grubbe, 2007; Morrissey, 2008; Swartz and Watermeyer, 2008) yet in the Paralympic world this body is the most highly celebrated. It appears that in Paralympic track and field athletics the closer a body is to a cyborg the more capital it holds, which is the opposite to the world articulated by Haraway (1991) in relation to the boundaries between humans and non-humans. Wheelchair users and amputees who use prostheses are tied explicitly to sport technologies and therefore blur the lines between 'natural' and 'artificial' and are perhaps the best example of the cyborg in contemporary society. Butryn see the nexus between the natural and legal and the artificial and illegal as hegemonic humanness (2003: 28). Hegemonic humanism can be seen to have been practised when Oscar Pistorius was initially excluded from competing in able-bodied athletics (Howe, 2008). His right to compete on his prostheses was restored because he has no other option but to run on man-made legs and by the fact they were not advantaging him in the context of competition. In a sense, Paralympic sport celebrates 'transgressing the taboo boundary between blood, sweat, and tears, and blood, sweat and gears' (Butryn, 2003: 28). Here the cyborg wheelchair user and the prosthetic limb wearer are the role models and supercrips the Paralympic Movement triumphs, in a way that Olympic and other mainstream sport has failed to achieve. This is largely because the Paralympics Games were designed to celebrate difference that is distinct from the able-bodied norm. Yet today it appears that Paralympic difference must increasingly take on a cyborg form.

Where does this leave *les autres*? They certainly have a part to play in the Paralympic Movement, but the more marginal the physicality of the body, the further away it is from the potential of cyborgification and the more likely a tragic rather than a heroic allegory will follow them. This analysis tells us a great deal about the politics of disablement. While it is considered an infringement for the able to become too cyborg, for the disabled it is highly advantageous because technology can normalize their 'inferior' bodies to the point where in the case of elite wheelchair racers they can produce super-human results. Of course there is a tension here. MacIntyre (1999) tells us that vulnerability and affliction and the related facts of dependence are central to the human condition. The susceptibility to injury and misery, distress and pain is likely to befall us all at some point in our existence. We all will be reliant on others from time to time. It begs the question why impaired bodies are so harshly disabled by society and, at least in the context of Paralympic sport, only those that are cyborgs are celebrated at length. Of these cyborgs the winners are put on a pedestal as supercrips.

CONCLUSION

The classification system at the centre of the Paralympic Movement was established by the now defunct International Stoke Mandeville Wheelchair Sports Federation but lives on in the International Wheelchair and Amputee Sport Association. This system classifies bodies that use wheelchairs to compete in the sport of athletics and creates *les autres* who are unable to use this mobility technology. In the last 20 years the associated development of biomechanically and ergonomically responsive prostheses has meant that many athletes who in the past would have competed from a wheelchair are now able to compete from a standing position. While the development of mobility technology that enhances sport performance is understandably beneficial for the impairment groups concerned (at least for those that can afford them), it marginalizes further those athletes that do not use technologies directly in their competitive performance. Because the high-end wheelchair athlete is able to perform at the same level or better than an able-bodied athlete, to the public the abilities of these athletes is obvious. On the other hand, it might be difficult to see the ability of an athlete who has cerebral palsy which affects both legs and who runs 100m much slower than his/her able-bodied counterpart.

The possibility of a re-embodiment for certain athletes with disabilities is provided through acquiring expensive sporting technologies. This economic exclusion makes ineligible much of the world's population of potential Paralympians. In elite sport for the disabled, there are increasing numbers of athletes with mechanical, artificially designed bodies creating new sporting potential. These athletes are the most celebrated in part because the sport for the disabled movement developed around them. The technology they use has the capacity to 'normalize' their bodies, and in so doing produces 'sporting cyborgs'. Unlike in mainstream sport, these athletes are celebrated both inside and increasingly outside the Paralympic Movement. A technocentric ideology has led to a cyborgification that is celebrated within Paralympic sport and has made celebrities of the athletes who are successful in using the state-of-the-art movement technologies to achieve super performances (Howe, 2008). Such elevated status of handpicked cyborgs can be problematic for the communities of impaired individuals who can never achieve such a position. As Kama argues:

> ... (w)ell-known, successful disabled people are put on a pedestal for their demonstrated ability to triumph. This triumph is used to validate the disabled individual and to alter societal perceptions. Consequently, the wish to see disabled who 'have done it' is particularly intense while the pitiful disabled trigger antipathy because they reproduce and reinforce disabled people's inferior positionality and exclusion. (2004: 447)

The celebration of the supercrip, which is manifest in the cyborg bodies of the best wheelchair and prosthetic-wearing athletes, is good for the individuals placed on the pedestal but may lead to the (dis)empowerment of other athletes with impairment who cannot take advantage of the explicit use of technology. Ultimately the Paralympics risk becoming a show of technology, rather than a show of athleticism, leaving behind those from the developing world without performance-enhancing technology at their disposal, and those from the West whose bodies are inappropriate for its use. Technological advancement in relation to Paralympic sport is not dissimilar to other changes in society; it is clearly a mixed blessing. Technology empowers some while leaving the status of others at best unaltered and at worst increasing their liminality.

ACKNOWLEDGMENT

I would like to thank Dr. Carol Morris and the two anonymous referees for helpful comments on earlier versions of this article.

NOTES

1. I am aware this approach is not favoured in social scientific circles but it is important here to accurately reflect Paralympic culture.
2. The federations are the Cerebral Palsy International Sport and Recreation Association, International Blind Sport Association, International Sports Federation for Persons with Intellectual Disability, and the International Wheelchair and Amputee Sport Association (IWAS). This last is a federation that was launched in September 2004 at the Athens Paralympic Games. It is the result of a merger of two federations, the International Stoke Mandeville Wheelchair Sports Federation and the International Sport Organisation for the Disabled, which have been part of the IPC since its inception.
3. Les Autres is a French phrase used within disability sport circles meaning 'the others'. Originally the term refers to athletes with a disability who did not directly fit into the classification system established by IWAS. Today Les Autres is used to highlight any athlete who is not specifically referred to in the classification systems of the IOSDs and who is able to be slotted into an existing classification system. I use the term here specifically to refer to athletes with a disability who do not use either a wheelchair or prosthesis while competing in athletics.
4. In the early days of Paralympic sport, athletes with amputations would have more often than not competed from a wheelchair and, as such, the group of athletes I consider to be at the centre of the Paralympic Movement are those with spinal cord injuries and amputations.

5. Club is an event for class F32/F51 athletes who either have very involved and severe cerebral palsy (F32) or a very high lesion on their spinal cord (F51) and as a result throwing a javelin is impractical and dangerous.

6. The connection between the prosthesis and the upper body obviously does have gravity to deal with, but the lack of 'weight bearing' means that pressure ulcers and the like are less troublesome. Also, arm prostheses are much less prevalent in the sport of track and field athletics.

7. I use the term 'able-bodied' here because it is the term used by athletes within the cultural context of the Paralympics.

REFERENCES

Berger RJ (2004) Pushing forward: Disability, basketball, and me. *Qualitative Inquiry* 10: 794–810.

Berger RJ (2008) Disability and the dedicated wheelchair athlete: Beyond the 'supercrip' critique. *Journal of Contemporary Ethnography* 37(6): 647–78.

Burkett B (2010) Technology in Paralympic sport: Performance enhancement or essential for performance. *British Journal of Sports Medicine* 44: 215–20.

Butryn TM (2002) Cyborg horizons: Sport and the ethics of self-technologization. In: Miah A and Easson S (eds) *Sport, Technology: History, Philosophy, and Policy.* Oxford: Elsevier Science, 111–34.

Butryn TM (2003) Posthuman podiums: Cyborg narratives of elite track and field athletes. *Sociology of Sport Journal* 20: 17–39.

Chaloner EJ, Flora HS and Ham RJ (2001) Amputations at the London Hospital, 1852–1857. *Journal of the Royal Society of Medicine* 94: 409–12.

Charles JM (1998) Technology and the body of knowledge. *Quest* 50: 379–88.

Cole CL (1993) Resisting the canon: Feminist cultural studies, sport, and technologies of the body. *Journal of Sport and Social Issues* 17: 77–97.

Cole CL (1998) Addiction, exercise, and cyborgs: Technologies and deviant bodies. In: Rail G (ed.) *Sport and Postmodern Times.* Albany: State University of New York Press, 261–75.

Davis R and Cooper R (1999) Technology for disabilities. *British Medical Journal* 319: 1–4.

DesGroseillers J-P, Desjardins JP, Germain JP and Krol AL (1978) Dermatologic problems in amputees. *Canadian Medical Association Journal* 118: 535–7.

Dupré J (2006) Scientific classification. *Theory, Culture and Society* 23(2–3): 30–2.

Frossard L, O'Riordan A and Goodman S (2006) Applied biomechanics for evidence-based training of Australian elite seated throwers. *International Council of Sport Science and Physical Education Perspectives series.* Available at: http://eprints.qut.edu.au/2713/

Haller B (2000) If they limp, they lead? News representations and the hierarchy of disability images. In: Braithwaite DO and Thompson TL (eds) *Handbook of Communication and People with Disabilities: Research and Application.* Mahwah, NJ: Lawrence Erlbaum, 273–88.

Haraway DJ (1991) *Simians, Cyborgs, and Women: The Reinvention of Nature.* London: Routledge.

Hoberman J (1992) *Mortal Engines: The Science of Human Performance and the Dehumanization of Sport.* Oxford: Free Press.

Howe PD (2006) The role of injury in the organization of Paralympic sport. In: Loland S, Skirstad B and Waddington I (eds) *Pain and Injury in Sport: Social and Ethical Analysis.* London: Routledge, 211–25.

Howe PD (2007) Integration of Paralympic athletes into Athletics Canada. *International Journal of Canadian Studies* 35: 134–50.

Howe PD (2008) *The Cultural Politics of the Paralympic Movement: Through the Anthropological Lens.* London: Routledge.

Howe PD and Jones C (2006) Classification of disabled athletes: (Dis)empowering the Paralympic practice community. *Sociology of Sport Journal* 23: 29–46.

Hughes B (2000) Medicine and the aesthetic invalidation of disabled people. *Disability and Society* 15(4): 555–68.

Hunt-Grubbe C (2007) The Blade Runner generation. *The Sunday Times.* Available at: http://timesonline.co.uk/tol/life/_and_style/health/article2079637.ece?print=yes

Jones C and Howe PD (2005) Conceptual boundaries of sport for the disabled: Classification and athletic performance. *Journal of Philosophy of Sport* 32: 133–46.

Kama A (2004) Supercrips versus the pitiful handicapped: Reception of disabling images by disabled audience members. *Communications* 29(4): 447–66.

MacIntyre A (1999) *Dependent Rational Animals: Why Human Beings Need the Virtues.* Chicago: Open Court.

Mastro JVM, Burton AW, Rosendahl M and Sherrill C (1996) Attitudes of elite athletes with impairments toward one another: A hierarchy of preference. *Adapted Physical Activity Quarterly* 13(2): 197–210.

Morrissey R (2008) Fast-moving technology: Prosthetics, physical ability merging in a blur. *Chicago Tribune*. Available at: http://dispatch.com/live/contentbe/dispatch/2008/02/03/20080203-C11

Mott S (2000) Impaired logic keeps heroes off the stage. *The Daily Telegraph*, 11 December.

Rossi LFA (1974) Rehabilitation following below-knee amputation. *Proceedings of the Royal Society of Medicine* 67: 37–8.

Schell LA and Rodriguez S (2001) Subverting bodies / ambivalent representations: Media analysis of Paralympian, Hope Lewellen. *Sociology of Sport Journal* 18: 127–35.

Seymour W (1998) *Remaking the Body: Rehabilitation and Change*. London: Routledge.

Sherrill C (1999) Disability sport and classification theory: A new era. *Adapted Physical Activity Quarterly* 16: 206–15.

Sherrill C and Williams T (1996) Disability and sport: Psychosocial perspectives on inclusion, integration and participation. *Sport Science Review* 5(1): 42–64.

Shogun D (1998) The social construction of disability: The impact of statistics and technology. *Adapted Physical Activity Quarterly* 15: 269–77.

Swartz L and Watermayer B (2008) Cyborg anxiety: Oscar Pistorius and the boundaries of what it means to be human. *Disability and Society* 23(2): 187–90.

Tweedy SM and Vanlandewijick YC (2011) International Paralympic Committee position stand—Background and scientific rationale for classification in Paralympic sport. *British Journal of Sports Medicine* 45: 259–269.

Webling DD'A and Fahrer M (1986) Early bent knee prostheses: Ancestors of K9. *British Medical Journal* 293: 1636–7.

Yilla AB (2000) Enhancing wheelchair sport performance. In: Winnock J (ed.) *Adapted Physical Education and Sport*, 3rd edn. Leeds: Human Kinetics, 419–31.

CHAPTER TEN

Tour du Dopage

Confessions of Doping Professional Cyclists in a Commodified Work Environment

BY **CHARLOTTE SMITH**

INTRODUCTION: UNDERSTANDING 'CHEATING' IN CYCLING

The commodification of sport and the vast financial expenditure devoted to it have reinforced sport's capacity as a form of spectatorship and entertainment (Furst, 1971), even though there are many accounts of the capitalist system being cheated. One example is 'drug doping' that according to Johanson (1987) has become a realistic feature of professional cycling given that 'good' performance can only be denoted by winning. 'Drug doping' pertains to performance enhancement that is commonly represented as the antithesis to sport: 'the potential to enhance or enhances the sport performance and/or presents an actual or potential health risk to the athlete and/or violates the spirit of the sport' (WADA, 2009: 14). Perhaps the most high-profile example illustrating this impurity came to light on the 13th of June 2012, when the United States Anti-Doping Agency (USADA) wrote to the seven time Tour de France (TDF) winner Lance Armstrong, charging him with conspiring in 'drug doping' between 1998 and 2011 (USADA, 2012). Since Armstrong's charge and acquittal, many more doping confessions and scandals have shown that this deemed illegitimate practice maintains prevalence among professional cyclists, despite zealous anti-doping campaigns that are costly, but yet do not eradicate the private motives for usage (Jones, 2010). These fallacies often translate to an inefficiency of testing. For example, Hermann and Henneberg (2014) have determined that to detect 100% of doping instances over a one-year period, 16–50 tests would need to be carried out on each athlete. Perhaps unsurprisingly the prevalence of doping in cycling remains, and especially in Grand Tours. From 1996 to 2010 thirty-six out of forty-five top three finishers in the TDF were caught doping (USADA, 2013).

As well as convincing statistics on its prevalence, discussions of doping are so overpowering that even those who have won clean—such as Chris Froome winning the TDF in 2013—have their victory tarnished by being located in contexts that are infiltrated by moral panics and previous scandals, such as the Lance Armstrong case (Groves and Griggs, 2014). Of course, not all cyclists are dopers and as Morente-Sánchez and Zabala (2013) note, most athletes at least acknowledge the practice as cheating. In panic laden environments, high profile cyclists often deny doping through press releases and autobiographies. For example, Bradley Wiggins (2012) stated he has never doped because the risks for his family and life are too great. However, despite this denial, Wiggins' (2012) sympathizes with dopers arguing that it is not a personality issue but instead the sport's culture and peer pressure. Further ambiguity also ensues as the implications of an enforced doping ban mean it becomes difficult to garner the true extent of the problem within professional cycling because acknowledgement of drug use carries severe career consequences for those concerned (Jones, 2010; Pitsch and Emrich, 2012). Despite this unknown, evidence highlights that both corporization and scientization mean there are great pressures imposed on athletes to adopt any means necessary to win (Stewart and Smith, 2010). The voices of athletes who face such pressure, and who inevitably use banned substances have, however, seldom been heard (Pappa and Kennedy, 2013). There are polarized views towards doping, one-side views it as a moral indignation and the other expresses it as a necessary part of performance in top sport. The behavior of sports persons and sport as a phenomenon generally however are far from located in their own system of behavior; instead being found amongst many other multi-facetted developments whose beginnings lie amongst the early-capitalist bourgeois society (Rigauer, 1981). This paper focuses on understanding how drug use and cheating is cultivated, and legitimated, by professional cyclists within the spectacle of the TDF. It begins by reviewing literature on early capitalist beliefs, framings of work performance, and cheating, before addressing the commodification of work and the sporting spectacle. Prior to outlining its methods, technique and approach towards analyzing doping cyclists' confessions, it explains it's theoretical adaptation of neutralization theory that provides a framework for understanding normalized wrongdoing. There are then three findings sections showing how and why cyclists legitimate their behavior at an individual, team and spectacle/society level, before a discussion and concluding section highlighting the contribution of 'performance egoism' at work.

EARLY CAPITALIST SOCIETY, PERFORMANCE, AND CHEATING

Early capitalist beliefs are based on a 'performative principle' historically founded on both economic alienation and repressive disblimination. This equates to the execution of specific workplace tasks in the most efficient manner, produced by the dominant values and instrumentalities of the capitalist market, most often associated with Scientific Management and Taylorism. Rationalized and commodified performances then potentially become a spectacle form comprised of the structural aspects of performance that responds and adapt to market criteria. Adopting this framing of work it is clear that athletic ability can be a quantifiable commodity like any other form of social labour or performance produced by capitalist firms for profit under the conditions of market exchange (Moller, 2010). As Loland (2004) suggests, in sport, the athlete is a postmodern subject with chances to maximize their performance with whatever means they consider appropriate. This produces a competitive arena whereby individuals' objectives are not merely performing their job, but instead aiming to be 'the best that they can be'. Consequently this also produces an agenda of winning that breeds a darker side and a cult of vengeance (Alt, 1983), demonstrating much similarity with the historical trajectory of sporting behaviors in cycling.

Continuing to draw an analogy between work and sport, the recalcitrant worker or 'cheat' has been a defining theme in British sociology (Thompson and Ackroyd,

133

1995). Deviant or 'cheating' employees are termed 'outsiders' who impose a threat to the 'social' or 'moral' order of the company (Vardi and Weiner, 1986), but who also engage in behavior that intentionally benefits the self. Despite emphasizing the moral indignity of the employee, in literature on employee deviance it also remains evident that the way work is organized determines the form of occupational crime, deviance or cheating (Mars, 1994). This idea has become clearer more recently wherein scholars suggest that there has been a shift from a dark 'outside' that impinges upon action inside organizations, towards a dark 'inside' that is situated within the boundaries of organizations and its practice (Linstead et al., 2014). Given the revenues required for testing doping cyclists (Maennig, 2014) there is a case for understanding how these dark 'insides' are reproduced and/or how they are derived from social and cultural factors outside to organizations.

THE COMMODIFICATION OF WORK AND THE SPORTING SPECTRE OF CULTURAL PERFORMANCE

Since 1960 the capitalist market has transformed from one that values material goods towards a society of spectacle, resulting in more people investing time, money and energy partaking in and embracing multi-faceted phenomena such as sports (Furst, 1971). Spectacle in this sense is something visible to the eye that is large scale and impressive (Cheska, 1978) and has taken on a much more theatrical conceptualization in recent decades. One notable area of difference has been the increased emphasis of individual's embodied enactment (Mckenzie, 2001), whereby the motif becomes performative, requiring the individual to 'act out' in particular places, especially when working. With cultural performance increasing in the modern workplace, the competitive struggle remains striving for similar socially determined desirables: personal prestige and recognition (Moller, 2010). This necessitates a broader definition of performance that encompasses both what a person does, but also being an expression of what they are. Such can also be applied to athletes, and as Birrell (1981: 373) suggests: 'the athlete is now an exemplary figure who embodies the moral values of the community and thus serves as a symbol of those values'. Following this symbolism, sporting culture has been transformed from a ritualized moral order to one concerned with the production of mass spectacles (Alt, 1983), integrating individual's enacted embodied performance. Walsh and Giulianotti (2001) refer to this spectacle as part of the 'hyper-commodification of sport' whereby both the quantitative value of sports have increased rapidly in addition to the secondary, non-play aspects that have become commercialized. This certainly applies with the TDF that over its 21 stages has 4700 hours of television coverage, 12 million spectators and circa 2000 reporting journalists. Subsequently, given the commodified nature of sport and work, and the spectacle that they have become, incidents of doping can no longer be meaningfully located solely within a discussion of each cyclist's inappropriate moral standing (Barthes, 1997) as doing so negates equal determinants concerned with the competitive and spectating environment in which they are located. In support of this there has been much research highlighting that doping is not a solitary act and that many stakeholders including professional athletes, the media, officials and team doctors all play a significant role in the definitional process (Lauber et al., 2010). However, rather than look at why cyclists dope, and the procedural institutional measures that help manifest the phenomenon, this study focuses on the strategies that individuals use to legitimate their consumption in the public arena, showing what purpose this serves for them, and the effects it has on their self-presentation of their performance whilst doing their job.

NEUTRALIZATION THEORY: NORMALIZING ORGANIZATIONAL WRONGDOING

The designated deviant or 'cheater' in sport and work is often framed as lacking moral awareness, knowing their behavior is 'wrong' but deciding to continue with it. However, this framing closes down in-depth understandings of how these individuals may locate their behavior within social and cultural contexts. One mechanism that can be used to overcome these concerns is the neutralization theory of Sykes and Matza (1957). This theory is applied herein and highlights the motifs and performance morals that are made explicit by professional cyclists. It does this through considering the strategies cyclists use to legitimize their doping behavior with the norm-conforming attitudes of sporting society. In particular the first three of these include a 'denial of responsibility' whereby delinquents pass on responsibility for their actions, a 'denial of injury' whereby delinquents argue that there is no harm caused by their actions, and a 'denial of victim' whereby the injury caused is not seen as wrong in light of the other person's behavior. The latter three include 'condemning of the condemners' where the delinquent blames those who disapprove of his actions, an 'appeal to higher loyalties' where more importance is placed on the delinquent's own social group rather than larger society and lastly the 'metaphor of ledger' where the benefits of the delinquent act are offset by the damaged caused.

METHODS

This study focuses on the use of the two most common performance enhancing techniques in cycling: blood-doping and Erythropoietin (EPO). The former concerns the removal, storage and re-injection of an athlete's own blood to increase the amount of oxygen that they are able to intake via an increase in red blood cells (Schjerling, 2005). The latter, EPO, is a type of growth hormone that stimulates the athlete's bone marrow to produce more red blood cells, also increasing the level of oxygen in their blood (Waddington and Smith, 2000). Owing to the difficulties in collecting primary data on doping cyclists (Ohl et al., 2013) this study analyses ad verbatim quotations from 112 cyclists' confessions in the media. Studies have already emphasized how the negativity of cycling and doping are exacerbated through the lay press who portray a damaging image of doping (Lopez, 2013). Therefore an understanding of the confession herein is one which is appropriated with Sykes and Matza's (1957) theory and which incorporates the notion that doping cyclists know their practice is perceived as cheating or impure throughout society and the cycling world. Whilst there have been debates concerning the degree of truth in confessionary statements for many decades, there is evidence that self-reported drug use is a reliable indicator of individuals' actual drug use (Mazanov et al., 2008).

Regarding access, statements have been acquired via a Google news search directed towards each cyclist, with the list of names being supplemented via two means. First, via an online database 'dopeology.org'—a database that is a topology of doping in European professional road cycling, listing all doping admission statements since 1980. Second, all names used in the United States of America Doping Agency's (USADA, 2014) case against Armstrong case were integrated. As these statements are widely available on the Internet and with the riders' real names attached, the author has not subjected these accounts to

136

further anonymisation in the findings section. All of the cases investigated in this paper refer to professional road cycling males, as opposed to amateurs and young cyclists where doping is less common (Ohl et al., 2013). Males are chosen because they represent the greater sample size, and whilst the female professional cycling population is growing (British Cycling, 2014), this is still substantially disproportionate in comparison to males. To understand individuals' accounts in a non-judgmental manner, 'cheating' and 'doping' are not understood as cultural universals, but instead as modern concepts that have emerged and developed as part of broader pattern of social relationships in sport and work (Waddington and Smith, 2000). Rather than offering an apology or justification for cyclists' doping, the focus is on how their drug use within the competitive and performative arena of their work is legitimated. The agenda is therefore unpicking how doping cyclists tell their stories and the positions and understandings these demonstrate about sport and work as a mode of cultural performance.

Whilst there are an increasing range and variety of techniques available for analyzing media materials such as quantitative forms of content analysis and more qualitative forms of analysis such as discourse analysis, given the meanings and 'morals' conveyed, the approach favored a more general interpretive analysis. This approach was able to note in more detail individuals' thoughts, feelings and behaviors surrounding their doping practices. Early on in the analysis the author noted frequent disjunctions in cyclists' quotations whereby they outlined their behavior and then exemplified this with statements such as 'this was necessary because' or 'but it was impossible to compete without'. Following these justifications and the known cultural context of cycling, it was then clear that Syke's and Matza's (1957) theory would be an apt lens to apply in the analysis. The quotations were separated from the media documents and analyzed using NVivo. First they were grouped and coded into each of the neutralization strategies, they were then coded a second time to break down each strategy to a finer level. This was needed to identify the key motives for cyclists justifying their doping within each particular strategy.

FINDINGS

The findings of the study are now presented and show how doping cyclists suggest their drug-taking behavior is justified and legitimate to their work performance and not something they consider cheating. To do this cyclists locate their consumption as part of the production and maintenance of their performance and TDF spectacle: occurring on an individual, team-based and broader capitalist level. Considered as a whole these three instances of doping show how individuals present themselves as performative subjects who respond to the challenges of sport through legitimated cheating.

SUSTAINING THE SPECTACLE OF SELF

Avoiding Damage to Bodies

Sykes and Matza (1957) suggest that one of the ways classified delinquents justify their behavior is through denying harm is caused to others. In the study, rather than deny that they are hurting others, cyclists took on a more self-centered role, doping to avoid damaging effects from participation in pro cycling. They also wanted to maintain the normal functioning of their bodies following heavy exertion. Their accounts drew on legitimized medical discourses, and statements often began with cyclists rejecting an identity of a doper. Instead they framed their drug use as a necessity:

> 'I was not a doper, I told myself—I just injected myself to recover and needed pills to sleep' (David Millar).

> 'In the pack you never use the word doping but medical help' (Richard Virenque).

By speaking of medical discourses this lead to a more individualized form of performance repatriation whereby cyclists also suggested doping was necessary to prolong and protect their own individual future performance and careers. Without these drugs cyclists would be hurt and end up with lower results when compared to non-dopers. They argued that every other cyclist neutralizes job effects by doping:

> 'If you hadn't taken it you would have been slaughtered. You didn't do it to cheat. You did it to survive. To fight the battle with the same arms as everyone else' (Paul Kimmage).

138

Whilst cyclists' accounts emphasized equality in their chances to perform their job effectively, these narratives did not suggest that performance was 'spectacular' but rather that it was equated with mere career survival. Doping was therefore a means of maintaining cyclists' exchange value to hold their performance and job:

> 'It was a matter of survival, just keeping up, not getting dropped, having my place in the peloton' (Frankie Andreu).

> 'It felt like I'm trying to survive and there's a little raft and I can stop treading water and hoist myself up on that' (Jonathan Vaughters).

This highlights performance infused arrogance whereby cyclists suggest their work should not have any damaging effects on their body, despite risk and occurrence of injuries being a normalized expectation of participation in top-level sport (Albert, 1999).

Protecting Careers

As well as allowing them to avoid harming their body, cyclists suggested doping was needed to prevent unnecessary physical damage on themselves, and which could impede upon their careers. They were against moving to a career that they associated with less credibility:

> 'My alternative would have been to drive the bicycle in the garage and stop the career' (Bo Hamburger).

> 'Everybody knew that the whole peloton was taking drugs and I had a choice. Either I buckle and go with the trend or I pack it in and go back to my old job as painter' (Alex Zulle).

Cyclists' conceptualized their self-understanding through a fear of failure and a vision of an idealized self that links the present to the future, and the future to the past (Schmitt and Leonard, 1986). Also, clearly whilst venalisation, where the pursuit of money becomes the modus operandi for action is at stake here, what also seems important is a collective memory that is public and shareable, containing episodes of success and failure. It is not the acquisition of the most financial capital that matters to cyclists but instead their public identity.

Furthermore the performative identity of being a successful cyclist carries little exchange value in the capitalist market once the cyclist ends their sporting career, even though the intrinsic value of being a cyclist is hard for individuals to forget.

Appealing to Career Loyalties

The consequences of suggesting their doping is justified to avoid self-injury on both a physical and career progression level was that it enabled cyclists to appeal to higher loyalties in their statements. Syke's and Matza (1957) argue delinquents justify their behavior by suggesting they sacrifice the demands of the larger society, choosing instead to favor their own social groups. This justification was also similarly represented with the cyclists' accounts, however, whereas Syke's and Matza (1957) suggest individuals attended to group level needs in their justifications, cyclists instead provided more self-centered justifications pertaining to their own self-esteem in society. Here they presented their job as an eternally dreamed of profession:

> 'I was closest to my dream than I had ever been so I never stopped to think because I had already justified it in my mind and I had already accepted it' (Floyd Landis).

> 'Cycling has always been a part of my life. As a boy my dream was to become a professional cyclists who raced at the highest level in Europe' (Michael Barry).

Cyclists' accounts emphasised a personal right to achieve their dream and which they could only achieve if they doped. Whilst dreaming of success, and perceiving one's aspirations on a visionary level are often requisite for realizing actual performance in sport (see Morris et al., 2005) cyclists used this as a mechanism for justifying continual doping. They built on their dreams by placing their job performance as the pinnacle tantamount to their life-world and existence. It allowed them to suggest that any alternative career; or social existence will always be secondary class to them:

> 'I started this point with the greatest dreams in the world, because I set myself a goal and I wanted to work or win money or to be someone' (Jesus Manzano).

140

'Cycling is my life and has been ever since I can remember. I have loved and lived this sport but more than a decade ago, I chose the wrong path' (Ryder Hesjedal).

There is an implicit assumption within accounts that cycling is like other normalized professions whereby each individual has the same chance of success in their role and should not be denied this opportunity. Cyclists therefore articulated reward as being commensurate with effort and believe they have a right to this reward, provided they put in their perception of the required amount of effort.

TEAM SPECTACLE AND 'BADGE OF HONOR'

Fulfilling Team Expectations

Whilst cyclists' accounts justified their doping as a way of maintaining and incorporating a spectacle of performance to the self, they also demonstrated how this spectacle to self was a necessary part of the normal functioning of their teams. There was a performative element to their drug use whereby there was value in showing to other team mates that they were prepared to risk taking drugs to support the team's overall performance. Syke's and Matza (1957) suggest that even if delinquents accept their responsibility for their deviant actions hurting others, people attempt to neutralize this moral indignation by insisting that the injury cannot be defined as wrong within the broader environment. As with the strategy of denying self-injury, cyclists here also presented a self-regulatory and commodified position of themselves, as opposed to considering the effects that their actions might have on other riders. It was clear from their accounts that they felt there was an expectation within the team that they would dope to perform at their best.

Cyclists justified this out of necessity by highlighting that doping was an important part of being allowed to do the job. Not taking this risk would mean they were seen as abnormal counterproductive citizens to the performative team culture and would not be allowed to race. The uncertainty and manner of this risk-taking also reinforces the spectacle whereby this willingness for risk becomes an important part of team level spectacle performance. On one level doping was presented as necessary to be accepted, or allowed to race in the team:

141

> 'It became obvious that if I wanted to stay competitive and be selected to do all the big races, I had to participate in a team-doping program' (Stephen Hodge).

> 'Because of my career and the team I ended-up on, if I wasn't willing to do that (dope), I wasn't going to be there' (Floyd Landis).

Beyond this, there was also an additional performative narrative in cyclists' accounts whereby being seen to be performing the risks of doping was necessary to maintain an acceptance by fellow team members:

> 'One speed bag later, I was back in the safe zone. It's a team sport' (Tyler Hamilton).

> 'The pressure not to let myself and my team down saw to it that I took refuge in EPO' (Tom Lotz).

Therefore the spectacle also operates at the level of teams and provides an arena for cyclist's to justify their cheating within. Here it is the visualized process of doping that is commodified in the performance of the act itself, as opposed to the potential effects of doping on a cyclist's performance. This suggests that doping is a 'cultural' symbol expressing an 'ideology' of performative risk that sustains the overall dominant performative team culture. Such presents a different view to the frequent perception of immoral characters as narcissists (e.g. Raskin and Hall, 1979) because here cyclists outwardly behave in ways that support the team and its members.

Negligence of the Cycling 'System'

Whilst riders justified their doping by suggesting they had to be seen to be taking drugs within their teams, they continued to shift responsibility for drug taking by blaming the cycling 'system' that is infiltrated with capitalist motives. In particular, cyclists discussed the disposable nature of their career as a result of the capitalist spectacle:

> 'Why haven't they made every possible effort to eliminate this cancer? It's as if the riders are entirely disposable, wheel them in for the show and then discard them.

It's time to put a stop to the massacre ... I was disgusted... I blamed the system. The race organisers, the directeurs sportifs, the sponsors—the men in power who knew what was going on but turned a blind eye to it. And when his career ended the system would spit him out as a penniless ex-pro' (Paul Kimmage).

Leading on from their dissatisfaction for the cycling 'system', cyclists also suggested they should have been told to stop doping by the 'system' and team management hierarchy. As this act of paternalism had not materialised, they therefore suggested it was legitimate for them to carry on with their performance enhancement:

There was no dissenting voice. Doping was a way of life and a way of riding. It was easy to be influenced, doping was widespread. They should have told me to be patient and to stay clear of doping, but that wasn't the case (Thomas Dekker).

Since we are constantly asked to go faster and to make even greater efforts, we have no choice but to take stimulants (Jacques Anquetil).

Whilst this does actually show narcissistic tones as a result of blaming others, cyclists are alluding to a spectacle on a team level whereby the team managers are subject to the same performative requirements as cyclists themselves. The overall pressure of the TDF therefore infiltrates down the cycling managerial hierarchies and as a way of overcoming this, individuals drew on egoistic tones of their own ideological position of selves to demonstrate how doping becomes legitimated at the team level.

SPECTACLE AND SPECTATORSHIP OF CYCLING GRAND TOURS

Performing Tour Exceptionality

The final level on which doping was framed in cyclists' accounts was at the broader level of the spectacle in society and spectatorship. As well as shifting responsibility for their doping and cheating onto the team culture and cycling 'system' infiltrated by capitalism, cyclists also justified their doping by blaming the exceptional measures required by grand spectacles such as the TDF, using this to take responsibility off themselves. The cyclists presented doping as behavior they are compelled to engage in because of the competitive environment in which they work in:

> 'But without EPO you can ride only ten stages at a very high level. Afterwards the fire is out' (Rolf Jarmann).

> 'In cycling, you get dropped in 99 out of 100 races, even when you give it everything. It hurts all the time; but you still are successful only a few times' (Jorg Jaksche).

Another key way that cyclists legitimated their doping at this level was to blame the landscape and terrain of the Tour that places exceptional requirements on their body, and which could not be accomplished without doping. Cyclists' highlighted that the level of performance required was impossible to achieve without performance enhancement:

> 'Well it's hard to imagine the endurance demanded by the Tour de France—21 days, 2000 miles and a vicious vertical climb totalling some 50,000 feet in all. This ordeal is one reason that cycling became a dirty sport' (Tyler Hamilton).

Doping as framed in cyclists' accounts therefore is represented as the material object that transpires their performance into a commodity and that in turn carries an exchange value enabling them to achieve tour exceptionality. By attributing blame to the Tour landscape and terrain it allows cyclists to uphold their own position and ego of seeing their performance as successful from their own perception. A second way that riders denied responsibility was by presenting the Tour as an impossible task that could not be completed without doping:

> 'My experiences during that first week made me question whether it was even possible to compete in a race like that without doping' (Michael Barry).

> 'You don't understand, this is the only was I can even finish the Tour' (Frankie Andreu).

'The Tour de France was no ordinary race. It made superhuman demands on the human body. Riding six hours a day for twenty-three days was not possible without vitamin supplements, mineral supplements, chemicals to clean out a tired liver, medication to take the hardness out of rock-hard leg muscle' (Paul Kimmage).

Balancing the Effort and Reward Ledger

Syke's and Matza (1957) use the metaphor of the ledger where acceptable behavior is perceived by the delinquent as an accrual of credits that are traded to frame their cheating behavior as legitimate. This operated by individuals suggesting their doping was legitimate due to the level of performance and effort that they had to put in. They thought this effort was very high and therefore warranted doping. Here they focused on the many sacrifices that they have made, including their long hours training and strict diet:

'I felt that I had been putting in a great deal of work, but not getting the results that I should have been able to achieve. Lance told me that he would contact Dr. Ferrari on my behalf' (George Hincapie).

'We speak a lot about doping when we speak about cycling. But don't often speak about the hours of training or about the sacrifices that most cyclists make' (Fabien Tallefer).

'Cycling per se is not fun. It always hurts. The sport is a lot about pain, physical pain' (Jorg Jaksche).

Cyclists use their intrinsic effort as an exchangeable commodity that enables them to engage in doping. As well as suggesting the more materialized sacrifices, cyclists also suggested they were legitimated to dope due to the many years that they have had to sustain their effort over. The consequences of presenting their performance in this way shows how cyclists self-brand and commodify their performance as a means of overcoming the difficulties encompassed in performing for the spectacle and which they articulate as being above the normal call of duty. Emphasizing their performance in this quantifiable manner therefore is a means through which cyclists search for an authentic self at work (Hoberman, 2000).

DISCUSSION AND CONCLUSION: PERFORMANCE EGOISM IN SPORT AND WORK

This paper has shown that in professional cycling the nature of the spectacle defined cultural performance drives individuals' legitimate goal seeking through the illegitimate means of doping. In agreement with Walsh and Giulianotti (2001), the commodification of cycling appears to bring with it a radical overthrow of prior social, economic, political and cultural arrangements in the service of maximizing profit and in response to the wider cultural aspects of competition and work. The findings lead to three more specific conclusions concerning the consequential effects of the commodification of cycling.

First, despite using means that are often perceived illegitimate by key stakeholders, the cyclists engaged in a process of self-commodification that enabled them to appropriate an identity that they understand as being fundamentally existent in the successful cyclist or employee (Dale, 2012), and certainly not one that 'cheats'. Throughout the study, this lead to the development of a 'performance ego' on three levels and which allowed cyclists to defend the legitimacy of their cheating. First, this occurred at the individual level whereby cyclists suggested they engaged in doping practices to avoid damage to their bodies. Here their ego was at play whereby they wanted to show to themselves that they could continue to perform their ideal career. Second, cyclists suggested their doping was necessary to show that their performance was adequate to their fellow teammates, but also to show that they were willing to take risks to perform at their best for the team. Their egos came into play here whereby their cheating was a means to show how serious they were with regard to producing the best possible performance for the team. Third, cyclists emphasized the spectacular exertion required by the Tour and doing so allowed them to protect their performance egos by suggesting that what they were engaging in was beyond the 'normal' parameters of the human body. In this sense they represented their doping as a tool that enabled them to perform beyond the 'normal' and to continue to perform spectacularly within the Tour spectacle.

Second, in the same way that an analogy can be drawn work to sport, it can also be drawn from sport to work in a modern era of elitism and exceptionality. The findings of the study have shown how achievement, performance and success have become an ideology that are rendered as integral to individuals' success, regardless of the style or moral arena in which this is achieved. As Motion (2000) argues, image management can be considered as a productive process, whereas impression management is more performative. In this sense

146

cyclists are more concerned with the overall impression they give, instead of the means in which this is produced. Therefore, ultimately the findings have paved the way for more in-depth study of the mechanisms and strategies that are used in sport in contextualized areas of elitism and exceptionality. This carries further resonance for understanding how high impact scandals in sport and athletic teams continue to place increasing pressure on organizations, communities and governments to manage athletes' behavior in ways that are non-detrimental to the financial and social performance of sport in the contemporary economy. This is further important given that prolonged research suggests that most adults' decision making is highly susceptible to the external environment in which they are located, making the management of cultural norms imperative (Trevino et al., 2006). If the more performative and subjective elements of performance are measured, as opposed to the productive and quantitative means, this opens a large ontological lacuna requiring debate of the nature and measurement of success in sport.

Third, it is also important to think about the reflexive agendas used by these cyclists. Broadly their accounts highlight the self-imposed value attached to the importance of reflexivity and self-presentation in modern times (Giddens, 1971). Whilst there are elements of a narcissistic tone echoed throughout, as cyclists do not call into question their own performance and do not hold themselves accountable, implicitly these cyclists must ultimately have a reason for sharing this self-knowledge in the public domain. Personal branding is ever prominent (Wee and Brooks, 2010) and therefore it is hard to fathom, given the narcissistic tone and personalities demonstrated that cyclists do not attach some value to this process, whether that be for the benefit of themselves or others. Supporting this, as Cluley and Dunne (2012) note, at the moment of consumption consumers may be faced with an 'as if' moment whereby they realize that their decision may not have been the best possible choice. Consequently many continue to consume what their aspirations attract them to, as if they did not know the uncomfortable facts about the production process. Therefore whilst one limitation of the study might be that too much weight has been placed onto individuals' accounts, a common criticism of self promotion (e.g. company reports (Koller, 2008)), the fact that athletes and individuals feel the need to publicise a bolstered self-identity highlights the modern sporting and working environment whereby self promotion is tantamount to fulfilling the ever performative nature of being seen as ubiquitously successful in the job.

REFERENCES

Albert E (1999) Dealing with danger; the normalization of risk in cycling. *International Review for the Sociology of Sport* 34: 157–171.

Alt J (1983) Sport and cultural reification: from ritual to mass consumption. *Theory, Culture and Society* 1: 93–107.

Barthes R (1997) *The Eiffel tower and other mythologies*. University of California Press: California.

Birrell S (1981) Sport as ritual: interpretations from Durkheim to Goffman. *Social Forces* 60: 354–376.

British Cycling (2014) A journey of inspiration and opportunity: Our vision for women's cycling. British Cycling: Manchester.

Cheska A (1978) Sports spectacular: a ritual model of power. *International Review for the Sociology of Sport* 14: 51–72.

Cluley R and Dunne S (2012) From commodity fetishism to commodity narcissism. *Marketing Theory* 12: 251–265.

Dale K (2012) The employee as 'dish of the day': The ethics of the consuming/consumed self in human resource management. *Journal of Business Ethics* 111: 13–24.

Furst R (1971) Social change and the commercialization of professional sports. *International Review for the Sociology of Sport* 6: 153–173.

Giddens A (1971) *Modernity and self-identity: Self and society in the late modern age*. Polity: Cambridge.

Groves M and Griggs G (2014) Riding in the shadows: The reaction of the British print media to Chris Froome's victory in the 2013 Tour de France, *International Review for the Sociology of Sport* DOI: 1012690214534848.

Hermann A and Henneberg M (2014) Anti-doping systems in sports are doomed to fail: A probability and cost analysis. Available at: http://road.cc/content/news/89328-anti-doping-systems-sport-doomed-fail-says-study (accessed 15th August 2014).

Hoberman J (2000) *Testosterone dreams; Rejuvenation, aphrodisiac, doping*. University of California Press: California.

Johanson M (1987) Doping as a threat against sport and society: The case of Sweden. *International Review for the Sociology of Sport* 22: 83–97.

Jones C (2010) Doping in cycling: Realism, antirealism, and ethical deliberation. *Journal of the Philosophy of Sport* 37: 88–101.

Koller V (2008) Identity, image, impression: Corporate self-promotion and public reactions. In: Wodak R Koller V (eds.) *Handbook of communication in the public sphere.* Berlin: Walter de Gruyter: 155–180.

Lauber M Jamieson K and Krohn M (2010) Newspaper reporting and the production of deviance: Drug use among professional athletes. *Deviant Behaviour* 14: 317–339.

Linstead S Marechal G and Griffin R (2014) Theorizing and researching the dark side of organizations. *Organization Studies* 35: 165–188.

Loland S (2004) Normative theories of sport: A critical review. *Journal of the Philosophy of Sport* 31: 111–121.

Lopez B (2013) Creating fear: The social construction of human growth hormone as a dangerous doping drug. *International Review for the Sociology of Sport* 48: 220–237.

Maennig W (2014) Inefficiency of the anti-doping system: Cost reduction proposals. *Substance Use and Misuse* 49: 1201–1205.

McKenzie J (2001) *Perform or else: From discipline to performance.* Routledge: London.

Mars G (1994) *Cheats at work: Anthropology of workplace crime.* Allen & Unwin: Aldershot.

Mazanov J Petroczi A Bingham J and Holloway A (2008) Towards an empirical model of performance enhancement supplement use. *Journal of Science and Medicine in Sport* 11: 185–190.

Moller V (2010) *The ethics of doping and anti-doping: redeeming the soul of sport.* Routledge: London.

Morente-Sánchez J and Zabala M (2013) Doping in sport: a review of elite athlete's attitudes, beliefs and knowledge. *Sports Medicine* 43: 395–411.

Morris T Spittle M and Watt A (2005) *Imagery in sport.* Human Kinetics: Leeds.

Motion J (2000) Personal public relations: Identity as a public relations commodity. *Public Relations Review* 25: 465–479.

Ohl F Fincoeur B Lentillon-Kaestner V Defrance J and Brissonneau C (2013) The socialization of young cyclists and the culture of doping. *International Review for the Sociology of Sport* DOI:1012690213495534.

Pappa E and Kennedy E (2013) 'It was my thought … he made it a reality'. *International Review for the Sociology of Sport* 48: 277–294.

Pitsch W and Emrich E (2012) The frequency of doping in elite sport: Results of a replication study. *International Review for the Sociology of Sport* 47: 559–580.

Raskin R and Hall C (1979) A narcissistic personality inventory. *Psychological Reports* 45: 590-590.

Rigauer B (1981) *Sport and work*, Columbia University Press: New York.

Schjerling P (2005) The basics of gene doping In: Tamburrini C and Tännsjö T (eds.) *Genetic technology and sport: ethical questions*. Routledge: London.

Schmitt R and Leonard W (1986) Immortalizing the self through sport. *American Journal of Sociology* 91: 1088–1111.

Stewart B and Smith A (2010) The role of ideology in shaping drug use regulation in Australian sport. *International Review for the Sociology of Sport* 45: 187–198.

Sykes G and Matza D (1957) Techniques of neutralization: A theory of delinquency. *American Sociological Review* 22: 664–670.

Thompson P and Ackroyd S (1995) All quiet on the workplace front? A critique of recent trends in British Industrial Sociology. *Sociology* 29: 615–633.

Trevino L Weaver G and Reynolds S (2006) Behavioural ethics in organizations: A review. *Journal of Management* 32: 951–990.

USADA (2013) Report on proceedings under the World anti-doping code and the USADA protocol. Available at: http://d3epuodzu3wuis.cloudfront.net/ReasonedDecision.pdf (accessed 2nd November 2014).

Vardi Y and Wiener Y (1996) Misbehaviour in organizations: A motivational framework. *Organization Science* 7: 151–165.

WADA (2009) World Anti-Doping Code 2009. Available at: https://www.wada-ama.org/en/resources/the-code/world-anti-doping-code-2009#.U-5Rpqi7n9s (accessed 15th August 2014).

Waddington I and Smith A (2000) *Sport, health and drugs: A critical sociological perspective*. Routledge: London.

Walsh A and Giulianotti R (2001) This sporting mammon: A normative critique of the commodification of sport. *Journal of the Philosophy of Sport* 28: 53–77.

Wee L and Brooks A (2010) Personal branding and the commodification of reflexivity. *Cultural Sociology* 4: 45-62.

Wiggins B (2012) *My time: An autobiography*. Yellow Jersey Cycling Classics: London.

CHAPTER ELEVEN

Does the Game Really Change?

How Students Consume Mediated Sports in the Age of Social Media

BY **JAN BOEHMER**

The role of social media in the distribution and consumption of sports content is a topic of constant debate. Although sports ranks among the most read topics on social media (Mitchell, Kiley, Gottfried, & Guskin, 2013), and most broadcast outlets have adopted Facebook and Twitter for various purposes (e.g., Cameron & Geidner, 2014; Elmer, 2013; Herrera-Damas & Hermida, 2014; Larsson, 2013), it is not quite clear how the availability of information on social media changes the ways in which the audience consumes sports on traditional distribution systems, such as television.

On one hand, the argument has been made that social media draw audiences away from traditional distribution systems and create "a whole new ballgame" (Sanderson, 2011). Researchers have argued that social media, and especially Twitter, are fundamentally changing the nature of sport media consumption (e.g., Hull & Lewis, 2014; Sanderson, 2011). Even a "shift in the audience marketplace, away from the traditional newspaper and television" (Clavio & Walsh, 2014, p. 262) has been anticipated. As a matter of fact, social media have become major places to encounter news (Mitchell, Holcomb, & Page, 2013), with media organizations, sports teams, and athletes allocating significant resources to harness these new tools and gaining substantial followings.

On the other hand, the degree to which this shift is actually happening remains unclear. The increased quality of sports broadcasts and the integration of new features—including social media—have rejuvenated television as a distribution system and kept it appealing to younger audiences (Galily, 2014; Whannel, 2014). As a result, researchers recently have raised questions about the ability of social media to meaningfully change the sport media landscape (Wenner, 2014b) and emphasized the sustained power of television in the realm of sports (Billings, 2014; Boyle, 2014).

Despite this controversy, however, few attempts have been undertaken to quantify the use of Twitter and other social media platforms in comparison to television for the consumption of sports content. This study aims at addressing this gap in the literature and has two main goals. The first is to provide an account of how Twitter is currently used to consume sports content by college students, a demographic that is assumed to be at the forefront of the digital revolution (Valenzuela, Park, & Kee, 2009) and should therefore be particularly receptive of Twitter. The second is to investigate personal characteristics that might lead audience members to rely more or less on a particular distribution system.

TWITTER AND SPORTS

Social media have gained significant importance in the sport media ecosystem. Media organizations, teams, and athletes increasingly turn to social media to engage their audiences, making sports the third most popular topic on Facebook (Matsa & Mitchell, 2014). Despite its smaller user base, Twitter has been ascribed an even greater importance in the context of sports news (Reed, 2013) for several reasons. First, while exposure to news remains incidental on Facebook (Matsa & Mitchell, 2014), Twitter is said to resemble many characteristics of traditional news media (Kwak, Lee, Park, & Moon, 2010). Especially in the case of current events, the micro-blogging platform becomes an important medium for instant communication between individuals that have not necessarily been connected before (Highfield, Harrington, & Bruns, 2013). This connected activity among strangers is different from Facebook where users usually communicate with individuals they already know. As a result, Twitter allows for broader discussions, with up to 95% of public social media conversations about current televised events happening on the microblogging platform (Graver, 2012). Finally, Twitter itself has been pushing the use of the platform in the realm of sports, resulting in major sporting events continuously setting new records for the most tweeted about events (Rogers, 2014). Overall, Twitter has quickly become one of the most popular social media tools for athletes (Schultz & Sheffer, 2010) as well as fans.

Consequently, Twitter has been ascribed a primary role at the intersection of social media and sports—not only by professionals but also in academia. Studies focusing on the various uses and effects of the micro-blogging platform in the realm of sports have increased (Wenner, 2014a), covering a wide range of topics including athletes' messaging styles (e.g., Pegoraro, 2010), their self-presentation (e.g., Lebel & Danylchuk, 2012), relationship promotion (e.g., Frederick, Lim, Clavio, Pedersen, & Burch, 2014), regulatory issues (e.g., Sanderson & Browning, 2013), as well as the overarching effects of Twitter on sports journalism (e.g., Sheffer & Schultz, 2010) and sport media culture (Hutchins, 2011). For a detailed analysis of the existing body of knowledge of social media in the field of sport management and communication, see Filo, Lock, and Karg (2015) as well as Witkemper, Blaszka, and Chung (2014).

However, although many recent studies explore how Twitter is used by fans, athletes, and organizations on a quality academic level, there seems to be a tendency to "overestimate the adoption of Twitter in the sporting context and overlook the staying power of sport on television" (Billings, 2014, p. 107). Clavio and Walsh (2014) recently urged researchers "to examine the usage characteristics of college sport fans on social media to begin to understand why audiences choose to engage in sport-focused social media usage" (p. 263). They found that social media participation was relatively low, while traditional media remained prevalent. Clavio and Walsh's (2014) findings echo notions of television's overlooked staying power in the realm of sports (Billings, 2014; Gantz & Lewis, 2014; Wenner, 2014a), as well as recent developments in the industry. For example, despite the increased use of social media and suggested models of displacement of traditional sports broadcasts (i.e., Hull & Lewis, 2014), Super Bowl XLIX became the most watched broadcast in U.S. history (Pallotta, 2015).

Despite these two seemingly contradictory trends, quantifiable evidence for how individuals actually use different distribution systems in the context of sport media is scarce. This study therefore aims at establishing a foundational understanding of usage patterns by

153

identifying the content distribution systems college students most frequently use to consume sports content, and where Twitter ranks among alternatives. In addition, it is investigated where obtaining sports information ranks among other popular uses of Twitter. To address these issues, the following research questions were asked:

Research Question 1: Where does Twitter rank compared to other content distribution systems in terms of college students' consumption of sports content?

Research Question 2: Where does the consumption of sports content rank compared to other popular uses of Twitter among college students?

USE OF MULTIPLE DISTRIBUTION SYSTEMS

One of the trends in previous research has been to pit social media against traditional media, suggesting that the increased use of one (social media) would harm or diminish the use of the other (traditional media and particularly television). This argument, however, seems out of place. Media consumption is not an either/or situation (Greer & Ferguson, 2011). Instead, the audience uses multiple distribution systems to fulfill different needs that cannot be satisfied by one system alone. In the case of Twitter and television, individuals often use a second screen to simultaneously engage with both distribution systems, offering "their own running commentary on the universally shared media text of the event as it unfolds live" (Highfield et al., 2013, p. 315). In fact, between 50% (Nielsen, 2013) and 80% (Tribbey, 2014) of smartphone and tablet owners report the supplementary use of their devices during television consumption, making the discussion of televised events the most prominent use of Twitter.

With the use of second screens having become a widespread practice (Cameron & Geidner, 2014; Giglietto & Selva, 2014; Harrington, 2013; Mukherjee & Jansen, 2014), it needs to be stated that television consumption is not likely to be diminished by the use of social media, but that users' experience is rather enhanced (Harrington, 2013). Furthermore, television should not lose its role as primary distribution system but rather remain the main medium considered by the audience (Mukherjee & Jansen, 2014), as it provides the content for discussion. Overall, social media will not replace mainstream media, but complement them, providing users with alternate opportunities to engage with content (Harrington, Highfield, & Bruns, 2013). As a result, the use of television and social media as distribution systems for sports content should be positively correlated. To test this assumption, the following hypothesis was tested:

> **Hypothesis 1:** There will be a positive correlation between the uses of television and social media applications for sport media consumption.

VARIABLES AFFECTING THE CHOICE OF A DISTRIBUTION SYSTEM

Although the use of different distribution systems is likely to be correlated, individuals might still prefer one relative to the other. More specifically, the reliance on a specific distribution system will likely depend on a series of platform, content, reception, and lifestyle factors (Gantz & Lewis, 2014). For example, given that only about 16% of the U.S. population actively uses Twitter (Mitchell, Holcomb, et al., 2013) and that the portion of individuals using the micro-blogging service for the consumption of sports content is likely to be even lower, there needs to be a set of certain characteristics that make individuals rely more or less on this particular distribution system. However, although a considerable amount of research has focused on potential reasons for social media becoming a functional alternative for television for parts of the population (e.g., Gantz & Lewis, 2014; Hull & Lewis, 2014), no quantitative test of the potential individual characteristics that might cause such a preference has been undertaken. Therefore, a more detailed analysis is warranted.

Assuming that individuals select a distribution system based on the needs they seek to fulfill, researchers have frequently employed a uses and gratifications approach (Katz, Blumler, & Gurevitch, 1973) to examine individuals' motivations to use different distribution systems in the realm of sports. For the purpose of the present study, especially the literature on Twitter and television is of interest, as it allows a comparison and possible distinction between the two distribution systems based on the underlying motivations for their use. Looking at investigations into the uses and gratifications of Twitter, it becomes apparent that individuals are often driven by the desire to interact with athletes and media personalities, a sense of camaraderie with other sports fans, and the intention to obtain information that cannot be obtained via traditional media (i.e., Clavio & Kian, 2010; Frederick, Lim, Clavio, & Walsh, 2012; Gibbs, O' Reilly, & Brunette, 2014; Sanderson, 2011). Findings also indicate that individuals wanting to express themselves and/or obtain additional information tended to supplement their television consumption with social media (Cameron & Geidner, 2014). These results mirror the general motivations found for Twitter use in the overall population (Chen, 2011), and among news users in particular (Greer & Ferguson, 2011).

When comparing this set of motivations to the uses and gratifications found in research on sports-related television consumption, a clear distinction can be made. When watching sports on television, excitement, entertainment, and relaxation were found to be some of the greatest motivators (e.g., Gantz, 1981; Raney, 2006; Trail & James, 2001).

For the purpose of this study, then, the argument can be made that individuals might rely more or less on a distribution system based on the gratifications they seek to obtain. More specifically, the case can be made that individuals seeing themselves as general sports enthusiasts/fans should be more interested in the relaxation and entertainment gratifications provided by television (Gantz, 1981; Gantz & Wenner, 1995). On the other hand, individuals seeing themselves as sports experts should be more interested in the opportunity to obtain additional, timely information through Twitter and use the micro-blogging service to disseminate their own commentary, presenting themselves as experts (Hull & Lewis, 2014). This is in line with Gantz and Lewis (2014) have mentioned the interactive capabilities of social media as an upside of Twitter when compared to television. They argue "fans who want to share their views are likely to turn to social media" (p. 763). To test this relationship, the following hypotheses were devised:

Hypothesis 2: Participants with greater general interest in sports will be more likely to prefer television to Twitter than participants with lesser general interest in sports.

Hypothesis 3: Participants with greater perceptions of sports expertise will be more likely to prefer Twitter to television than participants with lesser perceptions of sports expertise.

PARASOCIAL INTERACTIONS

Finally, Hull and Lewis (2014) suggest that the concept of parasocial interaction could play an important role in individuals' preference for a distribution system. More specifically, individuals who develop and value parasocial interactions with sport media personalities would prefer micro-blogging to television, as it allows them to engage in such behavior. This is in line with findings about general motivations to use social media in the context of sports, which often include the development of parasocial relationships between athletes and fans (Frederick et al., 2012; Kassing & Sanderson, 2009, 2010).

The concept of parasocial interaction was first formulated by Horton and Wohl (1956), who suggested that the audience of mass media would engage in a new form of social interactions with media figures they watched on television. They discussed how audiences could experience the illusion of an interpersonal relationship with actually remote mass media communicators. They labeled this type of relationship parasocial and proposed that the audience would respond to mass media characters as though they would encounter them in a typical social/interpersonal relationship. Individuals would eventually learn to interact with the stylized images presented by mass media (Levy, 1979), even without actual two-way communication taking place. The development of such relationships has been primarily studied with television characters, such as soap opera stars (R. B. Rubin & Mc Hugh, 1987) and news anchors (A. M. Rubin, Perse, & Powell, 1985), but has also been extended to talk radio hosts (A. M. Rubin & Step, 2000), weblogs (Thorson & Rodgers, 2006), and websites (Hoerner, 1999).

In the realm of sports, several studies have found parasocial relationships developing between sports media characters and their audiences. Hartmann, Stuke, and Daschmann (2008), for example, found that positive parasocial relationships between Formula 1 drivers and their fans increased the level of suspense in the audience. Similarly, a study by Spinda, Earnheardt, and Hugenberg (2009) revealed that parasocial interaction among NASCAR fans led to greater fan activity, as well as increased fandom. Kassing and Sanderson (2009, 2010) investigated fan–athlete interaction on Twitter, as well as athletes' websites in the realm of professional cycling. Finally, researchers have also investigated how motivations to follow social or parasocial athletes differ on Twitter (Frederick et al., 2012), and what traits affect the formation of parasocial tendencies in individuals (Sun, 2010; Sun & Wu, 2012).

157

Parasocial interactions and social media. With the lack of actual two-way communication being one of the main characteristics of parasocial interaction, the argument has been made that the concept would be outdated in an era of social media. Social media seem to contradict the initial premise of a distant relationship by offering a way to make direct connections between individuals (Boyd & Ellison, 2007). However, while social media generally facilitate social interaction, this potential is not consistently exerted in the realm of sport. Although there is an increase in actual interactions between sport media personalities and fans (Hull & Lewis, 2014; Kassing & Sanderson, 2010; Pegoraro, 2010), this is not yet the norm. Fan–athlete interaction occasionally becomes social, but it often reverts back to parasocial interaction. Kassing and Sanderson (2015) coined the term circumsocial to describe "how new media facilitate orbital or spherical patterns of fan-athlete interaction—moving between and capitalizing on relational attributes that are more or less para-social/social in nature" (p. 12). For the most part, though, research suggests that celebrities and mass media characters do not engage in direct social interactions with the majority of their followers. In fact, 77.9% of user pairs with any link between them are connected one way, and 67.6% of users are not followed by any of their followings on Twitter (Kwak et al., 2010).

For example, in a previous study employing the data set underlying this study, only 3 out of 943 participants reported one of the sports media personalities they follow ever having personally reacted to their tweets. Therefore, most interactions on Twitter should be regarded as parasocial. Hartmann (2008) revised the original conceptualization of parasocial relationships accordingly and suggested the concept "should also apply to encounters with characters in new media settings, if they are perceived as sufficiently authentic and distant" (p. 193). This is the case on Twitter. Media characters often reveal what appears to be personal information to create a sense of intimacy between participant and follower (Marwick & Boyd, 2011), which gratifies a need for an informal sense of camaraderie even with remote media characters (Chen, 2011). However, most audience members will remain aware of the mediated nature of the relationship and perceive the originators of the messages as distant.

Since the degree to which individuals engage in parasocial interactions and value the resulting relationships varies from person to person (Sun, 2010), it might play an important role in individuals' choice for a distribution system. Individuals who engage in parasocial interactions should be more likely to rely on Twitter than on sport broadcasts on television (Hull & Lewis, 2014). The present study tests this proposed relationship by assessing students' tendency to engage in parasocial interactions and relating the results to their preference of Twitter to television, testing the following hypothesis:

> **Hypothesis 4:** Participants with a greater desire to engage in parasocial interactions with sport media personalities will be more likely to prefer Twitter to television than participants with a lesser desire to engage in parasocial interactions with sport media personalities.

METHOD

Participants were recruited from undergraduate and graduate classes at a large public university in the Midwestern United States. The university's registrar's office sent out an invitation to a random sample of 10,000 students who were incentivized by the chance of being entered into a raffle of two US$50 gift certificates on Amazon. 1,005 participants completed the survey. However, cases with missing values in the survey instrument were dropped. This resulted in a final sample size of 943. To ensure that this sample represented the overall student population of the university, demographics were compared. Both sample and student population were predominantly white (sample = 78%, population = 79%), followed by Asian (sample = 10%, population = 11%) and African American (sample = 6%, population = 7%). About 70% of participants reported having an active Twitter account, which they used at least once a week. Research Question 1 examined the entire sample. For Research Question 2 and Hypotheses 1–4, only the subset of participants with an active Twitter account ($n = 666$) was examined.

Although the use of a student sample in many cases limits the ability to generalize findings beyond the surveyed demographic (Abelman, 1996; Cunningham, Anderson, & Murphy, 1974), it was deemed appropriate for this study for multiple reasons. First, college students are at the forefront of the digital revolution (Valenzuela et al., 2009), which makes them particularly receptive of Twitter (i.e., 70% adoption in this study). Although this differs significantly from the general population (i.e., 16% Twitter adoption), studying early adopters who are most likely to be affected by the processes under investigation allows to make preliminary observations about issues that subsequently might affect a larger demographic. In addition, although students certainly differ from the general population in many univariate values (such as Twitter adoption), multivariate relationships between variables (such as the influence of parasocial interactions on Twitter use) are believed to be stable across different samples and therefore generalizable to broader populations (Basil, Brown, & Bocarnea, 2002).

MEASUREMENT OF KEY VARIABLES

Media use. To assess which delivery system college students use to consume sports content, participants were asked to indicate how frequently they used the following systems to consume sports content on a 7-point Likert-type scale ranging from *never* to *daily*: newspaper, radio, television, Twitter, Facebook, YouTube, news websites, other social media (Tumblr, Instagram, etc.), and blogs. Television in this study was defined as traditional broadcasts (i.e., cable and satellite) consumed through the television screen. Moving images consumed online (i.e., webcasts, streams, and highlight videos) were included in the survey-item description for news websites.

Twitter use types. To identify where consuming sports content ranks among college students' uses of Twitter, participants were asked to indicate how often they used Twitter for the following five uses most frequently mentioned during qualitative responses in a pretest (*n* = 75). Participants indicated how often they used Twitter to "read tweets posted by friends," "get in touch with friends," "get sports related news," "get in touch with media/journalists/celebrities," and "start a conversation about issues" on a 5-point Likert-type scale ranging from *never* to *always*.

Parasocial interactions. The degree to which participants develop and value parasocial interactions was measured using an adaptation of the 22-item Audience–Persona Interaction (API) Scale (Auter & Palmgreen, 2000). Participants were asked to indicate whether they agreed or disagreed with statements such as "I can identify with the sport media personalities I follow" and "The tweets of the sport media personalities I follow are similar to the ones I send" on a 5-point Likert-type scale ranging from *strongly disagree* to *strongly agree*. Although the Parasocial Interaction Scale (A. M. Rubin et al., 1985) is still the most frequently cited instrument for measuring parasocial interactions, the API scale was deemed a better fit for this research. Not only is it less focused on a particular media environment, it is also easier to adapt to the context of this study. Unlike many univariate measures, the API scale also taps into the four dimensions of PSI suggested by theorists: identifying with a persona, interest in the persona, group identification, and liking the persona's methods of solving problems (Horton & Wohl, 1956; Nordlund, 1978; Rosengren & Windahl, 1972). This provides the opportunity to address potential issues with the multidimensional concept of parasocial interaction and how individual aspects of it might relate differently to certain outcome variables (Giles, 2002). Principal axis factoring with a Promax rotation (oblique) of the 22 items was conducted to confirm the adequacy of the measure (Kline, 2011). An examination of the Kaiser–Meyer–Olkin (KMO) measure of sampling adequacy suggested that the sample was factorable (KMO = .960). Four factors were extracted representing the theoretical dimensions of the scale, explaining 74% of the variance. One item each of the "persona identification" and "interest" dimensions that were not applicable to this research were dropped. The reliability of the scale was further tested using Cronbach's α. The individual scores of the four dimensions ranged from .85 to .93.

Preference of Twitter to television. To assess participants' potential preference of Twitter to television, a new variable was constructed by subtracting the "television" score obtained from the media use scale from the "Twitter" score obtained from the same scale. Participants who indicated using Twitter more frequently than using television (by marking Twitter higher on a 7-point Likert-type scale) obtained a positive score. Participants who indicated using television more frequently to consume sports content received a negative score. For example, a participant using Twitter *daily* (a score of 7), and using television *once a week* (a score of 5), would receive a Twitter preference score of 2. If participants used Twitter and television equally, the score was 0.

Sports interest and expertise. Interest in sports was assessed using four 7-point Likert-type items including "I am interested in sports" and "I enjoy watching sports," measuring the degree to which participants identified themselves as being interested in sports. Results of confirmatory factor analysis (CFA) and reliability analysis for the scale were satisfactory (single factor, KMO = .844, 85% of variance explained, Cronbach's α = .93), confirming the adequacy of the measure. Similarly, the perceived sports expertise of participants was measured using four 7-point Likert-type items including "I consider myself knowledgeable about sports" and "My friends ask me for advice about sports," indicating the degree to which participants identified themselves as experts on sports-related issues. Results of CFA and reliability analysis were satisfactory (single factor, KMO = .851, 86% of variance explained, Cronbach's α = .92).

CONTROL VARIABLES

In order to control for potentially confounding variables, several items that could influence the results of this study were assessed during the survey.

Perceived authenticity of sport media personalities' Twitter account. Important for the concept of parasocial interactions is an individual's belief in the authenticity of the content (Hartmann, 2008). Individuals believing that the tweets they read have actually been sent by the sport media personality, and that the sport media personality might read them and respond, could be more likely to prefer Twitter to television. This study controls for this potential effect by asking participants whether they believe that the sport media personalities they follow create their own tweets, read direct replies, and respond to audience feedback on a 7-point Likert-type scale ranging from *strongly disagree* to *strongly agree*. The 3 items of the scale were averaged to form a measure of authenticity beliefs. Results of CFA and reliability analysis were satisfactory (single factor, KMO = .645, 71% variance explained, Cronbach's α = .81), confirming the adequacy of the measure.

Twitter use. Individuals reporting greater use of Twitter in general might also be more likely to prefer Twitter to television for the consumption of sports content. To address this potential confound, the present study collected three measures of Twitter use. Participants indicated how frequently they log on to Twitter using a 7-point scale ranging from *less than once a month* to *more than 3 times a day*. They also reported how many people they follow on Twitter on a 7-point scale ranging from *less than 50* to *more than 1,000*. Finally, participants were asked to indicate how long they have been using Twitter using a 4-point scale ranging from *1 year or less* to *more than 5 years*. All three variables were entered into the regression model.

Demographics. The audience using social media has been found to be generally younger— and in some cases, such as Twitter, more educated (Matsa & Mitchell, 2014) than the general U.S. population. Given this, age and education might also affect the degree to which individuals potentially prefer Twitter to television. Therefore, this study asked participants for their age as well as their highest completed level of education. Since the sample was comprised of college students, the level of education reflects their advancement through higher education (from freshmen to doctoral/professional degree).

DATA ANALYSES

To address the question of where Twitter ranks compared to other distribution systems for college students' sport media consumption (Research Question 1), as well as where the consumption of sports content ranks compared to other uses of Twitter (Research Question 2), simple descriptive statistics were used. For both research questions, the mean of all responses served as the analytical measure. In addition, a repeated measures analysis of variance (ANOVA) was computed to further illuminate the differences in the use of distribution systems. Finally, this study compared the use of different distribution systems between participants that indicated having an active Twitter account and those that did not report having an account to test whether there exist differences between these two groups.

To test if there was a positive relationship between the uses of different distributions systems (Hypothesis 1), correlations between the media use variables were calculated.

To investigate the role that interest in sports (Hypothesis 2), perceived expertise in sports (Hypothesis 3), and parasocial interaction (Hypothesis 4) play in students' potential preference of Twitter to television, an ordinary least squares (OLS) regression model was computed. Sports interest, perceived expertise, and the four dimensions of parasocial interaction were used to predict participants' potential preference of Twitter to television for the consumption of sports content, while controlling for the perceived authenticity of sport media personalities' Twitter accounts, participants' Twitter use, as well as their age and education. All analyses were conducted using IBM SPSS statistical software version 22.

RESULTS

To address the question of where Twitter ranks compared to other distribution systems (Research Question 1), the means of the corresponding survey items were compared using a one-way repeated-measures ANOVA (see Table 11.1). Overall, the data underlying this study indicate that television is the most popular distribution system to consume sports content ($M = 4.86$, $SD = 1.91$) and that Twitter only ranks fourth overall ($M = 3.41$, $SD = 2.49$) behind news websites ($M = 4.46$, $SD = 2.20$) and Facebook ($M = 3.84$, $SD = 2.41$). Mauchly's test indicated that the assumption of sphericity had been violated, $\chi^2(35) = 754.89$, $p < .001$; therefore, Greenhouse–Geisser corrected tests are reported ($\varepsilon = .82$). Overall, results show that the preference for a distribution system differs significantly within subjects, $F(6.55, 6166.75) = 327.93$, $p < .001$, $\eta^2_{partial} = .71$. Planned repeated contrasts (comparing the item ranked first to the item ranked second, the 2nd item to the 3rd item, etc.) using the Bonferroni correction revealed that the differences between all of the distribution systems ranked next to each other—except the difference between radio and YouTube—were statistically significant ($p < .05$). Of particular interest to the research questions asked in this study is the difference between television and Twitter. This difference, -1.45, bias-corrected and accelerated 95% confidence interval = [1.224, 1.685], was significant ($p < .001$).

Table 11.1 Repeated Measures Analysis of Variance Comparing College Students' Frequency of Use by Distribution System.

		FULL SAMPLE ($N = 943$)			
RANK	SYSTEM	MEAN	SD	F	$\eta^2_{partial}$
1	Television	4.86	1.91	15.59***	.02
2	Websites	4.64	2.20	163.42***	.15
3	Facebook	3.84	2.41	33.63***	.04
4	Twitter	3.41	2.49	5.58*	.01
5	Radio	3.20	1.97	2.53	.00
6	YouTube	3.10	2.10	6.89**	.01
7	Other Social Media	2.94	2.29	18.22***	.02
8	Newspaper	2.59	1.74	48.94***	.05

9	Blogs	2.14	1.84	—	—

Note. *F*-values and $\eta^2_{partial}$ from within-subjects repeated contrasts comparing distribution systems ranked next to each other (i.e., 1 vs. 2, 2 vs. 3, 3 vs. 4, etc.). *SD* = standard deviation; Min = 1 (*never*), Max = 7 (*every day*) for all items.
*p < .05. **p < .01. ***p < .001.

In addition, an independent samples *t*-test was used to compare the use of different distribution systems between participants who reported having an active Twitter account and those who did not (see Table 11.2). The frequency of use differed significantly for all distribution systems except newspaper and radio. Overall, participants with an active Twitter account reported significantly more media use for television, $t(941) = 5.77$, $p = .000$; Facebook, $t(941) = 6.32$, $p = .000$; YouTube, $t(941) = 4.50$, $p = .000$; news websites, $t(941) = 2.97$, $p = .003$;, and other social media platforms, $t(941) = 8.21$, $p = .000$. The relative importance of distribution systems also differed across users and nonusers. For example, individuals not using Twitter ranked radio (Rank 2, $M = 3.14$, $SD = 2.05$) and newspapers (Rank 5, $M = 2.53$, $SD = 1.84$) as relatively more important. This goes hand in hand with a significant difference in age. Twitter users ($M = 23.7$, $SD = 4.62$) were on average about 2 years younger than nonusers ($M = 25.8$, $SD = 6.8$).

Table 11.2 Use of Distribution System by Twitter Users/Nonusers.

	Twitter Use						
	Yes (n = 666)		No (n = 277)		95% CI for Mean Difference	*t*	*df*
	M	SD	M	SD			
Television	5.09	1.81	4.31	2.03	[.511, 1.04]	5.77***	941
Websites	4.78	2.15	4.31	2.32	[.158, .775]	2.97**	941
Facebook	4.26	2.41	3.08	2.36	[.736, 1.40]	6.32***	515.77
Twitter	4.15	2.36	1.36	1.15	[2.60, 3.19]	19.09***	941
Radio	3.32	1.97	3.14	2.05	[−.181, .372]	.662	489.37
YouTube	3.29	2.11	2.62	2.01	[.378, .962]	4.50***	941
Other Social Media	3.23	1.93	2.01	1.88	[.992, 1.62]	8.21***	941

Newspaper	2.62	1.71	2.53	1.84	[–.163, .335]	.699	483.51
Blogs	2.26	1.89	1.87	1.70	[.131, .646]	2.96**	941

Note. SD = standard deviation; Min = 1 (*never*), Max = 7 (*every day*) for all items.
*p < .05. **p < .01. ***p < .001.

When looking at popular uses of Twitter (Research Question 2), the 5 items derived from the pretest were compared using a one-way repeated-measures ANOVA. Overall, the data indicate that obtaining information about sports ranked third among the five popular uses (see Table 11.3). Reading tweets posted by friends ($M = 3.90$, $SD = 1.21$) was the most popular activity among students, followed by "getting in touch with friends" ($M = 3.18$, $SD = 1.26$). Obtaining sports-related news ($M = 2.57$, $SD = 1.32$) ranked slightly ahead of "starting a conversation" ($M = 2.52$, $SD = 1.22$) and "getting in touch with media organizations" ($M = 2.40$, $SD = 1.18$). Mauchly's test indicated that the assumption of sphericity had been violated, $\chi^2(9) = 226.17$, $p < .001$; therefore, Greenhouse–Geisser corrected tests are reported ($\varepsilon = .87$). Overall, results show that uses of Twitter differ significantly within subjects, $F(3.47, 2287.93) = 290.47$, $p < .000$, $\eta^2_{partial} = .59$. Planned repeated contrasts (comparing the item ranked first to the item ranked second, the 2nd item to the 3rd item, etc.) using the Bonferroni correction revealed that the differences between all of the distribution systems ranked next to each other—except the difference between getting information about sports and starting a conversation about current topics—were statistically significant ($p < .05$).

Table 11.3 College Students' Primary Uses of Twitter.

RANK	ACTIVITY	MEAN	SD	F	$\eta^2_{partial}$
1	Reading tweets posted by friends	3.90	1.21	339.23***	.34
2	Getting in touch with friends	3.18	1.26	248.15***	.15
3	Getting information about sports	2.57	1.32	.727	.00
4	Starting a conversation about current topics	2.52	1.22	5.91*	.01
5	Getting in touch with media/personalities	2.40	1.18	—	—

Note. F-values and $\eta^2_{partial}$ from within-subjects repeated contrasts comparing distribution systems ranked next to each other (i.e., 1 vs. 2, 2 vs. 3, 3 vs. 4, 4 vs. 5). N = 666. SD = standard deviation; Min = 1 (*never*); Max = 7 (*every day*) for all items.
*p < .05. **p < .01. ***p < .001.

Investigating whether the uses of multiple distribution systems are related (Hypothesis 1), bivariate correlations were computed. Significant positive correlations were found among all distribution systems (see Table 11.4). Most relevant for this study, there was a statistically significant positive relationship between television consumption and the sports-related use of Twitter, $r(943) = .53$, $p < .001$; and Facebook, $r(943) = .55$, $p < .001$. These results indicate that if the use of one distribution system increases, the use of other distribution systems increases as well. Addressing the premise of this study, an increase in Twitter use should not relate to a decrease in television consumption. Thus, the results of this study support the relationship posed in Hypothesis 1.

Table 11.4 Summary of Correlations Among Use of Distribution Systems.

	1	2	3	4	5	6	7	8	9
1. Television	1								
2. Websites	.68***	1							
3. Facebook	.55***	.65***	1						
4. Twitter	.53***	.50***	.56***	1					
5. Radio	.53***	.55***	.48***	.33***	1				
6. YouTube	.51***	.69***	.66***	.50***	.46***	1			
7. Other SM	.44***	.55***	.59***	.60***	.41***	.63***	1		
8. Newspapers	.42***	.46***	.34***	.27***	.47***	.39***	.28***	1	
9. Blogs	.34***	.49***	.42***	.41***	.36***	.53***	.52***	.41***	1

Note. *$p < .05$. **$p < .01$. ***$p < .001$.

Finally, the OLS model predicting participants' preference for Twitter to television from the four dimensions of parasocial interaction (Hypothesis 4), as well as sports interest (Hypothesis 2) and perceived sports expertise (Hypothesis 3), while controlling for the perceived authenticity of sport media personalities' Twitter account, Twitter use, as well as age and education, revealed a significant equation ($F = 19.941$, $df = 12,647$, $p < .001$) with an adjusted R^2 of .256 (see Table 11.5). Interest in sports predicted a statistically significant decrease in Twitter preference ($\beta = -.430$, $p < .000$), yielding support for Hypothesis 2. Individuals who identify themselves as interested in sports rely more on television. When looking at perceived expertise in sports, a different picture emerged. A significant positive relationship was found (β = .305, p < .000), supporting Hypothesis 3. Individuals who see themselves and sports experts, more frequently turn to Twitter. From the four dimensions of parasocial interaction, only the relationship between "group affiliation" and the preference of Twitter to television was significant at the p < .05 level. It had a regression coefficient equal to .271 and a β weight of .112. The regression coefficient shows that individuals who see themselves as members of the group of sport media personalities and other Twitter users they communicate with are more likely to rely on Twitter than television for the consumption of sports content. As a result, Hypothesis 4 needs to be considered partially supported. Finally, some of the control variables emerged as statistically significant predictors. Although age and education were not statistically significant, the relationship between the frequency of Twitter use (β = .437, p < .000) and the number of individuals followed on Twitter (β = .088, p = .049) were statistically significant predictors of Twitter preference. This suggests that individuals following more people and using Twitter more frequently for general purposes are also more likely to use it for their consumption of sports content, even more so than television.

Table 11.5 Predictors of Twitter Preference.

	B	SE	β
Constant	−2.521	.508	
Age	−.022	.021	−.051
Education	.006	.077	.004
Interest in sports	−.485	.097	−.430***
Expertise in sports	.343	.098	.305***
Length of Twitter use	−.013	.087	−.005
Frequency of Twitter use	.390	.039	.440***
Number of people followed	.119	.060	.088*
Perceived authenticity	.041	.052	.028
Parasocial identification	−.077	.129	−.032
Parasocial interest	.098	.135	.038
Parasocial group affiliation	.271	.134	.112*

Parasocial problem solving	.003	.139	.001
Adjusted R^2	.256		
F(12, 647)	19.941***		

Note. N = 666.
*$p < .05$. **$p < .01$. ***$p < .001$.

DISCUSSION

There has been much discussion about the presumed importance of Twitter in the sport media ecosystem. Social media in general, and Twitter in particular, have often been ascribed a primary role in replacing traditional media as the main source of sports-related content. This is not the case. Even though the sample of college students utilized in this study reported an exceptionally high adoption of Twitter with about 70%, television remained the primary distribution system for sports content. Twitter only ranked fourth, even among these early adopters. Given the much lower adoption rate in the general population (16%), it needs to be assumed that Twitter plays an even smaller role when it comes to the general public. This is in line with initial research conducted by Clavio and Walsh (2014), who found "a surprising prevalence of traditional media usage for informational purposes" (p. 261) and lends support for arguments about the enduring power of television in the sport media landscape (Boyle, 2014; Wenner, 2014b).

The results of this study also lend support for the notion that most arguments of Twitter displacing television are misplaced (Greer & Ferguson, 2011). Although Facebook and Twitter have certainly gained importance and surpassed radio stations and newspapers as sources of sports content among most college students, social media still take on a supplementary role to television as suggested by Harrington, Highfield, and Bruns (2013). As the increase in second screening (Nielsen, 2013; Tribbey, 2014) and the significant positive correlations found in the present study indicate, Twitter is used in conjunction with television and not as a replacement. In fact, Twitter users in this study consumed significantly more sports content on television than nonusers.

The interrelation between televised sporting events and peak uses of Twitter found in previous literature also points out an interesting dynamic between social media platforms. Although Twitter seems to be an event-driven distribution system individuals turn to in case of breaking news and other shared media events, Facebook rather fulfills a day-to-day role. As a result, individuals are more likely to point towards Facebook than Twitter when being asked about the distribution system they use to encounter/consume news on a daily basis. This is in line with research on news consumption in the realm of politics, where 61% of online Millennials reported getting political news on Facebook in a given week while Twitter did not play a major role (Mitchell, Gottfried, & Matsa, 2015).

This has implications for future studies on social media and sport. Although Twitter has been the primary focus of many studies and has received much attention in the popular press, the results of this study suggest that Facebook plays a more important role in students' overall consumption of sports-related content when it comes to their average daily use. To shed further light on the use of different social media platforms in the realm of sports, a distinction needs to be made between punctual event-related and everyday information/entertainment-driven media use. During events, Twitter is heavily used in conjunction with television to discuss the events unfolding on the screen (e.g., Graver, 2012; Highfield et al., 2013). During nonevent periods, though, Twitter seems to be used in a more interpersonal way. Although obtaining sports-related information only ranked third among popular Twitter uses, the two main uses (reading friends' posts, getting in touch with friends) are both inherently social. Even during event-related use, the primary goal of many individuals' Twitter use is likely the discussion of unfolding events rather than the acquisition of information.

This strong social component might be related to the difficulty for many users—especially nonexperts—to locate sport-specific information on Twitter. If individuals are using Twitter mainly for social reasons (as indicated by the results of this study), they are unlikely to have an established network of sports information sources available. Most hard news content is therefore likely to be stumbled upon. While this incidental exposure to content also applies to Facebook, individuals are more likely to be exposed to quality content on the social network site. Not only is Facebook more frequently used for longer periods of time but shared news content also remains visible for a longer period of time than it does on Twitter. Overall, although Twitter seems to be a venue for sports experts to obtain current information from their established networks, Facebook is more popular among the general population for everyday use. Still, sports experts' relative preference of Twitter makes sense given that some affordances of the distribution system, such as its instantaneity (Petrovic et al., 2013), satisfy the need of perceived experts to obtain information quickly better than television. Twitter is often the first venue through which athletes, organizations, and media outlets provide information, making it a valuable resource for individuals aspiring to be up-to-date with current developments.

On the other hand, participants indicating high levels of sports interest were less likely to rely on Twitter. This makes sense as far as individuals with general sports interest can be seen as the more casual users than sports experts. As a result, they would be more motivated by the benefits such as entertainment, escape, and aesthetic gratifications (Raney, 2006), which can be better obtained from television than Twitter given the affordances of the distribution system (see Gantz & Lewis 2014).

Finally, the group affiliation dimension of the parasocial interaction construct was an important predictor of Twitter preference. Individuals who see themselves as members of the community of sport media personalities and other Twitter users they interact with are more likely to rely on Twitter than television. This at least partially confirms some of the assumptions about parasocial interactions (Hull & Lewis, 2014) and interactivity (Gantz & Lewis, 2014) being important factors in individuals' decision to rely more on social media for the consumption of sports content. It can also be seen as a further indicator for different usage patterns between experts and casual users. Expert users are more likely to have established a solid presence on Twitter, which can be seen as a prerequisite to engage in any parasocial interaction with that group. Overall, more research on the use of different distribution systems in the realm of sport is warranted, especially comparing them to each other and taking the differences in event-related versus daily use, as well as differences between user groups and purposes into account.

LIMITATIONS AND FUTURE RESEARCH

Although this study offers valuable insights into college students' sport media consumption, it is not without limitations. First of all, although a student sample was chosen on purpose to investigate the use of Twitter in the realm of sports among early adopters to shed light on a phenomenon that might later affect a broader demographic, future research should investigate this issue with further audiences to determine if the multivariate relationships found here indeed translate beyond this sample.

In addition, the present study was part of a larger investigation on sports content on Twitter and therefore did not always employ measures specifically designed to fit the purpose of this investigation. Most prominently, media use was measured rather broadly. Future studies should employ a more fine-grained measure, assessing the actual time individuals spent consuming sports content through different distribution systems rather than the broad increments used in the present study. This would yield even more detailed insights into the relative importance of individual distribution systems. Similarly, this study did not specifically ask participants how frequently they were using multiple distribution systems at the same time and therefore cannot make a definitive argument about the conjunct use of Twitter and television beyond correlations. In addition, this study did not differentiate among different types of television (i.e., Internet protocol television, on-demand, smart TV, and mobile screens) but rather focused on traditional broadcasts. Therefore, it is only differentiated between traditional broadcasts and all other forms of moving images often consumed through the Internet. Follow-up studies could take into account the changing nature of television and whether audiences perceive online streaming and other new formats as television—or a separate, blurred form of sport media consumption.

Finally, this study used parasocial interaction as a framework to identify a subgroup of the population that might be more likely to rely on Twitter for the consumption of sports-related content. Although parasocial interaction has frequently been utilized to study social media and sport, the use in the present context might be problematic. Although the overall regression model was significant, only the group affiliation dimension of the parasocial interaction construct was a significant predictor of Twitter preference. Furthermore, it only contributed a small amount to the overall variance explained. This is potentially related to the primary use of Twitter during events, where much of the conversation takes place among regular users focusing on the event itself and only in fewer instances on individual athletes or media personalities that might join the conversation. Instead of focusing on a particular media character, as it is often done in studies using the concept of parasocial interaction, the present study also asked participants to generally think of the sport media personalities and media institutions they follow on Twitter. It might have been more difficult to represent parasocial interactions with an unspecified individual or group rather than a named individual. Future studies could address this issue by presenting participants with one particular sport media personality, or priming participants to think of their favorite sport media personality and also differentiating between event-driven and day-to-day relational Twitter use.

172

CONCLUSION

Twitter will not displace sports broadcasts—and arguments pitting social media against television are often misplaced. Although this study finds that social media play an important role in students' sport media consumption, they are not taking the place of television as the most frequently used way of consuming sports-related content across a broader population. Twitter, for example, is rather taking a complementary role, striving as a second screen for users to provide their own commentary about events unfolding on television and aiding them in obtaining additional information. Furthermore, social media use in the realm of sports is surely a multifaceted phenomenon. Distinctions need to be made between different types of users (casual vs. expert) and uses (event-driven vs. daily browsing) of various social media platforms and how they are related.

From a practical standpoint, this study points out the need to question the overwhelming focus on Twitter in industry and academia. Ease of access and data collection should not determine whether a distribution system becomes a research priority. Rather, a strong rationale needs to be provided for focusing on a particular platform. That also applies to the sport media industry, where a more focused use of different social media platforms might yield beneficial results. Communication designed to engage casual users on a daily basis on Facebook needs to be different from materials designed to join the conversation around specific mediated events on Twitter.

From a theoretical standpoint, this study points out the need to take a closer look at parasocial interaction and how it is used to study social media and sport. Results suggest that the different dimensions of the construct might relate differently to some outcome variable. In addition, not all communication on social media falls under the parasocial interaction framework. Much of the communication on Twitter, for example, seems to be either interpersonal or mass-oriented—especially when discussing major televised events with other regular Twitter users or broad mass media institutions. Even when individual athletes or sport media personalities are joining the conversation, the concept of circumsocial interaction (Kassing & Sanderson, 2015) seems to be a more accurate way to describe interactions on many social media platforms.

173

DECLARATION OF CONFLICTING INTERESTS

The author(s) declared no potential conflicts of interest with respect to the research, authorship, and/or publication of this article.

FUNDING

The author(s) received no financial support for the research, authorship, and/or publication of this article.

REFERENCES

Abelman, R. (1996). Can we generalize from generation X? Not! *Journal of Broadcasting & Electronic Media, 40,* 441–446. doi:10.1080/08838159609364365

Auter, P. J., & Palmgreen, P. (2000). Development and validation of a parasocial interaction measure: The audience-persona interaction scale. *Communication Research Reports, 17,* 79–89. doi:10.1080/08824090009388753

Basil, M. D., Brown, W. J., & Bocarnea, M. C. (2002). Differences in univariate values versus multivariate relationships. *Human Communication Research, 28,* 501–514. doi:10.1111/j.1468-2958.2002.tb00820.x

Billings, A. (2014). Power in the reverberation: Why Twitter matters, but not the way most believe. *Communication & Sport, 2,* 107–112. doi:10.1177/2167479514527427

Boyd, D. M., & Ellison, N. B. (2007). Social network sites: Definition, history, and scholarship. *Journal of Computer-Mediated Communication, 13,* 210–230. doi:10.1111/j.1083-6101.2007.00393.x

Boyle, R. (2014). Television sport in the age of screens and content. *Television & New Media, 15,* 746–751. doi:10.1177/1527476414529167

Cameron, J., & Geidner, N. (2014). Something old, something new, something borrowed from something blue: Experiments on dual viewing TV and Twitter. *Journal of Broadcasting & Electronic Media, 58,* 400–419. doi:10.1080/08838151.2014.935852

Chen, G. M. (2011). Tweet this: A uses and gratifications perspective on how active Twitter use gratifies a need to connect with others. *Computers in Human Behavior, 27,* 755–762. doi:10.1016/j.chb.2010.10.023

Clavio, G., & Kian, T. M. (2010). Uses and gratifications of a retired female athlete's Twitter followers. *International Journal of Sport Communication, 3,* 485–500.

Clavio, G., & Walsh, P. (2014). Dimensions of social media utilization among college sport fans. *Communication & Sport, 2,* 261–281. doi:10.1177/2167479513480355

Cunningham, W. H., Anderson, W. T., Jr., & Murphy, J. H. (1974). Are students real people? *The Journal of Business, 47,* 399–409. doi:10.2307/2352457

Elmer, G. (2013). Live research: Twittering an election debate. *New Media & Society, 15,* 18–30. doi:10.1177/1461444812457328

Filo, K., Lock, D., & Karg, A. (2015). Sport and social media research: A review. *Sport Management Review, 18,* 166–181. doi:10.1016/j.smr.2014.11.001

Frederick, E. L., Lim, C. H., Clavio, G., Pedersen, P. M., & Burch, L. M. (2014). Choosing between the one-way or two-way street: An exploration of relationship promotion by professional athletes on Twitter. *Communication & Sport, 2,* 80–99. doi:10.1177/2167479512466387

Frederick, E. L., Lim, C. H., Clavio, G., & Walsh, P. (2012). Why we follow: An examination of parasocial interaction and fan motivations for following athlete archetypes on Twitter. *International Journal of Sport Communication, 5,* 481–502.

Galily, Y. (2014). When the medium becomes "well done": Sport, television, and technology in the twenty-first Century. *Television & New Media, 15,* 717–724. doi:10.1177/1527476414532141

Gantz, W. (1981). An exploration of viewing motives and behaviors associated with television sports. *Journal of Broadcasting & Electronic Media, 25,* 263–275. doi:10.1080/08838158109386450

Gantz, W., & Lewis, N. (2014). Sports on traditional and newer digital media: Is there really a fight for fans? *Television & New Media, 15,* 760–768. doi:10.1177/1527476414529463

Gantz, W., & Wenner, L. A. (1995). Fanship and the television sports viewing experience. *Sociology of Sport Journal, 12,* 56–74.

Gibbs, C., O' Reilly, N., & Brunette, M. (2014). Professional team sport and Twitter: Gratifications sought and obtained by followers. *International Journal of Sport Communication, 7*, 188–213. doi:10.1123/IJSC.2014-0005

Giglietto, F., & Selva, D. (2014). Second screen and participation: A content analysis on a full season dataset of tweets. *Journal of Communication, 64*, 260–277. doi:10.1111/jcom.12085

Giles, D. C. (2002). Parasocial interaction: A review of the literature and a model for future research. *Media Psychology, 4*, 279–305. doi:10.1207/S1532785XMEP0403_04

Graver, F. (2012, October). *90 days at Twitter: What I learned from the inside.* Paper presented at the Ad Age Social Engagement/Social TV Conference, Los Angeles, CA.

Greer, C. F., & Ferguson, D. A. (2011). Following local television news personalities on Twitter: A uses and gratifications approach to social networking. *Electronic News, 5*, 145–157. doi:10.1177/1931243111420405

Harrington, S. (2013). Tweeting about the telly: Live TV, audiences, and social media. In K. Weller, A. Bruns, J. Burgess, M. Mahrt, & C. Puschmann (Eds.), *Twitter and society* (pp. 237–247). New York, NY: Peter Lang.

Harrington, S., Highfield, T., & Bruns, A. (2013). More than a backchannel: Twitter and television. *Participations: Journal of Audience & Reception Studies, 10*, 405–409.

Hartmann, T. (2008). Parasocial interactions and paracommunication with new media characters. In E. A. Konijn, S. Utz, M. Tanis, & S. B. Barnes (Eds.), *Mediated interpersonal communication* (pp. 177–199). New York, NY: Routledge.

Hartmann, T., Stuke, D., & Daschmann, G. (2008). Positive parasocial relationships with drivers affect suspense in racing sport spectators. *Journal of Media Psychology: Theories, Methods, and Applications, 20*, 24–34. doi:10.1027/1864-1105.20.1.24

Herrera-Damas, S., & Hermida, A. (2014). Tweeting but not talking: The missing element in talk radio's institutional use of Twitter. *Journal of Broadcasting & Electronic Media, 58*, 481–500. doi:10.1080/08838151.2014.966361

Highfield, T., Harrington, S., & Bruns, A. (2013). Twitter as a technology for audiencing and fandom. *Information, Communication & Society, 16*, 315–339. doi:10.1080/1369118X.2012.756053

Hoerner, J. (1999). Scaling the web: A parasocial interaction scale for world wide web sites. In D. W. Schumann & E. Thorson (Eds.), *Advertising and the world wide web* (pp. 135–147). Mahwah, NJ: Lawrence Erlbaum.

Horton, D., & Wohl, R. R. (1956). Mass communication and para-social interaction: Observations on intimacy at a distance. *Psychiatry, 19*, 215–229.

Hull, K., & Lewis, N. P. (2014). Why Twitter displaces broadcast sports media: A model. *International Journal of Sport Communication, 7*, 16–33. doi:10.1123/IJSC.2013-0093

Hutchins, B. (2011). The acceleration of media sport culture: Twitter, telepresence and online messaging. *Information, Communication & Society, 14*, 237–257. doi:10.1080/1369118X. 2010.508534

Kassing, J. W., & Sanderson, J. (2009). You're the kind of guy that we all want for a drinking buddy: Expressions of parasocial interaction on Floydlandis.com. *Western Journal of Communication, 73*, 182203. doi:10.1080/10570310902856063

Kassing, J. W., & Sanderson, J. (2010). Fan-athlete interaction and Twitter tweeting through the Giro: A case study. *International Journal of Sport Communication, 3*, 113–128.

Kassing, J. W., & Sanderson, J. (2015). Playing in the new media game or riding the virtual bench: Confirming and disconfirming membership in the community of sport. *Journal of Sport & Social Issues, 39*, 3–18. doi:10.1177/0193723512458931

Katz, E., Blumler, J. G., & Gurevitch, M. (1973). Uses and gratifications research. *The Public Opinion Quarterly, 37*, 509–523. doi:10.2307/2747854

Kline, R. B. (2011). *Principles and practice of structural equation modeling* (3rd ed.). New York, NY: Guilford Press.

Kwak, H., Lee, C., Park, H., & Moon, S. (2010). *What is Twitter, a social network or a news media?* Proceedings of the 19th International Conference on the World Wide Web, 591–600. doi:10.1177/0193723512458931

Larsson, A. O. (2013). Tweeting the viewer—use of Twitter in a talk show context. *Journal of Broadcasting & Electronic Media, 57*, 135–152. doi:10.1080/08838151.2013.787081

Lebel, K., & Danylchuk, K. (2012). How tweet it is: A gendered analysis of professional tennis players' self-presentation on Twitter. *International Journal of Sport Communication, 5*, 461–480.

Levy, M. R. (1979). Watching TV news as para-social interaction. *Journal of Broadcasting & Electronic Media, 23*, 69–80. doi:10.1080/08838157909363919

Marwick, A., & Boyd, D. (2011). To see and be seen: Celebrity practice on Twitter. *Convergence: The International Journal of Research into New Media Technologies, 17,* 139–158. doi:10.1177/1354856510394539

Matsa, K. E., & Mitchell, A. (2014). *8 key takeaways about social media and the news* (PewResearch Center). Retrieved from http://www.journalism.org/2014/03/26/8-keytakeaways-about-social-media-and-news/

Mitchell, A., Gottfried, J., & Matsa, K. E. (2015). *Millennials and political news: Social media—the local TV for the next generation?* (PewResearch Center). Retrieved from http://www.journalism.org/2015/06/01/millennials-political-news/

Mitchell, A., Holcomb, J., & Page, D. (2013). *News use across social media platforms* (Pew Journalism Project). Retrieved from http://www.journalism.org/2013/11/14/news-useacross-social-media-platforms/

Mitchell, A., Kiley, J., Gottfried, J., & Guskin, E. (2013). *The role of news on Facebook: Common yet incidental* (PewResearch Center). Retrieved from http://www.journalism.org/2013/10/24/the-role-of-news-on-facebook/

Mukherjee, P., & Jansen, B. J. (2014). Social TV and the social soundtrack: Significance of second screen interaction during television viewing. In W. G. Kennedy, N. Agarwal, & S. J. Yang (Eds.), *Social Computing, Behavioral-Cultural Modeling and Prediction* (Vol. *8393,* pp. 317–324). New York, NY: Springer International Publishing.

Nielsen. (2013). The cross-platform report: A look across screens. *Nielsen Wire.* Retrieved from http://www.nielsen.com/us/en/insights/reports/2013/the-cross-platform-report-a-lookacross-screens.html

Nordlund, J.-E. (1978). Media interaction. *Communication Research, 5,* 150–175. doi: 10.1177/009365027800500202

Pallotta, F. (2015, February 2). Super bowl XLIX posts the largest audience in TV history. *CNNMoney.* Retrieved from http://money.cnn.com

Pegoraro, A. (2010). Look who's talking—Athletes on Twitter: A case study. *International Journal of Sport Communication, 3,* 501–514.

Petrovic, S., Osborne, M., Mccreadie, R., Macdonald, C., Ounis, I., & Shrimpton, L. (2013). *Can Twitter replace Newswire for breaking news?* Proceedings of the 7th International Conference on Weblogs and Social Media (ICWSM), 713–716.

Raney, A. A. (2006). Why we watch and enjoy mediated sports. In A. A. Raney & J. Bryant (Eds.), *Handbook of sports and media* (pp. 313–329). New York, NY: Lawrence Erlbaum.

Reed, S. (2013). American sports writers' social media use and its influence on professionalism. *Journalism Practice, 7,* 555–571. doi:10.1080/17512786.2012.739325

Rogers, S. (2014, July 14). *Insights into the #WorldCup conversation on Twitter* [Web log post]. Retrieved from https://blog.twitter.com/2014/insights-into-the-worldcup-conversation-on-twitter

Rosengren, K. E., & Windahl, S. (1972). Mass media consumption as a functional alternative. In D. McQuail (Ed.), *Sociology of mass communications: Selected readings* (pp. 119–134). Harmondsworth, England: Penguin.

Rubin, A. M., Perse, E. M., & Powell, R. A. (1985). Loneliness, parasocial interaction, and local television news viewing. *Human Communication Research, 12,* 155–180. doi:10.1111/j.1468-2958.1985.tb00071.x

Rubin, A. M., & Step, M. M. (2000). Impact of motivation, attraction, and parasocial interaction on talk radio listening. *Journal of Broadcasting & Electronic Media, 44,* 635–654. doi:10.1207/s15506878jobem4404_7

Rubin, R. B., & Mc Hugh, M. P. (1987). Development of parasocial interaction relationships. *Journal of Broadcasting & Electronic Media, 31,* 279–292. doi:10.1080/08838158709386664

Sanderson, J. (2011). *It's a whole new ballgame: How social media is changing sports.* New York, NY: Hampton Press.

Sanderson, J., & Browning, B. (2013). Training versus monitoring: A qualitative examination of athletic department practices regarding student-athletes and Twitter. *Qualitative Research Reports in Communication, 14,* 105–111. doi:10.1080/17459435.2013.835348

Schultz, B., & Sheffer, M. L. (2010). An exploratory study of how Twitter is affecting sports journalism. *International Journal of Sport Communication, 3,* 226–239.

Sheffer, M. L., & Schultz, B. (2010). Paradigm shift or passing fad? Twitter and sports journalism. *International Journal of Sport Communication, 3,* 472–484.

Spinda, J. S., Earnheardt, A. C., & Hugenberg, L. W. (2009). Checkered flags and mediated friendships: Parasocial interaction among NASCAR fans. *Journal of Sports Media, 4,* 31–55. doi:10.1353/jsm.0.0041

Sun, T. (2010). Antecedents and consequences of parasocial interaction with sport athletes and identification with sport teams. *Journal of Sport Behavior, 33,* 194–217.

Sun, T., & Wu, G. (2012). Influence of personality traits on parasocial relationship with sports celebrities: A hierarchical approach. *Journal of Consumer Behaviour, 11,* 136–146. doi: 10.1002/cb.1378

Thorson, K. S., & Rodgers, S. (2006). Relationships between blogs as eWOM and interactivity, perceived interactivity, and parasocial interaction. *Journal of Interactive Advertising, 6,* 5–44. doi:10.1080/15252019.2006.10722117

Trail, G. T., & James, J. D. (2001). The motivation scale for sport consumption: Assessment of the scale's psychometric properties. *Journal of Sport Behavior, 24,* 108–127.

Tribbey, C. (2014). CEA, NATPE Study Offers Second Screen Viewing Insights [Web log post]. *2ndScreenSociety.com.* Retrieved from http://www.2ndscreensociety.com/blog/2014/01/14/cea-natpe-study-offers-second-screen-viewing-insights/

Valenzuela, S., Park, N., & Kee, K. F. (2009). Is there social capital in a social network site?: Facebook use and college students' life satisfaction, trust, and participation. *Journal of Computer-Mediated Communication, 14,* 875–901. doi:10.1111/j.1083-6101. 2009.01474.x

Wenner, L. A. (2014a). Much ado (or not) about Twitter? Assessing an emergent communication and sport research agenda. *Communication & Sport, 2,* 103–106. doi: 10.1177/2167479514527426

Wenner, L. A. (2014b). On the limits of the new and the lasting power of the mediasport interpellation. *Television & New Media, 15,* 732–740. doi:10.1177/1527476414532957

Whannel, G. (2014). The paradoxical character of live television sport in the twenty-first century. *Television & New Media, 15,* 769–776. doi:10.1177/1527476414551180

Witkemper, C., Blaszka, M., & Chung, J. (2014). Establishing a typology of social media uses in the sport industry: A multidimensional scaling study. *Communication & Sport.* doi:10. 1177/2167479514544951

SECTION 4
Amateur Sports

For decades, millions of Americans have participated in amateur sports. At the youth level, organizations such as AYHA soccer, Little League baseball, and CYO basketball have been great sources of fun, success, and togetherness for kids and family members alike. In middle and high school, sports are also very important for American youth. Lettering in a sport is a big accomplishment, and millions of fans attend high school sporting events on a regular basis. In college, elite athletes play NCAA sports, while others play club and intramural sports. As adults, millions of people play in recreational softball, hockey, and basketball leagues all over the country. In this section, two different perspectives are outlined. The first examines the many benefits of amateur sports, and the second looks at the growing concerns that many have concerning amateur sports.

THE BENEFITS OF AMATEUR SPORTS

There are, of course, numerous benefits associated with playing sports. For many people of all ages, sports are social, fitness oriented, and—among many other things—very enjoyable to both play and watch. Think of how social sports are for athletes of all levels and spectators alike. Millions of people around the country love the camaraderie that comes with their weekly pick-up basketball game or men's league hockey game. Recreational athletes often joke with each other before, during, and after games. They go to restaurants and bars after games, and they enjoy spending time together. Clearly, a huge number of lasting friendships have been established among players and parents who are part of youth teams.

The health benefits of amateur sports are also very important. Of course, it depends on the sport, but people who play basketball, hockey, water polo, and other fast-paced sports will likely get an aerobic workout while they play. People of all ages burn hundreds of calories and promote cardiovascular health when they participate in aerobic activities. Although working out at the gym does not really fit the definition of a sport, it still represents a physical activity that can improve health.

Third, many people really enjoy playing sports and watching sporting events either live or on television. For many, it is time well spent attending a sporting event. They love the crowd, the food, the smells, and the energy that is not generally captured on television. Going to a game is also a social thing. People meet friends or go with family members and really spend quality time together bonding over a team. Watching games on television is also a huge source of enjoyment for millions of Americans. Watching football on Sunday afternoons or hockey on Saturday nights is a vastly popular pastime in this country. Again, there is also a social dimension to watching games on television, as many people do so with others. Finally, there is a host of additional benefits of playing sports. For many people, sports will push athletes to become better time managers. Playing sports is a commitment, and players need to know how to carve out the necessary time to commit themselves to that team.

Several studies have also shown that being a successful athlete has the potential to improve a person's self-confidence and self-esteem. In their chapter entitled "Come out and Play: Shyness in Childhood and the Benefits of Organized Sports Participation," Leanne Findlay and Robert Coplan establish that sports promote a greater sense of mental and emotional well-being among participating youth. Using baseline survey data and data collected after 1 year of playing sports, this study shows that participating in organized youth sports is positively linked with several measures of positive adjustment, including social skills and self-esteem. Findlay and Coplan also found that when shy kids participate in sports, they experience a significant decrease in anxiety.

CONCERNS ABOUT AMATEUR SPORTS

There are also various concerns about amateur sports. More and more people are worried about the heightened level of competitiveness, the potential for injury, the costs, the in-fighting, and the increased professionalization of many amateur sports. There is no question that winning is very important to most amateur athletes. Just like many professional athletes, some amateur athletes taunt opposing players and fans and take the games very seriously. Many referees who officiate everything from youth to beer-league games are often abused and threatened by players, parents, and fans who disagree with their calls.

A related issue pertains to the high potential for player injuries in amateur sports. Many contend that we are in a concussion crisis when it comes to high school and college football. Due to bigger, stronger, and faster players, the rates of youth football players being concussed is so much higher than it has ever been. Kids are also practicing and playing more as seasons are longer and practice regimens are more intense. In the news, for example, we hear stories of kids blowing out their arms from throwing too many curve balls and needing Tommy John surgery as teenagers. In part, more kids are getting hurt because they are not playing a given sport seasonally, as was historically the case.

A third concern is connected to how expensive amateur sports have become. At the youth level, many athletes play on travel teams and are required to pay hundreds—if not thousands—of dollars for league fees, equipment, and uniforms. Numerous people are concerned that only a small segment of the population is able to pursue these athletic opportunities. It is not just that more and more youth players are on travel teams; many elite athletes have private coaching, attend prestigious development camps, and even go to special schools that prioritize their athletic development.

Youth sports organizations are also frequently rife with drama and in-fighting. It is very common to hear stories of parents quarrelling with their kid's coach over their child's playing time and game strategies. Many parents invest heavily in their children's athletic endeavors and want to see them shine. But, sometimes, coaches see things differently. Maybe the coach thinks the player is better suited to a different position than his or her parent does. In any case, this is an emotional issue for many coaches and parents. It is an age-old story: Parents threaten to pull their kids from teams if they do not get more playing time.

A final issue relates to the increased professionalization of amateur sports. Think of how professionalized the Olympics and March Madness have become. Not only have the Olympics begun to allow professional athletes to participate in events, but the whole feel of the games is much different than it has been previously. Similar developments have occurred within the NCAA. March Madness and the end-of-season bowl games feel like professional events.

In his piece entitled "The Professionalization of Youth Sports in America," Jordan Cox examines the negative impacts concerning the pressure that many of today's parents place on their children to succeed in sports. Many of today's sports parents devote inordinate amounts of time and money to their children's athletic careers. This prompts them to micromanage their children's sporting careers and push them toward constant improvement. Unfortunately, this can backfire. All of the yelling, training, travel, and coaching that elite youth athletes often endure simply take their toll on many kids and prompt them to burn out—and ultimately quit. In his selection "The Professionalization of College Sports: The Case of College Basketball," Sean Kaukas argues that college football and men's basketball meet the criteria for being professional sports. He also outlines the perspective that favors paying college athletes and its corresponding counterargument, which is that college athletes should not be paid beyond their scholarships.

CHAPTER TWELVE

Come Out and Play

Shyness in Childhood and the Benefits of Organized Sports Participation

BY **LEANNE C. FINDLAY** AND **ROBERT J. COPLAN**

P ositive peer relations in childhood are consistently associated with positive social and psychological adjustment (Rubin, Bukowski, & Parker, 2006). Although the literature on children's peer relations is quite extensive, much of the research has focussed on peer interactions and relationships in the school context. However, this focus "provides a narrow view of childhood social relations, and reflects neither the breadth nor the dynamic nature of children's peer interactions" (Hymel, Vaillencourt, McDougall, & Renshaw, 2002, p. 273). Other social milieus, such as the sport context, provide opportunities for peer interaction and also provide an environment that fosters social support, security, and self-esteem. Sport is clearly tied to developing peer relations because children who have increased opportunities for social interaction are expected to be more socially skilled and have higher functioning.

Sport has previously been associated with such positive benefits as improved peer relations, increased self-esteem, and decreased anxiety (Kirkcaldy, Shephard, & Siefen, 2002; Marsh, 1998; Smith, 2003). However, relatively little is known about the potentially unique influence of sport participation for different "types" of children, such as shy children. It was the objective of this research to investigate the interplay between sport and social behaviour in the prediction of adjustment outcomes. In particular, we explored the role of sport as a potential protective factor in the socioemotional adjustment of shy children by examining sports participation as a moderator (see Baron & Kenny, 1986) between shyness and psychosocial outcomes.

BENEFITS OF SPORT PARTICIPATION

Fostering and developing relationships with peers are key reasons cited by children for participating in sports; however, the impact of sport peer relations on child adjustment is highly understudied (Ebbeck & Weiss, 1998; Smith, 2003). Although there is little empirical literature addressing children's social behaviour characteristics (e.g., shyness) and sport, there is evidence to suggest that sport has a positive effect on children's social well-being overall, with respect to both peer relations (Smith, 1999) and psychological functioning (Kirkcaldy et al., 2002; Marsh, 1998). Sport involvement has been associated with increased social status, particularly for boys (Chase & Dummer, 1992), and children's perceived as well as actual physical competence (Weiss & Duncan, 1992). Furthermore, Page, Frey, Talbert, and Falk (1992) found that children aged 6 to 11 years with higher physical activity scores reported lower scores on loneliness. They suggested that children who withdraw from their peer group are less likely to participate in social activities, including sport.

Aggressive behaviour has been suggested to be a potentially negative social consequence of sport involvement. Gender is particularly relevant; boys not only participate in a greater number of contact sports, but have also been shown to be more adversely affected by participation (Bredemeier, 1988). More recent research suggests that aggressiveness is not necessarily related to sports involvement, even if that involvement is in contact team sports. McHale, Vinden, Bush, Richer, Shaw, and Smith (2005) found that middle-school-age children who had engaged in sport over the previous year were not more likely to be rated as aggressive by their physical education teachers. However, a sport-by-gender interaction

188

revealed that sport-involved girls were more likely to be rated to be aggressive than were non-sport-involved girls, and sport-involved boys were rated to be less aggressive.

Sports participation has also been studied in terms of the potential effects on self-esteem and anxiety. Marsh and colleagues (Marsh, 1998; Marsh, Perry, Horsely, & Roche, 1995) have repeatedly demonstrated that adolescent and adult athletes have higher self-esteem than do nonathletes. Marsh et al. (1995) found that elite athletes had significantly higher physical ability self-esteem, social self-esteem, and global self-esteem. Finally, Kirkcaldy and colleagues (2002) found that German adolescents who frequently participated in endurance sports displayed significantly lower anxiety than did adolescents who never participated or seldom participated. To date, however, there is no literature to address the impact of sport on younger children's social anxiety in particular whether or not sport can have differential effects based on personal characteristics. It was therefore of particular interest to examine the benefits of sport participation for particular "subgroups" of middle-school-age children, namely those with peer relations difficulties.

SHYNESS IN CHILDHOOD

Shyness is often conceptualized as social anxiety accompanied by behavioural responses, such as inhibition and withdrawal, in response to social and novel situations (Henderson & Zimbardo, 2001). Asendorpf (1990) characterised shy children as being trapped in an approach-avoidance conflict; they are motivated to play with others (i.e., have a desire to approach) but are apprehensive or wary due to anxiety. Hence, many shy children may have limited social experience. It is this latter point that leads to the investigation of participation in sport, a venue for social interaction, as a protective factor for shy children.

Shyness has been associated with peer relation difficulties, including peer rejection (Coplan, Arbeau, & Armer, in press; Fordham & Stevenson-Hinde, 1999) and internalizing difficulties such as anxiety and loneliness (Coplan, Closson, & Arbeau, 2007; Crozier, 1995; Eisenberg, Shepard, Fabes, Murphy, & Guthrie, 1998). Hymel, Woody, and Bowker (1993) found that children in Grades 4 to 6 who were identified as withdrawn by their peers had more negative overall self-esteem, lower athletic competence, and reported greater dissatisfaction within the peer group. The research therefore suggests that shy children have lower self-perceptions, especially in the areas of peer relations and athletic competence.

Links between shyness and sport. Very little research is available on the social outcomes of sport participation in terms of children's individual characteristics. It might be expected that children would respond to the sport environment differently based on their social preferences and/or characteristics. In terms of rates of participation, Page and Zarco (2001) reported that shy adolescent boys and girls participated in fewer vigorous activities than did average or low-shy children, in particular team sports. They argued that shy individuals may have less self-confidence and avoid participating in sport out of fear. McHale and colleagues (2005) also found that middle-school-age children who participated in sport were reported by their physical activity teacher to be less shy-withdrawn and to have higher social competence than their nonparticipating peers. These results were maintained even after controlling for teacher perceptions of athletic ability.

Other research has pointed to a link between sport anxiety and social anxiety. In a sample of Hispanic fifth and sixth graders, Storch, Bartlas, Dent, and Masia (2002) found that social anxiety was significantly related to sport anxiety and that girls experienced greater sport anxiety than did boys. Anxiety in sport could be linked to decreased participation, which would result in fewer social opportunities. Storch and colleagues suggested that sport anxiety be further investigated as one manifestation of more general social anxiety and that psycho-social interventions to address social anxiety should include sport as a domain of treatment.

THE CURRENT STUDY

The goal of the current study was to examine the protective role of sport participation in the psychosocial outcomes of shy children. To address this goal, a short-term longitudinal study was undertaken, tracking children's sport participation, social behaviour (shy and aggressive tendencies) and socioemotional adjustment over a 1-year period. Previous research in this area has relied primarily on cross-sectional data (e.g., Ebbeck & Weiss, 1998). It was hypothesised that sport participation would have unique benefits for shy children in terms of their peer relationships, socioemotional functioning, and general well-being. That is, shy children who participate in sport were expected to report higher psychosocial functioning than did shy children who did not participate in sport. It is also possible that the positive outcomes associated with sport participation might be beneficial to children with peer relations difficulties in general (and not shy children in particular). In order to investigate this possibility, a group of physically aggressive children were also included.

METHOD

PARTICIPANTS

The participants in this study were 355 children in Grades 4 and 5 (181 boys, 174 girls), recruited from public elementary schools in and around Ottawa, Canada. At the beginning of the study (Time 1), children ranged from 8.9 to 11.8 years of age (M_{age} = 10.1 years, SD = 0.6). At Time 2 (approximately 1 year later), 96 boys and 105 girls (n = 201) remained in the study, which represented a retention rate of approximately 56% from Time 1 to Time 2. No significant Time 1 differences were found between children who did/did not participate in the study at Time 2 on measures of shyness, aggression, sports participation, or parental education.

MEASURES

Social skills. Parents completed the *Social Skills Rating Scale* (SSRS; Gresham & Elliot, 1990), which has previously been shown to have adequate internal consistency (α's ranging from .65 to .87), good test-retest reliability, and good criterion validity. Of particular interest for the present study were the externalizing problem behaviours subscale (6 items, Time 1 α = .79, Time 2 α = .81) and the four social skills subscales (10 items each): cooperation (Time 1 α = .80, Time 2 α = .79), assertion (Time 1 α = .66, Time 2 α = .75), responsibility (Time 1 α = .51, Time 2 α = .71) and self-control (Time 1 α = .83, Time 2 α = .84).

Shyness. Crozier's (1995) 27-item *Children's Shyness Questionnaire* (CSQ) was administered to the children to assess shyness in middle childhood. As suggested by Crozier (1995), one item ("I enjoy singing aloud when others can hear me") was eliminated. Previous research has found the measure to have good reliability (α = .82, Crozier, 1995). Scores were summed to create a value for total shyness, and internal consistency was found to be adequate (α = .77 at Time 1, α = .80 at Time 2).

Aggression. Children's physical aggression was measured with a self-report scale based on the *Conflict Tactics Scale* (CTS; Strauss, 1979) and modified for the current research to reflect physically aggressive behaviour engaged in by the child over the last six months. The CTS has previously been shown to have adequate reliability (α's ranging from .56 to .82) and shows construct validity with similar scales of aggression. In the modified version used for the current study, children were asked to respond along a 5-point Likert scale (1 = *never*, 5 = *always*) with reference to 9 behaviours. Items were summed to create a mean score for physically aggressive behaviour (ranging from 9 to 45). Internal consistency in the current study was found to be good (Time 1 α = .83, Time 2 α = .86).

Sport participation. Information on children's sport participation was collected using the *Sport Participation Information Sheet* (Bowker, Gadbois, & Cornock, 2003). At Time 1, children were asked to list all of the sports that they had ever participated in, including information on the number of years they had participated and the level of participation ("just for fun", "at school", "recreationally" or "competitively"). At Time 2, children were only asked to indicate the sports that they had participated in over the past year, the purpose being to report any additional sport participation. Total years in sports were then summed to create a summary score of children's participation. For instance, if the child had participated in organised soccer for 3 years and hockey for 2 years, his or her total sports score was 5. In this way, sports were represented along a continuum with more sports representing a greater number of sport (i.e., peer) experiences. As a further step, coding allowed for the creation of groups of nonparticipants (list no sports or sports just for fun) versus participants (participated in some organised sport at the recreational or competitive level).

General well-being. Children were asked to complete a 10-item well-being questionnaire designed by Allison and Furstenberg (1989; see also Coplan, Wilson, Frohlick, & Zelenski, 2006). Children rated their social dissatisfaction and distress; items were summed to create an overall well-being score (Time 1 α = .76; Time 2 α = .79).

Self-system. Based on the Shavelson, Hubner, and Stanton (1976) hierarchical model of the self-system, the *Self-Description Questionnaire* (SDQ) is one of the most commonly employed measures of the self (e.g., Hymel, Bowker, & Woody, 1993; Marsh, 1984). Children were asked to respond along a 5-point scale (1 = *false* to 5 = *true*). Four subscales were of interest for the current study, including those pertaining to physical ability (α = .83 and .84 at Times 1 and 2, respectively), physical appearance (α = .89 and α = .91), peer relationships (α = .86 and α = .88), and general self (α = .78 and α = .84).

Social anxiety. Children's social anxiety was measured using the Social Anxiety *Scale for Children Revised* (SASC-R; La Greca & Stone, 1993). The measure consists of 22 items and reflects three subscales: fear of negative evaluation (FNE; 8 items, e.g., "I worry about what other kids think of me"), social avoidance and distress in new situations (SAD-New; 6 items, e.g., "I get nervous when I meet new kids"), and social avoidance and distress in general (SAD-General; 4 items, e.g., "I feel shy even with kids I know well"). Each item was rated in terms of how much the item was "true of you" on a 5-point Likert-type scale (1 = *not at all*, 5 = *all the time*). Social anxiety was summed across the three subscales, and internal consistency was found to be good (Time1 α = .90, Time 2 α = .91).

Loneliness. Asher, Hymel, and Renshaw's (1984) *Loneliness and Social Dissatisfaction* measure was employed to assess children's loneliness and social dissatisfaction. The measure consists of 16 items (plus 8 filler items), and children respond on a 5-point scale indicating how much each statement is true. Items were summed to create a total loneliness and social dissatisfaction score ranging from 16 to 80. All 16 items have been found to load onto one principal factor (Asher et al., 1984). In the current study, internal consistency was adequate (α = .74 at Time 1, α = .73 at Time 2).

Positive and negative affect. Finally, children's affect was measured using the *Positive and Negative Affect Schedule for Children* (PANAS-C). The PANAS-C, designed for use with preadolescent children, is the child version of the PANAS (Watson, Clark, & Tellegen, 1988), a common tool used to assess adult symptoms of poor adjustment, such as anxiety and depression. Characteristics of positive affect include interest, engagement, and energy, whereas negative affect reflects moods such as fear, sadness, and guilt (Laurent et al., 1999).

The PANAS-C consists of 30 items, half representing each of the two factors (positive and negative affect). Children were asked to retrospectively indicate the extent that they had felt certain feelings or emotions over a 2-week period on a scale of 1 to 5 (1 = *very slightly*, 5 = *extremely*). Items were summed for each subscale (Positive Affect: Time 1 α = .83, Time 2: α = .83; Negative Affect: Time 1 α = .88; Time 2 α = .90).

PROCEDURE

Upon obtaining University Ethics, School Board, and individual school approval, parental consent was obtained via permission letters sent home through the child's classroom teacher.

Children were given the opportunity to deny participation if they so desired. Parent-provided demographic information (child age, gender, parental education) was collected at Time 1 only. Information regarding parental income could not be collected; therefore, parental education was used as a proxy for socioeconomic status. Written parental consent and all other measures were collected at both Time 1 and Time 2. For those children with positive consent, group testing was employed. Task instructions were read aloud by the researcher and children independently read and responded to the questionnaires unless assistance was requested.

RESULTS

PRELIMINARY ANALYSES

An aggregate index of parental education was calculated by summing maternal and paternal education scores. Parental education was not significantly correlated with sport participation. However, parental education was significantly correlated with many of the dependent variables, as well as shyness ($r = -.15$, $p < .01$). Thus, parental education was included as a covariate in subsequent analyses.

To explore gender differences in shyness and aggression over time, a 2 × 2 Repeated Measures MANOVA was conducted for shyness and aggression with Time as a within-subjects variable and Gender as a between-subjects variable. Results indicated a significant main effect of Gender, $F(2, 197) = 15.79$, $p < .001$, and of Time, $F(2, 197) = 4.85$, $p < .01$. Follow-up univariate analysis revealed a significant effect of Gender for both shyness, $F(1, 198) = 20.57$, $p < .001$, and aggression, $F(1, 198) = 11.48$, $p < .001$. An examination of means indicated that boys reported being less shy ($M = 15.60$, $SD = 7.82$) and more aggressive ($M = 14.38$, $SD = 5.47$) than girls ($M_{shy} = 19.85$, $SD = 8.13$, $M_{agg} = 11.80$, $SD = 4.02$). Univariate analyses also revealed a significant effect of Time for shyness, $F(1, 198) = 9.71$, $p < .01$, with shyness decreasing from Time 1 ($M = 17.38$, $SD = 8.24$) to Time 2 ($M = 15.83$, $SD = 8.28$). Finally, shyness ($r = .68$, $p < .001$) and aggression ($r = .60$, $p < .001$) were relatively stable from Time 1 to Time 2. Shyness and aggression were not significantly correlated at either Time 1 or Time 2.

Shy and aggressive groups. Following previous research (Hymel et al., 1993; Page & Zarco, 2001), a categorical approach to the assessment of shyness and aggression was taken by creating extreme groups of shy and aggressive children. Given the gender differences found for both shyness and aggression and following the procedures of Rubin, Chen, & Hymel (1993) and Prakash and Coplan (2007), percentile scores were calculated within gender. An 85th percentile was selected to indicate extreme groups of children (see Kagan, 1989). Children who reported shyness scores in the top 15% within gender and below the mean on aggression were classified as shy (n = 48 at Time 1); children who scored in the top 15% within gender on aggression and below the mean for shyness were classified as aggressive (n = 42). Finally, children who scored below the mean on both shyness and aggression comprised the comparison group (n = 110). One hundred and fifty-five children were therefore excluded from the analyses at Time 1.

Sport participation. Children had previously participated in M = 2.45 (SD = 2.87, range = 0 to 15) sports at Time 1, and an additional M = 1.00 (SD = 1.03) sports at Time 2. Overall, boys (M = 3.97, SD = 3.35) had participated in significantly more sports than had girls (M = 3.08, SD = 3.15), $t(193)$ = 1.51, p = .05. Results from partial correlations (controlling for parental education) indicated that participation in organised sport at Time 1 was significantly and negatively associated with shyness (r = –.22, p < .001) but not aggression (r = .02, *ns*).

SPORT PARTICIPATION, SHYNESS, AGGRESSION, AND OUTCOMES AT TIME 1

Overview. The first set of analyses concerned Time 1 data only. Following this, a repeated measures design was employed to investigate the longitudinal effects of sport participation over a 1-year period. Outcomes related to sport, shyness, and aggression were assessed with a series of Multivariate and Univariate Analyses of Covariance. Dependent variables were grouped conceptually for multivariate analyses and their associations were checked empirically using factor analysis. Each grouping loaded onto a single principle factor with loadings above .60 (ranging from .69 to .86). Parental education and gender were included as covariates for all analyses. The main effects of Sport Participation (no organised sport, some organised sport) and Behaviour Group (shy, aggressive, comparison) were examined, as well as interaction effects. Although power is limited by the relatively small sample size of the extreme groups, three-way interactions were interpreted with some caution given that they were of particular theoretical interest in the current study. Only significant results are presented (accepted at the $p < .05$ level) and effect sizes are reported for significant univariate results. Trends at the $p \leq .07$ level are also noted due to the small sample size of the groups.

Social skills. Significant multivariate effects were found for Behaviour, $F(8, 356) = 3.79$, $p < .001$, and Sport, $F(4, 178) = 5.82$, $p < .001$. Univariate analyses for Sport revealed a significant main effect for assertion, $F(1, 181) = 12.18$, $p < .001$, $\eta = .06$, and for self-control, $F(1, 181) = 7.38$, $p < .01$, $\eta = .04$. An examination of means indicated that children who had participated in organised sport were reported to be more assertive and had more self-control than did children who had not participated in sport (see Table 12.1 for a comparison of means).

Table 12.1 Mean (SD) Outcomes for Sport and Non-Sport Participants

	SPORTS M (SD)	NO SPORTS M (SD)
Social skills		
Assertion	16.20[a] (2.34)	14.80[b] (2.72)
Self-control	14.13[a] (3.60)	12.23[b] (3.63)
Cooperation	12.88 (3.41)	12.13 (3.45)
Responsibility	13.44 (2.86)	13.25 (2.28)
Self-esteem		
Physical ability	38.25[a] (5.39)	32.86[b] (8.17)
Physical appearance	32.39[a] (8.41)	29.30[b] (8.46)
Peer	34.31[a] (7.06)	29.75[b] (9.05)
Internalizing		
Anxiety	43.21 (15.60)	49.01 (18.52)
Loneliness	29.88 (10.34)	34.83 (13.25)
Negative affect	28.24 (10.05)	31.03 (11.70)
Positive adjustment		
Well-being	43.43[a] (5.60)	40.77[b] (6.43)
Positive affect	56.75[a] (9.07)	50.49[b] (11.30)

Externalizing behaviours	2.62^a (2.20)	4.02^b (2.68)

Note. Differences in subscripts indicate a significant difference at *p* < .05 level.

In terms of the main effect of Behaviour group, follow up univariate tests revealed a significant effect for assertion, $F(1, 181) = 5.46$, $p < .05$, $\eta = .03$; self-control, $F(1, 181) = 5.58$, $p < .01$, $\eta = .06$; and cooperation, $F(1, 181) = 4.51$, $p < .05$, $\eta = .04$. As shown in Table 12.2, results from Tukey's post hoc testing indicated that aggressive children were reported to display less cooperation and self-control than were comparison children (whereas shy children did not differ from either group). Shy children were reported to be significantly less assertive than were aggressive or comparison children (who did not differ).

Table 12.2 Mean (SD) Outcomes for Shy, Aggressive, and Comparison Children

	SHY M (SD)	AGGRESSIVE M (SD)	COMPARISON M (SD)
Social skills			
Assertion	14.39^a (2.96)	16.10^b (2.06)	15.95^b (2.47)
Self-control	12.63^{ab} (4.02)	11.78^a (3.12)	14.23^b (3.57)
Cooperation	11.96^{ab} (3.87)	11.30^a (3.13)	13.27^b (3.21)
Responsibility	13.30 (2.52)	12.94 (2.85)	13.54 (2.58)
Self-esteem			
Physical ability	33.47^a (7.44)	35.34^{a*} (6.38)	37.30^b (7.14)
Physical appearance	28.35^a (8.28)	29.82^{a†} (9.85)	32.74^b (7.79)
Peer	28.33^a (8.09)	30.91^a (8.48)	34.69^b (7.47)
Internalizing			
Anxiety	62.67^a (14.16)	44.95^b (13.61)	38.63^c (14.19)
Loneliness	40.22^a (10.46)	34.57^b (11.15)	27.43^c (10.52)
Negative affect	33.54^a (10.22)	33.52^a (9.95)	26.08^b (10.34)
Positive adjustment			
Well-being	39.36^a (6.87)	40.31^a (6.53)	44.33^b (4.81)
Positive affect	48.91^a (9.43)	53.55^b (12.35)	56.56^b (9.38)
Externalizing behaviours	3.65^a (2.39)	4.29^b (2.45)	2.68^a (2.47)

Note. Differences in subscripts indicate a significant difference at *p* < .05 level ($^\dagger p < .07$).

Self-esteem. Turning to self-esteem outcomes, significant multivariate effects were found for Sport, $F(4, 178) = 7.30$, $p < .001$, and Behaviour, $F(8, 356) = 3.35$, $p < .001$. In addition, a significant multivariate interaction was seen between Behaviour and Sport, $F(8, 356) = 2.01$, $p < .05$. To examine the highest order effect (i.e., the interaction between Behaviour and Sport), results were examined at the univariate level; only general self-esteem demonstrated a significant interaction effect, $F(1, 181) = 9.76$, $p < .01$, $\eta = .05$. To examine the interaction for general self-esteem further, analyses were performed for each Behaviour group (shy, aggressive, comparison) separately, collapsed across gender. For shy children, a univariate effect of Sport was found for general self-esteem, $F(2, 43) = 5.96$, $p < .02$, $\eta = .12$. For aggressive children, a significant trend was also shown, $F(2, 43) = 3.57$, $p = .07$, $\eta = .09$; however, a significant effect of Sport for general self-esteem was not found for comparison children, $F(2, 43) = 1.52$, *ns*. As shown in Figure 12.1, shy and aggressive children who had participated in sport had higher general self-esteem than children who had not participated in sport. For comparison children, the effect of sport on self-esteem was not significant.

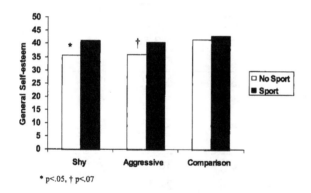

* p<.05, † p<.07

FIGURE 12.1 General self-esteem for shy, aggressive, and comparison sport and nonsport participants.

Given the nonsignificant Behaviour by Sport interactions for physical ability, physical appearance, and peer self-esteem, main effects of Behaviour and Sport were examined. All three types of self-esteem displayed a significant effect of Sport: physical ability, $F(1, 181) = 25.46$, $p < .001$, $\eta = .12$; physical appearance, $F(1, 181) = 5.86$, $p < .05$, $\eta = .03$; and peer self-esteem, $F(1, 181) = 7.36$, $p < .01$, $\eta = .04$. An examination of means revealed that children who participated in sport had higher physical ability self-esteem, physical appearance self-esteem, and peer self-esteem than did children who had not participated in organised sport (see Table 12.1).

Turning to the main effect of Behaviour on self-esteem, again all three remaining types of self-esteem displayed significant effects of Behaviour: physical ability, $F(2, 181) = 4.90$,

$p < .01$, $\eta = .05$; physical appearance, $F(2, 181) = 3.80$, $p < .05$, $\eta = .04$; and peer self-esteem, $F(2, 181) = 8.55$, $p < .001$, $\eta = .09$. As shown in Table 12.2, shy and aggressive children reported significantly lower physical ability, physical appearance, and peer self-esteem than did comparison children (with no differences between shy and aggressive children).

Internalizing problems. For Internalizing Problems, Significant Multivariate Effects Were found for Behaviour only, $F(6, 358) = 16.30$, $p < .001$. Univariate analyses indicated significant effects for social anxiety $F(2, 181) = 45.20$, $p < .001$, $\eta = .33$; loneliness, $F(2, 181) = 20.42$, $p < .001$, $\eta = .18$; and negative affect, $F(2, 181) = 9.86$, $p < .001$, $\eta = .10$. As shown in Table 12.2, shy children were significantly more anxious and lonely than were aggressive children, who were in turn more anxious and lonely than comparison children. Finally, shy and aggressive children reported greater negative affect than did comparison children.

Positive adjustment. The final MANCOVA for positive adjustment revealed significant effects for Sport, $F(2, 180) = 6.71$, $p < .01$, and for Behaviour, $F(4, 180) = 7.65$, $p < .001$. For the multivariate main effect of Sport, univariate analysis indicated a significant effect for both positive affect, $F(1, 181) = 12.69$, $p < .001$, $\eta = .07$, and well-being, $F(1, 181) = 6.92$, $p < .01$, $\eta = .04$. As shown in Table 12.1, children who had participated in organised sport experienced greater positive affect and well-being than did children who had not participated in sport.

In addition, the main effect of Behaviour was further examined for both well-being and positive affect. A significant main effect of Behaviour was found for positive affect $F(1, 181) = 7.76$, $p < .001$, $\eta = .08$, and well-being, $F(2, 181) = 13.73$, $p < .001$, $\eta = .13$. Follow-up Tukey's tests revealed that shy children had significantly lower positive affect than did aggressive or comparison children (with no differences between aggressive and comparison children). Shy and aggressive children were found to have significantly lower well-being than comparison children (see Table 12.2).

Externalizing problem behaviours. The final analysis at Time 1 was a 3 x 2 ANCOVA, with Behaviour (shy, aggressive, comparison) and Sport (none, some) as independent variables and externalizing problems as the dependent variable. A significant effect was found for both Sport, $F(1, 181) = 12.98$, $p < .001$, $\eta = .07$, and for Behaviour, $F(2, 181) = 5.56$, $p < .01$, $\eta = .06$. A comparison of means indicated that children who had participated in organised sport were reported to have significantly fewer externalizing problems than did nonsport participants (see Table 12.1). With respect to Behaviour, Tukey's post hoc testing revealed that aggressive children displayed more externalizing behaviour than did comparison or shy children (see Table 12.2).

LONGITUDINAL ANALYSES

Overview. The next set of analyses sought to answer whether participation in sport over a 1-year period impacts child outcomes. Four Repeated Measures MANCOVAs and one RM-ANCOVA were conducted to examine the effects on social skills, self-esteem, internalizing problems, positive adjustment, and externalizing problems. Given that the interest of the analyses were only in the specific effects of Sport participation over Time, only significant main effects of Time and interactions that involved both Time and Sport Participation are reported. No significant effects were found for social skills, self-esteem, positive adjustment, or externalizing problem behaviours; therefore, these outcomes are not reported herein. Also to note is that Sport reflects only the organised sports that the child had participated in over the 1-year period (none: $n = 52$; some: $n = 143$). In addition, due to attrition sample sizes at Time 2 were reduced (shy children: $n = 25$, aggressive: $n = 24$, comparison: $n = 69$).

Internalizing problems. In examining the internalizing outcomes of social anxiety, loneliness and negative affect, a significant multivariate Time by Behaviour by Sport interaction was revealed, $F(6, 188) = 2.57$, $p < .05$. In order to interpret the interaction, univariate results were examined. A three-way interaction was found for anxiety, $F(2, 96) = 6.27$, $p < .01$, $\eta = .12$; however, loneliness, $F(2, 96) = 1.83$, *ns,* and negative affect, $F(2, 96) = 1.56$, *ns,* were not found to be significant. Thus, analyses were conducted separately by Behaviour (collapsed across gender), looking

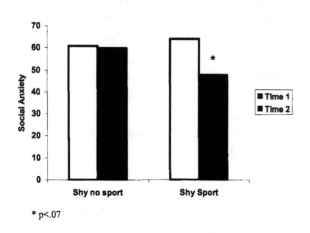

* p<.07

FIGURE 12.2 Shy sport and nonsport participants' social anxiety over time.

at the effects on social anxiety only. Beginning with shy children, a trend was shown for the Time by Sport interaction, $F(1, 19) = 3.80$, $p < .07$, $\eta = .17$. For aggressive, $F(1, 19) < 1$, ns, and comparison, $F(1, 62) = 1.31$, ns, children, no significant univariate interactions for anxiety were shown. As shown in Figure 12.2, Tukey's post hoc testing revealed that shy children who participated in sport over a 1-year period demonstrated a decrease in anxiety over time.

DISCUSSION

The aim of the current study was to explore the protective role of sport participation in the psychosocial outcomes of shy children. Overall, our results indicated that shyness was negatively associated with sport participation. Sport participation was associated with positive psychosocial outcomes, including higher positive affect and well-being and greater social skills. Shy children were found to have greater internalizing problems, whereas aggressive children displayed more externalizing and internalizing difficulties than comparison peers. It is most interesting to note that shy and aggressive children who participated in sport were found to report higher self-esteem (unlike their nonsport participating peers). In addition, shy children who participated in sport demonstrated a trend whereby social anxiety decreased over time.

BENEFITS OF SPORT PARTICIPATION

Participation in organised sports was related to various positive psychosocial outcomes. For example, children who participated in sport were found to be more assertive and exert more self-control than did children who did not participate in sport and to report more positive affect and well-being than did nonparticipants. Children who had participated in sport were also found to have higher physical ability self-esteem, physical appearance self-esteem, and peer self-esteem than did children who had not participated in organised sport. These findings coincide with previous research linking sport participation with positive self-esteem (Marsh, 1998; Marsh et al., 1995) and well-being (Kirkcaldy et al., 2002). It can be suggested that sport provides children with opportunities for mastery, which in turn leads to greater well-being. Alternatively, children who participate in sport may have a greater number of peer contacts or peer experiences.

Children who participate in sport may feel more competent and more physically fit (and perhaps attractive) and thus report higher physical ability and physical appearance self-esteem. It is also possible that children who are already higher in self-esteem are more likely to participate in sport. Children may previously possess certain attributes or characteristics that drive them to participate in sport or that may influence their choice of activities rather than sport itself fostering such characteristics (Page & Hammermeister, 1995). Sport may attract certain types of children; sport may also provide an opportunity to demonstrate these attributes. Longer term longitudinal studies would better be able to address the issue of directionality in future research.

CORRELATES OF SHYNESS

Shy children were found to be more anxious and more lonely than were aggressive or comparison children; reported higher negative affect and less positive affect than did comparison children; and were found to have lower physical appearance, physical ability, and peer self-esteem than did comparison children. Finally, shy children were found to be less assertive than their aggressive or comparison counterparts. This is not surprising given that shy children are by definition wary in social situations and are thus less likely to act in a sociable or outgoing way. These findings are in accordance with previous research suggesting that shy children are more likely to report greater internalizing problems, such as loneliness, anxiety, and lowered self-esteem (Coplan et al., 2007; Eisenberg et al., 1998; Hymel et al., 1993).

Shyness and sport. Given the positive impact of sport for all children, it was particularly of interest to investigate the value of sport for specific subgroups of children based on their social behaviour. Indeed, our findings suggest that sport participation may be particularly advantageous for shy children as a buffer for some of the negative correlates of shyness.

As expected, shyness was negatively associated with participation in sport. Previous research has focussed on the relation between sport and shyness in an adolescent or adult population (Page & Hammermeister, 1995; Page & Zarco, 2001). However, the current results support the notion that shy children are less likely to engage in sport in middle childhood.

Two interesting interaction effects were found with respect to sport participation and shyness. Shy children who participated in sport were found to have higher general self-esteem than did shy children who did not participate in sport. By contrast, this effect was not seen for comparison children; that is, whether the comparison child did or did not participate in sport did not appear to impact general self-esteem. This would suggest that by participating in sport, shy children in particular do not report the negative effects on self-esteem typically seen for shy children (Coplan, Findlay, & Nelson, 2004; Eisenberg et al., 1998). Perhaps this benefit to self-esteem is a reflection of the importance of sport participation as a social status determinant for children. That is, shy children who participate in sport may feel valuable or competent in their social network, thus increasing their self-esteem.

Moreover, shy children who participated in sport over a 1-year period demonstrated a significant decrease in social anxiety. That is, shy children had higher social anxiety than did their aggressive and comparison peers, but for those who participated in sport, their anxiety decreased over this one year period to the point that it did not differ from comparison children.

Children who participate in organised sport have greater opportunities for peer interaction, be that only for a couple of hours every week. In the sport context, children have specific experiences: they are given a role within the team or group; they must communicate with other members of the social group; they learn similar skills/tasks; and they work toward common goals. This experience could provide a social context to practise interacting with their peers and for peer-mediated learning of both physical and social skills. Participation in a sport provides children with a common ground, a context that is shared with a select group of other children. Not only can this provide children with a sense of belonging (that may be particularly relevant for shy children), but it may also give them a subject matter to discuss with peers.

It is also possible that shy children who participate in sport are merely exposed to an additional source of social anxiety to which they become conditioned, thus extinguishing the fear response. Norton, Burns, Hope, and Bauer (2000) found that adults who experience a higher degree of social evaluative fear in general also experience such fear in sport situations. It is possible that children who experience both social and sport-related anxiety

203

develop mechanisms to deal with this anxiety, which translates into decreased anxiety over time.

Finally, sport participation may also provide the shy child with mastery experiences that contribute to self-esteem. Although all children benefit from triumphs, for shy children this may be particularly important considering their high degree of anxiety in social situations. Nonshy children may not need as many experiences to feel good about themselves, whereas shy children are particularly fearful or self-conscious. Thus, shy children benefit from repeated success in various domains in order to buffer the typically negative effect of shyness on self-esteem.

AGGRESSION AND SPORT

Although aggression was not a primary focus of this investigation, we comment briefly on our results related to aggression. Aggressive children were found to be less cooperative and have less self-control than did comparison children, and they were found to utilise more externalizing strategies than shy or comparison children. Moreover, they reported greater anxiety, loneliness, and negative affect than did comparison children (but less anxiety and loneliness than shy children) and lower physical ability, physical appearance, and peer self-esteem than did comparison children. These findings coincide with previous research linking aggression with heightened "acting out" behaviour and maladaptive social problem solving skills (see Dodge, Coie, & Lynam, 2006, for a recent review), and reaffirm that there are both internalizing and externalizing ramifications of aggressive behaviour.

In terms of psychosocial functioning, the only significant (trend) interaction between aggression and sport occurred for self-esteem; aggressive children who participated in sport reported higher general self-esteem than did aggressive children who did not participate in sport. These findings coincide with those for shy children. What this again suggests is that for socially "deviant" groups, sport participation seems to have a positive impact on self-esteem, perhaps because of the pervasiveness of sport as a positive social status determinant.

CAVEATS AND DIRECTIONS FOR FUTURE RESEARCH

The current findings have important implications in terms of the benefits of sport participation, in particular for shy children; however, certain limitations should be considered. For example, data collection for the present study relied primarily on child self-reports. This may have heightened interassociations amongst variables because of shared-method variance. Future research might consider multisource assessments of both social behaviours and outcomes. In addition, some of the subscale internal reliability values were low (e.g., $\alpha = .51$ for the Time 1 *SSRS* responsibility subscale), although overall internal consistencies of the scales were adequate and thus accepted for the current study.

The assessment of sport participation may have also had some limitations. For example, children may have had difficulty recalling all of the sports they had participated in or may have been influenced by the seasonal nature of participation. However, other researchers have also employed self-report measures, including 7-day recall of physical activity (e.g., Sallis, Prochaska, Taylor, Hill, & Geraci, 1999) and self-report questionnaires of activity (e.g., Smith, 1999).

Future researchers might also consider exploring other outcome variables of conceptual interest. For example, it could be argued that a measure of competence would allow researchers to determine the role of aptitude in children's sport experience. Sport competence might be particularly important for shy children who are already lower in feelings of competence (Hymel et al., 1993).

Finally, a cautionary note should be made regarding attrition. Whilst the children who selectively chose to participate at Time 2 were not different on any of the independent variables than the participants who were lost, the children who ceased to participate were found to be less cooperative, less assertive, and more socially anxious at Time 1. Some variability in these outcomes may have been lost at Time 2, which may have limited statistical power to detect differences across time.

The results from the current study provide evidence of the benefits of sport participation for children including higher positive affect and well-being as well as social skills. In addition, shy children were found to be at risk for internalizing difficulties; in particular they were more anxious and lonely than their peers, experienced more negative affect and were less assertive. These findings reaffirm the notion that middle childhood aged children who are deviant from the peer group seem to be vulnerable to psychosocial health risk factors.

Unique to the current study is that sport participation was found to play a protective role against some of the negative outcomes associated with shyness. In particular, it was revealed that shy children who participated in sport reported greater general self-esteem than did shy nonparticipants. In addition, shy children who participated in sport were found to experience a decrease in social anxiety not evidenced by their nonsport-participating shy peers. The results have both theoretical and practical implications in the fields of developmental psychology and physical education, as sport can be suggested not only as a protective factor, but a potential intervention strategy for shy children. In essence, one could suggest that for shy children, the psychosocial benefits of sport are particularly evident, and as such shy children should be encouraged to come out and play.

REFERENCES

Allison, P. D., & Furstenberg, F. F. (1989). How marital dissolution affects children: Variations by age and sex. *Developmental Psychology, 25,* 540–549.

Asendorpf, J. B. (1990). Beyond social withdrawal: Shyness, unsociability and peer avoidance. *Human Development, 33,* 250–259.

Asher, S. R., Hymel, S., & Renshaw, P. D. (1984). Loneliness in children. *Child Development, 55,* 1456–1464.

Baron, R. M., & Kenny, D. A. (1986). The moderator-mediator variable distinction in social psychological research: Conceptual, strategic, and statistical considerations. *Journal of Personality and Social Psychology, 51,* 1173–1182.

Bowker, A., Gadbois, S., & Cornock, B. (2003). Sports participation and self-esteem: Variations as a function of gender and gender role orientation. *Sex Roles, 49,* 47–58.

Bredemeier, B. J. (1988). The moral of the youth sport story. In E. W. Brown & C. F. Branta (Eds.), *Competitive sports for children and youth: An overview of research and issues* (pp. 285–296). Champaign, IL: Human Kinetics.

Chase, M. A., & Dummer, G. M. (1992). The role of sports as a social status determinant for children. *Research Quarterly for Exercise and Sport, 63,* 418–424.

Coplan, R. J., Arbeau, K. A., & Armer, M. (in press). Don't fret, be supportive! Maternal characteristics linking child shyness to psychosocial and school adjustment in kindergarten. *Journal of Abnormal Child Psychology.*

Coplan, R. J., Closson, L., & Arbeau, K. A. (2007). Gender differences in the behavioral associates of loneliness and social dissatisfaction in kindergarten. *Journal of Child Psychology and Psychiatry (Special Issue on Preschool Mental Health)*, 48, 988–995.

Coplan, R. J., Findlay, L. C., & Nelson, L. J. (2004). Characteristics of preschoolers with lower perceived competence. *Journal of Abnormal Child Psychology*, 32, 399–408.

Coplan, R. J., Wilson, J., Frohlick, S. L., & Zelenski, J. (2006). A person-oriented analysis of behavioural inhibition and behavioural activation in childhood. *Personality and Individual Differences*, 41, 917–927.

Crozier, W. R. (1995). Shyness and self-esteem in middle childhood. *British Journal of Educational Psychology*, 65, 85–95.

Dodge, K. A., Coie, J. D., & Lynam, D. (2006). Aggression and antisocial behavior in youth. In W. Damon & R. M. Lerner (Eds. in Chief) & N. Eisenberg, (Vol. Ed.), *Handbook of child psychology: Vol. 3. Social, emotional and personality development* (6th ed., pp. 719–788). New York: Wiley and Sons.

Ebbeck, V., & Weiss, M. R. (1998). Determinants of children's self-esteem: An examination of perceived competence and affect in sport. *Pediatric Exercise Science*, 10, 285–298.

Eisenberg, N., Shepard, S. A., Fabes, R. A., Murphy, B. C., & Guthrie, I. K. (1998). Shyness and children's emotionality, regulation, and coping: Contemporaneous, longitudinal, and across-context relations. *Child Development*, 69, 767–790.

Fordham, K., & Stevenson-Hinde, J. (1999). Shyness, friendship quality, and adjustment during middle childhood. *Journal of Child Psychology and Psychiatry*, 40, 757–768.

Gresham, F. M., & Elliot, S. N. (1990). *Social Skills Rating System Manual*. Circle Pines, MN: American Guidance Service.

Henderson, L., & Zimbardo, P. (2001). Shyness, social anxiety, and social phobia. In S. G. Hofmann & P. M. DiBartolo (Eds.), *From social anxiety to social phobia: Multiple perspectives* (pp. 46–64). Needham Heights, MA: Allyn & Bacon.

Hymel, S., Bowker, A., & Woody, E. (1993). Aggressive versus withdrawn unpopular children: Variations in peer and self-perceptions in multiple domains. *Child Development*, 64, 879–896.

Hymel, S., Vaillencourt, T., McDougall, P., & Renshaw, P. D. (2002). Peer acceptance and rejection in childhood. In P. K. Smith & C. H. Hart (Eds.), *Blackwell handbook of childhood social development*, (pp. 265–284). Great Britain: Blackwell Publishers.

Hymel, S., Woody, E., & Bowker, A. (1993). Social withdrawal in childhood: Considering the child's perspective. In K. H. Rubin & J. B. Asendorpf (Eds.), *Social withdrawal, inhibition, and shyness in childhood* (pp. 237–262). Hillsdale, NJ: Erlbaum, Inc.

Kagan, J. (1989). Temperamental contributions to social behaviour. *American Psychologist, 44,* 668–674.

Kirkcaldy, B. D., Shephard, R. J., & Siefen, R. G. (2002). The relationship between physical activity and self-image and problem behaviour among adolescents. *Social Psychiatry and Psychiatric Epidemiology, 37,* 544–550.

La Greca, A. M., & Stone, W. L. (1993). Social Anxiety Scale for Children—Revised: Factor structure and concurrent validity. *Journal of Clinical Child Psychology, 22,* 17–27.

Laurent, J., Catanzaro, S. J., Joiner, T. E. Jr., Rudolph, K. D., Potter, K. I., Lambert, S., et al. (1999). A measure of positive and negative affect for children: Scale development and preliminary validation. *Psychological Assessment, 11,* 326–338.

Marsh, H. W. (1984). *Self-Description Questionnaire (SDQ): An instrument for measuring multiple dimensions of preadolescent self-concept.* Sydney, Australia: University of Sydney.

Marsh, H. W. (1998). Age and gender effects in physical self-concepts for adolescent elite athletes and non-athletes: A multicohort-multioccasion design. *Journal of Sport and Exercise Psychology, 20,* 237–259.

Marsh, H. W., Perry, C., Horsely, C., & Roche, L. (1995). Multidimensional self-concepts of elite athletes: How do they differ from the general population? *Journal of Sport and Exercise Psychology, 17,* 70–83.

McHale, J. P., Vinden, P. G., Bush, L., Richer, D., Shaw, D., & Smith, B. (2005). Patterns of personal and social adjustment among sport-involved and non-involved middle-school children. *Sociology of Sport Journal, 22,* 119–136.

Norton, P. J., Burns, J. A., Hope, D. A., & Bauer, B. K. (2000). Generalization of social anxiety to athletic situations: Gender, sports involvement, and parental pressure. *Depression and Anxiety, 12,* 193–202.

Page, R. M., Frey, J., Talbert, R., & Falk, C. (1992). Children's feelings of loneliness and social dissatisfaction: Relationship to measures of physical fitness and activity. *Journal of Teaching and Physical Education, 11,* 211–219.

Page, R. M., & Hammermeister, J. (1995). Shyness and loneliness: Relationship to the exercise frequency of college students. *Psychological Reports, 76,* 395–398.

208

Page, R. M., & Zarco, E. P. (2001). Shyness, physical activity and sports team participation among Philippine high school students. *Child Study Journal, 31,* 193–203.

Prakash, K., & Coplan, R. J. (2007). Socio-emotional characteristics and school adjustment of socially-withdrawn children in India. *International Journal of Behavioural Development, 31,* 1–10.

Rubin, K. H., Bukowski, W., & Parker, J. G. (2006). Peer interactions, relationships, and groups. In W. Damon & R. M. Lerner (Eds. in Chief) & N. Eisenberg, (Vol. Ed.), *Handbook of child psychology: Vol. 3. Social, emotional and personality development* (6th ed., pp. 571–645). New York: Wiley and Sons.

Rubin, K. H., Chen, X., & Hymel, S. (1993). Socioemotional characteristics of withdrawn and aggressive children. *Merrill-Palmer Quarterly, 39,* 518–534.

Sallis, J. F., Prochaska, J. J., Taylor, W. C., Hill, J. O., & Geraci, J. C. (1999). Correlates of physical activity in a national sample of girls and boys in grades 4 through 12. *Health Psychology, 18,* 410–415.

Shavelson, R. J., Hubner, J. J., & Stanton, G. C. (1976). Self-concept: Validation of construct interpretations. *Review of Educational Research, 46,* 407–441.

Smith, A. L. (1999). Perceptions of peer relationships and physical activity participation in early adolescence. *Journal of Sport and Exercise Psychology, 21,* 329–350.

Smith, A. L. (2003). Peer relationship in physical activity contexts: A road less travelled in youth sport and exercise research. *Psychology of Sport and Exercise, 4,* 25–39.

Storch, E. A., Bartlas, M. E., Dent, H. C., & Masia, C. L. (2002). Generalization of social anxiety to sport: An investigation of elementary Hispanic children. *Child Study Journal, 32,* 81–87.

Straus, M. A. (1979). Measuring intrafamily conflict and violence: The Conflict Tactics (CT) Scales. *Journal of Marriage and the Family, 41,* 75–88.

Watson, D., Clark, L. A., & Tellegen, A. (1988). Development and validation of brief measures of Positive and Negative Affect: The PANAS scales. *Journal of Personality and Social Psychology, 54,* 1063–1070.

Weiss, M. R., & Duncan, S. C. (1992). The relationship between physical competence and peer acceptance in the context of children's sports participation. *Journal of Sport and Exercise Psychology, 14,* 177–191.

CHAPTER THIRTEEN

The Professionalization of Youth Sports in America

BY **JORDAN D. COX**

INTRODUCTION

More children than ever before are participating in youth sports in the United States. The National Council of Youth Sports estimates that about 44 million girls and boys play on organized teams in the United States, a number that has steadily increased over the past 20 years (National Council of Youth Sports, 2008). While other research places the participation numbers closer to 35 million, studies consistently show that approximately seven out of ten adolescents drop out of organized youth sports by age 13, primarily because it was no longer fun for the children or they felt too much pressure to win. Fred Engh (2002), author of *Why Johnny Hates Sports* and president of the National Alliance for Youth Sports says, "Studies show than an alarming 70 percent of the approximately twenty million children who participate in organized out-of-school athletic programs will quit by the age of thirteen because of unpleasant sports experiences. That's 17.5 million unhappy, dispirited children. It's a frightening statistic that paints a rather bleak picture of organized youth sports in America today. The culprits are the adults who, in their roles as coaches, administrators, and parents, have misguided motives and ideals of what youth sports are all about."

Adult behavior has become extreme for a variety of reasons, including the desire for college athletic scholarship monies. What parents want and what parents hope to gain from their children's participation in organized youth sports is often the polar extreme of what their kids want. These different motives frequently cause much of the stress encountered by both adults and children involved in youth sports (Fraser-Thomas and Cote, 2009; Harwood and Knight, 2007). This shift has come at an extremely high cost to kids and their families. The formation of select or elite travel teams, particularly for younger ages, combined with a drive toward early specialization in a specific sport has led to physical and emotional trauma for millions of young people. Overuse injuries and emotional burnout because of a high pressure to win or succeed has reached well past alarming rates. While this evolution has been consistent, it has been rapid. The combination of these and additional factors has created the professionalization of youth sports in America.

ADULT FACTORS

The wishes of parents who allow their children to become active in youth sports are frequently very different from those of their kids. Parental requirements from the experience are often very different from those of many adolescents. The needs of adults are distinct. Author and psychologist Shane Murphy suggests generally well-meaning parents begin to act out of character as they become caught up in their child's competition, riding an emotional roller coaster. There is seductiveness in the youth sports experience and a narcissistic appeal in sports competition, which draws in parents when their own kids are involved (Murphy, 1999).

These adult factors, in conjunction with their corresponding behaviors, are a main cause of problems present in America's organized youth sports programs. Parental behavior often becomes detrimental toward children, noxious, and even injurious toward coaches, officials, and other adults. Their conduct often leads to litigation because of the fevered pitch at which their emotions often run. Lawsuits spring forth from incidents ranging from assault and battery to damages being sought for a college scholarship or professional contract parents believe may never be attained. Reality is overlooked with the understanding that the existence of youth sports programs is just for children. These endeavors are every bit as much for the parents and other adults, perhaps even more so. Adults direct these enterprises. They coach the children. They organize the leagues. They show up to watch. Because sight of this fact has been lost, it has become increasingly arduous to bring forth youth sports programs that meet the needs of the adults involved while remaining beneficial to children. "Such is often the case in youth sports," writes former pro basketball player and author Bob Bigelow. "What adults want and need from youth sports is often not what children want and need. It's as though the adults and the children live in different worlds and speak different languages" (Bigelow, Moroney, and Hall, 2001).

Dissecting the adult motives related to youth sports uncovers an emotional minefield. In a July 7, 1997, story which appeared in the *Dayton Daily News*, the coach of a highly competitive third-grade boys' basketball team described his efforts to writer Susan Vinella. "We don't want to lose a ballgame because we played the kids equally. It's sort of like a business. I'm trying to put the best product on the floor." The league director added, "We tell them our philosophy right up front. If parents don't like it, it's America and there are other places to play" (Vinella, 1997). Adults are often overly zealous in relating to their children's sports involvement. This over-investment can lead to an increasingly active role—to the point of manipulation.

Sports psychologist Alan Goldberg, who was interviewed for an October 2000 story which appeared in *Parents* magazine, concludes, "Raising kids is the most emotionally evocative experience you will ever have, and rearing an athlete—no matter how amateur— is particularly intense. Even if you think you're well adjusted, it can bring up a lot of stuff" (Bigelow, Moroney, and Hall, 2001). The tipping point for parental involvement reaching unhealthy levels for both adult and adolescent seems to occur when the natural instincts a parent possesses for their child becomes obsessive. This behavior is described by medical experts as "achievement by proxy" (Tofler and Knapp, 1999).

Many adults live vicariously through the success of their children. Parental deeds can take on varying degrees of intensity, moving from a loving encouragement to a willful neglect of the child in order to serve the needs of the adult. According to psychiatrist Ian Tofler, secretary of the International Society of Sports Psychiatry, parental actions move along a spectrum of progressive over-involvement. In the beginning, parents feel pride and offer their children support. The dynamic then moves to a level of sacrifice on the part of the parent. For example, a parent may skip work or neglect some of his or her professional responsibilities because of the parent's interest level in the child's sport experience. Often, over time, this commitment on the part of the adult develops into obsession. The pressure placed on the child to perform borders on abusive, as the identity of the child becomes lost in the goals set forth by the parent (Tofler, Knapp, and Drell, 1998). Psychologist Richard Ginsberg states, "The question isn't whether we're emotionally invested in our children, because we are. It isn't whether we see ourselves in our children, because we do. It's when the investment becomes so great that what is good for the child is forgotten that real problems happen. When it becomes bragging rights or the parents finding meaning in their lives through the sports successes of their children, that's when you've entered the gray area" (Hyman, 2009).

Anxiety for adults can easily occur since they are merely able to watch once their youngsters have donned their leotard, swimsuit, or uniform and stepped forward to compete with others on the gymnastics mat, in the pool, or on the court or field. Murphy (1999) asserts that, "A big game becomes a powerful emotional experience for both parent and child. Also, parents know how much effort their child has exerted to reach their current level of skill and competitiveness. The greater the effort that has been expended, the more it means to the parent." Thus, parents and other adults are a tremendous source of support for adolescent athletes in organized youth sports, and an equally great source of stress for children.

Because of this natural attachment between parents and children involved in sports experiences, there is also a significant adult investment socially and financially as well. Parents are trapped when they over-identify with their own child because they can easily lose sight of what the child wants, expecting their own investments to somehow pay off and yield results that are tangible to an adult mind-set. A child's participation is no longer a chance to better their physical fitness or improve their social skills. For parents, it can be viewed as the means to greater ends. These ends might be the goal of a college scholarship or a professional sports career with product endorsements and the financial windfall that accompanies these achievements. Parents increasingly view their child's participation and their own outlay as an investment in the future.

Professor Harry Edwards of the University of California–Berkeley believes that over the past 30 years—since the onset of television as the principal tool of highly saturated media presentation and intrusion—youth has been increasingly seen as a more productive period culminating in 18-year-olds coming out of high school signing $10 million basketball contracts and $90 million shoe deals. "You have high school girl singing groups like Beyoncé and Destiny's Child at 17, 18, 19, coming out of high school signing multimillion-dollar record deals. You have rappers 18, 19 years old, driving $150,000 Lamborghinis with $100,000 diamonds around their necks living in fifteen million dollar homes, all projected by the media into the living rooms" (McMahon, 2007).

This attitude and approach by parents is becoming increasingly disturbing, especially to collegiate coaches, who recognize many parents can be downright delusional about athletic scholarship monies. Ray Reid, men's soccer coach at the University of Connecticut, who has seen his teams win several Big East Conference titles and advance to the National Collegiate Athletic Association (NCAA) national championship, has a sense teenagers have an easier time accepting the bad news related to opportunities at the college level than their parents (Hyman, 2009). Moms and dads have long been involved in their children's sports careers as bankers, carpool drivers, travel agents, and sideline pacers. The conversations, he says, are often, "'Coach Reid, we invested a lot of money in my son's career—thirty thousand dollars in ten years. We'd like a soccer scholarship to get some of it back.' It angers me. I'm appalled by the attitude. My reaction is: That's interesting. Your son is a mutual fund!" (Hyman, 2009).

The parents with whom Coach Reid comes in contact are not unique. In 2006, Wisconsin pediatrician Dr. Robert Rohloff surveyed 376 mothers and fathers of sports players in elementary and middle school about their goals for their children's participation in sports. Almost 40 percent of them told the doctor they hoped their children would someday play for a college team. Twenty-two parents said they expected their children to become professional athletes (Hyman, 2009).

A growing number of parents are running themselves and their children ragged pressing for a scholarship that, statistically speaking, does not exist. Based on participation of organized youth sports in the United States, combined with those state organizations that compile the participation of high school athletics in the various states of the union, only about 5 percent of kids will ever play at the varsity level at some high schools. This refers to the varsity level at a high school of any size. Statistics from there should be even more sobering to the parents of children in youth sports. The figures of the National Collegiate Athletic Association (NCAA, 2010), which are estimates based on the numbers of scholarships and

215

their respective related dollar figures at an institution, combined with participation estimates from the National Federation of High Schools, are surprising to the undereducated about such matters. For example, approximately 3.5 percent of female high school basketball players will play at the college level. Of those athletes, less than one in a hundred will be drafted to play professionally, so only one player in five thousand will make it to the pros. For male basketball players, the percentage is the same.

Approximately 2 percent of high school athletes will earn an athletic scholarship to play at any level of college sports (NCAA, 2010). Even the NCAA advises "that this small number means high school student-athletes and their parents need to have realistic expectations about receiving an athletic scholarship to play sports in college. Academic, not athletic, achievement is the most reliable path to success in life" (NCAA, 2010). Research by Sandy Baum of Skidmore College and Luci Lapovsky of Mercy College compiled for the College Board show that of the overall scholarship aid given each year to college students, sports awards are a thin slice of the financial pie. Athletic scholarships, for example, account for 18 percent of scholarship money at public colleges and universities and just 7 percent of scholarship money at private institutions (Baum and Lapovsky, 2006). Being a gifted chemistry major has much better prospects (Baum and Lapovsky, 2006). The climb to the top for a chance at an athletic scholarship is steep.

In addition to the unrealistic expectations that many parents have related to the number of college athletic scholarships offered, another misunderstanding they have is the dollar amount of aid often given and the length of term of the award provided by a school. As it relates to scholarship awards, college sports are divided into two categories: Head count sports and equivalency sports. For all intents and purposes, head count sports could be considered full scholarship endeavors up to the limit set for each sport by the NCAA. Football and men's and women's basketball are among these sports. Most sports at the college level, however, are equivalency sports. That is, there is a limit on the value or equivalency an institution may award. In these programs, fractional awards are presented to student-athletes to reach the total number of available scholarships. For example, in men's golf, five players represent a university or college and participate in competition, yet a maximum of only 4.5 athletic scholarships may be awarded in a given year (NCAA, 2010). Still, men's golf programs generally have substantially more than five student-athletes on their respective golf rosters, meaning scholarship amounts are usually divided into fractional amounts. The fractions do not have to be distributed to student-athletes equally.

In 2008, the NCAA estimated the average yearly value of a full scholarship at just less than $14,000 at a public school. For an out-of state public institution, the value was approximately $24,000. Full scholarships at private universities were more than $32,000 (NCAA, 2008). Hyman (2009) notes that "The average athletic scholarship for the 138,216 athletes in Division I or Division II schools in 2003–2004 was $10,409, about half the cost of attendance at some state universities and a fifth of tuition at pricier private ones." One mother, whose daughter is a University of Delaware swimmer, talking about the lengths to which parents might go in hopes of landing a scholarship, was quoted by reporter Bill Pennington of the *New York Times* in an article published March 10, 2008. The mother said, "They're going to be disappointed when they learn that if they're very lucky, they will get a scholarship worth fifteen percent of the $40,000 college bill. What's that? $6,000?" (Pennington, 2008).

Lehigh University Soccer Coach Dean Koski says parents tell him they want their son to get a scholarship because college is so expensive. He shares with them that with only two hundred Division I programs and twenty to thirty thousand boys coming out of high school each year that each school is able to offer—at most—three scholarships. There are only about three hundred total scholarships to be awarded among every kid in the country. He believes parents are chasing dreams for their kids that just are not there (McMahon, 2007). In effect, many parents basically end up buying their children scholarships with all the money trying to develop them. And ironically, even with all the money, time, and effort spent, often they do not even earn scholarships.

This delusional fog in which parents operate relative to desired outcomes can often cause the caregivers to direct their children to excel in these competitive endeavors at significant risk to themselves and their kids. Jessica Dubroff, her father, and a flight instructor were killed when her plane crashed on take-off near Cheyenne, Wyoming, as she attempted to become the youngest pilot to fly across the United States. She was seven years old (Alter and Glick, 1996). The allure of competition can be great for the adults, who in turn, go to extremes with their children. The former head of Northfield Youth Baseball Association in Northfield, Minnesota, said he was asked by a kindergartner's parent if he was teaching the child to switch hit because the parent wanted the youngster to be prepared for the pros (McMahon, 2007). Focus is often misplaced by the adults. Instead of enjoying their child's sports experience, parents are expecting some sort of payoff down the road. The adults spend a great

217

majority of their time, effort, energy, and money worrying about whether progress is being made on the long-term goal of all their investment.

All of this misplaced devotion by parents has created a tremendous amount of pressure on both parent and child. Incidents of violence have occurred, and crimes have been committed, all from the venue of youth sports. Many parents take out their frustrations on their children and on other adults. In a 2003 *SportingKid* magazine survey of 3,300 parents, kids, and coaches, 84 percent of the kids polled said they had witnessed violent parental behavior toward children, coaches, or officials in the form of shouting, berating, or using abusive language (National Alliance for Youth Sports, 2003). In August 2001, a *Sports Illustrated for Kids* survey revealed that 74 percent of the youth who responded had observed out-of-control parents at their games (Bach, 2006).

In a well-publicized case in Massachusetts in July 2000, a hockey father died after a fight with another dad following a confrontation between the two over what one father saw as rough play during a scrimmage game involving their sons. *New York Daily News* writer Tara George published a story on September 11, 2000, recounting a soccer game between eight- and nine-year-old boys in South Brunswick, New Jersey, that ended in a brawl among dozens of parents and coaches. It began with an argument about whether one coach should have been allowed to stand behind the goal during a tie-breaker shootout (George, 2000). A year earlier, in suburban Swiftwater, Pennsylvania, between 50 and 100 adults became combatants after a football game involving 11- to 13-year-olds. During a ten-minute melee caught on videotape and later shown on local news, the adults kicked, punched, and screamed at each other (Nack, Munson, and Dohrman, 2000). The list of incidents similar to these, occurring all over the United States, is of staggering length. While violent parental behavior toward other parents has reached ridiculous levels, there is also a rise in violence against the coaches of youth teams, many of whom are volunteers.

In an article appearing in the *Los Angeles Times* on January 26, 2001, a Northridge, California, father was sentenced to 45 days in jail, three years of probation, and six months of anger management counseling after being convicted of slamming the manager of his son's youth baseball team against a truck. Prosecutors say Mitchell Craig Gluckman threatened to kill the manager for taking the 11-year-old out of a game after only three innings. The judge ordered the father to refrain from "any verbal dispute at any sporting event" (Fausset and Rhone, 2001). In Torrance, California, the father and uncle of a high school football player were sentenced to 45 days in jail for attacking the team's coach in October 2000.

Police say the father and uncle were upset that the high school student had not been given more playing time (ABC News, 2000). In a report that appeared in the *Stockton Record* on February 4, 2007, Barry Mano, president of the National Association of Sports Officials, said, "The biggest problem isn't really the coaches or the players, it's really the parents/fans. We get reports here every week of an assault against a sports official on some level. The problem has been getting worse and has been getting worse over the last five years." Mano's association reports more than 100 attacks of violence are recorded against members of the organization each year (Phillips and Sudhalter, 2007).

Attacks on sports officials have become so commonplace that in 2007, 23 states adopted laws to protect those individuals. For example, the state of Illinois passed legislation that went into effect in January 2005 that afforded sports officials the same status as police officers, jail guards, and other public employees in cases of assault and battery. In California, the penal code specifies that battery against a sports official carries a maximum punishment of a $200,000 fine and a one-year jail sentence (McMahon, 2007). No doubt the law was employed in May 2005 when the coach of a girls' rugby team was beaten until bloody and unconscious during a championship tournament game in Rohnert Park, California. The violence erupted when the coach came to the aid of a referee after a spectator, the brother of the opposing coach, strongly disagreed with a call, came onto the field, and punched the official. Waiting for police, the first coach was restraining that man, when the opposing coach and seven or eight men came and began beating and kicking him, sending him to the hospital to receive treatment for his injuries. When an assistant coach came to his aid, he, too, was kicked and punched, leaving the assistant coach with three broken ribs. The teenage female players also began to fight with one another before police arrived (National Association of Sports Officials, 2000).

This incident demonstrates one of the major emotional flashpoints for parental outbursts at youth sports contests. Virginia clinical psychologist Robert Nay suggests that lack of sleep, sustenance, and alcohol can be a factor in how parents act, in addition to disagreeing with calls by the officials. Incidents during the same month in various states show this to be true when school parents attacked high school coaches. In addition to the factors Dr. Nay suggests might be contributors, each occurrence involved the issue of playing time for the parent's child (Still, 2002).

A second trigger is stress and arousal for parents attending events. Parents are very energized and adrenaline flows through them, just as it does for the athletes participating in the contest. Still, another item is what Oliver Ross calls "unmet expectations" (Ross, 2002). Parents have extremely high expectations about how things should progress in these environments for their children; when anything occurs to disrupt this, the potential to unleash this stored emotional cache in adults becomes high. After an incident involving a violent father toward his own daughter in January 2011, John Gardner, president of the Greater Toronto Hockey League, said, "It used to be parents got their kids into hockey for the right reasons, to support the team. Now it's a very singular thing where it's about my kid, my kid, my kid" (Cribb, 2011).

Due to these extreme levels of parental behavior, the National Association of Sports Officials offers assault protection insurance to its members. The organization makes this "Sports Officials Security Program" benefit available when an official becomes the victim of an assault and/or battery by a spectator, fan, or participant (National Association of Sports Officials, 2000). It may not be enough to help, though. In 2001, at a youth basketball game between seven- and eight-year-olds in Fayetteville, Georgia, police say tensions built during a game to the point an official felt the need to defend himself against some hostile adults. The official slashed a coach with a knife, causing a wound that required 17 stitches to close (Wilcoxen, 2001).

A head sports official in Texas told a *Wall Street Journal* reporter the antics of parents had reached a point such that before games, he introduces himself to police or security guards at the venue before he starts any game. He tells them from which section of the court or field he will leave. Following the contest, he immediately removes his whistle from around his neck to reduce the chance that someone will grab it and try to choke him (Bigelow, Moroney, and Hall, 2001). In an effort to combat this trend, in February 2000, Florida's Jupiter Tequesta Athletic Association became the first league in the country to require parents to sign a pledge and attend a course on behavior before enrolling their child in youth sports (Nolin, 2000). Societal factors are involved, but the boundary is clear. When youth sports become lifestyle and not leisure, it affects how adults and parents relate to each other.

Intensive investment and the accompanying motivations on the part of parents point to the cause of this misbehavior toward other adults. However, parental actions are also increasingly aggressive—and even criminal—toward their own children and other kids. This manifests in many ways, including how parents communicate and interact with their own children. Police in East Pennsboro Township, Pennsylvania, arrested the father of an 11-year-old following the boy's wrestling practice (Hyman, 2009). He was charged with harassment of his son.

The man became angry because his child cried during the workout. As the pair sat in their car outside a Wal-Mart store, police say the man struck his son in the face and punched him in the chest. Later, he ordered the boy to run laps around the car (Hyman, 2009).

Similarly, authorities in Lincoln, Nebraska, reported that a mother and her 15-year-old daughter argued as they returned home from a soccer game. Police said the woman was upset over her daughter's performance in the contest and her attitude after the game. The woman pulled over the car to the shoulder of Interstate 80 at one of the Lincoln exits and demanded her daughter get out of the car, then drove away. Fortunately for the teenager, a teammate's parent spotted her and transported her to safety (Schnoes, 2008). This type of behavior is not confined to what might be considered a sideline stalking parent. Adults in positions of authority leverage their power against other adolescents to attain their desired results on behalf of their own children. A Little League coach in suburban Pittsburgh allegedly paid one of his eight-year-old players $25 to assault a fellow teammate, a nine-year-old autistic boy (Ayad, 2006). He did this so he would not have to let the autistic child play the league-mandated three innings in a playoff game. According to court testimony, the adult, Mark Downs, told Keith Reese two different times to hit Harry Bowers Jr., first in the groin, and then in the side of the head so he would be too sore to play. Downs was convicted of corruption of minors and conspiracy to commit simple assault and sentenced to one to six years in prison (Ayad, 2006).

In another instance, a high school football game in Albuquerque, New Mexico, was forcibly stopped by referees after they discovered the helmet of Mike Cito contained a buckle that had been sharpened like a razor (Thomson, 1996). The fashioned instrument had gashed several players during the game. One of the wounds required a dozen stitches to close. Cito was dismissed from the team and expelled from the school following the incident. His father, a dentist, admitted he had been the one who had sharpened the buckle because of unfair treatment he felt his son received from officials the previous week (Thomson, 1996).

Overzealous parents come in all shapes and sizes and from professions of all kinds. Those making our laws are not immune from the behavior the laws are intended to curb. Daniel Foley, the Republican whip in the New Mexico House of Representatives, was arrested at a high school basketball game for disorderly conduct, resisting arrest, and obstructing a police officer in the line of duty (Haussamen, 2007). The politician rushed onto the court when his 14-year-old son was restrained by a coach after attempting to join in a fight which had broken out on the court. According to police, the older Foley was screaming profanities and spitting chewing tobacco (Haussamen, 2007).

A nationally prominent case of a parent in a position of power exercising influence on behalf of his children occurred in New Jersey. The state supreme court censured one of its own jurists. Justice Roberto A. Rivera-Soto improperly used his influence to settle a score between his sons and the captain of their high school football team (Lat, 2007). When his twin sons claimed they had been struck by an older teammate, the judge filed a juvenile delinquency complaint for assault and then improperly intervened in the case by contacting two judges and asking a prosecutor to review the case (Lat, 2007).

Youth sports experts and psychologists put forward a number of reasons parents might behave in these ways. Parents might believe that a child's athletic success or failure reflects on them as parents. Some parents are simply anxious in a highly competitive world. Some love the attention or glory gained when their kids are successful in youth sports. Still other parents become hooked on protecting their kids from failure or discomfort. Madeline Levine, author of *The Price of Privilege*, contends that a parent's involvement is good, but being overly involved is not good. According to Levine (2006), when a parent says things like, "I know you tried hard, but I can't understand why you're not ashamed to hand in a paper that still has errors," it means the parent mistakenly believes that shame will motivate her child to try harder. Promoting guilt and shame invariably works against progress. More importantly, they weaken the ties between child and parent (Levine, 2006).

Many parents go to radical excesses to try and aid their children's future success in youth sports. Unfortunately, these trends are becoming widespread in children's academic lives. Parents are enrolling their children in kindergarten a year later than the age norm in order to give the child greater strength and maturity for youth sports competition. Older children are being made to repeat eighth grade to give them an extra edge in high school sports. Many school districts across the country have established strict transfer regulations to thwart the attempt of adults to move to a particular school so the child will be able to participate in athletics there. Many private schools do not have the same restrictions, which creates problems between public and private schools that may compete against each other, especially in less-populated states in America.

Psychotherapist Elayne Savage suggests some parents say they are going to extremes for the benefit of their child, but sometimes it is not in the child's best interests. Instead, it is in the best interest of the parents or the coach and can, in fact, be detrimental to the child

(Alberts, 2008). The lengths to which parents will go to see their child have success in youth sports seem endless. Felipe Almonte was banned for life from Little League baseball after he doctored his son's birth certificate to allow the youngster to pitch for the team from the Bronx in New York in the 2001 Little League World Series (Wong, 2001). Prosecutors in the Dominican Republic filed criminal charges against the elder Almonte for falsifying a birth certificate (Wong, 2001).

In other instances, parents and children have brought arguments to court over dashed athletic dreams. The legal genre of these cases, which are becoming less obscure because of their number, is called "disappointment lawsuits." These fascinating cases find young athletes and their parents seeking redress for damage inflicted to their sports reputations and college sports playing prospects. Rarely does a plaintiff win, but it does not seem to dissuade people from arguing their matter in court. In the Texas case of *Rutherford v. Cypress-Fairbanks Independent School District*, a high school senior and his parents filed suit alleging due process under the Texas constitution when the high school baseball coach scratched the young man as the starting pitcher for a regional quarterfinal playoff game. The young man had used a student publication to ridicule two school coaches, which baseball coach Archie Hayes judged to be "unsportsmanlike, disruptive, demoralizing, and disrespectful" (Hyman, 2007).

Two related state court cases appeared in Missouri in *Wellsville-Middletown School District v. Miles*. In the first case, the school district sued the Missouri State High School Activities Association, claiming its basketball team suffered an unjust defeat because the official scorer made a mistake (Feiner, 1997). In the second case, the aggrieved players sued the head referee, asserting that by failing to follow proper procedures in running the game, the referee harmed their chances of getting college scholarships. The second suit was dropped after the first was dismissed (Feiner, 1997).

Nineteen-year-old Cheryl Reeves filed a $700,000 lawsuit against her club softball coach alleging his "incorrect" teaching style had ruined her chances to earn a college athletic scholarship (Susquehanna Valley Center for Public Policy, 2002). She claimed her personal softball tutor, to whom she paid $40 per hour for private lessons, taught her an "illegal pitch technique," and when she complained, the man, who was also her club coach, replaced her with other players. The teenager maintained she was gripped by stress and forced to quit the team, unfairly ending her career as an elite athlete (Susquehanna Valley Center for Public Policy, 2002).

223

These varying motivations for parents, which are certainly different from the children's, who primarily play for fun, are creating increasingly unhealthy environments for youth sports in America. Whether it is seeing their son with the good arm or great hands as their personal winning lottery ticket or threatening to sue their six-year-old youngster's coach—like the dad in New Jersey did, feeling his son's professional baseball future would be diminished because the coach used a nonregulation baseball designed to reduce injuries—these parents are not just wrecking the youth sports landscape; they are also damaging the children who play the sports. They are hurting their own kids.

COST TO KIDS

The injuries to children caught in this tornadic activity of organized youth sports in America are occurring in several facets of their lives. Adolescents suffer mentally and emotionally from the toll of their participation in sports. They also hurt physically in grand numbers. The numbers of overuse injuries to young athletes is frightening. There is tremendous pressure to win or otherwise be successful; however, that pressure is being measured by adults, which often leads to emotional burnout on the part of the youth. Children also pay a devastating price developmentally. This loss occurs in the emotional realm of the child, as well as his or her social and physical development. Because of overcrowded schedules of youth sports, youth participants are losing their childhood play. This is also causing erosion to the fabric of family well-being, which further injures children. Kids become impacted to the point where they lose their sense of fair play and sportsmanship, because of what they are being taught by adults. Many children are literally tired and ragged on the inside and out.

A predominant theme encountered among young athletes is that parents are seen as both a tremendous source of support and as a source of great stress. The perception of the adolescent as to whether there is support or stress frequently relates to the current performance of the athlete. Children want to please and often deeply feel their parent's disappointment, which is interpreted as rejection. One teen describes this feeling by stating, "My mother's face turns off whenever I don't play well" (McMahon, 2007).

This is a central paradox of families of young athletes, according to sports psychologist Jon Hellstedt (1987). He suggests the greatest strength of these families is their unwavering emotional support of the child athlete, including their willingness to make sacrifices for the

224

athletic advancement of the kids. Ironically, however, this is also their greatest weakness. Parents' deep love and support for their young sports participant may help a talented child reach high levels of success, but may also cause a talented child to rebel or even burn out. Ray Lamb, an award-winning instructor of young golfers and a member of the Professional Golfers Association, related the story of one of his top teenage female students, who quit her sport in dramatic fashion at a Texas high school state championship tournament. The young prodigy had previously won a state title and finished as runner-up in another in her prep career. She had apparently accomplished these feats with the full emotional and financial support of her mother and stepfather. Spectators at her senior year championship tournament witnessed an outburst aimed directly at the parents, complete with profanities, and the young woman purposely hitting her golf ball the wrong direction in order to sabotage her score and further sink her chances of winning. According to Lamb (2006), "... it was her theatrical way of saying, 'I've had all I want and I'm done!' I think it was a combination of rebellion against her parents and emotions of potentially not winning her last high school tournament."

Although not as dramatic—but every bit as final—a top soccer recruit at Lehigh University in Pennsylvania told Coach Dean Koski on the third day of preseason practice, "I don't want to do this anymore ... because I've been playing since I was five and I thought this was going to be fun, but it's not fun anymore. I'm sorry" (McMahon, 2007). Playing sports becomes increasingly stressful for children because they often want to quit, but feel they cannot because it will anger or disappoint their parents. In an article that appeared on December 10, 2000, in the *San Francisco Chronicle*, former professional baseball player Erik Johnson said, "I see a lot of burnout. It used to be high school, but now it's ten-, eleven- and twelve-year-old kids. The kids get fried. They quit. They resent the game. They don't want to see the game" (Nevius, 2000).

A crucial change in perspective for a young athlete can occur when sports ceases to be what the youngster does for intrinsic pleasure and becomes something done for a reason. The child does not need a reason to do gymnastics. She loves it. There is nothing she would rather do than tumble, perform cartwheels, or do somersaults. When her gymnastic practice must be done for a reason, like to win a meet or impress a college coach in order to receive a scholarship, then often the fun is suddenly sucked away from the activity.

If the intrinsic drive is predominating, then the athlete stands to remain healthy in participation. When the external reasons for playing begin to take over, the sport becomes more of a chore. Some experts refer to this as the externalization of sports, and when this occurs, burnout becomes more likely. Coach Kirk Mango, a former Division I gymnast, contends that many athletes do seek external rewards from their respective sports endeavors, like trophies, popularity, scholarships, and admiration from parents and coaches. He says the problem occurs because of what he calls an "outside-in" mind-set. The rewards are fleeting and they do not sustain young athletes. Mango says, "When you value something from the inside, when you're striving to reach your potential, master a skill, or do well, regardless of whether you win or lose, you're climbing that ladder and reaching achievement or a level of accomplishment." He suggests if adults want kids to be properly motivated and sustain sports participation for a long period of time, then internal rewards must be promoted—not external rewards (Cohn and Cohn, 2010).

It is important to consider that children do not lose interest if they are learning and being challenged appropriately. Psychologist Mihaly Csikszentmihalyi (2008) captures this idea in his theory of "flow." His supposition is that people are happiest when the challenge they are facing is equal to the skills they have. Young athletes should be provided with challenges that are commensurate with their sporting ability. Anxiety is a likely outcome for those who are confronted with undertakings beyond their athletic ability. There is a balance to be struck, however. If the challenge is not great enough for the skill set present for a youngster, then boredom may occur. As kids develop their athletic prowess, they gain confidence. As these characteristics grow, greater challenges must be provided so they may have the opportunity to stay in the flow (Csikszentmihalyi, 2008). Children, like adults, desire to be good at something. This desire is a significant motivator and determinant in whether young athletes stay in sports. Sport psychologists call this notion "competence" motivation (Murphy, 1999).

Dr. Thomas Tutko, professor of psychology at San Jose State University who authored multiple works on the subject, believes if children go to practice, perform painful drills, and improve their skills, but have no fun, and if the coach constantly hammers at their mistakes, after a while, they are going to think, "Do I really want to be here?" Dr. Tutko also suggests kids who reach that stage and decide they really do not want to participate are conditionally labeled. They are called quitters. The children do not have fun and are insulted with a derogatory term. He suggests that what is being communicated to the children is that they are not worthwhile. He contends that kids quit because their needs are not being met. In fact, they are meant to feel miserable (Tutko, 1976).

Experts contend that the extreme pressures placed on children engaged in organized youth sports competition is stunting their development physically and emotionally. Development is also being retarded because of the children's lack of unstructured play. Kids do not ride their bikes to the park or play in backyards with other neighborhood children much anymore. Unstructured play time decreased almost 25 percent between 1981 and 1997, according to a study conducted by the University of Michigan Institute for Social Research. The work also revealed children's time spent playing organized youth sports during the same period *increased* by 25 percent. The research also found that kids have 12 fewer hours of free time per week, eat fewer family dinners, have fewer family conversations, and take fewer family vacations (MacPherson, 2002).

For many kids, childhood has become its own rat race in which they are rushed from school to practice to home with fast-food dinner in the car on the way to one place or the other, squeezing in homework while riding in the backseat in transit. They awaken the next day to do it all over again or multiple times over the course of a weekend while traveling to a tournament or other competition. Jeff Green, an assistant coach of the California State Girls Under 16 soccer team, says, "the biggest crime is there's too much organized sport and not enough kids going out into the yard and kicking the ball around. Things are out of balance in that regard. Kids don't think about it. They'd be much more inclined to pick up their PlayStation than to grab a ball, call up some friends and say, 'Hey, let's go to the school yard,' and play basketball, football, or soccer. If it's not an organized game, they don't do it" (McMahon, 2007).

Professional ice hockey great Wayne Gretzky suggests that players in hockey at the highest level have lost their creativity and imagination because super-organized youth systems have taken over control of the game. He surmises the creativity of Hall of Fame players like Bobby Orr, Gordie Howe, and Jean Béliveau is gone (Gretzky, 2000). According to Gretzky, the creativity of those players, "... was basically founded by the fact they would go on ponds and skate for six, seven, or eight hours a day, choose up sides and have two nets and no goalies. We need to get back to the basics of just having fun. That would go a long way toward getting back a lot of the imagination in our game" (Gretzky, 2000).

The demands on children as they participate in organized youth sports create trauma, stress, anxiety, and other injuries whether or not parents realize the young athletes are affected. Kids have this tremendous pressure not to let down or disappoint their parents, often recognizing the investment their parents have made both emotionally and financially on their behalf. Dr. Joel Fish, founder and director of the Center for Sports in Philadelphia, tells the shocking story of a young girl who had stopped eating because she felt she did not

227

"deserve" food. She explained to Dr. Fish that because she had not been performing well at her track meets and her times had not improved as she and her coach had hoped, she had taken this action. Her parents had expressed their disappointment in her athletic results, and subsequently, she had lost confidence. According to Dr. Fish, she began thinking of herself as "not good enough." This loss of esteem began a viciously unhealthy cycle for this adolescent. The little girl was ten years old (Engh, 2002).

CONCLUSION

Corporate America uses sports lingo as an everyday, common part of doing business. Workers are called team members. They labor together as part of a unit. Productivity is visually displayed in offices and factories on scoreboards. There is talk of sacrifice and teamwork in order to win victories. It would be difficult to imagine someone growing up in America since the 1950s without having his or her life affected by sports in one manner or another.

This mind-set has permeated our culture. Adult-driven motives have set forward an insatiable national appetite for success in organized youth sports in America. This journey occurred because professional educators saw dangers for adolescents involved in athletic environments that were too competitive. Those educators stepped away when they saw warning signs. Untrained parents filled the void, and the unhealthiness increased for youth in organized sports. The trend continues to be perilously unhealthy for young athletes. The near-disposable approach toward young athletes borders on child exploitation and is, in fact, occurring with a growing number of youth. Many parents and adults have become blinded by their own personal visions and agendas and have forgotten about the desires and needs of their children.

REFERENCES

ABC News. (2000). "Player's dad, uncle allegedly assault high school coach." Retrieved May 10, 2010, from ABC News Internet Ventures. http://abcnews.go.com/US/story?id=95117&page=1

Alberts, H. R. (2008). "Handling rejection." Retrieved April 2, 2015, from *Forbes*: http://www. forbes.com/2008/04/01/admissions-letters-rejection-oped-cx_hra_0401rejection.html

Alter, J., and D. Glick. (1996). "Jessica's final flight." *Newsweek* 127, no. 17.

Ayad, M. (2006). "Jury convicts t-ball coach of beaning." *Pittsburgh Post-Gazette*, September 15.

Bach, G. (2006). "The parents' association for youth sports: A proactive method of spectator behavior management." *Journal of Physical Education, Recreation and Dance* 77, 6, 16–19.

Baum, S., and L. Lapovsky. (2006). "Tuition discounting not just a private college practice." College Board: http://www.collegeboard.com/prod_downloads/press/tuition-discounting.pdf

Bigelow, B., T. Moroney, and L. Hall (2001). *Just Let the Kids Play: How to Stop Other Adults from Ruining Your Child's Fun and Success in Youth Sports*. Deerfield Beach, FL: Health Communications.

Cohn, P., and L. Cohn (2010). "The advantages of an inside-out mindset for young athletes." Retrieved July 1, 2010, from http://www.youthsportspsychology.com/ youth_sports_psychology_blog/?p=708

Cribb, R. (2011). "Should hockey dad be 'ashamed' after girl's humiliating departure?" Retrieved February 21, 201, from the *Toronto Star*: http://www.Parent central.ca/ parent/sports/hockey/article/920859-should-hockey-dad-be-ashamedafter-girl-s-humiliatingdeparture+paul+dennis+parents+sports&cd=8&hl=en&ct=clnk&gl=us&source= www.google.com

Csikszentmihalyi, M. (2008). *Flow: The Psychology of Optimal Experience*. New York: Harper Perennial Modern Classics.

Engh, F. (2002). *Why Johnny Hates Sports*. Garden City Park, NY: Square One.

Eubanks, R. (2003). Personal interview. Spartanburg, SC.

Fausset, R., and N. Rhone (2001). "Man headed to jail after attacking son's coach." *Los Angeles Times*, January 26.

Feiner, S. (1997). "The personal liability of sports officials: Don't take the game into your own hands, take them to court!" *Sports Lawyers Journal* 4, 213–233.

Fraser-Thomas, J., and J. Côté. (2009). "Understanding adolescents' positive and negative developmental experiences in sport." *Sport Psychologist* 23, 1, 3–23.

George, T. (2000). "Brawling adults tie up soccer game." *New York Daily News*, September 11.

Gretzky, W. (2000). Interview with ASAP Sports. February 6. http://www.asapsports.com/show_interview.php?id=24373 (accessed April 16, 2015).

Harwood, C., and C. Knight. (2009). "Stress in youth sport: A developmental investigation of tennis parents." *Psychology of Sport and Exercise* 10, 4, 447–456.

Haussamen, H. (2007) "Rep. Foley arrested following fight at sporting event." Retrieved May 16, 2010, from Haussamen Publications: http://www.nmpolitics.net/index/2007/06/rep-foley-arrested-followingfight-at-sporting-event (accessed May 16, 2010).

Hellstedt, J. (1987). "The coach/parent/athlete relationship." *Sport Psychologist* 1, 151–160.

Hyman, M. (2011). "'Disappointment lawsuits' give athletes another legal option." Street and Smith Sports Group. http://www.sportsbusinessdaily.com/Journal/Issues/2007/10/20071029/From-The- Field-Of/Disappointment-Lawsuits-Give-Athletes-Another-Legal-Option.aspx

Hyman, M. (2009). *Until It Hurts: America's Obsession with Youth Sports and How It Harms Our Kids*. Boston: Beacon Press.

Lamb, W. R. (2006). Personal interview. Waco, TX.

Lat, David. (2007). "Judge of the day: Justice Roberto Rivera-Soto." Retrieved April 20, 2010, from Breaking Media, LLC: http://abovethelaw.com/2007/05/judge-of-the-day-justice-roberto-rivera-soto

Levine, M. D. (2006). "What price, privilege? Has our over-involved parenting style created a generation of kids with an impaired sense of self? If so, how can we work to get it back?" Retrieved May 1, 2011, from Hearst Communications, Inc. http://www.sfgate.com/cgibin/article.cgi?f=/c/a/2006/06/25/CMG5EJ6PF71.DTL&ao=

MacPherson, K. (2002). "Development experts say children suffer due to lack of unstructured fun." *Pittsburgh Post-Gazette*, October 1.

McMahon, R. (2007). *Revolution in the Bleachers: How Parents Can Take Back Family Life in a World Gone Crazy over Youth Sports*. New York: Gotham Books.

Murphy, S. M. (1999). *The Cheers and the Tears: A Healthy Alternative to the Dark Side of Youth Sports Today*. San Francisco: Jossey-Bass.

National Alliance for Youth Sports. (2003). "Parents speak out." *Sporting Kid Magazine*.

National Association Sports Officials (2000). "Sports officials security program." Retrieved May 2, 2011, http://www.naso.org/benefits/updated_benefits/sos.htm (accessed May 2, 2011).

NCAA (2010). *2010–2011 NCAA Division I Manual*. Indianapolis, IN: National Collegiate Athletic Association, 2010.

National Council of Youth Sports (2008). "National Council of Youth Sports report on trends and participation in organized youth sports, 2008 edition." http://www.ncys.org/pdf/2008/2008-marketresearch.pdf (accessed March 30, 2010).

Nevius, C. W. (2000). "Child's play no more." *San Francisco Chronicle*, December 10.

Nolin, Robert. "Youth league to police adults." Retrieved on February 8, 2011, from *Sun Sentinel*. http://articles.sunsentinel.com/2000-0225/news/0002250224_1_youth-sports-league-kids-parentscode

Pennington, B., and B. Weber. (2005). "Doctors see a big rise in injuries for young athletes." *New York Times*, February 22.

Phillips, R., and M. Sudhalter. (2007). "Violence increasingly part of youth sports brawls, assaults, even deaths part of troubling unsportsmanlike trend." Retrieved May 24, 2011, from http://www.recordnet.com/apps/pbcs.dll/article?AID=/20070204/A_SPORTS/702040318/0/RSS01

Ross, O. (2002). "Anatomy of anger." Retrieved May 5, 2011, from Resourceful Internet Solutions. http://www.mediate.com/articles/oliverR.cfm

Schnoes, D. J. (2008). "The perceptions about youth sports programs in Nebraskan communities." Doctoral dissertation, University of Nebraska, 2008. Retrieved May 11, 2010. In http://www.yutan.esu2.org/highschool/pdf/ds.pdf

Still, B. (2002). *Officials under Assault*. Racine, WI: National Association of Sports Officials.

Susquehanna Valley Center for Public Policy (2002). "Pennsylvania examples of lawsuit abuse." Retrieved June 4, 2010, from Affnigent, Inc. http://www.susvalleypolicy.org/policynews.asp?aID=500&p=2

Thomson, P. (1996). "In preps, sportsmanship should be valued more." *Orlando Sentinel*, December 15.

Tofler, I. R., and P. K. Knapp. (1999). "The achievement by proxy spectrum: Recognition and clinical response to pressured and high-achieving adolescents." *Journal of the American Academy of Child & Adolescent Psychiatry* 38, 2, 213–216.

Tofler, I. R., P. K. Knapp, and M. J. Drell. (1998). "The achievement by proxy spectrum in youth sports: Historical perspective and clinical approach to pressured and high-achieving children and adolescents." *Child and Adolescent Psychiatric Clinics of North America 7*, 4, 803–820.

Tutko, T. (1976). *Winning Is Everything and Other American Myths.* USA: Macmillan.

Vinella, S. (1997). "Paid coaches expected to perform." *Dayton Daily News*, July 7.

Wilcoxen, W. (2001). "Out-of-control parents threaten youth sports." Retrieved May 2, 2015, from http://news.minnesota.publicradio.org/features/200107/19_wilcoxenw_sports/

Wong, E. (2001). "Baseball; Little League tightens its rules." *New York Times*, December 12.

CHAPTER FOURTEEN

The Professionalization of College Sports

The Case of College Basketball

BY **SEAN KAUKAS**

INTRODUCTION

It is clear that Division I athletics have evolved tremendously over the past 100 years. College athletic teams draw bigger crowds, bring in more television money, and sell more merchandise than ever before. Both men's basketball and football have emerged as the two largest revenue-producing NCAA sports. Although these sports are very popular among fans, critics point out that there is so much pressure on schools to win that they often skirt NCAA rules to land elite recruits and keep them eligible while in school. Using the case of college basketball, this reading documents the increasing professionalization of college sports in the United States. Attention is also paid to the debate concerning whether or not college student athletes should be paid.

NCAA SCANDALS

In recent years, a number of NCAA scandals have been exposed and reported upon by the media. For example, reports revealed that the University of Southern California had given "lavish gifts" to standout athletes Reggie Bush and O. J. Mayo, players were selling game-worn jerseys at The Ohio State University, and the University of Alabama paid a high school coach to steer a star player to enroll at Alabama (CNN.com). There is so much pressure placed upon coaches to win that many of them are willing to bend and even break the rules in order to not only be successful, but to also keep their jobs.

One common practice is for universities to accept "special admit" students who excel at sports and to offer them phony curricula (Dowling, 2001). These special admits are often held to different standards than regular students and are expected to place their athletic performance at a higher priority than their academics. Dowling (2001) uses the case of the University of Minnesota as an example of this. At Minnesota, athletic tutors were found to have "written over 400 pieces of work for 20 basketball players over a 5-year period" in order to provide the athletes more time and fewer distractions to help carry them to the March Madness NCAA postseason tournament (Dowling, 2001). Similarly, Dowling (2001) documents the University of Miami's boosters paying players $500 a touchdown, "losing" positive drug test results, and steering $700,000 in government student loans to recruited athletes.

Harris and Mac (2011) uncovered similar goings-on at Stanford University, a highly regarded private academic institution. Although Stanford officials claimed that they were not violating NCAA rules, many others disagree. Harris and Mac (2011) document that Stanford athletes had access to a list of easy classes. Kira Maker, a women's soccer player at Stanford, claimed that the classes on the list were "always chock full of athletes and very easy A's" (Harris and Mac, 2011). The list, titled "Courses of Interest," was distributed by the Athletic Resource Center solely to athletes. Although "the list itself isn't a violation," according to Gerald Gurney, the president of the National Association of Academic Advisers for Athletics, he states that "promoting courses because they're easy isn't, ethically, something that academic advisers should do" (Harris and Mac, 2011).

A senior academic administrator at Tufts University asked the question, "Does anyone actually believe that a freshman varsity basketball player at Duke, Stanford, or Georgetown, handle a normal first year curriculum at these rigorously academic institutions?" (Dowling,

234

2001). Dowling (2001) examined statistics available in the 1997 graduation-rates report published by the NCAA and found that the average SAT score of a student entering Duke University was 1392, whereas the average for their basketball players was 887. This fact alone puts into question whether these student athletes can legitimately handle the demands of Duke University's curriculum and how these players are able to stay eligible. Dowling (2001) feels that a few schools such as Duke, which have commercialized their college sports programs, have legitimized what he calls "prostitution" for the less academically prestigious schools.

HOW MUCH MONEY DO NCAA BASKETBALL TEAMS GENERATE?

Although most NCAA athletic teams lose money, most D1A football and men's basketball teams generate millions of dollars every year through ticket sales, television revenue, and merchandise sales. Schools, including Penn State, Notre Dame, Duke, and Alabama and dozens of others, generate substantial profits year in and year out through these two sports. Many schools, including Michigan, Ohio State, and Oregon play in football stadia that have greater seating capacities than every professional stadium in the country. Moreover, schools like South Carolina, Kentucky, and Nebraska play in states/regions without any professional teams and are followed by legions of people with the same enthusiasm and passion as people in more populated states who follow professional teams. Many colleges have "team stores" that rival the biggest professional team stores in the country. In addition, the amount of money generated through playing in end-of-football-season bowl games and the NCAA basketball tournament rivals professional marquee events.

Sheehan (2000) conducted a study looking to break down this issue quantitatively in order to examine the professionalization—or lack thereof—of Division 1A sports. His main argument for whether or not a sport is professional is based on the athletic department's fundamental focus. If the athletic department's fundamental focus is on profits, then it operates professionally. If its fundamental focus is not for profit, then it does not operate professionally. Sheehan (2000) collected data from 1994 and 1995 gender equity reports to analyze the revenues, expenses, and profits of basketball, football, and other women's/men's programs. He compared data by conference and by division and concluded the only profitable sports were Division 1A men's basketball and football. The fact that these sports were profitable alone does not yet imply that their fundamental focus was profit. In order to dig deeper into the numbers, Sheehan (2000) ran a least squares regression of expenditures versus revenues in order to gauge whether the program is spending to generate profit. Running the regression with data from individual institutions yielded results of a $0.66 increase in revenues for every dollar spent on football (Sheehan, 2000).

When the regression model was run with data by conference, however, the results yielded a much higher dollar increase of $3.02 (Sheehan, 2000). This implies an obvious economic incentive to increase spending, but this appears questionable considering the contrasting results by institution. Men's basketball produced similar results for both the individual and by conference regression of expenses and revenues. By individual institutions, every dollar spent generates $2.04 in revenue, and by conference, every dollar spent generates $3.12 in revenue (Sheehan, 2000). Therefore, it seems that men's basketball programs are spending in pursuit of profit (Sheehan, 2000).

In addition to regressing revenues and expenses of football and men's basketball, Sheehan (2000) regressed football gross revenue versus other men's and women's expenditures, as well as men's basketball, by individual institution and conference. The results for individual institutions showed that an increase in football gross revenue leads to a statistically significant increase in expenditures for other men's and women's programs (Sheehan, 2000). More specifically, a dollar increase in football gross revenue resulted in a $0.04 increase for other men's sports and a $0.07 increase in women's expenditures (Sheehan, 2000). There was no impact on men's basketball expenditures.

These results also show that money made in football is being used to subsidize other men's and women's sports (Sheehan, 2000). This presents yet another incentive to make a profit in football. In this case, operating professionally in football allows for the rest of the athletic department to stay afloat. Although Sheehan (2000) did not perform the same regression for men's basketball concerning subsidization, he concludes that both collegiate football and men's basketball fit a professional mode, while others do not.

Brown and Jewell (2004) take this idea a step further by assessing the value of football and men's basketball players. Their goal is to evaluate the actual amount of money generated by these revenue-generating players and compare that to the value of an athletic scholarship. If the amount of money generated per player is greater than the value of their athletic scholarship, it suggests that the athlete is not being compensated adequately. Brown and Jewell

236

(2004) accomplished this by measuring the marginal revenue product (MRP) of acquiring one premium football or men's basketball player, while holding constant other factors that influence revenues through the use of Poisson regression. This study was done as an updated replication to one done previously that used 1988–1989 revenues and 1989–1992 draft data.

Brown and Jewell's (2004) study shows that the MRP of a premium football player exceeds $500,000 in annual revenues, where the MRP of a premium men's basketball player is approximately $1,000,000 in annual revenues. These results implied that the NCAA and the schools do not properly compensate some players for their services. Brown and Jewell (2004) used 1995–1996 revenues and 1996–1999 draft data to perform their updated version of the study. Their results were similar where the MRP of a premium football player was roughly $400,000 and the MRP of a premium men's basketball player was approximately $1,000,000 (Brown and Jewell, 2004). These results were consistent with those found in past studies.

In a follow-up study, Brown and Jewell (2006) have continued to measure the rents[1] collected by college athletic programs, not only from men's college basketball and football, but women's college basketball as well. Brown and Jewell (2006) followed the same methodology as they did in their previous studies in terms of the explanatory and result variables. In other words, Brown and Jewell (2006) inferred from their previous studies that a women's college basketball team's revenues are a function of its players' skill levels, the quality of its opponents, its market demand characteristics, and its past success. When using ordinary least squares (OLS) regression to explain the relationship, they estimated that acquiring one premium player generated $250,000 annually for their team. Although this is much less than what they estimated for a men's college basketball player, it is still significant when considering how much they receive in scholarship money. This would imply that college athletic programs are collecting over $150,000 a year in revenue from these premium players.

Brown and Jewell (2006) came up with different results when using quantile regression to explain the relationship. They felt that this form of regression had two advantages over ordinary least squares regression. The first advantage is that quantile regression estimators are efficient in the presence of outliers, while OLS estimators are not. The second is that quantile regression allows for analyzing different parts of the conditional distribution of team revenue, where OLS regression concentrates only on the conditional mean. Therefore, quantile regression gave Brown and Jewell (2006) the ability to estimate the marginal value of a premium player, depending on where their team fell in the revenue distribution. The results of the quantile regression showed that the magnitude of the rents depend on a team's location in the revenue distribution. More specifically, teams falling on the lower end of the revenue distribution extract little or no rents, while teams falling on the upper end of the revenue distribution (elite programs) extract sizable rents from premium players. Overall, Brown and Jewell (2006) were able to conclude that female basketball players generate much less revenue than their male counterparts. The average men's basketball team produces five times the revenues of a women's team, whereas premium men's basketball players generate two and a half times the revenues of women players at even the most elite programs (Brown and Jewell, 2006).

The MRP of acquiring a premium player is also referred to by Lawrence M. Kahn (2007) as the player's market value. The purpose of his work, *Cartel Behavior and Amateurism in College Sports*, was to examine how this discrepancy between market value and compensation is possible. Kahn (2007) uses Brown and Jewell's estimation of MRP above as the basis for the discrepancy. He feels that this assumed discrepancy is due to the NCAA acting as a cartel. More specifically, Kahn (2007) asserts that the NCAA has "enforced collusive restrictions on payments for factors of production, including player compensation, recruiting expenses, and assistant coaches' salaries" and also "restricted output" to "defeat potential rival groups." He notes that of all of these restricted inputs, restrictions on payments to players are the most important way that the NCAA restricts competition. In limiting the payment to athletes, it allows for athletic departments to turn a profit and disperse the earned rents elsewhere. Rents are usually spent on "facilities, nonrevenue sports, and, possibly, head coaches' salaries" (Kahn, 2007). Kahn (2007) feels that reinvesting into the athletic department has indirect benefits for its respective academic institution. The benefits he mentions include public and private contributions as well as a generated interest from students, which in turn strengthens the school as a whole.

SHOULD NCAA ATHLETES BE PAID?

Because so many Division 1A basketball teams are very profitable, many people think that high-profile college athletes should share in that revenue and be compensated financially. Although many basketball players get full scholarships that cover their tuition, books, and room and board, they are not provided with money to cover any incidental expenses like cell phone bills and clothing. Many people who support the idea of paying high-profile athletes do not necessarily believe that they should be paid huge sums of money. Rather, they think that they should be given an extra hundred or two hundred dollars a month to help them pay their cell phone bills and have money to go the movies or out for dinner. Of course, many people and organizations strongly oppose this idea. The NCAA, for example, has made it very clear that student athletes are amateur athletes who are students first. The argument here is that athletes should not be paid any more than members of the marching band, campus theater organizations, or other student organizations.

ARGUMENTS AGAINST PAYING STUDENT ATHLETES

There are numerous reasons that exist concerning why NCAA athletes should not be paid. Many of them relate generally to the idea that college students are amateurs who are no different than other amateur athletes who play high school sports or compete in amateur events like the Olympics. Simply put, advocates of this position contend that college athletes are above-all-else students, who should not be treated differently from other students. A related issue is that many high-profile college athletes receive full scholarships which cover most, if not all, of their college-related expenses. So, in a sense, they are already being paid. Plus, they are coached by experienced and successful coaches who can help them improve as players and have an even better chance of being drafted into the professional ranks.

Kahn (2007) stresses that although the NCAA's compensation restrictions on top-notch players in men's football and basketball are allowing for athletic departments to collect the rents they generate, the process is fair for everybody involved. He lays out several complicating factors that he feels deserve consideration for this viewpoint. The first is that not only are the players receiving direct compensation through scholarship, they are also getting indirect benefits such as access to high-level coaching, training, and media exposure, which enhances their future earning power. If the cost of providing these indirect benefits is equal to or exceeds the marginal revenue product a premium player generates, then the current compensation system appears to be appropriate. However, Kahn (2007) still feels that this is unlikely, and these indirect costs do not reach the necessary levels to make this argument convincing.

Another factor that Kahn (2007) mentions is that the competition that would arise from paying top college athletes would be wasteful from society's point of view. In other words, devoting resources to other university activities may be more beneficial overall. The validity of

239

this argument depends heavily on the fans' demand for relative or absolute playing quality. Demand for relative playing quality would allow for inefficiently high demand for inputs to playing quality, assuming competition was uncontrolled. A third consideration offered by Kahn (2007) applies to whether or not the restrictions on paying top college athletes cause inefficiency when looking at the labor supply curve. If the supply curve happens to be perfectly inelastic (playing college sports is the player's best use of time by a significant margin), then there would be no efficiency loss in restricting pay. More realistically, the supply curve is elastic to some extent, which implies an efficiency loss when restricting inputs (payment to athletes). Players are likely to consider other options like turning pro or playing overseas when their compensation is restricted. Therefore, there appears to be efficiency loss when considering the labor supply curve. The last point Kahn (2007) brings up is that the demand for amateur college sports may be much higher than the demand for professionalized college sports. Therefore, restricting pay and keeping the sport amateur may be in the best interest of the NCAA.

In their article "*USA Today* Analysis Finds $120K Value in Men's Basketball Scholarship," Jay Weiner and Steve Berkowitz (2011) offer an estimate of what a typical basketball player in Division I receives yearly. Rather than taking the average of a state school's tuition and room and board to value a player's scholarship, they quantify other factors to be taken into account. These factors include coaching, general administrative support, equipment, uniforms, marketing, promotion, game tickets, medical and insurance premiums, and future earnings power. When all of these factors are taken into account, Weiner and Berkowitz (2011) estimate that a Division I men's basketball player receives roughly $120,000 per year in value. This supports the notion that they are already being compensated very well for their athletic contributions and should not be "paid" on top of the compensation that they already receive.

ARGUMENTS IN FAVOR OF PAYING STUDENT ATHLETES

As with all controversial issues, many people dismiss the arguments against paying student athletes and feel strongly that they should be better compensated for their athletic endeavors. The main argument is that high-profile athletes generate so many profits for their schools that they should get a bigger cut than is provided through a full scholarship. High-profile athletes help to increase their schools' profiles by helping to sell more tickets to games and appearing more frequently on national television. Moreover, schools sell jerseys, posters, and DVDs with players' numbers and likenesses. Some cynics also believe that many well-known athletes are already being paid anyway, as they receive cars, cash, clothing, tattoos, etc., by sympathetic boosters and agents eager to represent them as professionals. The idea here is that if many athletes are already being paid, it should be done in a more standardized, regulated, and transparent manner.

Of course, the idea of paying athletes brings with it a host of challenges. For example, whom do you pay? Do you pay all athletes, or only those who play revenue-generating sports? Similarly, whom do you pay among the revenue-generating athletes? Do you pay only the stars? Do you pay only the starters? Is payment based upon performance? Do you pay only the men? Do you pay some female athletes? Obviously, these decisions will impact different players in different ways. Another issue relates to the amount of money that athletes should be paid. Do you pay them thousands of dollars per month? Do you pay them a couple of hundred dollars per month? Obviously, a lot of decisions would need to be made.

In his article "The NCAA's Slaves," Andrew Cline (2009) expresses the notion that Division 1A student athletes are exploited by the NCAA and receive none of the money and school recognition that they generate. Cline (2009) bases much of his analysis on CBS's agreement to pay the NCAA $6 billion from 2002–2013 for rights to broadcast the NCAA men's basketball tournament. Each school that appears in the final game takes home a million dollars, and each also has the ability to generate millions from sales of licensed products and contracts with sporting goods suppliers. The point Cline (2009) makes is that none of the athletes receives any of that money they collectively helped produce. He claims that this practice can be best described as a "modern form of slavery" and stresses that the athletes on these teams sign over their rights to profit financially from their own hard work.

When considering the NCAA constitution and its rules, Cline (2009) finds numerous troubling components. Rule 12.4.4 states, "A student-athlete may establish his or her own business, provided the student-athlete's name, photograph, appearance or athletics reputation are not used to promote the business." Cline (2009) finds it unfair that the NCAA would be able to launch its own photo store online, where people could purchase a picture of a player, and not have to share any profit with that player. Schools all over the country have stores that sell photographs, posters, and jerseys, while the players receive none of the profit. The last point that Cline (2009) makes is based on the NCAA constitution statement that reads, "student-athletes should be protected from exploitation by professional and commercial enterprises." He finds it interesting that the NCAA constitution never addresses exploitation by nonprofit enterprises, which he feels is precisely what the NCAA is doing.

While Sack (2008) and Dowling (2001) point out that there is an extremely small percentage of players who are the main revenue generators, Cline (2009) supports the idea that the entire team should be recognized and compensated. According to NCAA data, 1.2 percent of the nation's men's basketball players will go on to play professionally. With 68 teams that make the NCAA tournament, each allowing 13 scholarships, there is a total of 884 players who are showcased. Cline (2009) assumes a similar percentage of this population will make it professionally, meaning that more than 850 players will never earn anything from their efforts. Meanwhile, the NCAA, its member institutions, and athletic conferences will earn billions. The NCAA, as well as many others, oppose payment for play, claiming that the players receive quality educations and athletic opportunities that cannot be quantified in terms of cash.

Nevertheless, many players are recruited with the hope that they will not only bring success to their program, but also bring attention to the school, resulting in lucrative media contracts. Some feel that because of the attention and money generated from these players, student athletes should receive monetary awards beyond their athletic scholarships from their respective programs. With the current system in place where athletes are considered amateurs, this cannot happen. Cline outlines that if you were to monetize the value of an education, it would be worth roughly $100,000, the cost of an average state school, taking into account out-of-state and in-state students. Cline (2009) uses a North Carolina basketball player, Tyler Hansbrough, as an example and thought it reasonable to claim that his share of television royalties, jersey, poster, and T-shirt sales, etc., would be significantly larger than his payment of $100,000 through scholarship.

Dowling (2001) argues that the way many Division 1A schools and athletic programs operate lowers the standards for college-level performance and shifts "the symbolic center of values at an institution away from the pursuit of knowledge and towards sports as a commercial spectacle." His ultimate point, which is also driven home by Andrew Zimbalist's (1999) book, *Unpaid Professionals,* is that making Division 1A athletics openly professional is the only way out of this situation. An alternative is proposed by James L. Shulman and William G. Bowen (2001) in their paper *The Game of Life: College Sports and Educational Values,* who claim that transitioning to the Division III model—where athletic scholarships are not rewarded—is another viable option. Although this outcome is unlikely, Division III schools have been able to compete athletically while maintaining their academic integrity.

One can make the argument that college players are, in fact, employees of their athletic departments and should be compensated as employees. Athletic scholarships are the current form of compensation for these athletes, and many feel that, given the cost of a college education, this compensation is more than fair. Brown and Jewell (2006; 2004), however, contend that compensation through scholarship is not nearly enough when considering the magnitude of the revenues the student brings in. In 1994 and 2000, they estimated that premium football players and men's and women's basketball players (players who have been drafted into the NBA or WNBA) have marginal revenue products of $500,000, $1,000,000, and $250,000, respectively.

In his article "Should College Athletes be Paid?" Allen Sack (2008) explains that college athletes are not simply "engaged in their sport during their free time." Rather, he argues that many of these athletes are essentially employees who are, in many cases, contributing to the building of a "sports entertainment empire." As such, Sack (2008) feels that certain players should receive other forms of rewards for the benefits the school reaps from their hard work. He states that the NCAA has devised a payment system—athletic scholarships—which provides a "cheap and steady supply of blue-chip athletes" for the fast-growing business of collegiate sports, as well as giving coaches control over athletes, similar to what an employer has over its employees (Sack, 2008). Sack (2008) states that student athletes are not compensated appropriately and should have similar benefits to what employees would have. He feels that these benefits should include "medical benefits, workers' compensation when injured, and the right to use their God-given talents to build some financial security for their families while still in college" (Sack, 2008). In addition to this, athletes should have players' associations to bargain for their ability to "endorse products, accept pay for speaking engagements, and get a cut of the profits universities make by marketing their images" (Sack, 2008). Sack (2008) believes that these actions are reasonable and necessary for the players who drive much of the revenue that keep athletic programs afloat.

Mark Isenberg (2010) gives his own take on payment of student athletes in his article "NCAA Should Admit Its March Madness Players Are Professionals," which is consistent with both Cline and Sack's thoughts. Isenberg (2010) views the issue as being caused by a very small percentage of players. The revenue-generating sports, football and men's basketball, only make up 3 percent of all student athletes in the NCAA. In addition, an even smaller

243

percentage of that population will end up making it professionally and are who drive most of the revenues for the school. It is these players that Isenberg (2010) stresses are what create the dilemma of payment for play. He feels that high-profile athletes are part of a strictly business arrangement, where the school provides a showcase for the player's talents, while the player provides his athletic and marketing services. Isenberg (2010) explores ways to possibly minimize these types of players by implementing rules.

One feasible rule Isenberg (2010) proposes is to mandate at least three semesters of good academic standing before being eligible to play. This rule, he believes, would help to filter out those who have no interest in academics, also referred to as "one and dones." While this idea seems great, Isenberg (2010) realizes the economic incentives of attracting superstars who happen to be disinterested in academics are too great to be overcome by the implementation of rules. He feels that athletic directors, coaches, and athletes themselves will continue to game the system no matter what. Isenberg's solution to the problem is consistent with Cline and Sack's, in that big-time basketball and football should admit they are professional and allow for players to receive money in addition to their scholarships. He believes that compensating student athletes through the schools themselves may not be feasible, but allowing for them to market their own names and images may be. This would require the removal of amateur status from these athletes—a very bold step. Isenberg (2010) stresses this as the only solution to a very complicated problem. With this system in place, those who have already created a brand for themselves through their play will be able to reap the benefits of that.

CONCLUSIONS

The combination of the conclusions on the issues of professionalism and money generation could be used as a rationale for paying these premium male athletes. Spending by men's basketball in order to profit and the moderate relationship indicating signs of subsidizing "other sports" would indicate that these programs are operating professionally. With these programs labeled as professional, it implies that the athletes are, in fact, employees. Every professional organization must compensate their employees fairly, and in this case it appears that they are not. Estimates of marginal revenue product for men's players would be one way to determine their fair level of compensation. Theoretically, these players should be

244

receiving something reasonable in comparison to these MRP estimates. If the NCAA were to ever address this issue, men's and women's sports would be examined separately. Solving the discrepancy between money generated and money received seems to be impossible at this point when considering all the NCAA laws that deal with amateurism. In addition, figuring out a system to compensate everyone fairly would be extremely difficult, considering that premium and nonpremium players generate different amounts of money, although both generate significant amounts.

NOTE

1. Kahn (2007) explains that the difference between the compensation an athlete receives through scholarship and his or her market value is the rent that the athletic departments collect.

REFERENCES

Brown, R. W., and R. T. Jewell. (2006). "The marginal revenue product of a women's college basketball player." *Industrial Relations: A Journal of Economy and Society* 45, 1, 96–101.

Brown, R. W., and R. T. Jewell. "Measuring marginal revenue product in college athletics: Updated estimates." In *Economics of College Sports*. J. L. Fizel and R. Fort, eds. Westport, CT: Greenwood Publishing Group.

Cline, A. (2009). "The NCAA's slaves." Retrieved July 24, 2010, from *American Spectator*: http://spectator.org/archives

CNN.com. (2014). Photos: Notable NCAA scandals. Retrieved March 25, 2015.

Dowling, W. (2001). "Big-time sports as academic prostitution." *Academic Questions* 14, 4, 82–90.

Harris, A., and R. Mac. (2011). "Stanford athletes had access to list of 'easy' classes." *California Watch*.

Isenberg, M. (2010). "NCAA should admit its March Madness players are professional." Retrieved July 24, 2010, from usnews.com: http://politics.usnews.com/opinion/articles

Kahn, L. (2007). "Cartel behavior and amateurism in college sports." *Journal of Economic Perspectives* 21, 1, 209–226.

Sack, A. (2008). "Should college athletes be paid?" Retrieved September 14, 2010, from CSMonitor.com: http://www.csmonitor.com

Sheehan, R. (2000). *Higher Education in Transition.* Westport, CT: Bergin and Garvey.

Shulman, J. L., and W. G. Bowen. (2001). "The game of life: College sports and educational values." *Journal of Philosophy of Sport* 29, 1, 87–95.

Weiner, J., and S. Berkowitz. (2011). "*USA Today* analysis finds $120K value in men's basketball scholarship." Retrieved March 23, 2015, from http://usatoday30.usatoday.com/sports/college/mensbasketball/2011-03-29-scholarship-worth-final-four_N.htm

Zimbalist, A. (1999). *Unpaid Professionalism: Commercialism and Conflict in Big-Time College Sports.* Princeton, NJ: Princeton University Press.

Zimmerman, A. (2013). "Contending with Chinese counterfeits: Culture, growth, and management responses." *Business Horizons* 56, 141–148.

SECTION 5

Fan and Player Behavior

A great focus in the sociology of sports is fan behavior. After all, it is the fans who buy the tickets to games, purchase the merchandise, and watch the games on television. Without fan support, sports would be very different compared to the way they currently are. One issue that has been studied by sociologists is the connection between alcohol consumption and sports. Clearly, there is a culture of drinking among athletes and fans alike, and there are numerous accounts of excessive drinking among both groups. In fact, much of the sports-related violence that occurs is fueled by large quantities of alcohol. Ultimately, some fans can drink excessively without getting in trouble, while others cannot. This section examines fan behavior as it relates to violence, sports gambling, and fantasy sports.

VIOLENCE AND SPORTS

In many respects, sports and violence go hand in hand. Contact sports like football, hockey, lacrosse, and boxing are very physical and often violent. Although penalties are given when hockey players fight or boxers punch below the belt, the fact remains that many people would argue that contact sports are, by definition, violent. Consider, for example, how common it is now for players to jostle after the whistle is blown in basketball, hit players when they are out of bounds in football, and blatantly punch someone in hockey. Sociologists of sports have long been interested in this issue and have studied violence among players and fans alike.

FAN VIOLENCE

Violence is not limited to players on the field; fans engage in violence as well. It has become fairly routine for opposing fans to taunt each other and get into fights at games and bars. Part of this is that for many fans supporting their teams is a very emotional endeavor. When their team gets soundly beaten, loses to a rival, or plays poorly in a playoff game, it is upsetting for many fans. Just as many players engage in compensatory masculinity during losses, many fans do as well. It is almost like they feel better about themselves by going down swinging, if you will. Sociologists have observed the phenomenon that when play gets rough on the field, ice, or court, it can carry over to the fans. When referees appear to have lost control of a game, fans are more likely to become violent in the stands.

One outgrowth of fan violence is celebratory violence. It has become commonplace for the fans of teams that win big games and championships to act in a variety of inappropriate and illegal ways. For decades, excited fans have stormed college basketball courts and football fields after a thrilling upset by the home team. In recent years, fans of mostly professional teams have taken this behavior and elevated it to the next level. It is commonplace today for fans to set fires, flip cars, vandalize private property, and engage in looting. After the Montreal Canadiens won the Stanley Cup in 1989, for example, the city went into a state of chaos with riots, fires, vandalism, and physical altercations between fans and the police. More recently, similar events occurred after the Red Sox came back from being down three games to zero to beat the Yankees in 2004. Sociologists relate this to the mob mentality that develops among people who are so caught up in the moment that they are not concerned with the consequences of their actions.

PLAYER VIOLENCE

There have been dozens of violent episodes perpetuated by athletes both on and off the field over the years. One condition that often prompts on-the-field violence is when there is a lopsided score in either a meaningful game or a game between rivals. This happened in the recent

(2015) Super Bowl between the Seahawks and the Patriots. The Seahawks were on the Patriots' 1-yard line and the quarterback, Russell Wilson, threw an interception to essentially end the game and cement the Patriots' victory. On the next play, members of the Seahawks defense grabbed and punched players on the opposing team.

One sociological explanation for this is that it is so emasculating for athletes to lose games that they feel the need to compensate for that in other ways. The idea is that they may lose the game, but at least they are going down with a fight. It is almost as if players believe that acting out physically somehow preserves the honor of the team being beaten. This exact scenario unfolded during the infamous "Malice at the Palace" in the game between the Indiana Pacers and the Detroit Pistons. It also prompted Todd Bertuzzi to essentially attack Dominic Moore at the end of an NHL game between the Vancouver Canucks and the Colorado Avalanche. Simply put, many athletes are so competitive and hard-wired to win that they do not have the emotional maturity to deal with losing.

In recent years, there have been several news stories about active and retired athletes who have been arrested for committing violent acts. Ray Rice of the Baltimore Ravens was arrested for punching his fiancée in an elevator. Adrian Peterson of the Minnesota Vikings was charged with child abuse after he hit his young son repeatedly with a switch. Jovan Belcher of the Kansas City Chiefs shot his girlfriend to death and then committed suicide. Warren Sapp, a retired NFL player, assaulted a prostitute in a hotel room. This is worrisome to many people, including the commissioner of the NFL, Roger Goodell, who suspended Rice and Peterson from the league based on their actions. Clearly, Goodell is concerned that NFL players who are arrested for the possession of unlicensed firearms and assault could affect the profitability of the very lucrative NFL brand.

ALCOHOL AND VIOLENCE

Obviously, fan violence would not be anywhere near as prevalent if fans did not consume alcohol. Sober fans do not generally taunt opposing fans and get into fights. Fan violence is the provenance of inebriated fans who drink excessively before, during, and after games. Tailgating, for example, is an American tradition that prompts many fans to arrive at sporting venues hours before games begin. Tens of thousands of college football fans arrive to schools like Penn State, Florida State, and the University of Southern California 2 or 3 days prior to a game. Fans cook food, consume alcohol, play games like cornhole and rings, and socialize for hours in parking lots all over the country. Of course, many sports fans are responsible consumers of alcohol who know when to say when. Unfortunately, many others drink so heavily that they lose their capacity to make good decisions. It is this group of fans who gets into trouble by taunting fans, driving drunk, vandalizing property, and so on.

Efforts have been made to curb alcohol consumption by raising the price of alcoholic beverages, limiting the number of beers that a person can buy at a given time, and suspending alcohol sales before the game ends. At professional sporting events, a 22-ounce beer costs upward of $8, and the number of beers that a fan can purchase at any given time is generally limited to two. Major League Baseball suspends beer sales after the seventh inning; the NHL suspends sales after the second intermission; and the NFL suspends sales after the third quarter. Although the intention of these policies is to promote responsible alcohol consumption, people can still get around that by tailgating before and after the game and asking friends to purchase alcohol for them.

In their piece entitled "A Situational Understanding of Violence Occurring at Professional Sporting Events," Eric Lesneskie and Robert Moschgat use routine activities theory to explain the growing rates of fan and player violence at sporting events. Using this criminological theory, violence at sporting events is thought to occur because of people's willingness to fight, the plethora of people available to fight, and the general lack of security. Of course, this is all compounded by the vast amounts of alcohol that many fans consume before and during games, the hypermasculinity of many fans, large crowds, long lines, inclement weather, and poor refereeing on the field.

In a follow-up piece, "A Consideration of Domestic Risk Factors in Professional Football," Moschgat and Lesneskie define domestic violence, identify its risk factors, and outline reasons why rates of domestic violence are so high among professional football players. Football players have such a high propensity for domestic violence because violent sports appear to not only reinforce masculinity, but to also contribute to a sense of hypermasculinity that, when connected with narcissism, ego, status, and jealousy, results in anger, frustration—and, ultimately, violence.

SPORTS GAMBLING

Although the connection may not seem readily apparent, sports and gambling go together. Millions of Americans bet on the outcomes of college and professional sporting events throughout the course of the year. There are now 10 states that have legalized sports gambling and another 8 that look like they will have it very soon. In these states, gamblers can go to the sports book room of an approved casino and make bets from $2 on up. They can make a variety of bets relating to the outcome of games and total points scored to the performance of individual players during a game or an entire season. Although sports betting has been recently legalized in many states, it is important to note that most of the gambling that takes place around the country is either done between individuals or through what is known as a bookmaker. Commonly called bookies, they collect bets, post odds, and manage the accounts of clients who make bets through them.

As with drinking, there are responsible gamblers and problem gamblers. Responsible gamblers bet within their means and do so in order to make watching the game a little more exciting. Responsible gamblers may buy a $10 square at a Super Bowl party or lay a modest sports bet here and there, but they are not consumed by the activity. They do not really research their picks or study trends, for example. Problem gamblers, on the other hand, are less likely to gamble within their means and are likely to make bigger bets and study their picks.

Many athletes also like to gamble. Professional athletes in a number of different sports play card games like poker on planes and buses while traveling to road games and even bet during practice. It is well known in golf, for example, that players make high-stakes bets during the practice rounds. Similarly, many basketball players bet on games of H-O-R-S-E after the official practice ends. Athletes have also been known to play credit-card roulette to see who pays for meals and create betting pools for other sporting events like the Daytona 500, March Madness, and the Kentucky Derby. Michael Jordan has openly discussed his passion for gambling. When he played for the Chicago Bulls, Jordan and his teammates would each put $100 in a pot that would be won by the player whose off-loaded suitcase would enter the airport baggage carousel first.

In "A Sociological Examination of Point Shaving: Reflections on Sports Gambling Culture in the United States," Moschgat and Lesneskie identify the role of criminological theory in explaining sports gambling. Specifically, they use differential association theory to illustrate that in order for point shaving to occur, players need to establish personal relationships with people who offer them financial incentives to underperform in games. Using the point-shaving scandals at City College of New York, Boston College, and Arizona State University, Moschgat and Lesneskie demonstrate that college basketball players engaged in point shaving after being offered money to manipulate scores by someone they either knew or owed money to.

FANTASY SPORTS

Fantasy sports have grown tremendously over the past 2 or 3 decades. The advent of the Internet has made it very easy for millions of Americans to manage fantasy teams and compete in leagues around the country. There are many different formats of fantasy sports. Some people play in leagues with their friends, while others play in more anonymous leagues with people they do not know. Some people play for fun and bragging rights rather than money. Meanwhile, others play in high-stakes leagues with huge payouts. In recent years, 1-day and 1-week fantasy leagues have also emerged, where people compete over a much shorter period of time.

The Brandon Lang piece traces the history of fantasy sports and explains how fantasy sports represent a kind of conflict of interest for people. More specifically, many fans have been in the difficult position of having to choose between drafting the best player in a fantasy draft and being loyal to their favorite team. Because so many fantasy players have drafted players from teams that are rivals with their favorite teams, one can argue that fantasy sports are lessening the intensity of the rivalries that exist between teams such as the Red Sox and Yankees or the Cowboys and Eagles.

CHAPTER FIFTEEN

A Situational Understanding of Violence Occurring at Professional Sporting Events

BY **ERIC G. LESNESKIE** AND **ROBERT S. MOSCHGAT**

"It's like a version of prison ... If a guy messes with you one time and gets away with it, you're in trouble. So my rookie year, I got into two or three fights. You just can't back down. I don't care if you were scared or not. I don't care who it was, you don't let anyone disrespect you and you don't back down."

—Michael Strahan, NFL Hall of Fame, defensive end,
New York Giants, *Men's Journal* magazine (Rodrick, 2015)

INTRODUCTION

On Sunday, September 21 , 2014, at least two violent events occurred during the course of the NFL game between the Washington Redskins and the Philadelphia Eagles at Lincoln Financial Field. On

255

the field, players from Washington and Philadelphia engaged in violence beyond the explicit rules of the game. This fight was started when Eagles quarterback Nick Foles was aggressively tackled by the Redskins' defensive lineman Chris Baker after Foles threw an interception (Suskind, 2014). This type of play is common in professional football, as defenders are often taught to "hunt" the quarterback after a pass is intercepted. After Foles was hunted, an Eagles offensive lineman quickly came to Foles's aid by retaliating against the Redskins' defensive lineman. For a short period of time, there were punches, pushes, and shoves between the two teams near the Redskins' sideline until the referees separated the players (Suskind, 2014). There was nothing really unusual about this fight because similar situations occur each Sunday during the course of the NFL season. Yet, this game captured our attention, along with the other documented violent act that occurred in the seating sections between fans. The instigation for the fight is unknown, but it was not over team allegiances because the individuals involved were all fans of the Eagles.[1] Spanning numerous rows of seats, this brawl involved eight to nine individuals (two of whom were female) and resulted in ejections from the stadium, arrests, and injuries (Campitelli, 2014).[2]

Unfortunately, these two types of violent incidents do not just occur at the professional level, but at all levels. Moreover, football is not the only sport where these violent incidents occur.[3] As indicated by our opening quote, violence is believed to be a necessary part of sports (Rodrick, 2015; Shields, 1999; Bredemeier and Shields, 1984). The casual sports fan can recall incidents of a baseball player charging the mound after being hit by a pitch, a basketball player pushing an opponent after a hard foul, and a hockey player removing his gloves and throwing punches after being high-sticked. These are all common sports scenarios that result in spontaneous acts of violence outside the explicit rules of the respective games.

Often, these acts are viewed as just a normal function of sports. So much so, that the violence is quickly forgotten or in some instances celebrated by being shown repeatedly on sports highlight shows (see Fields, Collins, and Comstock, 2007). According to Paul (2003), NHL games with teams that are known for fighting produces an increase in fan attendance and approval, thereby lionizing violence between and among players. Additionally, Zillman and Paulus (1993) indicate a positive relationship between fan satisfaction and the levels of violence and aggression associated with a particular sport. As such, player violence is attractive, normalized, and glorified in the professional setting. For example, a simple Internet search can produce numerous accounts of fans engaging in violence either before, during, or after contests of all types. Fights between fans are the most frequent type of spectator violence occurring at sporting events (Kudlac, 2010).

This chapter identifies and explains the reasons why spontaneous violence occurs at professional sporting events. Within the context of sports violence, violent events occur in two different spheres. The first one is the playing surface,[4] when two or more players engage in unsanctioned physical violence after the end of a play or outside the explicit rules of the game. The second one is at the stadium[5] either before, during, or after a sporting contest, when two or more fans engage in physical violence. The focus of our understanding is on the situational characteristics of place, because these violent incidents take place in micro-places within the larger confines of the stadium. Specifically, routine activities theory is used to explain facets of both player and fan violence. Within this framework, subcultural theories of masculinity will be employed to help explain offender motivation. This chapter concludes with recommendations on how to reduce violence at professional sporting events.

THE IMPORTANCE OF PLACE

For decades, criminologists have noted the importance of the relationship between spatial neighborhood conditions and crime (see Weisburd, Groff, and Yang, 2012). This line of thought has remained strong, but newer research is now focused on smaller units of analysis by analyzing the effects of spatial and situational characteristics of micro-places (i.e., street corners, bars) on crime and violence within the macro-place level (i.e., city, neighborhood). Using this taxonomy, stadia can be viewed as macro-places consisting of a number of smaller sections of seats divided by barriers and levels. These smaller seating sections are micro-places that are analogous to street corners in a neighborhood. Each seating section is a socially unique micro-place with its own characteristics (see Madensen and Eck, 2008). For example, one seating section might have more families and children, with all the fans sharing the same team allegiances.[6] Another seating section in the stadium may have more fans who are male, ages 21 to 25, with mixed team allegiances. The social makeup of the seating section will therefore have an influence on the behavior that is associated with a particular section. The seating section with more male fans with mixed team allegiances, who are between the ages of 21 to 25, will most likely have greater alcohol consumption and a greater propensity for physical violence than the other section comprised of families and children with the same team allegiances (see Madensen and Eck, 2008). Intoxicated male fans may react violently to perceived slights compared to sober fans or those in the company of families and children (see Madensen and Eck, 2008; Johnson, 2004).

Other characteristics of the situational environment—crowded conditions, weather, guardianship, and space reputation—can also influence violence. Crowded conditions put limitations on mobility and increase unwanted physical contact between fans, which may increase the levels of aggression and violence for the seating section (Madensen and Eck, 2008; Russell, 2004). Research also indicates that there is a relationship between weather and fan violence. More specifically, as the temperature increases at a sporting event, the likelihood of violence increases (Reifman, Larrick, and Fein, 1991; Dewar, 1979). Additionally, each section of a stadium usually has some form of guardianship, typically an usher or security guard. The role that the guardian takes, either passive or aggressive, can vary, thereby influencing the behavior occurring in each section (see Madensen and Eck, 2008). If guardianship is passive, the area can get a reputation as a place where violence is tolerated, further increasing the commission of these acts (Stott and Adang, 2005). The field and sidelines are also micro-places within the greater macro-level of the stadium. Like the usher or security guard, how a referee controls the game and how a coach controls the crowded sidelines can influence the behavior in these spaces. Each micro-space is distinct with its own characteristics and forms of guardianship, which ultimately affects the behavior of fans seated in a given area.

THEORETICAL UNDERSTANDING OF STADIUM VIOLENCE

Most criminological theories have been developed to further understand street crime and violence such as theft, assault, robbery, and homicide. Often, the motives behind these crimes are rooted in economic or personal gain. In a sense, violence occurring at sporting events is unique because most of the incidents taking place are assaults or fights between players or fans that are not motivated by economic or personal gain. Moreover, the sporting environment is one where generally there is fierce competition and something at stake for both the players and the fans. Without question, the competitive orientation of sports, in conjunction with the ever changing emotional states of many fans in the stadium, contributes to a greater proclivity for violence in this venue compared to outside environments. Upon adding often copious amounts of alcohol consumed by the fans, the odds of violence increase even more (Johnson, 2004; Roberts and Benjamin, 2000). Within this vacuum of competition, emotion, alcohol consumption, and the unique situational characteristics of stadia, the opportunities for violent behavior can intensify drastically. Although the setting and the motives may be different, the mechanisms that lead to violent events at sporting venues are similar to violence that occurs on the street. Accordingly, aspects of existing theories used to understand street crime can be applied to stadium violence.

The routine activities perspective suggests that crime and violence are direct results of opportunities that are present in the situational environment (Cohen and Felson, 1979). Specifically, the opportunity to commit criminal acts occurs when there is a convergence in time and space of a motivated offender, suitable target, and the lack of capable guardianship (Cohen and Felson, 1979). According to this theory, anyone can be a motivated offender if the opportunity presents itself. A suitable target could be a person or physical object; the lack of capable guardianship could be the absence of lighting, security cameras, or a police officer. For example, let's imagine that it is two o'clock in the morning on a dark and deserted street with nonworking street lights (lack of capable guardianship). An intoxicated young woman is walking down the street with an expensive purse (suitable target). On the same street, a heroin addict is lying behind a dumpster and is in need of money to feed his addiction (motivated offender). The addict (motivated offender) sees the intoxicated young woman with the expensive purse (suitable target), and because the street is deserted and dark (lack of capable guardianship), the addict robs the purse from the young woman. This is an example of how a criminal or violent event takes place when the three components of routine activities theory converge in the same situational environment.

Using routine activities theory as a guide, we can adapt and apply the three components to understand the violence that occurs at professional sporting events. With the high stakes of professional athletic competitions, there will likely be verbal confrontations both on the field and off. The presence or absence of guardianship (a characteristic of the situational environment) at sporting events is a key factor which influences whether a verbal argument escalates to physical violence. Take an NFL football game as an example. Football is a highly violent game, and after a play, there is often "trash talk" between players. This is controlled by the rules, which are ultimately enforced by the referees. Like a police officer, referees have some discretion on whether or not to enforce a penalty.

Often, excessive trash talking leads to minor pushing and shoving after the play. Although referees often allow the players latitude in their physicality and trash talking by not throwing flags, giving warnings, or enforcing penalties, this latitude can quickly escalate to violence after the play. With hockey, for example, one of the reasons for the plethora of fights is due to a referee failing to or unwilling to call a penalty, and the hockey players feel that they must protect themselves from these uncalled fouls (Colburn, 1986). In these instances, the player who initiates the fight is doing so because of the lack of guardianship by the referee. On the field or ice, the referee's willingness to enforce penalties and control excessive trash talk is essentially guardianship or the lack thereof.

Similar to referees on the field, stadium personnel have the guardianship role in the seating sections. Usually, in a seating section, there is at least one usher or security guard who is tasked with keeping civility. When fights between fans occur, they often stem from verbal altercations that escalate into physical violence. If one of the fans decides not to continue or the verbal confrontation is noticed by an intervening usher or security guard, the escalation process often stops. However, if the fans are willing to continue and there is no intervention, there is an increased potential for physical violence. In sum, stadium personnel who give latitude to the fans may produce a lack of guardianship, which hastens the transition from verbal abuse to physical violence.

The motivated offender and suitable target components of routine activities theory are not directly applicable to violence at professional sporting events. These incidents often involve the willful use of violence by two or more individuals. The suitable target and motivated offender components might be simultaneously applicable to each of the individuals involved in the fight. For instance, when arguments escalate into physical violence, both of the individuals are motivated to continue with the confrontation (motivated offenders), and both believe that they have the advantage over the other individual, either physically or in terms of the rightness of the argument (suitable target). The players or fans in these situations can be both the motivated offender and the suitable target.

With street crime, an offender can be motivated by economic need or want. With regard to stadium violence, it is important to ask what makes an individual a motivated offender to engage in physical violence at professional sporting events. The initial reasons that instigate an argument between fans are often trivial and shaped by the characteristics of the situational

260

environment such as fan demographics, crowding, outside temperature, and alcohol consumption. These instigating acts, like spilling a beer of an opposing fan due to the crowded conditions, can provide the tipping point toward a verbal confrontation. Moreover, these instigating acts, in conjunction with a lack of guardianship, feed into and are exacerbated by a subculture, in particular, masculinity, which leads to violence after the initial verbal confrontation.

Traits of masculinity include aggression, strength, dominance, competitiveness, and the controlling of emotions (see Copes, Hochstetler, and Forsyth, 2013). At a young age, males learn masculinity, in part through sports by placing value on the aforementioned qualities (Messner and Sabo, 1994). When males exhibit any characteristics that are the opposite of the masculine qualities, they are viewed negatively and often sanctioned (Messner and Sabo, 1994). These masculine traits are exhibited on the field by male players and coaches, as well as off the field by male fans. Kreager (2007) found a positive relationship between adolescent involvement in masculine contact sports and people's likelihood of fighting off the field. In order to avoid the ultimate insult of being viewed as a "wuss," "pussy," or "fag" within the masculine subculture, males often feel compelled to prove their manhood by fighting. If the questioning or testing of manhood takes place in public spaces, males are more likely to try to validate and display their masculinity by engaging in violence and aggression (Copes et al., 2013; Pappas, McKenry, and Catlett, 2004; Weinstein, Smith, and Wiesenthal, 1995; Messner, 1990).

A central part of masculinity involves males being respected for being tough. When males do not stand up for themselves, their masculinity is often questioned, and they can lose their status in their own eyes and in the eyes of others (see Copes et al., 2013). In part, this parallels Elijah Anderson's research (1999) concerning how adolescents navigate violent inner-city neighborhoods. The code of the street is based primarily upon masculinity and respect. By not showing the ability or willingness to fight for material and nonmaterial possessions, this opens up vulnerability and a loss of status in the neighborhood. A key part of this code is retaliation or fighting back. If a male is punched in the face, then, to live up to the street code, he must retaliate violently.

According to Copes et al. (2013), there is a similar code of honor among middle-class males in the South. Bars or taverns can be seen as micro-places that are analogous to professional sporting events. They are public spaces, where men have the opportunity to display their masculinity (see Copes et al., 2013). In bars, with the help of alcohol, males frequently feel that they are incapable of turning away from simple slights or insults that may go ignored in the other venues. Consequently, in these hypermasculine settings, the only option is to fight. Similarly, a sporting event is a hypermasculine public setting, where slights and insults cannot be ignored. Add in alcohol to the mix, and the propensity for violence increases for the venue (Johnson, 2004; Roberts and Benjamin, 2000). The masculine subculture interacting with the situational environment of inner-city streets, bars, or stadia influences how males behave in these public spaces.

Comparable to behaviors in the stands, masculinity also shapes the behaviors of players on the field. Whether it is playing while injured, engaging in sanctioned acts of violence, or as the opening quote from NFL Hall of Famer Michael Strahan indicates, fighting to maintain a code of honor, the masculine subculture is ever present in male-based professional sports. Strahan's quote suggests that violence is a necessity for respect and protection in the NFL (see Rodrick, 2015). Just like there is a code of the street, there is a "code of the field," where players feel they must fight to be respected by others or risk being victimized. In hockey, for example, fighting is a semi-sanctioned event, where players who choose not to fight are chastised and emasculated. This is because males are taught from a young age to compete and not back down from a physical confrontation (see Copes et al., 2013). This is reflective of prevailing gender norms, which hold that males on the playing surface have a reputation to uphold.

Characteristics of the situational environment such as fan demographics, crowded conditions, weather, and guardianship provide the tipping point for small slights or verbal disagreements to turn to violent events. In the same space and time during this escalation process without guardianship, the fans or players involved with the verbal argument perceive that they are correct, that they can easily physically victimize the others involved, and/or that they must maintain the confrontation for fear of emasculation. The agitated fan or player has now morphed into the motivated offender, and a similar process can happen simultaneously for the others involved in the confrontation. In sum, motivated offenders, suitable targets, lack of capable guardians, and other characteristics of the situational environment intersect to produce a violent event.

ESCALATION TO BRAWLS

Up to this point, our discussion has simply concerned the confrontation between two individuals, but how does this interaction turn into a multi-person brawl at the sports venue?

In stadia, there is a large number of fans or players who are crowded—even sometimes overcrowded—into a small area. Off the field, the seating is often cramped, and fans are in close proximity to each other. If there is a confrontation between two fans in this confined area, other spectators can do one of three things. First, they can instigate the confrontation by encouraging or chanting at the infuriated fans. Second, they can ignore or try to distance themselves from the situation. Third, they can try to act as guardians and prevent or break up the physical act. Due to the confines, bystanders can become victimized by inadvertently being pushed, punched, kicked, or having food or drink spilled.[7] Now, the victimized bystander becomes a motivated offender because they have been wronged and must correct that wrong by becoming an actor in the fight.

Similarly, on a football field, if a quarterback is hit late and roughed up by the defender, often you see teammates coming to the aid of their quarterback by pushing or getting in the face of the defender.[8] This scenario can quickly escalate by the defender pushing or punching back, and then more players become involved within the tight confines of the field. We see comparable situations on the baseball diamond with bench-clearing brawls. In most incidents, the benches clear to try and separate the two opposing players, typically a pitcher and batter. But as the two groups mass, punches are missed and landed unintentionally on another individual. The unintentionally hit player feels that he has been wronged and becomes a motivated offender by engaging in the physical violence. Therefore, simple fights at professional sporting events, both on the playing surface and in the seating sections, can become contagious, which leads to a sequence of retaliatory acts.

EXAMPLES OF PLAYER-INVOLVED VIOLENCE

During the course of a season, across all professional sports, there are numerous examples of players engaging in violence on the field. Some of these incidents are so mainstream and common that they do not garner much attention. But some become glorified and are reminisced about on sports networks. The famous "Malice at the Palace" between fans and the members of the Indiana Pacers basketball team comes to mind, or when MLB Hall of Fame pitcher Nolan Ryan repeatedly punched Robin Ventura after he charged the mound.

Other violent incidents are recalled because of serious injuries or criminal charges that resulted. In 2004, Todd Bertuzzi of the NHL's Vancouver Canucks punched Steve Moore

263

of the Colorado Avalanche in retaliation for a "dirty" play that received no penalty weeks prior, resulting in a Canucks player missing games due to injury (see Kudlac, 2010). When Bertuzzi hit Moore on the side of the head, Moore fell to the ice, suffering a severe neck injury that ended his playing career (see Kudlac, 2010). Bertuzzi was suspended from the NHL and was criminally charged; he pleaded guilty and received one year on probation (see Kudlac, 2010). With this example, there was initially a lack of guardianship by the referees for the failure to enforce the penalty weeks prior. What resulted was Bertuzzi's belief that he must retaliate against the Avalanche and engage in violence to protect the team in the future because the referees were not enforcing penalties (see Colburn, 1986). By retaliating, the Canucks were sending a message that they were not going to back down, and that dirty plays against them will not be tolerated, living up to the informal code of the NHL.

Fights in Major League Baseball are relatively rare, but when they happen, benches often clear, and the incidents are given widespread attention on highlights shows. On April 20, 2014, in a game between the Pittsburgh Pirates and the Milwaukee Brewers, there was such an incident (see Jaffe, 2014). The incident started when the Brewers' Carlos Gomez hit what appeared to be a home run off of Pirates pitcher Gerrit Cole (Jaffe, 2014). Gomez celebrated the apparent home run by throwing his bat, but the ball fell short and he ended up with a triple (Jaffe, 2014). Cole took offense and had a verbal confrontation with Gomez. The benches and bullpen cleared for both teams. Punches were thrown on both sides, resulting in Gomez, a Pirates player coming off the bench, and a Brewers coach being ejected (Jaffe, 2014). Prior to this incident, Gomez had a history of inciting violence because of his perceived arrogance and admiration of his home runs.[9] This admiration is often seen as offensive by the opposing team. In order not to lose face, the opposing team members feel they must verbalize their displeasure to the batter. Specifically, with this situation, Cole calls out and insults Gomez. Gomez takes offense to this slight, and now we have two motivated offenders, because both have challenged each other's masculinity. When the benches clear, the teams are providing guardianship to their teammates, who are involved in the confrontation. The bench players try to separate and/or protect the two fighting players. The two teams crowd together at the scene, and when punches are thrown, individuals can be inadvertently hit. This, then, incites more motivated offenders because those who have been victimized feel they must retaliate—and the violence becomes contagious.

EXAMPLES OF FAN VIOLENCE

During the 2014 NFL season, there were numerous violent incidents that received considerable attention and called into question whether it was safe to attend these events. At the University of Phoenix Stadium in Arizona, there was a fight between fans of the San Francisco 49ers and the Arizona Cardinals.[10] During this brawl, there were about a dozen fans of both teams involved, and quickly the fighting spread throughout the area. With blood clearly visible on the stadium floor, the fans continued fighting while tumbling down the steps of the seating section. A security guard tried to intervene, but struggled to gain control over the brawlers and was struck and choked in the melee. With this fight, it appears that there was a lack of capable guardianship at the start of the incident; then, when security started to intervene, it was too late. At this point in the escalation process, the motivated offenders disregarded the role of the stadium personnel. Of course, this is speculative, but since fans of both teams were involved, the initial instigating factor might have been some slight against one team or the other. A slight of a fan's team could be seen as a challenge, and the fan may feel that he needs to react violently. The cramped and crowded seating in the section helped to expedite the escalation process. Fans who may have been trying to break up the fight or were simply bystanders unintentionally got punched or shoved; thus, they became motivated offenders and responded with subsequent physical violence. Similar to on the field, fan violence at sporting events can be catching.

Another incident during the 2014 NFL season occurred in a restroom at Levi's Stadium, home to the San Francisco 49ers. This incident made national headlines, with one victim being severely injured and partially paralyzed (CBS News, 2014). Like the incident in Arizona, the situational environment, especially the crowded conditions, helped to trigger the initial confrontation. Interestingly, this fight involved 49ers fans and appears to have nothing to do with the game itself. The incident apparently started when one of the victims tapped one of the perpetrators on the shoulder and pointed out an open urinal in the crowded restroom (CBS News, 2014). Offended in some way, the perpetrators (brothers) punched the victim and then attacked the victim's cousin, who appeared to be trying to intervene (CBS News, 2014). When viewing the video of the incident, throughout the confrontation, you can hear bystanders yelling for the fight to stop. Yet, the incident happened in a matter of seconds and too quickly for any real bystander intervention or guardianship. For masculine identity maintenance purposes, the two assailants (motivated offenders) may have felt that they could easily attack the victims (suitable targets) with little immediate consequences. The incident stops when both victims have been knocked to the ground.

By conducting a simple YouTube search, the videos of these incidents can be viewed online. These videos provide the opportunity to see the physical violence between fans. Unfortunately, with these videos and many others posted, it is not possible to determine what the initial causes of the fight were. Thus, the motivations for why a fan decides to become involved remains speculative. These videos do, though, offer insights into the level of guardianship and how an incident can quickly escalate into a brawl involving many fans.

CONCLUSION

In this chapter, we look to the situational characteristics of micro-places and used routine activities theory as a foundation for understanding violence at professional sporting events. Place characteristics such as weather, crowding, and fan demographics play a role, but guardianship is a key component, with presence or absence influencing whether an incident occurs or whether a minor altercation escalates into a major brawl. Individuals involved with the confrontation can simultaneously be the motivated offender and suitable target in situations when there is mutual hostility. Offenders, in these situations, become motivated when their manhood or masculinity is called into question and feel that they must fight to maintain their status. When a motivated offender perceives that the other individual (or suitable target) has wronged him or her and when there is a lack of guardianship, the violent event can occur. All of these components must converge at the same time and space in the situational environment in order for the escalation of verbal confrontation to morph into physical violence.

There is little doubt that violence at sporting events can be costly and produce negative results for all those involved (see Fields, Collins, and Comstock, 2007; Campo, Poulos, and Sipple, 2005). On the field, penalties, ejections, injuries, and monetary fines of players can result. In extreme cases, the negative outcomes can be the culmination of an athletic career and/or criminal charges filed against the offender. Negative collective team outcomes can also occur when key players are ejected or penalized and their absence of play contributes to a loss. Off the playing surface and in the seating sections, the costs can be criminal penalties, being removed from the venue, loss of ticket privileges, injuries, and also the disruption of the game environment for other spectators (see Madensen and Eck, 2008). With all of these negatives, the fans, media, and teams are paying more attention to how to prevent these acts and to provide a better overall experience.

One such effort was the creation of the Fans Against Violence (FAV) organization, established by fans to raise awareness and stop violence at sporting events. This national group grew out of the San Francisco Bay area in 2011, after two well-publicized incidents. First, a Giants fan was brutally beaten at a game at Dodger Stadium between the San Francisco Giants and the Los Angeles Dodgers, and later that same year, there were numerous fights and shootings occurring during and after an NFL game between the Oakland Raiders and the San Francisco 49ers. A big part of this group's efforts is to provide game day safety tips for fans and also to provide instructions on how to use the NFL, MLB, and MLS game day hotlines to report stadium disturbances (see www.fansagainstviolence.org). The ultimate goal of this organization is to provide a violence-free environment for fans.

Based on routine activities theory, to reduce violence, the situational environment needs more capable guardians.[11] These guardians can be informal, such as the fans who use the game day hotlines to report disturbances or formal guardians, such as uniformed stadium personnel. With more potential guardians, there will be fewer opportunities for verbal confrontations to escalate into physical violence. By increasing the visibility and availability of information about the game day hotlines, there will be additional informal fan guardians. Moreover, the training, visibility, and number of ushers or security guards needs to be increased in order to protect fans and also the stadium personnel themselves (Madensen and Eck, 2008; Heinzmann, 2002). The stadium personnel are often volunteers or part-time, minimally paid employees with limited enforcement powers (see Madensen and Eck, 2008). Not only does this reduce their authority in the eyes of fans, but the stadium personnel may not be willing to risk their safety in situations that could potentially lead to violence. Having visible sworn law enforcement officers at the stadium could reduce the number of potentially motivated offenders due to the respect of their authority. Further, with only one usher or security guard per section, brewing incidents might not be noticed until it is too late (Madensen and Eck, 2008). By incorporating CCTV, stadium personnel can be directed to disturbances more quickly, and this adds to the layers of guardianship (Madensen and Eck, 2008). On the field, the better training of referees to uniformly enforce penalties (guardianship) to increase player's perception of fairness will prevent players from taking to violence in order to protect themselves or their teammates.

Increased attention has been directed at violence occurring at sporting events of all levels, and examining the situational environment of stadia allows for a starting point to better understand this phenomenon. Although much attention is given, empirically current research is limited as to the true extent of violence and why or how these events originate. More descriptive knowledge is needed to gauge the state of violence at professional sporting events. For instance, are these events increasing, decreasing, or remaining stable? In the situational realm, future studies should investigate the types of guardianship that are effective at reducing violence and the reasons why a player or fan would become a motivated offender and perceive their opponents as suitable targets.

NOTES

1. The instigating factors could be related to the game, such as the disrespecting of teams or players. Or the starting factors could be by accidents such as spilling food or drink, bumping into other fans in the crowded seating sections, the blocking of another fan's view of the playing surface, or being inadvertently hit by a punch by an opposing player.

2. An innocent bystander was injured by being pushed into the seats. He reportedly suffered broken ribs (Campitelli, 2014).

3. Violent incidents happen at all levels; however, in this chapter, we will focus specifically on violence occurring at professional sporting events. Additionally, there are far too many scenarios of violence at sporting events to cover comprehensively in one chapter; thus, we will focus on only a few scenarios and sports.

4. In this chapter, we use the term "playing surface" to include the field, court, and ice.

5. Stadium and arena are used interchangeably in this chapter.

6. Female fans are also involved with violence at sporting events, as was the case with the fight between fans at the Redskins and Eagles game in September 2014, but the frequency in which females are involved is less than that of males (see Madensen and Eck, 2008; Coakley, 2007).

7. Family or friends who are inadvertently victimized can also cause someone to become involved in violence.

8. Recall the incident between the Philadelphia Eagles and Washington Redskins.

9. In 2013, Gomez got into a similar confrontation in a game with the Atlanta Braves (Jaffe, 2014).
10. As of March 9, 2015, the video of this fight is widely available on the Internet.
11. Other avenues to reduce violence by altering the situational characteristics include limiting sales and consumption of alcohol, implementing metal detectors prior to entering the stadium, and clearly displaying the consequences for creating a disturbance at the venues (see Madensen and Eck, 2008).

REFERENCES

Anderson, E. (1999). *Code of the Street: Decency, Violence, and the Moral Life of the Inner City*. New York: W. W. Norton.

Bredemeier, B., and D. Shields. (1984). "The utility of moral stage analysis in the investigation of athletic aggression." *Sociology of Sport Journal* 1, 138–149.

Campitelli, E. (2014). "Ugly fight broke out in stands at Sunday's Eagles game, too." *Comcast SportsNet*. Retrieved March 17, 2015: http://www.csnphilly.com/blog/700-level/ugly-fight-broke-out-stands- sundays-eagles-game-too

Campo, S., G. Poulos, and J. W. Sipple. (2005). "Prevalence and profiling: Hazing among college students and points of intervention." *American Journal of Health Behavior* 29, 137–149.

CBS News. (2014). Brothers charged with felonies in bathroom fight at 49ers game. *CBS News*. Retrieved March 15, 2015: http://www.cbsnews.com/news/brothers-charged-with-felonies-in-bathroom-fight-at 49ers-game/

Coakley, J. (2007). *Sports in Society: Issues and Controversies*. Ninth edition. Boston: McGraw-Hill.

Cohen, L., and M. Felson. (1979). "Social change and crime rate trends: A routine activity approach." *American Sociological Review* 44, 588–608.

Colburn, K. (1986). "Deviance and legitimacy in ice hockey." *Sociological Quarterly* 27, 63–74.

Copes, H., A. Hochstetler, and C. Forsyth. (2013). "Peaceful warriors: Codes for violence among adult male bar fighters." *Criminology* 51, 761–794.

Dewar, C. (1979). "Spectator fights at professional baseball games." *Review of Sport and Leisure* 4, 12–25.

Fields, S., C. Collins, and R. Comstock. (2007). "Conflict on the courts: A review of sports-related violence literature." *Trauma Violence Abuse* 8, 359–369.

Heinzmann, G. (2002). "Parental violence in youth sports." *Parks and Recreation* 37, 66–73.

Jaffe, J. (2014). "Carlos Gomez's celebration of non-homer provokes Brewers-Pirates brawl." *Sports Illustrated*. Retrieved March 15, 2015: http://www.si.com/mlb/strikezone/2014/04/20/carlos-gomez-brewers-pirates-brawl

Johnson, K. (2004). *Underage Drinking*. Washington, DC: US Department of Justice, Office of Community Oriented Policing Services.

Kreager, D. (2007). "Unnecessary roughness? School sports, peer networks, and male adolescent violence." *American Sociological Review* 72, 705–724.

Kudlac, C. (2010). *Fair or Foul: Sports and Criminal Behavior in the United States*. Santa Barbara, CA: Praeger.

Madensen, T., and J. Eck. (2008). *Spectator Violence in Stadiums*. Problem-Oriented Guides for Police. Washington, DC: Center for Problem-Oriented Policing.

Messner, M. (1990). "Boyhood, organized sports, and the construction of masculinities." *Journal of Contemporary Ethnography* 18, 416–444.

Messner, M., and D. F. Sabo. (1994). *Sex, Violence and Power in Sports: Rethinking Masculinity*. Berkeley, CA: Crossing Press.

Pappas, N., P. McKenry, and B. Catlett. (2004). "Athlete aggression on the rink and off the ice." *Men and Masculinities* 6, 291–312.

Paul, R. (2003). "Variations in NHL attendance." *American Journal of Economics and Sociology* 62, 345–364.

Reifman, A., R. Larrick, and S. Fein. (1991). "Temper and temperature on the diamond: The heat-aggression relationship in major-league baseball." *Personality and Social Psychology Bulletin* 17, 580–585.

Roberts, J., and C. & Benjamin. (2000). "Spectator violence in sports: A North American perspective." *European Journal on Criminal Policy and Research* 8, 163–181.

Rodrick, S. (2015). "Michael Strahan's mad rush." *Men's Journal* 24, 46–51, 82–83.

Russell, G. (2004). "Sport riots: A social-psychological review." *Aggression and Violent Behavior* 9, 353–378.

Shields, E. (1999). "Intimidation and violence by males in high school athletics." *Adolescence* 34, 503–521.

Stott, C., and C. Adang. (2005). "Crowd dynamics, policing, and 'hooliganism' at 'Euro2004.'" Research report for the Economic and Social Research Council.

Suskind, A. (2014). "Redskins, Eagles fight expected to draw a 'ton of fines.'" *Sports Illustrated*. Retrieved March 17, 2015: http://www.si.com/nfl/2014/09/21/redskins-eagles-fightafter-illegal-hit-nick-foles

Weinstein, M., D. Smith, and D. Wiesenthal. (1995). "Masculinity and hockey violence." *Sex Roles* 33, 831–847.

Weisburd, D., E. Groff, and S. Yang. (2012). *The Criminology of Place: Street Segments and Our Understanding of the Crime Problem.* Oxford, UK: Oxford University Press.

Zillman, D., and P. & Paulus. (1993). "Spectators: Reactions to sports events and effects on athletic performance." In R. Singer, M. Murphey, and L. Tennant, eds. *Handbook of Research on Sport Psychology* (pp. 600–619). New York: Macmillan.

CHAPTER SIXTEEN

A Consideration of Domestic Risk Factors in Professional Football

BY ROBERT S. MOSCHGAT AND ERIC G. LESNESKIE

"The most glorified sports in this society are those that emphasize physical domination and subjugation. In these sports, men's bodies, particularly as weapons of physical balance become sites of power."

—M.J. Kane and L.J. Disch, 1998

INTRODUCTION

The graphic video (released by TMZ on September 8, 2014) of former Baltimore Ravens running back Ray Rice knocking his fiancée unconscious in an elevator has brought considerable attention to the issue of domestic violence, especially among professional football players in the United States (Wertheim and Kaplan, 2014). Based on ex-Carolina Panthers defensive end Greg Hardy's convictions for two domestic violence charges in July 2014 and allegations that Ray McDonald, a defensive end for the San Francisco 49ers, struck his pregnant fiancée, the National Football League (NFL) continues to face tremendous scrutiny for its handling of players accused and convicted of domestic violence.

Interestingly, football is explicitly designed to allow men to express their masculinity and virility by physically dominating their opponents through "the sanctioned use of aggression/ force/violence" (Bryson, 1987). Welch (1997) argues that the American culture's fascination with the controlled violence in sports encourages violence outside the sports arena. A time-series analysis revealed the frequency of women's emergency room visits for injuries consistent with violence increases in Northern Virginia when the Washington Redskins win football games, even when controlling for days of the week, months, years, and special holidays (White et al., 1992). The authors of this study theorized "that viewing the successful use of violent acts may give the identifying fan a sense of license to dominate his surroundings" (White et al., 1992, p. 157).

It should be no surprise that athletes who compete in an arena where the ability to dominate their opponents through aggression and physical force is at an absolute premium likely results in hypermasculinity (Welch, 1997). Combined with the status and prestige awarded to football players, hypermasculinity exudes sexual virility (Messner, 1990; Messner and Sabo, 1990). Bryson (1987) argues that raising male athletes to heroic status serves to subjugate women, encouraging narcissism and creating a sense of entitlement among the athletes. The consequence may serve to encourage violence toward women (Welch, 1997). The purpose of this essay is to explore risk factors associated with domestic violence in theoretical terms and to provide a more comprehensive understanding of the proliferation of domestic violence among professional football players.

WHAT IS DOMESTIC VIOLENCE?

Domestic violence encompasses a wide range of crimes ranging from simple assault, aggravated assault, sexual assault, rape, and homicide. The damage done by domestic violence transcends physical harm and is usually accompanied by psychological trauma, anxiety, stress, sleep deprivation, social isolation, and fear for the victim and those who care about

274

her (Carrington and Phillips, 2003). For the purposes of this inquiry, our analysis is limited to theorizing about incidents involving male offenders and female victims.

In the United States, domestic violence constitutes 20 percent of the nonfatal violence toward women, compared to just 3 percent of nonfatal violence toward men (Rennison, 2003). Estimates indicate only 25 to 50 percent of female domestic victims report the incident to the police (Tjaden and Thoennes, 2000; Rennison and Welchans, 2000). The vast majority of these incidents are limited to shoving, slapping, and hitting and do not require medical attention. However, female victims are reluctant to seek medical attention even when it is necessary (Greenfield et al., 1998).

Due to the inconsistent operationalization of definitions of domestic violence, it is difficult to ascertain a reliable and valid measure of the extent of domestic violence in the United States (Mears, 2003). Quantifying domestic violence in professional football is an even more daunting task, as the teams attempt to insulate themselves from negative publicity and protect violent athletes (Welch, 1997). The National Violence Against Women Survey (NVAWS) found that nearly 25 percent of women experienced a physical or sexual assault during their lifetimes, and 1.5 percent of women had been assaulted in the 12 months prior to the survey (Tjaden and Thoennes, 2000). The National Crime Victimization Survey's (NCVS) estimates are approximately 33 percent lower for the same period of time.

Welch (1997) was able to compile a total of 100 cases involving former or current professional football players who came to the attention of police for violence toward women between 1989 and 1996 from the *Washington Post* by searching NFL teams cross listed with "domestic violence" or "rape" or "sexual assault." The data for Welch's study was limited to new stories, and he was unable to quantify professional football data in order to compare it to the estimates in the NVAWS or NCVS. Interestingly, at the time of Welch's (1997) study, O. J. Simpson, Warren Moon, Vance Johnson, and Lawrence Phillips, all of whom are former NFL players or draft picks, were making news headlines for violence against women. Each of these former players was alleged to have had extensive histories of violence toward women.

275

RISK FACTORS FOR DOMESTIC VIOLENCE

Estimates from the NCVS and other studies designed to capture domestic violence indicate that overwhelmingly, domestic violence offenders are male, and the victims are female (Rennison and Welchans, 2000). Women are also far more likely to be injured in incidents involving domestic violence. The data consistently indicates men tend to be the offenders in domestic violence (Tjaden and Thoennes, 2000). Females living with female partners report lower rates of violence than females living with male partners. Similarly, males living with male partners report higher rates of violence than males living with female partners. In short, males are far more likely to be the perpetrators in incidents of domestic violence.

Participation in sports—especially professional football—would be expected to amplify maleness from mere masculinity to hypermasculinity due to the societal value placed on the effective use of controlled violence and the spoils of wealth, status, and power (Welch, 1997). Sabo and Runfola (1980: xiii) even go so far as to suggest that violence and masculinity, in part created by sports, appear to "reinforce misogynistic elements of male sexuality and may be related to the prevalence of rape and wife beating." Statistics indicate younger females (between the ages of 16 and 24) have the greatest risk of becoming domestic violence victims (Rennison and Welchans, 2000; Greenfeld et al., 1998). The risk is even greater for undergraduate college students (DeKeseredy, 1997).

Domestic violence occurs across all socioeconomic strata. However, lower-income women are far more likely to be domestic violence victims (Rennison and Welchans, 2000). Professional football players earn vast sums of money for their gladiatorial efforts. It would be hard to argue that their spouses or girlfriends are lower-income women. However, their spouses/girlfriends are likely to be dependent upon them financially. The remuneration associated with professional football serves to reinforce hypermasculinity, entitlement, and narcissism (Bryson, 1987). Jackson (1991) found male collegiate athletes in high-profit sports such as basketball and football are more likely to be accused of sexual assault. Women with partners who express unhealthy levels of jealousy and control are at greater risk for domestic violence (Tjaden and Thoennes, 2000). In the case of Greg Hardy's assault on former on-and-off-again girlfriend Nicole Holder, a song by Nelly, a rapper with whom Holder had a fling during one of her breakups with Hardy, was played in a club that they frequented. Hardy immediately became enraged (Wertheim and Kaplan, 2014). An argument ensued, which continued as they returned to Hardy's residence and culminated in a vicious act of domestic violence fueled by jealousy.

EXPLAINING DOMESTIC VIOLENCE AMONG PROFESSIONAL FOOTBALL PLAYERS

In Welch's (2007) study, he discovered 38 of the 100 news accounts of professional football players involved "scoring" positions, running backs and receivers, followed by 21 defensive backs, 18 linebackers, 12 defensive linemen, 8 offensive linemen, 2 quarterbacks, and 1 placekicker. From this data, he created a heuristic theory based upon these descriptive statistics encompassing a wide array of psychological and sociological traits.

Welch (2007) notes that football has become increasingly specialized in recent years, and positions on the football field correspond to varying levels of masculinity and aggression that are associated with the ultimate goal of domination. By and large, running backs and receivers attempt to avoid the aggression and physicality of the defensive players. To accomplish their task of gaining yards and scoring, they "must run away from tacklers," leaving their masculinity in a constant flux (Welch, 2007: 402). In essence, they are less masculine. They must be protected by larger and stronger players. He notes this may translate into aggression off the field, including violence toward women. Some argue that violence toward women is an ego defense mechanism directed at resolving insecurities with masculinity as with power-reassurance rapists, who rape to resolve doubts about their masculinity (Groth, 1979).

Bryson (1987) equates touchdown celebrations with the release associated with avoiding the physicality of opponents and their own physical superiority. Within the sociology of sports, a celebration of this nature would be considered one of male physicality, which must be repeated in order to maintain the precarious balance between masculinity and femininity (Kane and Disch, 1993). Along similar lines, the violence against women literature has identified narcissism and a lack of empathy as psychological traits present in those who abuse women (Welch, 2007). Hamberger and Hastings (1990) find that men who abuse their spouses and score high on narcissism scales are more likely to recidivate. In essence, evading opponents, gaining yards, scoring touchdowns, and engaging in a gratuitous celebration is a narcissistic endeavor that must be repeated to maintain masculinity and avoid femininity. Welch (1997) further contends that running backs and receivers tend to demonstrate "protest masculinity" characterized by a fast lifestyle that includes substance abuse, driving fast, and womanizing due to the relatively short career in professional football (six to eight years).

Football is the ultimate celebration of masculinity. Only two of the 100 news accounts involving arrests for violence against women involved quarterbacks (Welsh, 1997). Although the position of quarterback is not overwhelmingly physical, the intelligence, leadership, and willingness to take responsibility for losses and share credit for victories symbolize the patient, even-tempered, and wise father willing to take control when necessary, but eager to let his family grow and prosper. The quarterback is the head of the family, and his masculinity is assured by being a leader of men. Any glory to be gained by winning must be shouldered by taking responsibility for losing.

Linemen are willing to sacrifice individual fame and fortune for the good of the team. They are large, strong, and supportive big brothers eager to protect their smaller siblings, knowing full well they are more than capable of taking care of themselves. Linemen get the job done, can enjoy the support of other linemen, and look forward to relatively long careers. By virtue of their sheer size and strength, linemen are innately masculine. Only eight offensive linemen and 12 defensive linemen were among the 100 news accounts involving violence against women. Offensive linemen are protectors and clear the way for others to make plays on offense. Defensive linemen occupy a similar role on defense, but still have the opportunity to make three of football's most sacred and masculine plays: stuffing the running back behind the line of scrimmage, forcing fumbles, and, of course, sacking the quarterback.

Linebackers constitute 18 of the 100 news accounts involving violence against women. By virtue of their position, linebackers are neighborhood bullies, always prepared to punish someone for being on their turf with physical aggression. Linebackers have ample opportunities to make big plays, stuffing running backs, quarterback sacks, punishing tackles, interceptions, and forced fumbles. Missing a tackle, misreading a play, and getting run over by an offensive player pose serious threats to their masculinity.

Defensive backs are predators engaged in a never-ending battle with the receivers preventing them from catching passes, having the ability to physically punish running backs who break away into the secondary, and the opportunity to intercept a pass, maybe even for a touchdown. According to Welch (1997), 21 of the 100 news accounts involved defensive backs. However, getting beaten by a receiver who catches a big pass or scores a touchdown is a definite threat to their masculinity.

Running backs and receivers are the playmakers. The opportunities for glory, fame, and fortune render these "skill" positions innately narcissistic. Success assures masculinity and a sense of entitlement. The inability to sustain success raises issues of insecurity and doubts about masculinity with the need for affirmation off the football field. These positions are volatile. They have the most to gain and the most to lose over the span of a relatively short career. All told, 38 of 100 news accounts of violence against women involved running backs or receivers.

CONCLUSION

High-profile incidents of violence toward women involving professional athletes garner a lot of media attention. Football is a product of American culture and provides a natural laboratory for the examination of masculinities, how risks/rewards impact this continuum, and ultimately, how hypermasculinity, status, narcissism, and entitlement may affect violence against women in the larger society.

Welch (1997) argues the status, prestige, and entitlement inherent in football positions translate into personality and physical typologies. The position of quarterback is equated with intelligence, being even tempered, and leadership. Defensive backs and linebackers are "assassins" who can gain considerable notoriety for physically punishing ball carriers. Because running backs and receivers score, they tend to be individualistic and reap benefits (money and women) associated with their privileged positions on the team. Meanwhile, linemen are simply part of a unit and exhibit a collective consciousness.

Although Welsh's (1997) study is largely descriptive, it sheds considerable light on domestic violence among professional athletes and society at large. Football is the most popular sport in the United States, and its patronage and viewership are predicated on its ability to appeal to our masculine natures, both good and bad. The most consistent finding in the domestic violence literature is that offenders are overwhelmingly male and victims over-whelmingly female (Rennison and Welchans, 2000). Perhaps the continuum of masculinity capable of explaining why males are involved in violence can be found on the football field.

279

REFERENCES

Brewster, M. (2002). "Domestic violence theories, research, and practice implications." In A. Roberts, ed., *Handbook of Domestic Violence Intervention Strategies*. Oxford, UK: Oxford University Press.

Bryson, L. (1987). Sport and the maintenance of masculine hegemony. *Women's Studies International Forum* 10, 349–360.

Carrington, K., and J. Phillips. (2003). "Domestic violence in Australia: An overview of the issues." E-brief. Retrieved March 1, 2015: www.aph.gov.au/library/intguide/SP/Dom_violence.htm

DeKeseredy, W., D. Saunders, M. Schwartz, and S. Alvi. (1997). "The meanings and motives for women's use of violence in Canadian college dating relationships: Results from a national survey." *Sociological Spectrum* 17, 2, 199–222.

Greenfeld, L., M. Rand, D. Craven, P. Klaus, et al. (1998). "Violence by intimates: Analysis of data on crimes by current or former spouses, boyfriends, and girlfriends." *Bureau of Justice Statistics Factbook*. Washington, DC: US Department of Justice, Bureau of Justice Statistics. Retrieved March 13, 2015: www.ojp.usdoj.gov/bjs/pub/pdf/vi.pdf

Groth, A. (1979). *Men Who Rape: The Psychology of the Offender*. New York: Plenum.

Hamberger, L., and J. Hastings. (1990). "Recidivism following spousal abatement counseling: Treatment programs and implications." *Violence and Victims* 5, 3, 157–170.

Jackson, T. (1991). "A university athletic department's rape and assault experiences." *Journal of College Student Development* 32, 77–78.

Jasinski, J. (2001a). "Pregnancy and violence against women: An analysis of longitudinal data." *Journal of Interpersonal Violence* 16, 7, 712–733.

Jasinski, J. (2001b). "Pregnancy, stress and wife assault: Ethnic differences in prevalence, severity, and onset in a national sample." *Violence and Victims* 16, 219–232.

Kane, M., and L. Disch. (1993). "Sexual violence and the reproduction of male power in the locker room: The 'Lisa Olsen' incident." *Sociology of Sport Journal* 10, 331–352.

Malamuth, N. (1986). "Predictors of naturalistic sexual aggression." *Journal of Personality and Social Psychology* 50, 953–962.

Malamuth, N., R. Sockloskie, P. Koss, and T. Tanaka. (1991). "Characteristics of aggressors against women. Testing a model using a national sample of college students." *Journal of Consulting and Clinical Psychology* 59, 670–681.

Mears, D. (2003). "Research and interventions to reduce domestic violence victimization." *Trauma, Violence, & Abuse 4*, 2, 27–147.

Messner, M. (1990). "When bodies are weapons: Masculinity and violence in sport." *International Review for the Sociology of Sport 25*, 203–218.

Messner, M. (1992). *Power at Play: Sports and the Problem of Masculinity*. Boston: Beacon.

Messner, M., and D. Sabo. (1990). *Sport, Men, and the Gender Order*. Champaign, IL: Human Kinetics Books.

Rennison, C., and S. Welchans. (2000). *Intimate Partner Violence*. Washington, DC: US Department of Justice, Office of Justice Programs, Bureau of Justice Statistics. Retrieved March 13, 2015: www.ojp.usdoj.gov/bjs/pub/pdf/ipv.pdf

Taylor, P. (2014). "The brutal truth." *Sports Illustrated*, September 24, 12–14.

Tjaden, P., and N. Thoennes. (2000). *Extent, Nature, and Consequences of Intimate Partner Violence*. Washington, DC: US Department of Justice, Office of Justice Programs, National Institute of Justice and Centers for Disease Control. Retrieved October 11, 2013: www.ncjrs.org/pdffiles1/nij/181867.pdf

US General Accounting Office (2002). *Violence Against Women: Data on Pregnant Victims and Effectiveness of Prevention Strategies Are Limited*. Report to the Honorable Eleanor Holmes Norton, House of Representatives. GAO-02-530. Washington, DC: GAO. Retrieved September 30, 2013: www.gao.gov/new.items/d02530.pdf.

Welch, M. (1997). "Violence against women by professional football players." *Journal of Sport & Social Issues 21*, 4, 392–411.

Wertheim, L., and E. Kaplan. (2014). "Hard choices." *Sports Illustrated*, September 22, 48–52.

White, G., J. Katz, and K. Scarborough. (1992). "The impact of professional football games upon violent assaults on women." *Violence and Victims 7*, 2, 157–171.

CHAPTER SEVENTEEN

A Sociological Examination of Point Shaving

Reflections on Sports Gambling Culture in the United States

BY **ROBERT S. MOSCHGAT** AND **ERIC G. LESNESKIE**

"Nothing has done more to despoil the games Americans play and watch than widespread gambling on them. As fans cheer their bets rather than their favorite teams, dark clouds of cynicism and suspicion hang over games, and [the] possibility of fixes is always in the air."

—A. Keteyian, 1986

INTRODUCTION

G ambling is a highly visible and generally accepted aspect of American culture. Millions of American adults of all ages go to casinos, play the lottery, and bet on horse and greyhound races. A substantial number of Americans also bet on the outcomes of sporting events. According to the American Gaming Association (2011), approximately $2.5 billion in legal bets are placed on sporting events in the United States in Nevada[1] every year. That number is much lower than the approximately $80 billion that are wagered each year illegally[2] on sporting events in the form of March Madness pools, bets between friends, bets made through bookies, and so forth (American Gaming Association, 2011).

In short, illegal sports wagering creates a substantial illicit economy creating opportunities for widespread corruption and scandal. The two main scandals are match fixing, when a team intentionally loses, and point-shaving schemes, where a player or players intentionally lowers the margin of victory. College and professional football are the most frequently wagered sports in the United States, followed by college and professional basketball. The purpose of this essay is to evaluate the plausibility of explaining three of the most notorious and highly publicized point-shaving scandals in NCAA basketball using established criminological theories.

WHAT IS SPREAD BETTING?

Point spreads are used to facilitate gambling on sporting events when the teams are not evenly matched. In other words, point spreads provide a handicap of sorts for gamblers that spots the underdog a certain number of points before the game even begins. Say, for example, a really successful basketball team like Kentucky was playing a mid-major conference school like Creighton in the first round of the NCAA tournament. Presumably, Kentucky would be favored to win the game. If there was not a point spread, most bettors would put their money on Kentucky, the favorite, to beat Creighton. What the point spread does is give added incentive for bettors to bet on Creighton. People who bet on Creighton to win are not betting that they will necessarily win the game. Rather, they are betting that they will not lose by more than the spread.

From a business standpoint, casinos—and bookies for that matter—use point spreads to attract similar levels of money bet on each team. This puts the casinos in a position where they are really facilitating betting between multiple parties in return for a commission. This is because sports bettors must pay in and around 10 percent of their winnings to the casino upon winning a bet. That is their commission, known as the vigorish or "vig." So, it is in the casinos' best interests to have similar amounts of money bet on each team. This means that they can take the money bet on the losing team and give it to the winning bettors, minus the vig. In short, casinos make 10 percent of all of the money that is paid out without taking much risk. All told, that amounts to hundreds upon hundreds of millions of dollars. This is why betting lines change over time. If more money is being bet on the favorite than on the underdog, the betting line will be adjusted to attract more money to be bet on the underdog.

When a bettor participates in spread betting, the favored team must exceed the spread in order for him or her to collect on the wager. If one were to bet on Random University (a nine-point favorite), the spread would be nine points. In order to win the bet, Random University would have to win by at least ten points. If Random University won by exactly nine points, it would be considered a push. No one would collect on the wager, and bettors would get their money back, minus the vig.

WHAT IS POINT SHAVING?

Point shaving involves players being paid by an outside agent to manipulate the score of a game. In general, a gambler seeks out a player on a strong team and offers him or her money to keep the score of the game close. More specifically, gamblers bet huge sums of money on the underdog and pay one or more players on the team that is favored to not cover the spread. In other words, teams that are favored are still allowed and even encouraged to win, but they simply cannot win by more points than are included in the point spread. That way, the team still wins the game, but loses the bet. In many respects, spread betting creates the ultimate win-win and/or lose-win scenarios for athletes who conspire to shave points from illegal gambling. Aside from having the ability to win the game, point shaving provides the additional challenge of keeping the score close enough to avoid covering the spread. Even if the conspirators' team loses, the athletes still stand to profit from illegal gambling or by collecting fees to shave points.

The first recorded match fixing event actually predated professional sports by four years and organized professional sports by 11 years (Seymour, 1960). In a pre–professional era baseball game, the Mutual Club of New York intentionally threw a game against the Eckford Club of Brooklyn in order to collect on gambling wagers. Match fixing is also said to have tainted the 1919 World Series between the Cincinnati Reds and the Chicago White Sox.

285

Several prominent White Sox, including Shoeless Joe Jackson, were accused of accepting large sums of money in return for throwing the series and were ultimately banned from the game. Disgraced NBA referee Tim Donaghy was also accused of match fixing and ended up losing his job and going to federal prison. Donaghy's recreational gambling debts were bigger than he could repay, so he decided to influence outcomes, thereby allowing his creditors to recoup their money.

Most of the existing research concerning match fixing has focused on NCAA collegiate basketball and the ability of the favored team to cover the point spread (Diemer and Leeds, 2013). Wolfers (2006) argues that point shaving may permeate collegiate sports as evidenced by data indicating that favored teams cover the point spread on a regular basis. Gibbs (2007) found similar evidence in analysis data of NBA games, but contends the exorbitant salaries of NBA players insulate them from the temptation of the relatively modest monetary rewards provided by point-shaving schemes. Existing research has found that heavily favored teams are less likely to cover the point spread (Borghesi, 2008; Borghesi and Dare, 2009; Diemer and Leeds, 2013).

CRIMINOLOGICAL THEORIES AND POINT SHAVING

Like many other social theories, criminological theories make assumptions about human nature and the relative importance of environmental forces. Hirschi's (1969) social bonding theory begins with the assumption that we human beings are innately selfish and will strive to fulfill our self-interest when social bonds, attachment, commitment, involvement, and belief are weak or nonexistent.

With regard to sports gambling, Hirschi's (1969) social bonding theory asserts that, athletes, like all human beings, are self-interested and would be inclined to participate in point shaving if it had the potential to fulfill their self-interest. Our inquiry begins with attachment. Does the athlete have emotional bonds to the other players on the team, the coaching staff, the student body, and/or the fans? Presumably, close, personal relationships would dissuade an athlete from participating in a nefarious and illegal scheme which would compromise his personal relationships. If the athlete is committed to his sport or education, the cost of getting caught in a scandal would be too great. Does the athlete have a stake in his education and future? Is the athlete making progress toward educational goals? Does the athlete have the potential to play professional sports? How much time and effort does the athlete dedicate to his sport or to his studies? Involvement in studying and practice would be expected to reduce the likelihood of point shaving. An athlete who believes in hard work, honesty, fairness, education, and playing by the rules would be unlikely to engage in point shaving, even for a substantial profit.

Strain theorists, on the other hand, believe that our culture determines what goals are worth pursuing. In Merton's (1938) strain theory, he argues that the United States is a materialistic and stratified society that emphasizes the goal of material success over the legitimate means to achieve it, hard work, honesty, and education. He theorizes that persons in the lower socioeconomic strata are more likely to experience strain, which leads to innovation (accepting the goal of material success and rejecting culturally approved means to obtain this goal) and, as a consequence, crime and deviance. An analysis of point shaving in strain theory would predict athletes from the lower socioeconomic strata would be more likely to experience strain and innovate by point shaving toward the goal of achieving material success. In spite of being a scholar athlete seeking a college degree, the athlete would have to perceive a bleak future in order to seek material success through point shaving.

Along similar lines, Cohen's (1955) status frustration theory holds that we seek status in lieu of material success. He, too, maintains that persons in the lower socioeconomic strata are more likely to experience strain in the form of status frustration—the inability to compete for status with the middle class—which leads to the formation of subcultures, thereby allowing participants to compete for status on their own terms. In terms of status frustration theory, the athlete would have to feel like he could not achieve status by simply competing. Perhaps the threat of a disappointing or losing season or a lack of opportunities in professional sports would cause the athlete to turn to point shaving, especially if he were surrounded by like-minded individuals.

Earlier strain theorists focused primarily on the lower classes. Agnew's (1992) general strain theory is a class-neutral theory. He conceptualizes strain as a negative emotional state induced by 1) failing to achieve a goal; 2) experiencing negative life events; or 3) losing something or someone of value. Coupled with a lack of coping mechanisms, strain may lead to involvement in crime and deviance. In its essence, collegiate sports offer tremendous opportunities to win and lose with so many trials and tribulations that can occur in any given season. An athlete may fail to make the starting lineup. She may come to the stark realization that she is not going to make a living as an athlete. A seemingly promising season ends with an injury to a key player. Athletics are rife with opportunities to fail. Even the finest athletes experience negative life events. An athlete or his family or friends may struggle with

287

addictions, finances, illness, and even death. Breakups with significant others, losing valued teammates to graduation, injury, or the pros can also be significant sources of strain. Close relationships with teammates, coaches, or other people may serve to counteract even the most serious sources of strain.

Sutherland's (1947) differential association theory views crime and deviance as being learned through the same mechanisms as any other behavior through definitions provided via our interpersonal relationships, which vary in terms of priority, duration, frequency, and intensity. Crime is the result of a surplus of definitions favorable to crime. Each of these theories serves to elucidate our understanding of human nature and the various forces which may affect athletes participating in point-shaving schemes. In order for differential association theory to explain point shaving, an athlete would have to be associated with people who provide definitions favorable to point shaving and foul play. These would have to be people whom the athlete admires and respects (intensity). The definition providers would exert a stronger influence if they occurred early in the career of a scholar athlete (priority) and had staying power (duration). Obviously, the amount of time spent with negative influence would increase the proliferation of definitions favorable to point shaving.

WHY DO COLLEGIANS PARTICIPATE IN SPORTS?

Curry and Jiobu (1995) surveyed 492 student athletes at two colleges and one university in the Midwest and examined 13 motivations to participate in college athletics on a Likert scale (strongly disagree = 1; disagree = 2; undecided = 3; agree =4; and strongly agree = 5). Excitement (4.49) and competition (4.47) were the two most important reasons. The respondents also agreed physical fitness (4.32), enjoying exercise (4.28), being on a team (4.17), winning (4.12), and meeting people (4.0) were important reasons for participating. Relaxation (3.36), being considered physically attractive (2.97), friends who also participated (2.40), and family expectations (2.09) were less important. Career (0.04) and money (0.02) were the least important. Of the 492 respondents, 29 percent indicated career and 21 percent answered that money were not applicable reasons for participation. Follow-up interviews with a subsample of the athletes revealed that most of them did not believe participating in athletics would enhance their career or financial prospects.

288

Interestingly, most of the athletes who agreed with the extrinsic motivation items attended the larger university presumably due to increased professional sport prospects.

Curry and Jiobu (1995) conducted a principal components factor analysis, reducing the 13 motivations into five explanatory variables. The first, *fitness*, encompasses enjoying exercise, physical fitness, enhancing physical attractiveness, and relaxation. This concept is similar to the coping mechanisms found in general strain theory. Feeling good about oneself would surely insulate a person from strain and other negative influences. The second, *sociability*, consists of meeting people, being a part of a team, and excitement. An openness to experience, cultivating social relationships, and being part of something bigger than yourself equates with the attachment of social bonding theory. The third, *competition*, is comprised of competition, and winning closely approximates Cohen's claim that we strive for status. The fourth, *other-directedness*, consists of family expectations and friends who participated, closely resembling differential association's definitions favorable to sport provided by interpersonal relationships. The fifth, *extrinsic motivations*, is a combination of career and monetary reasons. This concept could be subsumed by strain theory's goal of material success. It is worth reiterating that extrinsic motivations are identified as the least important reasons for competing in collegiate athletics.

Aside from the five motivations to compete in college athletics, Curry and Jiobu (1995) created control variables that are significant in the aforementioned criminological theories. The first variable is gender. Differential association theory explains the male propensity to take risks and develop definitions favorable to crime in terms of differential associations. Males are more likely to associate with deviant peers and have more opportunities to acquire definitions favorable to crime. Class rank (freshman through graduate student) equates with social bonding theory's commitment and involvement variables, as these scholar athletes have demonstrated a commitment to college and athletics and have more time invested with each passing year. Conversely, time spent each week watching or traveling to sporting events as a fan would be viewed as being less committed or involved in the athlete's own athletic or educational endeavors. Religiosity represents Hirschi's concept of belief in conventional values. The extent to which a person identifies him- or herself as an athlete would represent social bonding theory's concepts commitment and belief.

289

WHY DO COLLEGE ATHLETES GAMBLE ON SPORTS?

The vast majority of people who gamble on sports are male and tend to be younger than non–sports gamblers (Petry, 2003). Moreover, most people who gamble on sports can be described as social or recreational gamblers (Petry, 2003). It has also been found that college students interested in sports are more likely to bet on sporting events (Nelson et al., 2007). Ultimately, Curry and Jiobu (1995) were interested in explaining sports gambling among the same sample of college athletes. They had two dependent variables: betting frequency and largest wager. The first equation explains 27 percent of the variation in betting frequency. Time spent as a fan of other sports increased the frequency of betting and was the strongest explanation of betting frequency ($\beta = 0.24$). Consistent with social bonding theory, this would decrease the time and effort an athlete would put into his or her own athletic and education endeavors. One of the religiosity variables (say, attending a Baptist school) was associated with reduced betting frequency and was the second strongest explanation of betting frequency ($\beta = -0.24$), which is consistent with social bonding theory. In support of differential association theory, female scholar athletes did not bet as frequently as males ($\beta = -0.19$). Extrinsic rewards ($\beta = 0.14$) and competition ($\beta = 0.13$) increased the frequency of betting, consistent with strain and status frustration theories. Class rank ($\beta = -0.12$) decreased the frequency of betting, consistent with social bonding theories' commitment and involvement concepts. All of the other variables did not exert a statistically significant effect on betting frequency.

The second equation explains 32 percent of the variation in largest amount ever bet. One of the religiosity variables (attending a Baptist school) decreased the largest wager and was the strongest explanation ($\beta = -0.33$), consistent with social bonding theory. Time spent as a fan of other sports increased the largest wager and was the second strongest explanation of betting frequency ($\beta = 0.25$). Consistent with social bonding theory, this would decrease the time and effort an athlete would put into his or her own athletic and education endeavors. In support of differential association theory, female scholar athletes did not bet as large as males ($\beta = -0.23$). Extrinsic rewards ($\beta = 0.12$) and competition ($\beta = 0.13$) increased the largest wager consistent with strain and status frustration theories. All of the other variables did not exert a statistically significant effect on the amount of the largest wager.

In terms of explaining sports gambling among collegiate athletes, social bonding concepts such as attachment, commitment, involvement, and belief do appear to reduce involvement in sports gambling. Consistent with strain and status frustration theories, athletes motivated by competition and extrinsic rewards were more likely to engage in sports gambling. Males were more likely to bet on sports, consistent with differential association theory. Important variables missing from this analysis would be having relationships with other people who gamble on sports and definitions favorable to sports gambling. We next turn our attention to applying criminological theory to actual point-shaving incidents involving NCAA collegiate athletes.

A CRIMINOLOGICAL ANALYSIS OF COLLEGE BASKETBALL POINT-SHAVING SCANDALS

Since the early 1950s, three prominent point-shaving scandals have been exposed among NCAA basketball teams. City College of New York was a very successful team with players who were accused of point shaving in the early 1950s. Similarly, there was a point-shaving scandal at Boston College in the late 1970s. A similar point-shaving scandal emerged out of Arizona State University in the mid-1990s.

CITY COLLEGE OF NEW YORK IN 1951

The greatest point-shaving scandal in the history of college basketball involved City College of New York (Roy and Stern, 1998). In 1950, they were the first and only team in the history of college basketball to win the NIT and NCAA in the same year, an astonishing achievement that will be celebrated for decades to come. After three of CCNY's players were arrested for manipulating point spread during this monumental season, however, the CCNY basketball program was soon immortalized for perpetrating one of the most infamous scandals in the history of organized sports. As the scandal unfolded, three other New York City colleges—New York University, Long Island University, and Manhattan College—were implicated, as well as three other colleges in three different states: Bradley University (Peoria, Illinois), the University of Kentucky, and the University of Toledo (Ohio), spanning a total of seven colleges, 32 players, and 86 fixed games between 1947 and 1951.

College basketball players were often recruited to work in the Catskills in the 1940s to work in hospitality positions and to entertain affluent vacationers by playing competitive basketball (Rosen, 1999). It began rather innocently: a hotel chef wagered with other employees on the games. He recruited players to keep the margin of victory within the spread and rewarded them with steak and lobster dinners. One of the players, Eddie Gard, recruited Salvatore Sollazzo, a petty criminal and gambler, from New York City. Gard and Sollazzo organized a point-shaving ring. Sollazzo established point spreads for the games and took wagers from anyone who wanted to bet on basketball in the Catskills. Sollazzo would wager on Gard's games. Gard's role was to recruit other players to ensure his teams did not cover the spread by intentionally turning the ball over—after all, a win is a win. Gard paid his conspirators with a portion of his substantial winnings. Even when Gard's teams lost, he still profited by creating the quintessential lose-win situation by failing to cover the spread.

Eddie Gard played collegiate basketball at Long Island University and began to recruit his teammates, including Sherman White, one of the greatest players in NCAA history, to engage in point shaving under the guise of winning, while keeping the margin of victory within the spread (Rosen, 1999). The conspiracy continued to grow. One of Sollazzo's associates enrolled Norm Mager, a CCNY player, who recruited other players, eventually spreading to Kentucky, Illinois, and Ohio.

Only the concepts found in Sutherland's (1947) differential association theory have the ability to explain a point-shaving scandal of this magnitude. First and foremost, 32 players participated in point shaving across seven colleges and four states. The players came from very diverse backgrounds, including race, ethnicity, religion, and socioeconomic status. Strain and status frustration lack the ability to explain such widespread participation. Many of them were excellent prospects with lucrative professional careers ahead of them. Due to the fact that all of the players earned enough playing time to affect games through point shaving, they obviously demonstrated commitment and involvement to their sport, refuting social bonding theory. All of the participants played for nationally renowned programs. Gard, the initial participant, learned the art of point shaving from the chef. He solicited assistance from Sollazzo, who had the contacts to provide lucrative fees for participation. His ability to recruit other players was predicated on the power of being victorious, with the additional challenge of keeping the victory within the point spread and substantial financial remuneration. Surely, the athletes came to define point shaving as favorable, as it served to further fuel their already competitive natures and was passed on from player to player in interpersonal groups.

BOSTON COLLEGE IN 1978

Rick Kuhn, a player on the Boston College basketball team, became acquainted with Rocco Perla and Tony Perla, petty gamblers and brothers who convinced Kuhn to shave points and recruit other players to do so (Porter, 2000). As explained in the ESPN 30 for 30 documentary entitled *Playing for the Mob*, a small handful of players were paid relatively small sums of money to ensure that Boston College would not cover the spread in the games. The Perlas, in conjunction with Henry Hill and other Mafia members, used the inside information to their advantage and bet huge amounts of money against Boston College. In fact, so much money was being wagered that Hill and the Perla brothers had to devise a betting system that allowed them to spread their wagers across numerous bookmakers. In other words, they did not want to make bets that were so big that individual bookmakers would not be able to pay them. Moreover, they did not want to attract undue attention with large bets.

It did not take very long for Kuhn and his confederates to want out of this scheme. They were in over their heads and were afraid of getting caught. Unfortunately, their pleas fell on deaf ears. The mob made it clear to the players that if points were not shaved, the players and their loved ones would be physically harmed.

Throughout the first half of the 1978 season, Boston College won many games, but did not cover the spread. The scheme, however, ended when Boston College exceeded the point spread against Holy Cross. So much money was lost on the Holy Cross game that the Perla brothers felt that they could no longer trust the small group of players who were in on the fix. More than likely, the scandal would have gone undetected if not for Henry Hill becoming an FBI informant in 1980. Although the Boston College scandal pales in comparison to the CCNY affair, it shows that the production of interpersonal relationships and definitions favorable to competition and point shaving are consistent with differential association theory.

ARIZONA STATE UNIVERSITY IN 1994

In the early 1990s, Stevin Smith, an Arizona State University basketball player, owed Benny Silman, a bookmaker, $10,000 in gambling debts. As a means of repaying his debt, Silman offered to waive the debt and reward Smith an additional $20,000 for ensuring ASU did not cover a 15-point spread against Oregon State. He also offered Smith $80,000 to ensure that

ASU would not cover the point spread in four upcoming games (ESPN, 2002). Smith agreed to the deal and recruited Isaac Burton to assist him and paid him a total of $4,300 over two games. Smith was amazed at how easy it was to shave points, and the mutually beneficial relationship continued for three more games until Las Vegas casinos became suspicious when approximately $1,000,000 was bet on an ASU versus Washington State game.

One could argue that Smith's vice and substantial gambling debt led to his decision to shave points in support of strain theory. However, it was his underworld contact who exposed him to point shaving. It allowed him to continue to win basketball games and reap substantial profits from ensuring ASU did not exceed the margin of victory (ESPN, 2002). He enjoyed the easy money and did not believe he was jeopardizing his future as a top NBA prospect, consistent with differential association theory.

CONCLUSION

Participation in point-shaving schemes cannot be explained in terms of the mere motivations to compete in sports such as the excitement and thrills associated with competition. As it turns out, the lesser motivations for participating in athletics, extrinsic motivations, career and money do account for variation in gambling among student athletes (Curry and Jiobu, 1998). Differential association theory provides the essential ingredient in each of these scandals: interpersonal relationships. One illicit contact is all it takes. Athletes obviously define competition as favorable. When combined with monetary motivations, greed, or flat-out vice, point shaving fuels this competitive spirit, offering seemingly easy money to demonstrate their athletic skill is poignant enough to win, even when intentionally not performing at optimum levels to ensure the team does not cover the spread. Recruiting and conspiring with teammates simply reinforces these definitions.

As evidenced by the breadth of the CCNY scandal, athletes from all walks of life can be ensnared, regardless of professional potential or current socioeconomic status. Going forward, university officials and coaching staffs should take every precaution necessary to ensure their players do not succumb to these temptations, which only serve to reinforce their competitive spirits with illicit camaraderie and the spoils of point shaving.

NOTES

1. Although many states have legalized gambling, Nevada is the only state where people can legally bet on sports.
2. An illegal sports bet is one that is made either outside of the state of Nevada or outside of a casino in Nevada.

REFERENCES

Agnew, R. (1992). "Foundation for a general strain theory of crime and delinquency." *Criminology* 30, 1, 47–88.

American Gaming Association. (2011). "Sports wagering." Washington, DC. Retrieved March 23, 2015: http://www.americangaming.org/industry-resources/research/factsheets/sports-wagering

Associated Press. (1997). "Point-shaving scandal hits Arizona State." *Los Angeles Times*. Retrieved April 30, 2015: http://articles.latimes.com/1997/dec/06/sports/sp-61336

Borghesi, R. (2008). "Widespread corruption in sports gambling: Fact or fiction?" *Southern Economic Journal* 74, 1063–1069.

Borghesi, R., and W. Dare. (2009). "A test of the widespread point-shaving theory." *Finance Research Letters* 6, September, 115–121.

Cohen, A. K. (1955). *Delinquent Boys: The Culture of the Gang*. New York: Free Press.

Curry, T., and R. Jiobu. (1995). "Do motives matter? Modeling gambling on sports among athletes." *Sociology of Sport Journal* 12, 21–35.

Diemer, G., and M. Leeds. (2013). "Failing to cover: Point-shaving or statistical anomaly?" *International Journal of Sports Finance*, 8, 175-191.

ESPN. (2002). "Anatomy of a fix." *Outside the Lines*. ESPN.com. Retrieved April 12, 2015: http://espn.go. com/page2/tvlistings/show105transcript.html

Gibbs, J. (2007). "Point shaving in the NBA: An economic analysis of the National Basketball Association's point spread betting market." Stanford University mimeo.

Hirschi, T. (1969). *Causes of Delinquency*. Berkley: University of California Press.

Keteyian, A. (1986). "The biggest game in town." *Sports Illustrated*. Retrieved March 21, 2015: http://www.si.com/vault/search? term=the+biggest+game+in+town

Merton, R. (1938). "Social structure and anomie." *American Sociological Review* 3, 672–682.

Nelson, T., R. LaBrie, D. LaPlante, M. Stanton, et al. (2007). "Sports betting and other gambling in athletes, fans, and other college students." *Research Quarterly for Exercise and Sport* 78, 271–283.

Petry, N. (2003). "A comparison of treatment-seeking pathological gamblers based on preferred gambling." *Addiction* 98, 645–655.

Porter, D. (2000). *How Goodfellas Bought Boston College Basketball*. Taylor Trade Publishing.

Rosen, C. (1999) *Scandals of '51: How the Gamblers Almost Killed College Basketball*. Seven Stories Press.

Roy, G., and S. Stern. (1998). *City Dump: The Story of the 1951 CCNY Basketball Scandal*. Documentary film. March 24, 1998. Black Canyon Productions and HBO Sports.

Seymour, H. (1960). *Baseball: The Early Years*. London: Oxford University Press.

Sutherland, E. (1947). *Principles of Criminology*, 4th edition. Philadelphia: Lippincott.

Weiss, S. M., and S. L. Loubier. (2010). "Gambling habits of athletes and nonathletes classified as disordered gamblers." *Journal of Psychology* 144 (6), 507–521.

Wolfers, J. (2006). "Point shaving: Corruption in college basketball." *American Economic Review* 96, 2006, 279–284.

CHAPTER EIGHTEEN

Fantasy Sports and the Demise of Rivalries

BY **BRANDON LANG**

P eople have been playing fantasy sports for many years. Although not all sports fans play fantasy, many of those who do find that it helps to make watching and following sports more enjoyable. Now, fantasy sports is a multimillion-dollar industry that has become an important part of the sporting experience of many fans. Millions of Americans play everything from fantasy football and baseball to hockey, golf, and NASCAR. The purpose of this selection is to trace the origins of fantasy sports and explain how their growth has diminished the role that rivalries play in sports.

WHAT ARE FANTASY SPORTS?

Using the actual statistics of current professional athletes, fantasy sports give players the opportunity to manage a team in a competitive league of other "owners," as they are known. There is a variety of different formats, but the general idea is that players build a team

297

through a draft and compete in a series of games against other owners. At the end of the season, the owner with the most wins, or points, wins the league championship.

THE DRAFT

The first step in a fantasy sports is to hold a draft. Sometimes, this is done virtually over the Internet, while sometimes this is conducted face to face in a restaurant or bar or even a player's house. The general idea is that a draft order is established, and then players proceed to build their teams. In fantasy football, players must draft a quarterback, running backs, receivers, kickers, and a defense. In hockey, players need to draft goalies, forwards, and defensemen, while in fantasy baseball, all position players must be drafted, in addition to starting and relief pitchers.

If a league consists of ten teams, there would be one pick for each team in each round. What many people like about fantasy sports drafts is they can trade draft picks just like they do in the pros. Generally speaking, players go into fantasy drafts with the hope of drafting players that they think will help them win games. If some of those players are chosen by other teams, players often use the same logic as the general managers of professional teams and draft the best player available at that time. Part of the drafting process involves drafting back-up players who can play when starters are injured.

PLAYING GAMES

Once teams are drafted, the fantasy season is ready to begin. The fantasy season follows the season schedule of the league whose players are being used, and both commence at the same time. One thing that fantasy owners need to do in advance of each game is to create a starting lineup. In football, for example, a quarterback, receivers, running backs, and a defense would have to be selected. In hockey, a goalie and a number of skating players would also need to be chosen. If a fantasy owner starts a player who is injured, then no points can be generated at that position. In other words, if Eli Manning is my starting quarterback and he is injured, he will not generate any points for his fantasy team.

298

Next, points are allocated to different players based on their performance. Once the game is over, all of the individual scores are added together to create an overall team score. In basketball, players would generate points based on rebounds, steals, points, and assists, for example. In baseball, position players are awarded points based on their number of hits, total bases, and runs batted in. Pitchers, meanwhile, generate points for strikeouts and not allowing earned runs. In hockey, goals, assists, and plus-minus are used for skaters, while saves, save percentage, and goals would be employed for goalies. Players at different positions in football generate points in different ways. Passing percentage, yards, and touchdowns are used for quarterbacks, while running backs generate points with yards and touchdowns. Receivers generate points with number of catches, yards, and so forth. Different leagues weight many of the above variables differently. Some leagues may use four variables to measure performance, whereas others use six. Similarly, some use a combination of offensive and defensive statistics, yet others use only offensive numbers. All leagues have commissioners, whose role it is to arbitrate differences and both establish and enforce the rules.

The general format of fantasy is that players have head-to-head matchups over the course of the season. To model the 16-game NFL season, most fantasy leagues have 16 head-to-head games against other teams in their league. Similarly, Major League Baseball fantasy would consist of 162 games, and National Hockey League fantasy would consist of 82 games. In these matches, a win counts as a certain number of points; the win-loss records of teams determine their place in the standings.

Fantasy team owners have a group of starting and reserve players that make up their rosters. Backup players, who are generally drafted lower than starting ones, can be inserted into the lineup if a starter is injured or mired in a slump. Just like real-life general managers, fantasy team owners can release players, pick up players who have been waived by other teams, and make trades with other teams. Successful fantasy team owners tend to be very active and involved in the day-to-day operations of their teams.

There are several motivations that people have for playing fantasy sports. For many who play in leagues with their friends, they enjoy the social component of meeting for the draft and talking shop with others. Some also enjoy the thrill of victory. Many fantasy team owners have trophies for the winning owner, which bestow a sense of pride upon winning players. Others like the financial rewards of playing fantasy sports. More and more, players pay entry fees to join leagues and stand to win a lot of money. Websites like www.draftkings.

THE SOCIOLOGY OF SPORTS

com and www.fanduel.com allow players to assemble one-game fantasy teams that compete for very large sums of money. In this form of fantasy sports, players essentially wager a given amount of money and win back that amount and more based on the performance of their teams.

THE ORIGIN OF FANTASY SPORTS

As articulated in the film *Silly Little Game*, fantasy sports first emerged in 1980 when a group of friends living in New York City came up with an activity where they could manage MLB rosters and compete against each other in a league of sorts. Writers and editors living in New York City, including Daniel Okrent and Lee Eisenberg, drafted players and managed teams over the course of the 162-game season. Before the term fantasy baseball emerged, this was known as Rotisserie League baseball because the group often met at a restaurant called La Rotisserie Française. Just like today, trades were made, struggling players were released, and standings were kept. Using pencils, paper, and calculators, fantasy team owners spent hours keeping track of their players' statistical output using box scores from the newspaper. Standard measures like batting average, home runs, and strikeouts were used. In addition, Okrent invented the concept of WHIP (walks plus hits divided by innings pitched), which has evolved into a mainstream baseball stat (Di Fino, 2009). At the end of the regular season, the winner was awarded a small trophy and had chocolate milk poured over his head.

Over time, people adapted the idea of fantasy baseball to other sports like football and hockey. The original members of the Rotisserie League wrote about their experiences and influenced dozens of groups around the country to start their own leagues. Through the 1980s and early 1990s, fantasy sports were played among friends, and the time commitment was pretty extensive. The advent of the Internet in the mid-1990s, however, changed all of that. The Internet allowed for more people to join leagues and play without having to devote a huge amount of time to calculating statistics. People could join online leagues and devote as much or as little time to their fantasy teams as they wanted.

THE GROWTH OF FANTASY SPORTS

Fantasy sports have experienced a huge amount of growth over the last three decades. What started out as an activity among a small group of friends evolved into a multibillion-dollar empire. Clearly, the idea of managing one's own team appeals to tens of millions of sports fans who embrace the competitive components of fantasy sports. As with many popular pastimes, word spread, and more and more people not only gave fantasy sports a proverbial shot, but ended up becoming active participants.

The principal way that fantasy sports are different today from in the past lies in the resources available to players. In the 1980s, people playing fantasy baseball spent hours every week combing through box scores and compiling statistics by hand. Although this was fun for many participants, it was also very labor intensive. Today, computer programs crunch numbers more quickly than people ever could by hand. Moreover, the Internet provides people with the information they need very quickly. Fantasy players can join websites like cbssportsline.com and have access to more information than they could ever sift through. Analysts now provide fantasy owners with trends, projections, and insights that people simply could not access one or two generations ago.

Computers have allowed companies like ESPN to set up leagues consisting of members all over the world. Fantasy sports are no longer limited by physical geography. With a computer and Internet connection—even a smartphone, for that matter—people can join leagues, draft players, compete in games, track players, and be full participants in one or more fantasy leagues.

THE BENEFITS OF FANTASY SPORTS

There are numerous benefits of playing fantasy sports. One is that it is fun. Just like some people collect stamps or classic cars, playing fantasy sports is an important hobby for millions of Americans. Many sports fans like playing GM and setting lineups, managing rosters, making trades, etc. It is fulfilling for players when their teams do well and will likely increase their interest in the sport. All of a sudden, fans on the East Coast will be more likely to watch contests between West Coast teams if they have players on one of those teams.

Next, fantasy sports have a social dimension. Even if team owners play in virtual leagues with strangers, they are still likely to watch games and talk about goings-on in the league with friends. People feel gratified when their teams do well and win championships as well. In addition, people can win money playing fantasy sports. Championships can pay out anywhere from $20 or $30 in a small league among friends to tens of thousands of dollars in Internet-based leagues.

SOME CONCERNS ABOUT FANTASY SPORTS

Obviously, some people have a few concerns about fantasy sports. We have all heard stories of the fantasy-playing husband or boyfriend who is making trades and setting lineups while on a date or at a social event with his significant other. Clearly, fantasy sports can be time consuming and take away time that people—mostly men—spend with their kids or working, for example. Like anything, fantasy sports can be a very healthy and positive outlet for people who devote some time and energy toward it. There will, however, always be compulsive players who devote so much time and money toward fantasy sports that it detracts from other areas of their lives. Compulsivity, or even addiction, can be measured by the number of teams or leagues that a player plays in and the amount of time that s/he devotes to the activity.

Building on this point, fantasy sports are also becoming more and more money oriented. The seasons are shorter, and the stakes are higher than they have ever been. In recent years, websites such as fanduel.com, starfantasyleagues.com, and draftkings.com have emerged that allow people to play one-day fantasy seasons. In other words, players create teams that only participate in one game. The teams with the most points during those games win back an amount of money that is based upon their initial stake. These are explicitly designed for people who want to use their fantasy knowledge to try to make money.

In many respects, the line has really blurred between fantasy sports and gambling. Just like gamblers, many fantasy owners pay money up front in hopes of winning prize money. This is no different from playing in a poker tournament. Both involve a fee, and people use their knowledge and skills to beat others and finish "in the money." Of course, millions of recreational gamblers are able to gamble within their means and stop at any time. There are millions of others, on the other hand, who cannot do that. Just like many addicted gamblers

302

who max out credit cards for cash advances to gamble, surely people have loaded their accounts on one-day fantasy sports websites with money that they cannot repay. In this day and age of easy credit and high credit card limits, I have to think that Internet entrepreneurs are, in fact, banking on this happening.

FANTASY SPORTS AND THE DEMISE OF RIVALRIES

The biggest concern that exists regarding fantasy sports is that it is slowly eroding many of the rivalries that exist in professional sports. Let me use a personal example to help explain this point. A friend of mine is a passionate Philadelphia Flyers fan who watches every game and spends hundreds of dollars per year on tickets and merchandise. This friend often assembles one-game teams on fanduel.com hoping to win big. Like many fantasy sports players, he seeks to assemble the best teams that he can, and he often selects Sidney Crosby, the star center for the Pittsburgh Penguins, to be on his team. Generally speaking, Flyers fans do not like Sidney Crosby. In fact, the term *do not like* is really an understatement. The reality is that many Flyers fans would say that they hate him. When the Penguins play in Philadelphia, many fans chant "Cindy, Cindy, Cindy" in a manner designed to taunt Penguins fans and emasculate Crosby himself. In short, these two teams are huge rivals, and fantasy sports is ultimately lessening the significance of these rivalries.

Whom do you root for if the Penguins are playing the Flyers and you are a Flyers fan, but have Sidney Crosby or Evgeni Malkin, another world-class player for the Penguins, on your fantasy team? Do you hope that the Flyers win, but that Crosby or Malkin have good games? In some ways, this taps into how James van Riemsdyk's parents must feel when his team, the Philidelphia Flyers, play the Carolina Hurricane, the team that his younger brother plays for. Similarly, Mr. and Mrs. Harbaugh must have felt equally as conflicted when their sons were head coaches on opposite sides of the field during Super Bowl XLVII.

A huge percentage of fantasy players must feel conflicted when choosing players for their teams. One of the golden rules of fantasy is to draft the best player available when it is your turn. As such, many fantasy players end up drafting players who play for teams that have rivalries with their favorite ones. Obviously, Minnesota Vikings fans select Green Bay Packers, Boston Red Sox fans select New York Yankees, and Edmonton Oilers fans select Calgary Flames. This means that they have players who regularly play in games against their favorite teams.

303

There is no doubt fantasy sports have eroded some of the intensity of long-standing sports rivalries. One thought to ponder is that hard-core fantasy players are more and more likely to be sports fans, in general than to root solely for one team. This is evidenced by the huge numbers of people who watch the NFL Red Zone channel every Sunday, a station that switches to games where a team is on the verge of scoring. Although Red Zone ratings are not made public, hundreds of thousands of fans appear to prefer watching the action on the Red Zone Channel than to focus on one game. This makes sense for two reasons. One, Red Zone has more action and is a good fit for people who enjoy watching scoring on a league-wide level. Second, it helps fantasy players follow many of their players and keep tabs on their statistical output.

Personally, I am a big fan of sports rivalries. Although I would never condone the violence and egregious taunting that crosses the line, I enjoy the added excitement that comes with a rivalry game. As a graduate of North Carolina State University, I find basketball games against Duke and the University of North Carolina to always be a little more exciting than ones against other ACC schools. Of course, there is a rivalry between NC State and UNC, but for the most part, it is a healthy one that makes the games exciting to watch.

My hunch is that rivalries will erode as fantasy sports increase in popularity. Fantasy team owners will continue to choose the best players, and it will not matter which teams they play on. Research shows that millennials are different in many ways from their parents. Millennials study for school, communicate with others, find jobs, date, and do hundreds of other things differently from generations of people before them. As millennials come of age, maybe we will see that they watch sports differently as well. Just like they multitask when they pursue activities like homework, maybe they like switching channels and watching the Red Zone because it is faster paced and filled with more information.

CONCLUSIONS

In the span of four decades, fantasy sports went from a virtually unknown game to something that is played by millions of people all over the world. Today, fantasy sports bring joy to people who have made a meaningful hobby out of managing teams in fantasy leagues. In recent years, opportunities have emerged for people to play shorter seasons for higher stakes. Like many others, I suspect that this will grow in popularity and be very attractive to many members of the fantasy community who want to use their sports knowledge to make money. This carries with it some concerns. One is that some people will not be able to play in a responsible manner. The second is that as fantasy becomes a bigger part of American culture, the rivalries that exist in the big four sports leagues will be eroded.

REFERENCES

Di Fino, N. (2009). "The secret history of WHIP." Retrieved March 31, 2015, from the *Wall Street Journal*: http://www.wsj.com/articles/SB1000142405297020461900457431 8690805089868.

SECTION 6
Sports, Politics, and Business

ozens of current and retired athletes have used their celebrity status to speak out about social and political issues that they deem important. Think of all of the NBA players who wore warm-up jerseys displaying the messages "Don't Shoot" and "I Can't Breathe" following tensions between minorities and police officers in Ferguson, Missouri, and Staten Island, New York. As described below, sports and politics are intertwined in a number of different ways. A related issue is that sports represent a huge economic engine that has brought hundreds of millions of dollars to cities, regions, and countries that host the Super Bowl, the Final Four, World Cup soccer matches, and the Olympics. The purpose of this section is to identify how sports, politics, and business are interconnected.

SPORTS AND POLITICS

There is an inextricable link between sports and politics. For example, fans sing the national anthem before games and cheer for national teams in international competitions like the Olympics and the World Cup. When the United States and Mexico play in soccer games, fans fiercely show their national pride. American fans wear as much red, white, and blue to support the United States, and Mexican fans wear as much red, white, and green to show their support for Mexico. Although this is a good-natured rivalry, it is a source of pride for supporters of one team to beat the other, even if they are only playing an exhibition game.

Many communities around the country have highway signs that not only welcome people to their city, but also reference a championship team or successful athlete from there. It is quite common to see signs that read, "Welcome to _____. Home of the 2015 State 4A Football Champions" or "Welcome to _____. Birthplace of _____ _____."

Long-time Oakland Raider Fred Biletnikoff is from the city that I live in. In this city, there is Fred Biletnikoff Field and numerous signs and murals around the city.

Many athletes often use their athletic success to raise awareness about political issues. Think back to the 1968 Summer Olympics in Mexico City, when two African American medalists in the 200-meter race raised their fists in the air, engaging in a black power salute on the podium to raise awareness about racial inequality in the United States. Numerous countries have even boycotted international tournaments like the Olympics as a form of protest against another country's foreign policy. Due to Cold War tensions between the United States and the USSR during the Cold War, the United States boycotted the 1980 Summer Olympics in Russia, while the Soviet Union boycotted the 1984 Summer Olympics held in Los Angeles. Similarly, FIFA did not allow South Africa to participate in the World Cup during the era of apartheid.

Athletes have also used their elevated public profiles to endorse politicians, support political campaigns, and even run for public office. Many athletes, including Michael Jordan and Alex Rodriguez, have publicly supported political candidates. Curt Schilling, for example, actively supported presidential candidate John McCain when he ran for president against Barack Obama. Others, including Bill Bradley and Steve Largent, engaged in successful political careers once their professional athletic careers were over.

In their piece "Politics by Kayfabe: Professional Wrestling and the Creation of Public Opinion," Stodden and Hansen demonstrate the similarities between professional wrestling and modern politics. Both wrestling and politics manufacture storylines to attract people's attention and support. In wrestling, pro-American storylines, or kayfabes, are used to vilify foreign wrestlers like the Iron Sheik. Fans root against the Iron Sheik and other non-American wrestlers precisely because they are un-American. In the same way, in politics, both major parties use pro-American story-lines to vilify their opposition. What is so interesting is that does not matter if their opponents really are un-American. What matters is that they are *perceived* as being un-American by voters.

SPORTS AND BUSINESS

More than ever, people are recognizing the commercial basis of sports at all levels. Sports is a huge force in the American economy, accounting for millions of jobs and billions of dollars spent. It is not just that people spend vast sums of money on tickets and team merchandise. Teams are responsible for paying player salaries and municipalities often assume the responsibility of building and maintaining stadia. Simply put, sports account for a substantial percentage of spending in this country.

One economic dimension of sports relates to all of the money that fans spend on sports. Fans spend huge amounts of money on tickets, travel, hotels, concessions, and team gear. Going to games is more expensive than ever, and the costs of parking, buying concessions, and paying for gas can really add up quickly. Fans also spend a lot of money for cable television packages and Internet sites like NHL GameCenter Live for access to games involving their favorite teams. Municipalities and counties also spend vast amounts of money building and maintaining stadia and other sports facilities. Of course, not all stadia are publicly owned, but those that are publicly owned are very expensive to build and operate. In most cases, a $400 or $500 million stadium will cost more money to build and operate than it will generate for municipalities while it is being used.

Meanwhile, those cities seeking to host events like the NCAA Final Four or the Super Bowl put together lavish application presentations. When cities bid for national and international athletic competitions, they spend a lot of money putting together proposals. Unfortunately, an arms race of sorts has emerged, where cities believe that their chances of being chosen increase with the amount of money put into their application. This involves paying for architectural renderings of facilities, marketing costs, entertaining committee members, and so forth. Teams also spend exorbitant amounts of money paying players and coaches, traveling to road games, and paying for insurance. Professional teams have very high budgets needed to cover all of their expenses. It is very expensive to charter planes, secure hotel rooms for dozens of players, cover salaries, and the like.

Media outlets pay hundreds of millions of dollars for the rights to broadcast popular sporting events. The amount of money that CBS pays to air March Madness, NBC pays to air the Olympics, or FOX to air the World Series is higher than it has ever been. Broadcasting companies know that they can make so much selling commercial time during these events that it is worth paying whatever it takes to outbid their competitors. Knowing that sporting events account for virtually all of the highest-rated television shows, many companies, in turn, spend great amounts of money to pay these media outlets to air their commercials during big games. During events like the Super Bowl, it costs millions of dollars to air a commercial.

It is not just that professional sports teams have a number of expenses. Sports at the college, high school, and youth levels can be a very expensive proposition. At the college level, many schools pay football and men's basketball coaches millions upon millions of dollars to coach their teams. Many college teams travel extensively, play in expensive facilities, and have substantial operating budgets. At the high school and youth levels, parents pay a lot of money for equipment and fees, travel and hotels at tournaments, private coaching, just to name a few. Simply put, sports are a big part of America's Gross Domestic Product (GDP).

A related issue pertains to how commercialized sports have become. Professional stadia and arenas are often named after corporations and filled with advertising. Teams play in places like Heinz Field and FedEx Field that have advertising all over the scoreboard, bathrooms, cup holders, stair risers, and many other spaces where a sign can be displayed. Some North American professional sports teams have corporate sponsorship right on their jerseys. In Major League Soccer (MLS), teams have corporate logos right on the chests of their jerseys. Things are so commercialized in the MLS that one team even changed its name to that of an energy drink. The New York/New Jersey Metrostars changed their name to the New York Red Bulls. Many NFL and NHL teams have corporate logos on their practice jerseys. During televised sporting events, halftime shows are brought to you by company X, power plays are brought to you by company Y, and plays of the game are brought to you by company Z.

The Lang article entitled "The Relocation of Professional Sports Franchises and Sweetheart Stadium Deals" explains why so many professional sports teams have moved from one city to another. For teams that move, this is primarily a business decision that has been driven by three economic factors: League expansion, poor attendance, and the lure of moving into

309

newly built publicly subsidized stadia in cities that are desperate for a professional sports team.

Chapter 21, entitled "Ad Nauseam? Sports Fans' Acceptance of Commercial Messages during Televised Sporting Events" by Levin, Cobbs, Beasley, and Manolis is an empirical piece that chronicles the extent to which NFL and NASCAR fans are bothered by watching television commercials during games or races. Their results show that a fairly small number of fans are "annoyed" by commercials during televised sporting events, although this varies by sport, age, and gender. They also found that the more NASCAR fans identify with the sport, the more accepting they are of commercial messages during races. Interesting analyses are also conducted with regard to the relationship between brand perception and commercial acceptance.

The last reading in this section is called "The Growing Popularity of Counterfeit Jerseys among Sports Fans: A Critical Analysis." Counterfeit jerseys are omnipresent in the United States, and a high percentage of them are such good copies that many people likely wear them without even realizing they are fakes. In this chapter, Lang traces the history of counterfeit jerseys and establishes how and why they have become so popular. Lang also examines the potential effectiveness of several strategies that can be used to limit people's ability to purchase counterfeit jerseys.

CHAPTER NINETEEN

Politics by Kayfabe

*Professional Wrestling and the
Creation of Public Opinion*

BY **WILLIAM P. STODDEN** AND **JOHN S. HANSEN**

INTRODUCTION

Professional wrestling offers an excellent analogy for understanding the way politicians socially construct reality to produce changes in public opinion. In most cases, politicians will frame specific events in a way designed to elicit public support for their preferred policies or candidates. They will also use these same techniques to frame those they perceive to be negative in a way that generates fear and antipathy in the population. The creation of reality and incitement to action in a mass population are one function of political propaganda, which is nearly ubiquitous in the age of mass media, big data, and the 24-hour news cycle.[1]

In many ways, the process used by politicians to construct reality is similar to the creation of angles and storylines used in professional wrestling. Professional wrestling has grown into a world phenomenon alongside—and largely as a result of—mass media. In its current manifestation, professional wrestling, now called sports entertainment, requires the apparatus of mass media, as well as the audiences mass media generates to succeed financially. For their part, policy makers and political leaders also use the mass media. In fact, the modern mass-based political party, which appeals to huge swaths of the population using claims and narratives resonant with the average person rather than traditional political elites, would not exist without the mass media. Without widespread dissemination of news, parties would not be able to effectively propagate political propaganda or generate public opinion.

This article provides a brief overview of the analogue between public opinion creation and professional wrestling. Particularly important is the concept of the "kayfabe." The kayfabe is an accepted substitution of reality and willing suspension of disbelief that allows fans to buy into often fictionalized storylines, larger-than-life personalities, and match results, thereby turning modern professional wrestling into a form of entertainment instead of an actual sporting contest. When looking at various political contests and events of the recent past through the lens of the kayfabe, we can gain a better understanding both of how the political landscape in the United States can appear to be much more starkly polarized than it actually is, and how politicians are able to sell international conflict to even war-weary populations.

THE KAYFABE AND THE SOCIAL CREATION OF "GOOD" AND "BAD"

Central to the discussion of professional wrestling and politics is the concept of kayfabe.[2] The term itself is derived from a slang pig Latin–like word for "fake," which was originally used by workers at the carnivals, traveling circuses, and county fair venues where wrestling events were once held. Over time, kayfabe has come to refer to the ability of wrestlers to create an alternate reality and to have those viewing the show believe that what they are watching is, in fact, a real contest. To "break kayfabe" is to let on that the show is not a real contest, an act that could have serious financial consequences for the promoter and end wrestling careers.

Kayfabe was developed to boost the entertainment value of the spectacle (Beekman, 2006). The switch to a pure kayfabe show did not occur until the early 20th century. Before that time, wrestling was able to straddle both the entertainment realms and that of organized

312

martial arts sports such as boxing, judo, and gymnastics. Wrestlers are and always have been highly skilled athletes, many with a background in amateur wrestling or field sports.

Regardless of venue, for the professional wrestlers, the act was a job. As Kerrick (1980) points out, wrestlers and promoters consider professional wrestling to be first and foremost a business. Before the purely kayfabe era, it was not uncommon to have shoots, or legitimate wrestling bouts, for either a championship title or as a means to create crowd support for a wrestler who may be in line for a shot at a title. In a shoot, the outcome was never determined beforehand, and would often lead to a draw or some uninteresting, anticlimactic contest; in these events, bookers, or promoters, who came from an entertainment background, found that they had to answer to angry spectators, who felt they had paid for a spectacle that never materialized. An uninteresting or indeterminate match could, after all, prompt calls for a refund from the spectators, and these demands were often backed up with the threat of very real violence.

To prevent these boring non-spectacles, promoters began pushing for matches that were works—productions that were not factually true per se, but rather were true within the reality of kayfabe. These matches were complete with angles, or scripted feuds, designed to build programs. The earliest programs dating from the mid-to-late 19th century developed from the more organic aspects of competition found in boxing, itself a scandal-prone sport. A program often consisted of several scheduled bouts between various wrestlers or wrestling cliques. These bouts were scheduled based on the angles being run at that time within the promotion. In the days of territory wrestling, before TV became the primary medium through which the fan engaged with the sport, the angle was set to draw on local biases and interests. After wrestling became primarily focused on TV viewership, starting in the 1950s, the angles also incorporated national concepts of race, nationalism, xenophobia, and class. A perfect example of the sort of antiforeign, xenophobic angles that have been with professional wrestling since the advent of kayfabe is the 1980s feud between Sgt. Slaughter and the Iranian-born Iron Sheik.[3]

Wrestling promoters soon learned that by controlling the outcome, they could script or build up regional or national champions, which would have big draw potentials. With such capacity for revenue, it became important for promoters to protect—at all costs—the image of a champion wrestler or one who was being built up for a championship run. At this point, it became necessary for the industry to establish the norm of the kayfabe. With kayfabe, bookers could build heat, or in-ring hype, for a wrestler or storyline, ensure interesting programs, and protect the integrity of champions while still working the crowd. It soon

313

became in the industry's financial interest to keep kayfabe, as the scripted show became the most reliable source of revenue in professional wrestling.

It is natural therefore that pro wrestlers consider themselves to be workers. Those who were unable or unwilling to maintain kayfabe were known as "bad" workers, while those who could convincingly maintain kayfabe were "good" workers. Those wrestlers who were experts at keeping or building kayfabe, producing exciting matches and drawing public interest, were often known as carpenters. The primary endeavor of the professional wrestler was to work in the show. Sometimes, this meant doing a job, or selling the illusion, while losing the match. Hence, a jobber is a wrestler who routinely loses and often is used to build the image of a top-bill performer known as a main eventer or top man.

Kayfabe also established a system of good guys and bad guys known as faces and heels, respectively. These roles were completely angle based and could change several times over the course of a single wrestler's career. The faces were usually the crowd favorites, but heel wrestlers were also quite popular; these were characters that most fans loved to hate, but whom many fans also idolized because they represented the breaking of norms with impunity. As wrestling became more of a dramatic spectacle and less of a pure sporting competition, these roles, as well as the role of tweener—someone who could at any moment act as a face or a heel—became increasingly important to the maintenance of kayfabe.

One primary concern for promoters was a fear of shooters moving into their territory. A shooter was a wrestler who treated worked shows as if they were legitimate athletic contests. The shooter was particularly dangerous to the business model of professional wrestling because he was often unwilling to keep the established kayfabe of the territory. For example, occasionally, a shooter would beat the champion in a match, which undermined the integrity of the promotion and title. The fear of shooters led to tight control over who could be booked in a territory. There was even the cultivation of professional wrestlers who could actually beat any shooters and help to enforce kayfabe. Over time, the blacklisting of wrestlers who could not be trusted, as well as the apparent financial reward for those who were trustworthy, led to wrestling being primarily an entertainment spectacle consisting of scripted outcomes and promoted champions.

Given the financial incentives and the entertainment guarantee of worked shows, even spectators soon gained an interest in keeping kayfabe. Few watched professional wrestling because they wanted to observe athletic prowess. Instead, most relish in the spectacle, whether they know it is kayfabe or not. Today, everyone who watches and enjoys professional

314

wrestling understands that the show is almost completely scripted, and that the old kayfabe—which insisted that the matches were actual athletic events—is broken. Nobody who watches the WWE thinks that the match outcome is not determined in advance. In fact, a new kayfabe has taken the place of the old, where people willingly pretend that professional wrestling is something more than a soap opera being played out by people with large muscles. Today, a professional wrestler is as much an actor and businessperson as he or she is an athlete. And thus, like soap operas, enjoyment of professional wrestling with this new kayfabe becomes a form of escapism, in much the same way as reading comic books is. As such, kayfabe and fan interaction with professional wrestling have come to mirror the way many people engage with political discourse.

THE SOCIAL CONSTRUCTION OF POLITICS

Like professional wrestling, the world of politics employs a kayfabe to boost public support for policies and politicians. The public is propagandized on a constant basis by political leaders. Jacques Ellul (1965) notes that propaganda is ubiquitous, even when not intentionally employed, because it is quite functional. On the one hand, politicians cannot rely on the fickle nature of public opinion to guide their policies, but on the other hand, especially in Western democracies, politicians are constrained in their policy making to those policies that appear to have public support.

For its part, the public wants to feel like it supports the policies of the government, but at the same time, members of the public insist that they have some input in the matter, however illusory that input truly is. The result is that both politicians and the public have an interest in the political spectacle. The politicians require it to appear to have taken the interests of the people into account, while the people need it to feel a sense of ownership in the government and its policies without actually having to participate in any meaningful way (Ellul, 124–128).

Politics by kayfabe is not crass cynicism. Like professional wrestling, the kayfabe has become necessary for all interested participants. In wrestling, the kayfabe provides a vehicle for fans to accept the spectacle as real. The business itself relies on the public buying into the story just as much as the public requires a story to buy into. The fans at a wrestling match are, in a sense, there to be taken. They want the drama, which so happens to center on men and women throwing each other around in the ring.

315

But in the final analysis, the motivation for seeing a professional wrestling match is no different from the motivation for going to see a popular movie or play in the theater. At no point does the audience assume that anything they see on the stage or screen is actually real, as "real" is unimportant. Those actors, directors, and special effects artists who can make it *look real* are given awards for their talent. So, it is unreasonable that anyone should complain that professional wrestling is fake. Nobody involved—the wrestlers themselves, or the bookers, or the crowd—thinks professional wrestling is real in a strictly factual sense: kayfabe allows professional wrestling to *become* real by acting as a vehicle that allows fans to buy into the spectacle and enjoy it. When non-kayfabe accidents do happen in or out of the ring, this amounts to a tragedy or a scandal, partly because it breaks the illusion that the crowd has bought into.[4] Even when accidents are not involved, there is still a norm against breaking kayfabe, because it then denies the crowd their ability to enjoy the spectacle, which undermines the business model of the promotion in turn.

Conversely, what has come to be known as political theater is held up to a completely unrealistic standard. The problem with the political kayfabe is that most of those who make up the audience actually believe that what they are seeing before them is real, in the sense of treating political campaigns like shoot matches; this, in turn, guides their reactions to events. Possibly, the reason is that the policies made by the government, which themselves are only incidentally related to the political theater, actually affect people's lives. The difficulty comes when people attempt to divorce the experience they have when they are exposed to *political propaganda* crafted for them by interested actors from the *outcomes of policy making*, as they see those two things as intricately connected. In fact, the spectacle of a publicly aired political debate or a political campaign is as far removed from the actual policy outcomes as the worked program is from shoot wrestling.

And yet, it is that spectacle to which people tune in by the millions to experience. Millions of people will view MSNBC or FOX News for hours *every single day*. Rush Limbaugh's syndicated political talk show alone reaches 600 radio stations and as many as 20 million listeners daily. That figure says nothing of the vast assortment of other politically related talk shows that are somewhat less popular (Farhi, 2009). Political news and talk radio, it is important to note, do not offer much in the way of *policy education*. For that, one must tune into C-SPAN, which 47 million Americans do *at least once a week*, according to one recent survey (Harper, 2013).[5] These numbers aside, the audience for political entertainment, analogous to sports entertainment, dwarfs the audience for coverage of actual political policy making.

316

What we have then is a population largely conditioned to see heroes and villains in politics, the same way they see heroes and villains in professional wrestling. The script that casts our political leaders as faces or heels, domestic and foreign policies as angles, and the process of government in general as a worked program is written for the population by the bookers of politics. It is these people who gain from the population continuing to pay attention and continuing to buy into the political kayfabe.

The bookers may be the commentators who require political spectacle to generate revenues from commercials, but there can be no doubt that they contribute to the script. Bookers can also be the politicians themselves, and their combined staffs, who benefit electorally and financially from the manufactured outrage by significant segments of their constituencies, or from those who make their living raising money for political candidates. These people instrumentally benefit from the social construction of reality and use the fact that this exists to create the opinions of men and women in the same ways that wrestling bookers generate heat for pro-wrestling champions.

Political angles are scripted in much the same way as wrestling angles are. Political bookers make claims that are designed to produce both movement in public opinion and social action for a particular candidate or policy. In doing so, they present issues in a particular way that offers a coherent framework. A narrative is built on that framework, which is designed to generate a specific response in certain segments of the population by presenting relatively mundane policy disputes as if they were Armageddon scenarios. These narratives paint one's political opponents as reckless, corrupt, and malevolent others, while presenting one's friends as hardworking, patriotic, and legitimate. The "other" is an important concept in the social construction of political reality and identity. An other becomes a trope, something that defines a person by defining what that person is not.[6] Interestingly, a single person can be cast as a hero or a villain in politics, depending on who is doing the framing. What is important for the claim-makers in politics is that their selected segment of the audience buy into the narrative, whatever it happens to be.

It is important to note that the creators of political reality do not need to craft their narrative to attract all people, or even a majority of the population. Often, political bookers need only channel the interest and the ire of a small—but vocal—minority, who will then attract the media and make it appear that a nascent sentiment held by a marginal segment of the population is actually a full-fledged national social movement supported by a strong majority. The news media reports on this small group's activities because the news media require

317

viewers and need content to fill up space on their 24-hour news programs. That reporting, in turn, serves to reinforce the framework set up by the political claim-makers. As if on cue, a more general audience predictably responds in a way that translates to predictable news consumption habits, more reliable votes for candidates, and increased political activity, usually in the form of political contributions for campaigns. This response, reflected in endless polls, then generates more news coverage. Nothing is strictly true in this process, but then, from the standpoint of the audience, it *becomes* true, and they respond as if it is and has always been true, until they are somehow convinced otherwise. Even then, however, the kayfabe of politics has to be broken, often by a scandal of some sort or a consistently terrible public performance on the part of the politician, before a counter-narrative will begin to build heat and become salient.

As in professional wrestling, the audience benefits from the maintenance of the kayfabe, even if some people are not yet aware that it is all a scripted spectacle. It is possible that if they knew, they would not care anyway. The population, which is largely consumed by its own parochial interests, nonetheless craves the feeling that it is part of the collective political decision-making process, or as Ellul writes, "… to have wanted what the government is doing … the government almost always conducts its [policies] on its own initiative, but where the public is interested in a particular question, it can only proceed with the *apparent* support of a substantial majority of the people" (Ellul, 1965: 127–128). According to Ellul, this support in the population is manufactured by political propaganda—just as, we add, a wrestling program is scripted by bookers.

The political bookers, the news media, and the population, which gets to feel as if it is participating in a meaningful way in its democracy, all benefit from this. Nobody has any interest in altering this feedback loop created as a result of the complementary needs of politicians to generate public support for their activities, political news to raise revenue from advertisers, and the public to be quasi-involved in a democracy. Even the people who are perpetually shut out of the system benefit from the maintenance of the kayfabe. This is because they get to see their own struggle as just and everyone on the inside as somehow wicked or corrupt. For those who support third parties are the jobbers who serve to further validate and legitimate the hegemonic ideology of majoritarianism in a democracy.

Thus, political kayfabe represents political reality, as real as anything, for the vast majority of the interested population. Meanwhile, the mundane process of actually crafting and enacting public policy is not nearly so interesting, nor does it actually require the input of the public

318

at all. Not surprisingly, despite all the drama and polarization reported on by the political press and repeated back to reporters and pollsters by endless streams of frustrated and angry citizens, the government still functions: it still pays its bills; citizens still receive their social security checks on time; politicians still receive their paychecks; and the military still operates on dozens of bases overseas. It is as if nothing that happens in the political spectacle actually matters one bit when it comes to passing and executing policy at home and abroad.

FOREIGN POLICY BY KAYFABE

Two cases particularly illustrate the way politicians use kayfabes to craft attitudes among the population. The first is an example of the manner foreign policy makers use kayfabe angles to get the public to buy into policies over which they actually have very little input, as illustrated in the long-standing antipathy between the United States and Russia. The second involves the employment of racial and nationalistic prejudices of an audience to generate support for the narrative surrounding the 2008 election. In both politics and professional wrestling, these tropes are used because they work. In professional wrestling, they generate ticket sales and help the crowd develop an investment in the show. Meanwhile, in politics, these tactics help to drive popular support for policy and elections.

The use by promoters of racial, class, and xenophobic stereotypes to draw crowds is well documented. Since the early days of professional wrestling, the "foreign menace" has been a standard go-to tactic used by promoters to draw crowd interest. Examples of this can be seen in famous American-versus-foreigner rivalries such as Frank Gotch opposite George Hackenschmidt from the latter 19th and early 20th centuries. The appeal of the foreigner by new immigrants to the United States was also exploited in the early decades of the 20th century with wresters like Jim Londos, whose Greek heritage made him a hero to the immigrant populations in New York City. He would be regularly pitted against and defeat some foreign menace to the delight of the crowd (Shoemaker, 2013, 22–24).[7]

The best example of the usefulness of a foreign menace in wrestling as a reflection on foreign politics is the storyline featuring Hulk "Real American" Hogan and the Russian/Soviet tag team aptly named the Bolsheviks. The Hogan-Bolshevik kayfabe rivalry used the Cold War in the 1980s as its backdrop and coincided with a sharp rise in hostile public rhetoric between the United States and the Soviet Union. Following the Soviet invasion of

319

Afghanistan in 1979, the hopeful period of détente between the two superpowers suffered a major setback. With the 1980 election of Ronald Reagan to the US presidency, there seemed to be a new era of aggressive Cold War rivalry. Reagan, campaigning as a hardened Cold Warrior who would be tough on the Soviets, came into office and faced bad economic news at home and a seemingly aggressive Soviet Union abroad. This reality—that antagonism was increasing—was ripe for exploitation by the entertainment sector and those engaged in international diplomacy.[8]

Throughout the 1980s, the actual antagonism between the United States and the Soviet Union cooled. During Regan's presidency, there was an increase in both communication and cooperation between the two superpowers. For example, following the rise of Soviet leader Mikhail Gorbachev, the United States seemed more willing than ever to discuss and agree to nuclear weapons reductions in summits and to conclude trade deals with the Soviets. But this reality did not alter the anti-Soviet rhetoric coming from the White House. The Reagan administration famously described the Soviet Union as an "evil empire" and called Nicaragua under the leftist Sandinistas a "Communist dungeon." Interestingly, President Reagan is still given credit for being tough on the Soviets and for being a man who knew how to beat his foe into submission. His aggressive and militarized response to the Soviet Union is still seen in some political circles as being responsible for ending the Cold War. This position has become mythologized in modern American popular culture, especially among political conservatives. As is almost always the case when myth is put next to factual truth, the truth in all its nuanced and haphazard reality is much harder to identify and relate to than the straightforward and simplified myth.

Back in the ring in the late 1980s, Hogan and the WWF were in full xenophobic spin. The epic battles between Hogan and "Communist" foes Nikolai Volkoff and Boris Zhukov, better known as the tag-team the Bolsheviks, were packing houses and generating revenue in the new highly profitable, pay-per-view events. Hogan would whip the crowd into anti-Communist/anti-Soviet frenzy by waving the American flag in the ring, adopting and using extreme anti-Soviet rhetoric in promos, dressing in patriotic garb, and extolling viewers to be "real Americans"—something they could achieve by training, eating vitamins, praying, and remaining "true to themselves" and their country (Hogan in the WWF promo, 2012). Hogan went on to defeat his anti-American foes in a televised "Flag Match," where, to the delight of the crowd, he spat on the Soviet flag in disgust, used it to shine his boots, and then proudly waved the Stars and Stripes as he victoriously left the ring.

Hogan's fame also inspired various pro-American characters like the Hart Foundation, whose feud with the Bolsheviks led to a major anti-Soviet angle in the financially lucrative WrestleMania IV, as well as "Hacksaw" Jim Dugan, who famously brought the still widely used "U-S-A! U-S-A!" chant to professional wrestling. Along with these angles, other popular storylines seemed to be ripped from the international section of the *New York Times*. Americans cheered for Hogan in his epic battles with the Iranian-born Iron Sheik and applauded his in-ring crumbling of the portrait of Libyan leader Muammar Gaddafi because Hogan was seen as everything American, deserving of applause and praise, while the Bolsheviks and the Sheik were others, deserving of the crowd's hatred. In all, the us-and-them mentality of the crowd was exploited by promoters to generate interest—and more importantly, profits. It should be noted the biographies of wrestlers were always well known. Hogan was from Florida, the person who played Volkoff was from Croatia, and Boris Zhukov, the other half of the Bolsheviks tag-team, was born Jim Harrell in Roanoke, Virginia.

As the 1980s came to an end, progress toward nuclear disarmament between the Soviets and the United States became increasingly clear. The populations of both countries began to see each other less as enemies than they had before. This was in large part due to the fact that Mikhail Gorbachev was now leading the Soviet Union, and he was not subjected to intense US government vilification. Reagan's successor, George H. W. Bush, whose perceived Cold Warrior status was viewed as not as tough as Reagan's, was able to push and achieve the START Treaty of the early 1990s. With the fall of the Berlin Wall and the rapid retreat of the Soviet Union from eastern Europe, the American entertainment consumer was ready for a new bad guy. Thus, the foreign menace role began to shift from Soviet/Communist bad guys to other types of official antisocial imagery. Hogan himself would later become a heel, and while this reversal would be notable in other media, fans of wrestling took it in stride and learned to love to hate the new bad guy. In the end, just as in wrestling, the kayfabe antagonism between the United States and the Russians had run its course; and as in wrestling, the American people were startlingly quick to adopt a new narrative about their old enemies.

ELECTIONS BY KAYFABE

Domestic politics also benefit from framing a chronicle about one's opponent using an us-versus-them narrative to help create identity. The 2008 election provides an excellent example of politics by kayfabe. Before it was clear that Senator Barack Obama would be the frontrunner in the 2008 election, few people outside of the state of Illinois had heard of him. If Obama had been a professional wrestler in 2006, he would be a mid-card wrestler who only ever wrestled in local venues and rarely ever made it on to television. He would have had a small, dedicated fan base within his region, but would be nearly unknown outside of Illinois, thus drawing few supporters nationwide.

The 2008 primary contest with Hillary Clinton had the effect of battle hardening Obama and exposing him to a national audience for the first time. But the showdown with Clinton was essentially the show-before-the-show. And at this point, the real kayfabe kicked in. Early in the primary contest, questions about Obama's citizenship began to emerge. These questions were initially associated with Clinton's campaign (Smith and Tau, 2011), but the effect was to raise doubt in the minds of voters who were looking for some excuse to disqualify Obama from office. Wherever the challenge to Obama's citizenship began, it was ultimately picked up by the bookers on the political right, who inaugurated various whisper campaign tactics to spread the idea to the minds of Republican voters that perhaps Obama was not actually from the United States. The challenge around Obama's birth certificate was absolutely necessary to create a storyline that Obama was a dangerous other to be feared, then hated, and then opposed. For those who saw him in these terms, Obama became a Kenyan Muslim Socialist—someone not truly American.[9]

These insinuations, which did not necessarily need to be substantiated, were stoked nonetheless to some degree by the Republican campaign of John McCain and Sarah Palin, who were playing on the preexisting prejudices and fears common in certain segments of the American populace. This framework was reinforced by commentators on political radio. It got so bad that in mid-October, McCain went off script and tried to walk back comments from spectators at one Minnesota rally. There, several people vocally repeated the points coming from the McCain campaign and those who affiliated themselves with the campaign, which suggested that Obama was not American, and inspired fear among McCain's sup- porters. McCain, a long-time public servant and former POW, was by this point probably quite chagrined. But if he thought the optics of people repeating the talking points his own campaign had encouraged were bad, the results of him breaking the kayfabe angle were even worse. He grabbed the microphone from one woman who said she could not trust Obama because he was an "Arab," called Obama a "decent" man, and was subsequently booed by the crowd.[10]

322

But where did this perception come from? We argue that painting Obama in these terms, to the point where the argument that he was a foreigner, or a Socialist, or that he was pro-Islam was useful to both the McCain and Obama campaigns in 2008. McCain and Obama could have debated policy the entire campaign, and very few people would have tuned in. However, when the election became about the spectacle, this is when the temperatures rose and the activists came out in support for their chosen candidate. In other words, when the narrative was fixed that either Obama was some untrustworthy other in the minds of his opponents (and therefore a danger to the country) or conversely, that McCain courted the support of fanatical idiots (and therefore a danger to the country), then people became invested in the election. We can look at data to find out essentially when this happened. Gallup's Daily Tracking Poll for 2008 follows the trends from that year. Between March and late June, there was very little difference between popular support for the two campaigns. Obama looked like he would jump out ahead in the summer, but his lead was erased in time for the convention. It was not until after the conventions late in September that Obama began to pull away, and the undecided voters disappeared from existence, for all intents and purposes (Gallup, 2008).

Our argument is that at this point, the message of both campaigns became fixed in the minds of those answering the polls. The narrative had become a self-perpetuating story. The campaigns built talking points around it and crafted them into standard stump speeches. News media covered those stump speeches as if they were news, and then the talking points were repeated back to pollsters by the electorate as if they were a reflection of reality. In the 2008 elections, voters were acting like spectators to a wrestling event. For them, the storyline became real, and it generated action. The campaigns benefited because voters had internalized their message; the media benefited because people were glued to constant coverage of the campaign; and the voters benefited because they felt an ownership for their campaigns. Each group of supporters had their own face, and the opponent was the heel.

By the time the woman at the McCain rally called Obama an Arab, factual reality did not matter. She would proceed in her life as if he had always been an Arab, with all the connotations that go along with that term in the minds of those for whom that label is salient. In her mind, Obama was the heel of all heels, a completely untrustworthy and illegitimate foreign other. And when McCain broke the kayfabe and explained that he thought Obama was a decent man, he was ridiculed by that crowd. McCain had been thus far successful in framing Obama in terms he was now directly contradicting. He disabused the crowd—for

323

one moment—of their illusions that Obama was some sort of monster who needed to be stopped at all costs. After that day, he never did it again.

CONCLUSION

As these two cases demonstrate, politicians use the same techniques that wrestling promoters use when developing support for their chosen narratives and actors. Professional wrestling then becomes an excellent analogy for the creation and the mobilization of mass opinion, most especially in advanced democracies. The result can be called government by kayfabe, where everyone buys into the narrative that while the rivalries are not nearly as exciting as they appear to be, nonetheless, the people, political leaders, and news media outlets all benefit from a willing suspension of disbelief. The people get to feel as if they have some investment in public policy, when their opinion is actually rarely taken into account. The politicians can drum up support for both political campaigns and for policies, which is necessary in a democracy. And the news media outlets get to sell commercials and underwrite their own revenue stream. Like the knowledge that professional wrestling is all a work, government by kayfabe does not appear to present much of a problem for most of the players involved.

NOTES

1. Perhaps the most famous and comprehensive discussions on the creation and function of propaganda, and its effects on a mass population is found in Jacques Ellul's book *Propaganda* (1965). In this book, Ellul systematically defines propaganda, but more importantly, he also discusses the way that propaganda works in the individual to produce action. This work is instructive for those interested in social construction of reality.
2. When discussing wrestling jargon, it is important to remember that there is no one definitive authority. Many times, as in the use of all languages, the meaning is contextually defined. Often, there is mixing of the argot with specific meanings being transferred from term to term as the situation dictates. It is helpful, however, to have an understanding of the terms used in this paper.

3. During the 1980s, when suspicion of people from the Middle East was on the rise in the United States and United States-Iranian relations were at an all-time low, the Iranian wrestler known as Iron Sheik gained prominence as a notorious heel wrestler. His chief rivals were those who promoted the ideals of the "USA," especially Hulk Hogan, whose national fame and reputation as "the Real American Hero" was launched in a high-profile match against the Sheik, "Hacksaw" Jim Duggan, who riled up the crowd with the "USA! USA!" chant; and Sgt. Slaughter, whose character was based primarily on a US Army drill instructor. Later, following the First Gulf War, the Sheik, now known as Col. Mustafa, actually teamed with Slaughter as Iraqi sympathizers, despite their long-standing feud and despite the fact that Iran and Iraq were still bitter rivals in the non-kayfabe world.

4. For example, in 1999, a tragedy in the wrestling world occurred when a crowd favorite, Owen Hart, was set to make a comedic entrance on a line suspended above the ring. Hart was tethered to a line by a harness, which was equipped with a quick release. The quick release failed unexpectedly, and Hart fell from the line, suffering mortal injuries. As medical professionals attended to Hart, the announcer repeated that what was happening was not an angle. Hart subsequently died from his injuries.

5. Unfortunately, the survey does not differentiate between the coverage of political debates on the floor of the Congress and the various other programming and lectures presented on the channel.

6. An excellent discussion of the "other" as a construct is found in Schwalbe et al. (2000, 422–426). The other can be constructed for the instrumental purpose of gaining some economic or social advantage, but it can also be used to perpetuate social and political inequality. For our purposes, the creation of the other in professional wrestling is important to give the crowd someone to dislike for the purpose of generating support for the champion or contender, while in politics, the other is necessary to drum up support for a particular candidate by generating hate and fear of his or her opponent.

7. As current opinion and biases changed, so too would the home country of the foreign villain. In the immediate post–World War II era, the foreign villain would often come from Japan or Germany. One example is the wrestler Martin Hisao "Duke Kiamoka" Tanaka, whose ability to use "oriental trickery" to blind his opponents enraged crowds made up of former GIs just home from the war. His gimmick was later expanded upon very successfully by Akihisa "the Great Kabuki" Mera, who blew green mist into the face of his opponents, temporarily blinding them. The us-versus-them angle was profitable, and from it we get many famous wrestlers like the Von

Erich family, whose ring names came from the creation of the character Fritz Von Erich in an angle that set a tag-team of pseudo-Nazi characters against American good guys. Fritz von Erich's real name was Jack Adkisson, and he was born in Texas.

8. See, for example movies like *Rocky IV* (1985), where the Communist hero Ivan Drago, played by Dolf Lundgren, after delivering a lethal knockout to the American boxer Apollo Creed (who arrived at the ring dressed as Uncle Sam and wore American flag shorts for the match) famously and coldly says, "If he dies, he dies. ..." Another example of bellicose Cold War politics portrayed in film is the 1984 movie *Red Dawn*. This movie was particularly terrifying to audiences because it portrayed a scenario where Communists from Cuba and Nicaragua, supported by Soviet arms, advice, and tactical nuclear weaponry, were able to occupy most of the United States. That movie was also notoriously the product of US foreign policy planners. The director, John Milus, famously drafted former secretary of state Alexander Haig, then on the board of MGM-UA to consult on the realism of the scenario presented (Sirota, 2011). Haig, for his part, praised the realism of the final version of the film.

9. A Reuters article from January 2008 demonstrates that the association of Obama with a Kenyan Socialist who also seemed to support Islamic interests was already fairly widely trafficked, even by this time. The article went to great lengths to demonstrate that the connection was not accurate, according to an unnamed uncle. But this did not stop the rumor from spreading among Obama's opponents. In fact, it was useful to help them construct their own identity by constructing Obama as an other (Mukoya and Malherbe, 2008).

10. CBS news reported this, while making sure to also report Obama's connection to William Ayres, someone opponents have called a "terrorist" (Bentley, 2008).

REFERENCES

Beekman, S. (2006). *Ringside: A History of Professional Wrestling in America*. Santa Barbara, CA: Greenwood Publishing Group.

Bentley, J. (2008). "McCain booed for telling audience to be respectful of Obama." CBS News. Accessed online October 7, 2014, at http://www.cbsnews.com/news/mccain-booed-for-telling-audience-to-be-respectful-of-obama

Ellul, J. (1965). *Propaganda*. Translated by Konrad Kellan and Jean Lerner. New York: Vintage Books.

Farhi, P. (2009). "Limbaugh's audience size? It's largely up in the air." *Washington Post*, March 7. Accessed online October 7, 2014, at http://www.washingtonpost.com/wpdyn/content/article/2009/03/06/AR2009030603435.html

Gallup. (2008). Gallup Daily: Election 2008. Accessed online October 7, 2014, at http://www.gallup.com/poll/107674/Gallup-Daily-Election-2008.aspx

Harper, J. (2013). "C-SPAN the emerging hipster network: Its audience 'trends young.'" *Washington Times*, March 19. Accessed online October 7, 2014, at http://www.washingtontimes.com/blog/watercooler/2013/mar/19/c-span-emerging-hipster-network-its-audience-trend/

Hogan, H. (2012). *Hulk Hogan—Real American HD* (Official Video). Accessed online December 24, 2014, at https://www.youtube.com/watch?v=RKM1AAzeRCg

Kerrick, G. E. (1980). "The jargon of professional wrestling." *American Speech* 55, 142–145.

Mukoya, T., and V. Malherbe. (2008). "Some Kenyans forget crisis to root for Obama." Reuters.com. Accessed online October 7, 2014, at http://www.reuters.com/article/2008/01/08/us-usa-politics-kenya-idUSL0872724120080108

Schwalbe, M., S. Godwin, D. Holden, D. Schrock, et al. (2000). "Generic processes in the reproduction of inequality: An interactionist analysis." *Social Forces* 79, 419–452.

Shoemaker, D. (2013). *The Squared Circle: Life, Death and Professional Wrestling*. New York: Gotham Books.

Sirota, D. (2011). "How the '80s programmed us for war." Salon.com, March 15. Accessed online January 15, 2015, at http://www.salon.com/2011/03/15/sirota_excerpt_back_to_our_future/

Smith B., and B. Tau. (2011). "Birtherism: Where it all began." Politico.com, April 22. Accessed online November 8, 2014, at http://www.politico.com/news/stories/0411/53563.html

Stallone, S. (1985). *Rocky IV*. Los Angeles: MGM-UA.

CHAPTER TWENTY

The Relocation of Professional Sports Franchises and Sweetheart Stadium Deals

BY **BRANDON LANG**

Dozens of professional sports teams have moved from one city to another over the years. One reason for this is overexpansion. North American leagues such as the NHL, for example, have expanded into nontraditional hockey markets such as Atlanta and Arizona, where the new teams struggle financially. Another reason has to do with sweetheart stadium deals. Many teams, including the Hartford Whalers (NHL), Baltimore Colts (NFL), and Seattle Sonics (NBA), among others, have been lured to other cities with the promise of a new publicly financed stadium. The purpose of this reading is to fully explain reason why teams move and to discuss the positive and negative implications of these practices.

BACKGROUND

The number of professional sports teams that have relocated from one to city to another is astonishingly high. In Major League Baseball, 14 teams have relocated. For example, the Giants and the Dodgers moved to California in the late 1950s, and the Washington Senators relocated on two occasions, once to Minnesota and the other to Texas. Over the years, the St. Louis Browns moved to Baltimore and became the Orioles; the Philadelphia Athletics moved to Oakland by way of Kansas City; and the Expos moved from Montreal to Washington, DC, where they became the Nationals. In the cases of the Athletics, the Browns, and the Boston Braves, they moved because they were competing with other MLB teams in the same city. Over time, several cities that lost teams, including New York, Washington, Seattle, Milwaukee, and Kansas City were either awarded expansion franchises, or they lured away teams from other cities themselves.

In the National Football League, 14 teams have also relocated. The Chicago Cardinals, for instance, moved to St. Louis and then ultimately to Arizona. The Oilers moved to Nashville and became the Tennessee Titans; the Cleveland Browns moved to Baltimore after the Colts left town; and the Rams moved from Los Angeles to St. Louis and then back to a different stadium in Los Angeles. In the National Hockey League, 14 teams have relocated. For example, the Atlanta Flames moved to Calgary; the Kansas City Scouts moved to Denver and became the Colorado Rockies and then moved to New Jersey, where they became the Devils; the Quebec Nordiques moved to Denver and became the Colorado Avalanche; and the Winnipeg Jets became the Phoenix, now Arizona, Coyotes. The National Basketball Association has had the most team movement of the big four North American leagues. Many teams have moved cities. The Minneapolis Lakers, for instance, moved to Los Angeles; the New Orleans Jazz moved to Utah; and the Vancouver Grizzlies moved to Memphis.

If we include Major League Soccer, the Arena Football League, and the WNBA, a total of 70 North American franchises have moved over time. Around half of the teams that have moved kept their team names—the Milwaukee Braves became the Atlanta Braves, and the San Diego Clippers became the Los Angeles Clippers. Meanwhile, the other half rebranded themselves. This happened when the Montreal Expos became the Washington Nationals and the California Golden Seals became the Cleveland Barons. One last point pertains to team records. In most cases, teams that move and rebrand themselves honor the franchise records and retired numbers associated with the old city, such as when the Hartford Whalers moved to North Carolina and became the Hurricanes; they kept Gordie Howe's number retired and all of the team records intact. One example of this not happening applies to the Baltimore Ravens. As part of the deal that saw the Cleveland Browns move to Baltimore, the team colors and records were not allowed to be used by Baltimore.

WHY HAVE SO MANY TEAMS MOVED?

There are three main reasons why professional sports franchises have moved from one city to another. The first is that all of the main North American professional sports leagues have expanded since their inception. Second, some teams lost money and sought to move to cities where they could make money. The third is that other teams have been wooed away from cities with what can be termed sweetheart stadium deals.

REASON 1: LEAGUE EXPANSION

Since their inception, all of the main North American professional sports leagues have expanded. The NHL started out with four teams in 1917, expanded to six teams in the next decade, and operated as a six-league team until 1967, when they added six more teams. Since 1967, the league has continued to expand: there are now NHL teams in 30 cities. Similarly, the NBA, NFL, and Major League Baseball have expanded to 30 or more teams over the years.

Prior to World War II, professional teams were located in eastern North American cities such as Toronto, New York, Detroit, Philadelphia, and Chicago. Teams traveled by train, and rivalries were quickly established between these teams, in part because the leagues were so small and they played each other so frequently. Following World War II, air travel became more common. Fans in cities west of the Mississippi River such as Denver, San Francisco, and Los Angeles were craving their own sports teams. Moreover, most of these cities had the infrastructure, funding, and pool of fans needed to accommodate pro teams.

Professional sports hit the West Coast in the 1950s and 1960s. In some cases, expansion teams were created like the Los Angeles Kings and the Seattle Pilots. When the NHL expanded in 1967, two teams were located in California to help grow the game and nationalize the NHL brand. In other cases, existing teams moved west from the East Coast. A perfect example of this would be the Brooklyn Dodgers and New York Giants moving to California. The Dodgers and Giants were playing in dilapidated stadia and were courted by West Coast cities offering enthusiastic fans, state-of-the art facilities, and beautiful weather.

331

REASON 2: POOR ATTENDANCE

The second reason why teams move relates to poor attendance. In the NHL, for example, several teams, including the Atlanta Flames, Cleveland Barons, and California Golden Seals, really struggled selling tickets and merchandise. Although each of these teams had a small base of dedicated fans, games were under-attended, and team owners lost huge sums of money operating the teams. It is not just that these teams struggled selling tickets to games; the viewership of games on television and the listening to games on the radio were so low that not enough money was being generated through the selling of media rights to support the teams. Ultimately, many team owners decided to move to markets where they thought they could make more money.

In a small number of cases, teams have been moved even though they sell out games and have an enthusiastic fan base. The Seattle Sonics (NBA) and Winnipeg Jets (NHL) are both examples of teams whose games sold out and had a large pool of fans. In the case of the Sonics, a new person from Oklahoma City bought the team who felt strongly about putting a pro sports franchise in his hometown. In the case of the Jets, their arena did not have many luxury boxes, and the team could not generate the same gate revenue that they could in a stadium with more club seats and boxes.

REASON 3: SWEETHEART STADIUM DEALS

The majority of professional sports teams play in publicly owned stadia that they lease from the stadium authority in that city. In addition to rent, cities receive a share of the concession, advertising, and parking revenue. Like all landlords, however, they are also responsible for the upkeep, maintenance, and renovation of these facilities. Along the way, many team owners appealed to municipal authorities to renovate existing or build new stadia, only to be told that there was not enough money to do so.

The third reason that teams move is that many cities around the United States are desperate to either land professional teams or replace teams that they have lost. Having a professional sports team is not just a source of pride for residents of a city; teams create jobs, generate taxes, and help elevate a city to world-class status. As such, many municipalities have offered team owners so many incentives to relocate a professional team to their city that these owners felt they could not afford to say no. These can be termed sweetheart stadium deals.

Consider the case of the Cleveland Browns. The Browns played in an outdated stadium built in 1930, which was in what many would consider a state of disrepair. There were not enough bathrooms, many seats were far from the field, and support posts interfered with many fans' view of the game. For years, Art Modell, the team's owner, pleaded with the Cleveland city council to build a new stadium. The Browns were playing in one of the oldest stadia in the league, and he felt that the team deserved a new one. During this time, however, Cleveland was experiencing a high rate of deindustrialization and manufacturing jobs were rapidly being outsourced to Mexico, Korea, and China. Cleveland's tax base was in a state of decline, and there were clearly more pressing issues than the building of a new stadium. Consequently, Modell's requests always fell on deaf ears.

During this same period, Modell was approached by interests in Baltimore and told that the state of Maryland would build a new stadium and allow the team to play there rent free if he moved the team there. In addition, Modell was told that the team could keep the advertising, parking, and concession revenues. The city of Baltimore lost the Colts after the 1983 season to Indianapolis and wanted to restore the proud football tradition of the city. As such, the state of Maryland, the county of Baltimore, and the city of Baltimore were all desperate to have an NFL franchise and willing to pay whatever it took to make that happen. No matter how Modell felt about Cleveland, this deal was so generous that it almost seemed too good to be true. Looking back, Modell would have been crazy to turn down this deal.

This exact scenario characterizes the types of offers that were given to the Hartford Whalers to move to North Carolina, the Quebec Nordiques to move to Colorado, the Seattle Sonics to move to Oklahoma City, and the St. Louis Cardinals (NFL) to move to Arizona. These team owners felt strongly about needing new facilities, but were met with resistance in their home cities. Rather than continuing to play in an older stadium, owners like Peter Karmanos Jr. of the Whalers decided to shop his team around, knowing that other cities were very interested in having an NHL team of their own. Ultimately, they were offered such sweetheart stadium deals by other cities that they invoked their right to relocate the team.

WHAT DOES THIS MEAN FOR FANS?

At the risk of sounding dramatic, tens of thousands of dedicated fans throughout North America have been heartbroken when their favorite team moved to another city. In spite of protests, media campaigns—and even political intervention—fans do not have much say about their favorite team moving. When the Cleveland Browns moved to Baltimore in 1996, many Clevelanders were crushed. They were bitter, angry, and very discouraged. Above all, they felt betrayed by the team owner, Art Modell, whom they viewed and treated as one of their own. After he moved the team, his life was threatened numerous times by Cleveland fans, and he needed security guards to accompany him to games to make him feel safe.

All told, during the three years when there was no football in Cleveland, Sunday was a depressing and sad day in this industrial city on the shore of Lake Erie. Browns fans felt alone. They could not root for the Ravens and the city that pulled them away from Cleveland. They certainly could not root for the Pittsburgh Steelers, their long-time rivals. Rooting for the Cincinnati Bengals was a stretch, as there was such a cultural and geographic gulf between those two cities. To make matters worse, the once great but long-suffering former Browns won the Super Bowl in 2000, four years after moving from Cleveland.

Many of the cities that have persuaded teams to move there have lost teams themselves. Baltimore is a perfect example of this. The Baltimore Colts played in Baltimore for over 30 years. The fan base was rabid, and the team was successful. In many respects, the team fostered a sense of pride and togetherness among people who were living in a city that was racially divided and in the throes of deindustrialization. In 1983, the Colts suddenly moved to Indianapolis, where they played as the Indianapolis Colts. They were persuaded to move by the promise of playing in a new stadium in front of fans very eager to support a team of their own. Needless to say, after the team moved, many fans were crushed. Many were too bitter to root for the team in Indianapolis, and it would have been very difficult for them to root for the rival Redskins in nearby Washington, DC. In any case, 12 years later, the Cleveland Browns were wooed to Baltimore with a sweetheart stadium deal. The Browns fans now felt all of the betrayal and anger that Baltimore fans felt one decade prior.

THE BENEFITS OF MOVING CITIES

Clearly, there are several benefits of a team moving from one city to another. The first benefit is that when teams move, they are generally promised newly built and publicly funded stadia and arenas. As with the Cleveland Browns, the Hartford Whalers, the St. Louis Cardinals (NFL), the original Winnipeg Jets, many others were lured to other cities with the promise of a new stadium. For teams like the Whalers who played in the Hartford Civic Center, a building in dire need of renovation, the prospect of moving to a new location and playing in a brand-new, publicly funded state-of-the-art stadium was, obviously, very enticing. So, the Whalers ended up moving to North Carolina where they played in the Entertainment and Sports Arena, now the PNC Arena, one of the nicest arenas in the NHL. The power brokers in Raleigh bought into the idea that world-class cities need professional sports teams and believed that the presence of an NHL team would elevate their status.

The building of new stadia has helped promote a sense of urban renewal in scores of cities with dilapidated neighborhoods. Many recent stadia and arenas have been built in conjunction with surrounding shops, hotels, condominiums, and restaurants that are designed to promote tourism and encourage more people to move downtown. The two classic examples are Camden Yards in Baltimore and Coors Field in Denver. Camden Yards, for example, was one of the first retro-ballparks with brick facades and other features of older ballparks. Camden Yards was built in the Inner Harbor district of the city and helped transform a neighborhood with abandoned buildings, drug dealers, and general blight to a hip, entertaining, and safe place to be. Similarly, Coors Field helped to transform the Lower Downtown region of Denver from a crime-ridden, dangerous place to an entertainment destination.

An interesting phenomenon is that many teams who have never won a league championship have done so upon moving cities. As documented above, the Ravens won a Super Bowl after moving from Cleveland. Similarly, the St. Louis Rams won a Super Bowl after being relocated from Anaheim. In the NHL, the Hurricanes won the Stanley Cup after moving from Hartford, and the Avalanche won the Stanley Cup shortly after moving from Quebec City. This has also happened in Major League Baseball with the Orioles, Twins, and A's and in the NBA with the Lakers.

When teams relocate, they often change divisions and establish new rivalries. Although the Hartford Whalers left behind a tremendous rivalry with the Boston Bruins, they switched

335

divisions and established fierce rivalries with the Washington Capitals, Florida Panthers, and Tampa Bay Lightning. Similarly, when the Quebec Nordiques moved to Denver and became the Colorado Avalanche, they switched conferences and quickly established fierce rivalries with many western teams, including the Vancouver Canucks and Calgary Flames. This is good for the sport and has the potential to really increase people's degree of support for a given team.

A final benefit is that when teams move cities, the sport's fan base will likely expand. When the Houston Oilers moved to Nashville by way of Memphis and became the Tennessee Titans and the Sonics moved to Oklahoma City and became the Thunder, for instance, fans living in cities without professional franchises finally had professional teams of their own to follow and root for. All of a sudden, people were buying Titans and Thunder merchandise in droves. The level of support for the teams was very high. Although leagues are likely to lose fans in cities like Hartford and Cleveland when they lose teams, they will probably gain more fans, at least in the short term, in their new cities, especially if they do well.

CONCERNS WITH MOVING CITIES

Obviously, there are numerous concerns with relocating teams. It is very expensive to build and manage new stadia. Municipalities around the country have spent hundreds of millions of dollars to build new stadia as a way to encourage other teams to move there. In some cases, all of this money is spent, an arena is built, and a team does not even move there. This happened in Kansas City, where a brand-new arena was built in hopes of luring the Penguins away from Pittsburgh. In spite of all the money that was spent, they could not lure any teams to move there.

It is widely documented that many people have concerns with the public funding of sports stadia. It is not just that most municipalities raise sales and hotel taxes in order to help come up with the money needed to finance new stadia; many also feel strongly that all that money could be better spent on other things like education, infrastructure, and the arts. Nobody could deny that half a billion dollars would go a very long way toward improving test scores and graduation rates in inner-city schools. Similarly, very few could deny that the building of community centers, basketball courts, and parks would not be very beneficial for cities with high poverty rates. Some people liken the public funding of professional stadia

336

to corporate welfare. The main beneficiaries are the people who own teams. Cities do not build restaurants for restaurateurs or car dealerships for people who sell cars. This raises the question of why should they build stadia.

An additional concern is that when teams move, their histories are often played down. Even though the Hartford Whalers retired Gordie Howe's number, there are few references to Gordie Howe in Raleigh. Many current fans are probably not even aware that Gordie Howe is one of the most celebrated members in the history of the Hurricanes/Whalers. Similarly, Tennessee Titans fans do not pay much homage to Earl Campbell, one of the best players in the history of the Houston Oilers. In short, when teams move, they tend to downplay their history. This is unfortunate for fans who could really benefit from knowing more about the history of their teams. Just like it is nice to see people wearing Babe Ruth and Joe DiMaggio jerseys at Yankee Stadium, it would be nice to see more people wearing Whalers jerseys at Hurricane games or Oilers jerseys at Titans games.

A final concern is that when teams move, it can be very hard on the fans who have supported the team. Winnipeg Jets fans supported the team through thick and thin. When the team moved to Arizona, fans must have been devastated. For someone to grow up rooting for a team—only to have that team move—is a very difficult thing to contend with. Most sports fans are very loyal to their favorite team(s). It must be very difficult for people when that loyalty is not reciprocated. A related issue revolves around the question of whom to root for. Chances are, if your favorite team moves to another city, you will no longer root for them. This is especially true if they change their name and rebrand themselves. What are fans left to do? Do they just pick a team out of thin air and root for them? Of course not. They probably become very bitter and angry and lose interest in that sport altogether.

MY PERSONAL THOUGHTS

Let me begin by stating I fully understand that professional sports teams and leagues are businesses. Just like people who own restaurants or car dealerships, it is the prerogative of team owners to make money and be successful. The problem for many fans, however, is that many business decisions are made concerning issues to which they have an emotional connection. For huge fans, it is emotional when a fan favorite or team captain is traded or released from the team. Similarly, people can be very emotional when a team moves from one city to another. Simply put, many fans are loyal supporters of teams and expect teams to be loyal to them in return.

I would never take issue with a restaurateur closing a restaurant that was losing money. Restaurants, like sports teams, are not philanthropic organizations. They exist for reasons beyond making people happy. However, I strongly empathize with people whose favorite team has moved. I lived in Cleveland for four years and saw how supportive the fans were of their Browns. When the Browns played, the city essentially stopped, and a huge percentage of residents watched the game. I am not a Browns fan, but I respect the history of the team and feel for the people who lost their team. The Browns were part of the cultural fabric of Cleveland, and for that to be taken away is very sad for many people. I could not imagine how I would feel if my favorite teams moved cities. Even though I no longer live in the city that I grew up in, like many others, I would be devastated.

CONCLUSIONS

This selection identifies three reasons why professional sports teams relocate. One reason is that many leagues seek to expand their brand. A second is due to poor attendance. The third is based on what I term sweetheart stadium deals. There are, of course, many benefits and concerns associated with a team moving. Some benefits are that teams that move generally receive new publicly funded stadia, urban renewal can take place, and new rivalries are established. Some concerns are that building new stadia is very expensive, that money could be spent in other ways, and teams come across as being disloyal in the eyes of many fans. I understand why teams move, but am very sympathetic to fans.

CHAPTER TWENTY ONE

Ad Nauseam?

Sports Fans' Acceptance of Commercial Messages during Televised Sporting Events

BY **ARON LEVIN**, **JOE COBBS**, **FRED BEASLEY**, AND **CHRIS MANOLIS**

Advertising, sponsorships, promotions and other marketing communication vehicles have become ubiquitous in sports. The 42,500 hours of live sporting events broadcast on national over-the-air and cable television in just the United States (US) generated $10.9 billion in advertising expenditures in 2011, which represents a six percent increase from the previous year (Nielsen, 2012). International Events Group (IEG) projected that another $18.2 billion was invested in North American sponsorships in 2011, with sports sponsorships accounting for over two-thirds of this expenditure. Meanwhile, European and Asia Pacific sponsorship spending reached record levels at $13.6 and $11.1 billion respectively, with similar ratios committed to sports (IEG, 2011). Rance Crain, editor of *Advertising Age*, decries, "I've never seen things changing as much as they are now. Advertisers will not be satisfied until they put their mark on every blade of grass" (Petrecca, 2006). Indeed, artificial turf manufacturers are developing technology to imbed the plastic grass on sports field with fiber optics. One executive admitted, "we will be able to turn the football field into a giant Jumbotron" (Forbes, 2006).

Can the commercial messages in sports ever become too much for the audience to accept? Is there a point at which consumers, and more specifically sports fans, will become annoyed by all the advertising surrounding sports and express their dissatisfaction—a point at which advertisers and sponsors would experience negative repercussions?

The current level of consumer dissatisfaction with commercialization in sports is unclear. There is anecdotal evidence to suggest that many sports fans are becoming increasingly aggravated. On multiple occasions, Major League Baseball (MLB) considered adopting the international football (soccer) and rugby model of selling ad space on players' uniforms and the field of play, only to be flooded with negative fan reaction. Most notably in 2004, Columbia Pictures sought to cover the bases in major league stadiums with Spider Man II logos. The outcry of fans and negative votes at ESPN.com and AOL.com caused the movie studio to retract their promotional strategy (Petrecca, 2006). "We listened to the fans," said Geoffrey Ammer, president of worldwide marketing for Columbia; "We never saw this coming, the reaction the fans had. It became a flashpoint—the reaction was overwhelming. We don't want to do anything that takes away from a fan's enjoyment of the game." Nevertheless, MLB was later able to incorporate sponsor logos on the jerseys of some teams competing in the World Baseball Classic (Fisher & Lefton, 2008). Other major leagues have followed the trend by introducing corporate logos on practice jerseys (Lefton, 2009). Fifteen of the 19 teams in the MLS have jersey sponsors. Most prominently, the Los Angeles Galaxy of the MLS signed a 10-year, $44 million jersey sponsorship agreement with the Herbalife Corporation (Sandomir, 2012). The Women's National Basketball Association (WNBA) now fields several teams with commercial marks on their game uniforms (Neuman, 2009). Similarly, recent discussions in the NBA indicate that there may soon be corporate logos adorning the players' uniforms (Lombardo & Lefton, 2012).

This study investigates consumers' tolerance for commercial messages (e.g., sponsorship and advertising) within televised sports broadcasts and assesses the relationship between acceptance of commercial messages in two popular sports and the perceived brand equity of a common advertiser in those sports. Spectators watching a sporting event on television are exposed to an extensive array of official and unofficial commercial messages (McKelvey, 2006). In addition to advertising during commercial breaks, commercial messages embedded into the content of the broadcast may include actual and virtual signage in the stadium

340

or arena, sponsors' logos on the uniforms of players, coaches, and officials, as well as in-game broadcast billboards and sponsored segments (i.e., "brought to you by ..." messages from announcers) and even ambush marketing (Smolianov & Shilbury, 2005). These sports marketing elements originate from a network of relationships—advertiser soften contract with the media outlet and sponsors contract with the sports team or event directly (Cobbs & Hylton, 2012)—and each can have different consumer effects (Bennett et al., 2006; Meenaghan & Shipley, 1999). Nevertheless, the broadcast viewer is often exposed to this collection of commercial messages simultaneous to sport consumption.

As corporations continue to allocate more of their marketing communication dollars to sports programming (IEG, 2011; McClellan, 2009), marketers should be concerned with sport fans' reaction to this increasing commercial clutter (Bennett et al., 2006). To address such concerns, we develop a contemporary measure of consumers' tolerance for the collection of commercial messages accompanying a sport's television broadcast—the Sport Commercial Acceptance (SCA) scale—and we test the measure across fans of two different sports. The SCA scale is derived from and adds to established scales and contributes to the research literature by producing a measure of fans' attitude toward marketing communications within a specific sport's telecasts—a key consideration in evaluating a sport's mass marketing effectiveness.

LITERATURE REVIEW

The attitudes of consumers toward advertising in general has been extensively studied (e.g., Bauer & Greyser, 1968; Pollay & Mittal, 1993) and linked to advertising effectiveness (MacKenzie, Lutz, & Belch, 1986; Mehta, 2000). Consumers have often been asked about not only their general attitudes, but also their opinions about the trustworthiness, offensiveness, and informative value of advertising. Elliot and Speck (1998) found that among several different media, consumers believed television had the most advertising clutter. Li, Edwards, and Lee (2002) measured viewers' reactions to advertising clutter in various mediums and discovered that television commercials were also the most distracting, suggesting a high degree of intrusiveness. More recently, Logan (2011) noted that many consumers will do anything possible to avoid television advertising, as they often view it as distracting, interfering, and intrusive. While similar research in the domain of sports marketing is sparse,

341

Bennett and colleagues (2006) recognized the potential for television advertising during sporting events to be informative but also irritating and potentially intrusive. Yet not all commercial messages in televised sports programming take the form of traditional advertising (i.e., commercial breaks and broadcast billboards in and out of such breaks).

Various forms of sponsorship have become commonplace in contemporary spectator sports and several elements of sponsorship are aimed at television broadcast exposure (Meenaghan & Shipley, 1999). For instance, field sponsor signage is frequently placed and valued in sponsorship contracts according to the likely exposure time in televised event broadcasts (Lardinoit & Derbaix, 2001). Likewise, the cost of team jersey sponsorships can vary widely based on the team's visual media coverage (Lombardo & Lefton, 2012). However, sponsorship diverges from advertising in that the message and medium for sponsorship are more closely tied in the official relationship with the sponsored entity (e.g., team, league, event, venue), whereas advertising features a message crafted by the advertiser apart from the delivery medium (Meenaghan & Shipley, 1999).

Although marketers utilizing sports advertising and sponsorship often have similar communication objectives (Harvey, 2001), the persuasion process and effects can be quite different. Advertising frequently involves a more complex message that necessitates greater cognitive processing on the part of the consumer compared to sponsorship, which is more passive in nature and indirectly influences consumers through goodwill and an image transfer from sponsored entity to sponsoring brand (Gwinner & Eaton, 1999; Meenaghan, 2001). As a result, advertising is generally thought to be most useful for new brands and products; sponsorship is most effective for established brands; and combinations of sponsorship with moderate advertising support can maximize effects, but with considerable variation based on context (Olson & Thjømøe, 2009). Given that, collectively, over $20 billion is annually invested by marketers in sports sponsorship and advertising during sports television broadcasts (IEG, 2011; Nielsen, 2012), assessing fans' overall attitude toward these commercial messages in televised sports programming is an important gauge for sports marketers to judge commercial tolerance and potential saturation.

AD INTRUSIVENESS

Ad intrusiveness is the amount of interference of one's cognitive processes when exposed to an ad (Edwards, Hairong, & Lee, 2002). Factors affecting ad intrusiveness include the situational context, one's overall attitude toward advertising, and various characteristics of the commercial message (e.g., content, repetitiveness etc.). Edwards and colleagues (2002) also discussed moderating factors likely to influence perceptions about advertising intrusiveness. For example, consumers more focused on programming or content perceive interruptions by ads as more intrusive than less focused consumers.

For decades, advertising has been criticized for being intrusive (e.g., Bauer & Greyser, 1968; Pollay, 1986), and this intrusiveness contributes to ad irritation and ad avoidance (Speck & Elliott, 1997). Beyond intrusiveness, Greyser (1973) identified several factors that impact ad irritation in consumers, including demographics of the consumer, the advertising medium, the type of product, and the ad content and execution. In the little work done in sports on commercial acceptance, television ads have been described as more irritating but also more entertaining than virtual advertisements during a game (Bennett et al., 2006). However, given that viewers of televised sports programming are often exposed to a plethora of commercial messages of varying content and context, consumers' overall impression of the commercial messaging surrounding sports and its impact on brand attitudes are unknown.

This literature sparks the initial research question (RQ1): To what degree do sports fans accept the collection of commercial messages during sports events as being entertaining and informative as opposed to being invasive or annoying? We broadly define commercial messages as any advertising during the televised event or the commercial breaks, as well as event, team, venue, or broadcast sponsorships, billboards (including 'brought to you by…' messages), or ambush marketing within the sports programming. While advertising theory suggests that consumers are generally irritated with advertising, the use of commercial messages in sports beyond just traditional advertising (such as sponsorship embedded in the content) and the concept of fan identification provide rationale to suggest that commercial acceptance within the sports context may be unique. As an extension of RQ1, we also test the extent to which advertising acceptance translates into consumers' attitudes toward advertised brands.

SPORTS FAN IDENTIFICATION

Previous studies have developed the concept of fan identification (e.g., Shank & Beasley, 1998; Hunt, Bristol, & Bashaw, 1999; Funk & Pastore, 2000). Madrigal (2000, p. 14) describes fan identification as a "person's sense of connectedness" to a team, an event or a sport. In summarizing the literature, Wann and Pierce (2003) report that fan identification predicts several cognitive, affective, and behavioral responses. Related to corporate marketing through sport, greater fan identification enhances the recall and recognition of a sponsor's marketing stimuli (Cornwell, Relyea, Irwin, & Maignan, 2000), encourages favorable attitudes toward a sponsor's brand (Gwinner & Swanson, 2003; Levin, Joiner, & Cameron, 2001), and increases intentions to purchase a sponsor's product (Madrigal, 2000). Yet sponsorship is but one form of commercial communication in sports broadcasts, and the effects of all methods of televised sports marketing are not equivalent (Olson & Thjømøe, 2009). While fan identification may favor response to sponsors' messages, it is not clear if more highly identified fans are therefore more accepting of all commercial messages within their favorite sport, or fans simply appreciate the direct support sponsors offer teams, leagues, or events. In other words, investigation of the influence of fan identification on sports marketing beyond just sponsorship is necessary to assess if the same acceptance of commercial messages by highly identified fans exists on a broader marketing level.

To address the sparse research in this area, the study in this paper poses a second research question (RQ2): What is the relationship between acceptance of commercial messages in televised sports broadcasts and fans' level of identification with the sport? While general advertising research suggests consumers highly focused on the ad context would judge advertising within that context to be more intrusive (Edwards et al., 2002), fan identification research in sponsorship implies greater acceptance of commercial messages by highly identified fans (Gwinner & Swanson, 2003). By exploring RQ2, we begin to reconcile these somewhat contrary perspectives of the influence of identification by investigating the tolerance for the collective commercial messages in a sport's telecasts based on different identification levels.

Just as fan identification research emphasizes differences across fans, research across sports also highlights the fallacy of treating all sports as homogeneous. For example, Wann and colleagues (2008) explicated extensive differences in fan motivations across not only several sports, but also various types of sports (e.g., individual vs. team). Similarly, Milne and colleagues (1996) mapped the overlap and unique market positions of over 30 sports, thereby highlighting the perils of sports marketers that ignore differences between sports. In particular, other researchers have isolated motorsport as potentially more conducive to corporate promotional messages than other sports (Cobbs & Hylton, 2012; Levin, Beasley, & Gamble, 2004). Racing fans appear to especially appreciate the monetary and other support provided by corporate marketers in exchange for using motorsports as a promotional platform (Lapio & Speter, 2000). Thus, as a follow-up to RQ2, we offer the following question (RQ3): Do levels of acceptance of commercial messages during sporting events differ between fans of different sports? To investigate this final question, we compare fans of the National Association of Stock Car Auto Racing (NASCAR) to fans of the National Football League (NFL). Prior research in motorsports suggests that NASCAR fans may be more accepting of commercial messages than fans of the NFL.

METHODOLOGY

To empirically address our three research questions and thereby assess attitudes toward commercial messages in televised sports, we surveyed fans of the NFL and NASCAR. These two sports were chosen because their respective fans experience divergent types of marketing messages when consuming their chosen sport. Motorsport is rather unique (although increasingly being emulated by other sports such as professional skateboarding) among sports in its level of commercialization (Lapio & Speter, 2000). NASCAR fans watch three hours of 200 mile-an-hour "billboards" and drivers are adorned from head-to-toe with sponsors' logos (Yost, 2007). Conversely, the commercial messaging is less overt in the NFL, though many marketing messages are embedded in any given NFL game (e.g., corporate stadium name, sponsored coaches' headphones, Gatorade cooler). Regarding traditional commercial breaks, approximately one hour of a three hour televised NFL broadcast is devoted to commercial advertisements (Biderman, 2010). Similarly, in 13 NASCAR Sprint Cup races during the 2012 season, commercial break advertising composed 31.4% of TNT broadcasts and 23.6% of FOX's broadcasts (Gluck, 2012).

345

THE SAMPLE

A sample of 602 members of an online survey panel completed our questionnaire. The sample was purchased from the panel provider, e-Rewards, and response rate was 26%. Respondents were first screened to determine if they were a NASCAR or a NFL fan. More specifically, respondents were asked "How much of a fan of _____ (NASCAR / NFL) would you say you are" (1 = not at all a fan. ... 7 = a die-hard fan). Those who rated themselves above four on the scale were deemed to be a fan, and completed the questionnaire. In the cases in which respondents rated themselves above four on both sports, they were randomly assigned to either the NASCAR or NFL fan group. There were 300 completed surveys from NASCAR fans and 302 from NFL fans. Sixty-five percent of the respondents were male. The majority of the sample was between 25 and 54 years of age, and most respondents have attended at least some college. There was no difference in the age or gender of NASCAR and NFL fans, but there was a significant difference ($p < .05$) in the education levels of the two groups. A higher percentage of NASCAR fans were "high school graduates or less" (25% vs. 16% for NFL fans); while NFL fans were more likely to have some college education. Scarborough Sports Marketing also reports similarities in the demographic profile of NFL and NASCAR fans, with NFL fans having higher average household income (Sports Business Daily, 2010).

To extend the relevance of SCA assessment to a common sports advertiser, we also measured the relationship between SCA and customer perceptions of the Miller Lite brand. Of the original 602 respondents, 253 were found to be drinkers of Miller Lite beer. Miller Lite beer was chosen as the brand of interest in the study because of the brand's prominence in both sports studied (NASCAR and NFL). In 2011, MillerCoors spent $203 million, more than half of its media budget, on sports sponsorships (Crupi, 2012). At the time of data collection, Miller Lite was the primary sponsor of successful NASCAR driver Kurt Busch and also sponsored several NFL teams (e.g., Chicago Bears, Philadelphia Eagles, Dallas Cowboys) in addition to the brand's tailgating-themed, football promotional campaign. Of the 253 Miller Lite-drinking respondents, 55 percent (n = 139) were NASCAR fans and 45 percent (n = 114) were NFL fans.

MEASURES

Sport fan identification

The Wann and Branscombe (1993) fan identification scale was used in this study, which employed six items: 1) how big of a fan of (NASCAR/the NFL) are you, 2) how big of a fan of (NASCAR/the NFL) do your friends and family see you as, 3) how often do you follow (NASCAR/the NFL) on TV and radio, 4) how often do you follow (NASCAR/the NFL) in newspapers and magazines, 5) how often do you follow (NASCAR/the NFL) on the internet, and 6) how often do you wear or display (NASCAR/the NFL) related clothing. Responses were recorded on a series of seven-point Likert scales ($\alpha = .90$).

Table 21.1 Item Means and Standard Deviations for the Sport Commercialization Acceptance Scale (1 = strongly agree -5 = strongly disagree)

	OVERALL	NASCAR	NFL	DIFFERENCE
Distracting	3.26 (1.0)	3.37 (1.0)	3.16 (.97)	.21**
Interfering	3.18 (1.1)	3.25 (1.1)	3.12 (1.0)	.13
Disturbing	3.56 (1.0)	3.57 (1.0)	3.54 (.99)	.03
Intrusive	3.37 (1.0)	3.46 (1.0)	3.22 (1.0)	.24**
Forced	3.18 (1.1)	3.30 (1.1)	3.05 (1.1)	.25,**
Annoying	3.22 (1.1)	3.33 (1.1)	3.11 (1.1)	.22*
Invasive	3.35 (.97)	3.40 (.98)	3.30 (.98)	.10
Obtrusive	3.39 (1.0)	3.44 (1.0)	3.33 (1.0)	.11
Entertaining^	2.35 (.95)	2.39 (.95)	2.31 (.94)	.08
Informative^	2.73 (.94)	2.58 (.95)	2.88 (.90)	−.30**
Overall Mean	3.35 (.83)	3.42 (.84)	.27 (.81)	.15*

* p < .05
** p < .01
^reverse coded for analysis

Sport commercial acceptance

To assess fans' tolerance of commercial messages during televised sporting events, we introduce an extension of existing measures to be applied in the sports context. We define commercial messages as any marketing communication during the televised event or the commercial breaks, including advertising, event, team or venue sponsorships, virtual signage or other billboards within the broadcast (e.g., 'brought to you by...' messages) and ambush marketing. The Sport Commercial Acceptance (SCA) scale was adapted from Li and colleagues' ad intrusiveness scale (2002), which was designed to measure the intrusiveness of a specific advertisement (pop-ups versus television commercials versus magazine ads). In contrast, the SCA scale does not measure attitudes toward a specific advertisement, but to commercial messages in sports in general.

Items in the ad intrusiveness scale asked respondents how much they agree/disagree that ads are: intrusive, invasive, forced, distracting, disturbing, interfering, and obtrusive. Following Gaski and Etzel's (1986) index of consumer sentiment toward marketing, the adjective "annoying" was also added as a descriptor. Finally, given that messages in a sporting context might be seen by some fans to have positive attributes (Levin, Joiner, & Cameron, 2001), the adjectives "entertaining" and "informative" were added to the SCA scale.

Using a Likert scale (strongly agree-strongly disagree), respondents completed the measure of SCA by indicating their level of agreement that commercial messages within NFL/NASCAR telecasts are distracting, disturbing, forced, interfering, intrusive, invasive, obtrusive, annoying, entertaining, and informative. Table 21.1 presents the mean response and standard deviations for each of the scale's items ($\alpha = .83$).

Brand equity—Miller Lite

The Yoo and Donthu (2001) measure of multidimensional brand equity was employed to gauge the respondent's perceptions of this particular sports marketer. The measure consists of 10 items (5-point Likert scale, strongly disagree-strongly agree) which assess consumers' awareness of and loyalty to the brand as well as their perceptions of the brand's quality ($\alpha = .92$).

Emotional attachment—Miller Lite

The emotional attachment scale of Thomson, MacInnis, and Park (2005) was also utilized in the brand study. The scale consists of 10 items that ask respondents how well an adjective describes their feelings about a specific brand (1 = describes poorly, 7 = describes very well). The adjectives used are: affectionate, friendly, loved, peaceful, passionate, delighted, captivated, connected, bonded, and attached (α = .98).

RESULTS

To highlight the empirical results and usefulness of the concept of SCA, we address the three research questions along with the related question of how SCA impacts brand perceptions. To conclude, we offer discussion of the study's overall implications and three conclusions for sports marketers.

In regard to the first research question, sports fans overall showed moderate levels of acceptance of commercial messages during televised sporting events. When separated as a function of item valence, the mean score was 3.31 for the negative items and 2.54 for the positive items (t (601) = 12.3, p < .01 (paired-samples)) where 1= strongly agree and 5=strongly disagree. Fans were more likely to agree that commercial messages within their sport were entertaining and informative than any of the negative descriptors within the scale. Only 20 percent of fans believe that advertisements are intrusive and 26 percent feel that ads are annoying (strongly agree or agree). This finding in the sports context counters previous research that suggests consumers are generally frustrated with the level of advertising that has crept into their daily lives (Mittal, 1994; Ruskin, 2004). For product marketers, this result implies that sports may offer a context divergent from other promotional channels that have become too cluttered for consumers' taste. Marketers of certain sports have strived to create a commercial environment where their customers (fans) appreciate the support of sponsors and advertisers that make the sport widely available and more accessible to fans (Lapio & Speter, 2000). The response to this first research question suggests such efforts have been successful to some degree when compared to consumers' negative characterization of advertising in non-sports context. This generally positive reaction to commercial messages in televised sports programming also provides some substantiation for the escalating television rights fees of sports (Bee & Madrigal, 2012).

Across both the NFL and NASCAR fans, the mean score on the SCA index when the positive items were reverse scored was 3.35 on a 5-point scale where higher scores represent more accepting attitudes towards advertising messages. Women were found to have significantly higher SCA scores than men (t (600) = 2.7, p < .01), thereby demonstrating a greater acceptance of commercial messages in sports. Older fans were found to have significantly lower SCA scores (i.e., less tolerant of commercial messages) than their younger counterparts ($F_{5, 596}$ = 4.66, p < .01). The greatest level of irritation with commercial messages occurs among those respondents 60 years of age and older (SCA index = 2.89), which is particularly relevant to sports marketers targeting an older segment of sports consumers.

Results concerning the second research question demonstrate that the relationship between fan identification and SCA is mediated by sport in this study. To begin, NFL fans had higher levels of fan identification with their sport than did NASCAR fans (t (600) = 2.7, p < .01). Yet among NFL fans, there is not a significant correlation between fan identification and SCA score. The identification of football fans did not translate to acceptance of commercial messages in their sport's television broadcasts. Conversely, amongst NASCAR fans a significant *positive* correlation (r = .27, p < .01) exists between fan identification and SCA score. As fan identification with the sport increases, the NASCAR fan becomes more accepting of commercial messages. This finding suggests that although sports may offer the product marketer a more accepting context for commercial messages, all sports cannot be considered equal in their fans' responses to such messages. While the NFL fans were not intolerant of commercial messages, their acceptance was not related to their level of identification as it was for NASCAR fans. Certain sports may either be more conducive to commercial messages or have created a culture more accepting of commercial support that is most appreciated by highly identified fans. The response to the third research question offers further evidence of this proposition.

In evaluating the third research question, analysis of variance (ANOVA) of SCA scores demonstrated that NASCAR fans are significantly more tolerant of commercial messages during televised events than are NFL fans (Table 21.2: F (1, 600) = 5.00, p <.05). For example, only about one in five (21%) NASCAR fans feel that commercial messages during televised events are annoying (strongly agree or agree), compared to almost one in three (32%) NFL fans. Similarly, one in four (24%) NFL fans feel that commercial messages are intrusive, but less than one in five (16%) NASCAR fans feel the same. Over half (54%) of NFL fans agreed that advertisers/sponsors do not belong on the players or the playing field,

Table 21.2 Analysis of variance summary for Sport Commercial Acceptance between fans of NASCAR and the NFL.

SOURCE	SUM OF SQUARES	DF	MEAN SQUARE	F	P-VALUE
Between groups	3.39	1	3.39	5.00	.026
Error	407.06	600	.68		
Total	410.45	601			

whereas less than a tenth (7%) of NASCAR fans felt the same way about their sport, which already prominently features sponsors on the cars and track infield. These findings suggest that commercial messages in televised events are indeed more accepted by motorsports fans. As a result, sport marketers may be less concerned about commercial clutter in motorsports context where fans are less likely to be annoyed by marketing communications within their sport's broadcasts. Not only are commercial messages already prominent on the field of competition in motorsports, but such corporate support has been front-and-center since the earliest NASCAR competitions (Yost, 2007). On the contrary, commercial messages in many other sports have emerged over time and fans have been expected to adapt to the

Table 21.3 Analysis of variance summary for Miller Lite customers in NASCAR and the NFL.

MILLER LITE BRAND EQUITY					
SOURCE	SUM OF SQUARES	DF	MEAN SQUARE	F	P-VALUE
Between groups	2.49	1	2.49	5.39	.021
Error	116.04	251	.46		
Total	118.53	252			
EMOTIONAL ATTACHMENT TO MILLER LITE					
SOURCE	SUM OF SQUARES	DF	MEAN SQUARE	F	P-VALUE
Between groups	25.85	1	25.85	10.35	.001
Error	626.93	251	2.50		
Total	652.78	252			

growing necessity of commercial platforms for revenue generation (Lefton, 2009; Lombardo & Lefton, 2012).

In the total sample of Miller Lite consumers (i.e., both NASCAR and NFL fans) there was a significant positive correlation between the SCA index score and both the perception of brand equity (r = .19) and emotional attachment (r = .28) to Miller Lite beer. This positive correlation exists in the two fan sub-groups as well (i.e., NASCAR and NFL fans). Those less accepting of commercial messages have lower perceptions of brand equity and lower emotional attachment towards Miller Lite—an advertiser and sponsor in both sports.

Utilizing an ANOVA (Table 21.3), we compared Miller Lite customers in the two sports' fan groups. Both the perceived brand equity of Miller Lite beer (F (1, 251) = 5.39, p< .05) and the emotional attachment toward Miller Lite (F (1, 251) = 10.35, p< .01) were significantly higher among NASCAR fans. As previously discovered, NASCAR fans exhibit a significantly higher level of acceptance of advertising in their sport compared to NFL fans. Though further research is needed, these higher SCA scores may positively influence fans' perceptions of the brand equity of sponsors and advertisers within the sport.

DISCUSSION

This examination of corporate sports marketing found that fans of two of the most popular U.S. sports were generally tolerant of commercial messages. Although public opinion polls and previous research indicate consumers are bombarded with advertising, the results of this study demonstrate that NFL and NASCAR fans do not necessarily feel such sentiment about the commercial messages within the televised broadcast of their favorite sport. Perhaps sports fans are simply resigned to the fact that commercial messages are a necessity. As one respondent noted in an open-ended response, "commercials are a necessary evil in all sporting events ... they pay the bills."

NASCAR fans were significantly more tolerant of commercial messages than NFL fans; and as fan identification increases, NASCAR fans become more accepting of commercial messages and correspondingly more emotionally attached to Miller Lite—a sponsor within the sport. Such a finding provides evidence that NASCAR has conditioned its fans to accept advertising as part of the sport. Much has been written about the NASCAR fan culture (e.g., Amato et al., 2005). Gill (2008, p. 186) summarizes the results of studies of NASCAR fans and sponsors saying, "All of these studies produced similar results: NASCAR fans are extremely aware of who is sponsoring their sport, and fans support those sponsors." Highly identified fans support entities that help ensure the continued success of the object of their identification—the team, event, or sport. NASCAR takes pride in nurturing the emotional connections that fans have with the sport and extending those positive connections to the advertisers and sponsors of the sport (Levin et al., 2004). By conceptualizing and measuring fans' acceptance of commercial messages in televised sports programming, our study begins to bridge the gap between fans' connection to the sport and fans' perception of brands marketing through the sport. Recall that the perceived brand equity and emotional attachment toward Miller Lite were higher among NASCAR fans compared to NFL fans, even though Miller Lite is a sponsor and advertiser in both sports. Yet, NASCAR fans display a significantly higher acceptance of commercial messages within their sport compared to NFL fans.

RESEARCH CONCLUSIONS, LIMITATIONS, AND MAJOR IMPLICATIONS FOR SPORT MARKETERS

Conclusion #1: Sports fans are generally accepting of the current level of commercialization in televised sport.

Contrary to consumer research in a broader context (e.g., Edwards et al., 2002; Speck & Elliott, 1997), televised commercial messages in sports appear to be accepted as more informative and entertaining than disturbing or obtrusive. While our investigation was limited to two sport contexts—NASCAR and the NFL—the findings lend support to the suggestion that commercial messages embedded in engaging programming, such as sports, may be more effective than other advertising mediums. Wang and Calder (2006) offer a theoretical explanation for this assertion by describing a "media transportation" experience in which consumers become mentally absorbed. They propose that a high transportation experience will result in increased advertising effectiveness if the advertisement does not interrupt the transportation experience or intrude on the information processing going on in the transportation experience. Therefore, a level of commercial messaging deemed acceptable to a sport's fans is desirable to establish and maintain not only for the fan viewing experience, but also for maximum effectiveness of embedded advertising.

353

By utilizing the SCA scale, sports marketers can test for fans' acceptance of commercial messages across televised sports. Our results within a defined context indicate that fans do not yet perceive sports telecasts to be over-commercialized (i.e., intrusive, distracting, obstructive, etc.). According to the empirical results, female and younger fans are the most accepting of commercial messages within the sports tested. Such segmentation may be important to note for marketers defining their target consumers by gender or age. For example, marketers aiming to reach women or younger fans through sports might be justified in composing more aggressive promotional communications.

Conclusion #2: Acceptance of commercial messages is not identical across televised sports and the relationship between fan identification and the acceptance of commercial messages varies by sport.

Previous researchers have noted the benefits to sponsors of aligning with sports exhibiting high fan identification (Gwinner & Swanson, 2003), but how broadly this relationship extended was unknown. In this study, although NFL fans exhibited higher fan identification than fans of NASCAR, general acceptance of commercial messages in televised sports broadcasts was significantly higher among NASCAR fans. Stock car fans' acceptance of commercial messages was also positively related to their identification with the sport; whereas this relationship did not hold among NFL fans. The finding further confirms that NASCAR has successfully conditioned its fans to view brand marketers as an integral part of the success of the sport. This result is not surprising given the historical commercial integration of NASCAR (Lapio & Speter, 2000), but the finding is important for sports marketers because the results demonstrate that any assumption that greater fans (i.e., more highly identified) are more or less accepting of commercial messages needs closer examination by sport. Marketers in NASCAR now have more evidence that such an assumption does hold for their sport's more identified fans, who embrace current levels of commercial messaging. However, the same evidence has not materialized yet in other sports. As a result, marketers utilizing sports beyond NASCAR should temper any enthusiasm for commercial messaging beyond current accepted levels until further study can test potential thresholds of acceptance and fan backlash.

Conclusion #3: Fans' acceptance of commercial messages in televised sport may influence their perception of and attachment to brands marketing through sports.

Until further research employing a wider sample of brands is conducted, this conclusion remains rather tentative given the limited test here of just one brand that relies heavily on marketing through sports. That being said, the empirical results demonstrate a significant positive relationship between SCA scores and impressions of the Miller Lite brand across the subsample of Miller Lite drinkers. Such a correlation extends to professional sports the results previously found for collegiate athletics by Zhang, Won, and Pastore (2005). Their study in combination with the findings here lend strong support for the possibility that sports fans who are accepting of commercial messages within their sport are therefore more receptive to the brands utilizing that sport as a marketing platform. Other factors that might influence the relationship between SCA and perception of supporting brands are the existing brand prominence of an advertiser or sponsor and the congruence between the aligning brand and the sport property (Wakefield, Becker-Olsen, & Cornwell, 2007). Marketers of both the sports property and sponsoring brands should emphasize to fans the role of corporate sponsors and advertisers in the betterment of the sport. Specifically, sports marketers need to become more explicit in explaining to the fans how corporate support has advanced the fan consumption experience. For example, many sports facilities and the fan amenities therein are possible due to the funding secured through corporate naming rights (Clark, Cornwell, & Pruitt, 2002); yet, fans may not make such a connection without proper articulation by marketers.

In addition to expanding the scope of sports and brands studied, future research should attempt to distinguish the influence of different types of advertising strategies (e.g., humor, fear, spokesperson, etc.) and promotional platforms (e.g., broadcast billboards, product placement, 30 second commercial, etc.) on fans' perceptions of commercial messages. Sports consumers may be more accepting of some types of messages (e.g., product placements) versus others (e.g., commercial breaks), and such an effect may depend on the nature of the sport. There are many different methods for the delivery of commercial messages during NFL and NASCAR events and broadcasts. This study is limited in that it does not address the difference between these multiple methods and how the effect of each can be different. Furthermore, we have employed the measurement of SCA in only one (television) of

355

several potential sport consumption channels. Future research could study how SCA differs in other sport consumption context, such as live event attendance, radio, or online streaming.

While our investigation focused on surveying a relatively diverse sample of sports fans (i.e., not a student sample) removed from the viewing experience, future work utilizing experimental design could address the issues raised above and begin to explore causation within the relationships we uncovered. Nevertheless, this study has contributed to contemporary sports marketing research by producing evidence that sports as a corporate marketing channel has yet to reach a point of commercial saturation. To the contrary, many fans find commercial messages within their sports to be both entertaining and informative, rather than obtrusive or disturbing. Such findings across two different sports should be welcome news for sports marketers and encouragement to remain relevant to fans.

REFERENCES

Amato, C.H., Peters C.L.O., & Shao, A.T. (2005). An exploratory investigation into NASCAR fan culture. *Sport Marketing Quarterly, 14* (2), 71–83.

Bauer, R. A., & Greyser, S.A. (1968). *Advertising in America: the consumer view.* Boston, MA: Harvard University, Graduate School of Business Administration, Division of Research.

Bee, C. C. & Madrigal, R. (2012). It's not whether you win or lose, it's how the game is played: The influence of sports programming on advertising. *Journal of Advertising, 41*(1), 47–58.

Bennett, G., Ferreira, M., Siders, R., Tsuji, Y., & Cianfrone, B. (2006). Analysing the effects of advertising type and antecedents on attitude towards advertising in sport. *International Journal of Sports Marketing & Sponsorship,* (October), 62–81.

Biderman, D. (2010). 11 minutes of action. *Wall Street Journal,* (January 15).

Burke, M. (2006, November 27). Field of screens. Accessed October 15, 2012 at: http://www.forbes.com/forbes/2006/1127/058.html

Clark, J. M., Cornwell, B. T., & Pruitt, S. W. (2002). Corporate stadium sponsorships, signaling theory, agency conflicts, and shareholder wealth. *Journal of Advertising Research, 42*(6), 16–33.

Cobbs, J. & Hylton, M. (2012). Facilitating sponsorship channels in the business model of motorsports. *Journal of Marketing Channels, 19*(3), 1–20.

Cornwell, T.B., Relyea, G.E., Irwin, R.L., & Maignan, I. (2000). Understanding long-term effects of sports sponsorship: Role of experience, involvement, enthusiasm and clutter. *International Journal of Sports Marketing & Sponsorship, 2*(2):127–142.

Crupi, A. (2012). Bud Light suits up for 2012 NFL season. *Adweek,* (September 5).

Edwards, S.M., Hairong, L., & Lee, J. (2002). Forced exposure and psychological reactance: Antecedents and consequences of the perceived intrusiveness of pop-up ads. *Journal of Advertising,* 31(3): 83–95.

Elliott, M. T., & Speck, P. S. (1998). Consumer perceptions of advertising clutter and its impact across various media. *Journal of Advertising Research, 38,* 29–41.

Fisher, E. & Lefton, T. (2008, November 10). WBC expects higher ticket, retail sales numbers. *Street & Smith's SportsBusiness Journal,* pp. 4.

Funk, D. & Pastore, D. (2000). Examining the attitudinal component of loyalty toward a professional sports team. *Research Quarterly for Exercise and Sport. 71*(March), 118–128.

Gaski, J.F. & Etzel, M.J. (1985). A proposal for a global, longitudinal measure of national consumer sentiment toward marketing practice. *Advances in Consumer Research. 12*: 65–70.

Gill, M. (2008). Corporations brought to you by NASCAR: Rhetorical identification through sponsorship. *International Journal of Sports Marketing and Sponsorship.* (April), 180–192.

Gluck, J. (2012). Commercial interruptions make NASCAR viewing almost unbearable. *SB Nation (sbnation.com).* (July 12).

Greyser, S. (1973). Irritation in advertising. *Journal of Advertising Research.* 13(1): 3–7.

Gwinner, K. P., & Eaton, J. (1999). Building brand image through event sponsorship: The role of image transfer. *Journal of Advertising, 25*(2), 19–35.

Gwinner, K., & Swanson, S. (2003). A model of fan identification: antecedents and sponsorship outcomes. *Journal of Services Marketing, 17*(3), 275–294.

Harvey, B. (2001). Measuring the effects of sponsorships. *Journal of Advertising Research,* (January/February), 59–65.

Hunt, K. A., Bristol, K.& Bashaw, R.E. (1999). A conceptual approach to classifying sports fans. *Journal of Services Marketing. 13*(6), 439–452.

IEG (2011, January 4). Sponsorship spending: 2010 proves better than expected; Bigger gains set for 2011. *IEG Sponsorship Report,* pp. 1–4.

Lapio, R. & Speter, K.M (2000). NASCAR: A lesson in integrated and relationship marketing. *Sport Marketing Quarterly, 9*(2), 85–95.

Lardinoit, T., & Derbaix, C. (2001). Sponsorship and recall of sponsors. *Psychology & Marketing, 18*(2), 167–190.

Lefton, T. (2009, July 27). Many NFL clubs still perfecting approach to practice patches. *Street & Smith's Sports Business Journal,* pp. 9.

Levin, A.M., Beasley, F. & Gamble, T. (2004). Brand loyalty of NASCAR fans toward sponsors: The impact of fan identification. *International Journal of Sports Marketing and Sponsorship. 6*(1), 11–21.

Levin, A.M., Joiner, C. & Cameron, G. (2001). The impact of sports sponsorship on consumers' brand attitudes and recall: The case of NASCAR fans. *Journal of Current Issues and Research in Advertising. 23*(2), 23–31.

Li, H., Edwards, S.M., & Lee, J. (2002). Measuring the intrusiveness of advertisements: Scale development and validation. *Journal of Advertising, 31*(2), 37–47.

Logan, K. (2011). Hulu.com or NBC? Streaming video versus traditional t.v.: A study of an industry in its infancy. *Journal of Advertising Research, 51*(1), 276–287.

Lombardo, J., & Lefton, T. (2012, April 23). EPL model pushes estimates on NBA jersey rights to $20 million. *Street & Smith's SportsBusiness Journal,* pp. 1.

MacKenzie, S. B., Lutz, R. J., & Belch, G. E. (1986). The role of attitude toward the ad as a mediator of advertising effectiveness: A test of competing explanations. *Journal of Marketing Research, 23*(2), 130–143.

Madrigal, R. (2000). The influence of social alliances with sports teams on intensions to purchase corporate sponsors' products. *Journal of Advertising.29*(4), 13–29.

McClellan, S. (2009). MEC forecasts rise in sponsorships. *Adweek,* (June 1). Accessed June 2, 2009 at: http://www.adweek.com/aw/content_display/news/media/e3ic0507728e66c92e3d57615e ac57b791b

McKelvey, S. (2006). Coca-Cola vs. PepsiCo—a "Super" battleground for the cola wars? *Sport Marketing Quarterly, 15,* 114–123.

Meenaghan, T. (2001). Sponsorship and advertising: A comparison of consumer perceptions. *Psychology & Marketing, 18*(2), 191–215.

Meenaghan, T., & Shipley, D. (1999). Media effect in commercial sponsorship. *European Journal of Marketing, 33*(3/4), 328–347.

Mehta, A. (2000). Advertising attitudes and advertising effectiveness. *Journal of Advertising Research*, (40), 67–72.

Milne, G. R., McDonald, M. A., Sutton, W. A., & Kashyap, R. (1996). A niche-based evaluation of sport participation patterns. *Journal of Sport Management, 10*, 417–434.

Mittal, B. (1994). Public assessment of TV advertising: faint praise and harsh criticism. *Journal of Advertising Research, 34*(1), 35–54.

Neuman, M. A. (2009, June 22). Activation, accountability vital to future of jersey sponsorships. *Street & Smith's SportsBusiness Journal*, pp. 13.

Nielsen Corporation (2012, January 24). Year in sports advertising: TV ad spend grows to $10.9B. Accessed February 19, 2013 at: http://blog.nielsen.com/nielsenwire

Olson, E. L., & Thjømøe, H. M. (2009). Sponsorship effect metric: Assessing the financial value of sponsoring by comparisons to television advertising. *Journal of the Academy of Marketing Science, 37*, 504–515.

Petrecca, L. (2006). Product placement—you can't escape it. *USA Today* (Oct. 10).

Pollay, R.W. (1986). The distorted mirror: reflections on the unintended consequences of advertising. *Journal of Marketing, 50*, 18–36.

Pollay, R.W., & Mittal, B. (1993). Here's the beef: factors, determinants, and segments in consumer criticism of advertising. *Journal of Marketing, 57*, 99–114.

Ruskin, G. (2004). A 'death spiral of disrespect'; if the consumer is really king, why do marketers keep bombarding him," *Advertising Age*, April 26

Sandomir, R. (2012). NBA takes a look at jersey sponsorship. *The New York Times*, April 17.

Shank, M. & Beasley, F. (1998). Fan or fanatic: refining a measure of sports involvement. *Journal of Sport Behavior. 21*(4), 435–443.

Smolianov, P., & Shilbury, D. (2005). Examining integrated advertising and sponsorship in corporate marketing through televised sport. *Sport Marketing Quarterly, 14*(4), 239–250.

Speck, P. S., & Elliott, M. T. (1997). Predictors of advertising avoidance in print and broadcast media. *Journal of Advertising, 26,*(3), 61–76.

Sports Business Daily (2010). Fan demographics among major North American sports leagues. June 9.

Thomson, M., MacInnis, D.J., & Park, C.W. (2005). The ties that bind: measuring the strength of consumers' emotional attachments to brands. *Journal of Consumer Psychology, 15*(1), 77–91.

Wakefield, K. L., Becker-Olsen, K., & Cornwell, T. B. (2007). I spy a sponsor. The effects of sponsorship level, prominence, relatedness, and cueing on recall accuracy. *Journal of Advertising, 36*(4), 61–74.

Wang, J. & Calder, B.J. (2006): Media transportation and advertising. *Journal of Consumer Research, 33*(2), 151–162.

Wann, D.L. & Branscombe, N.R. (1993). Sports fans: measuring degree of identification with their teams. *International Journal of Sport Psychology.* 24(1), 1–17.

Wann, D. L., Grieve, F. G., Zapalac, R. K., & Pease, D. G. (2008). Motivational profiles of sport fans of different sports. *Sport Marketing Quarterly, 17*(1), 6–19.

Wann, D. L., & Pierce, S. (2003). Measuring sport team identification and commitment: An empirical comparison of the sport spectator identification scale and the psychological commitment to team scale. *North American Journal of Psychology, 5,* 365–372.

Yoo, B. & Donthu, N. (2001). Developing and validating a multidimensional consumer-based brand equity scale. *Journal of Business Research, 52* (April), 1–14.

Yost, M. (2007). *The 200-MPH billboard: The inside story of how big money changed NASCAR.* St. Paul, MN: Motorbooks.

Zhang, Z., Won, D., & Pastore, D.L (2005). The effects of attitudes toward commercialization on college students' purchasing intentions of sponsors' products. *Sport Marketing Quarterly, 14* (3), 177–187.

CHAPTER TWENTY TWO

The Growing Popularity of Counterfeit Jerseys among Sports Fans

A Critical Analysis

BY **BRANDON LANG**

Today, hundreds of millions of sports fans around the world wear their favorite teams' jerseys to games. This is a relatively new phenomenon that has been aided by a huge increase in the availability of team merchandise and the branding of sports fans around the world. Historically, sports fans did not purchase or wear sports jerseys through the late 1970s and early 1980s. Although a few professional teams sold game-used jerseys to collectors during this time, authentic and replica jerseys were not aggressively marketed or sold to fans. Buying branded sports apparel was very difficult, and team stores as we know them today simply did not exist. Generally speaking, fans did not have access to buying the many varieties of hats, jackets, T-shirts, and other branded team items that many fans take for granted today.

Another change within professional sports since the 1970s is that the cost of being a fan has dramatically increased (Coakley, 2009; Fried et al., 2013). The costs of tickets, concessions, souvenirs, and merchandise have soared (Carter, 2011; Coakley, 2009). What many fans call "nosebleed" seats cost $25 and up; soft drinks, hot dogs, and other food items are marked up hundreds of percent; and anything with the team's logo is generally pretty expensive. In North America, licensed baseball hats cost $35, and authentic Major League Baseball (MLB), National Football League (NFL), and National Hockey League (NHL) jerseys sell for upwards of $250. Needless to say, it has become prohibitively expensive for many families to attend professional sporting events, much less purchase team memorabilia.

Since the early 2000s, more and more fans around the world have been wearing counterfeit sports jerseys. Counterfeit, or knockoff, jerseys, as they are commonly known, cost around 90 percent less than licensed, authentic jerseys and in many cases, closely approximate the licensed versions they copy. They typically have all of the correct manufacturer labels in the collar and on the bottom front of the jersey, along with the same tags hanging from them that you would see in any store. William Henderson (2012), an expert in the game-worn jersey field, estimates that 75 percent of the jerseys that fans wear to North American MLB games are counterfeit. Henderson (2012) also contends that 75 percent of the jerseys sold on eBay are counterfeit.

The purpose of this chapter is threefold. One is to document the increased production and distribution of counterfeit jerseys. The second is to evaluate strategies that are used to reduce counterfeit jersey sales. Lastly, the third purpose is to consider future trends concerning counterfeit jersey sales.

MAJOR THEMES IN THE COUNTERFEIT CONSUMER GOODS LITERATURE

Although there are not any published academic studies that consider counterfeit sports jerseys, there are dozens of articles looking more generally at counterfeit goods. These studies examine the economic impacts that counterfeit goods have on businesses, people's motivations for buying counterfeit products, the demographic bases of counterfeit goods purchasers, and the effectiveness of strategies used to reduce counterfeiting.

Every year, billions of dollars' worth of counterfeit handbags, sunglasses, perfume, jewelry, alcohol, software, pharmaceuticals, and music is sold around the world. Norum and Cuno (2011) contend that global consumers spend $600 billion per year on counterfeit items. All told, estimates suggest that counterfeit items account for 5 to 7 percent of world trade (Norum and Cuno, 2011).

Green and Smith (2002) explain that there are two different types of counterfeiting. Nondeceptive counterfeiting takes place when there are little to no ill health effects to consumers; little effect on name-brand sales; items are known to be counterfeit; and sales provide some sort of benefit such as employment (Green and Smith, 2002). Conversely, deceptive counterfeiting happens when consumers are unaware that goods are counterfeit; there are potential health and safety risks associated with their use; the government experiences substantial financial losses; and companies experience substantial financial losses (Green and Smith, 2002).

Building upon this model, Hilton et al. (2004) discovered that most consumers generally find it difficult to differentiate between counterfeit and genuine items. Unfortunately, most studies focus on respondents who knowingly purchase counterfeit items because it has been difficult to identify respondents who unwittingly purchase counterfeit items thinking they are getting a good deal on a genuine item.

The ultimate challenge for counterfeiters is to invest enough money into a product to make it appear genuine while being able to sell it a low enough price to attract customers. Some counterfeiters opt to manufacture higher-end replicas that can be sold for more money, while others opt to manufacture lower-end copies that can be sold for less money. Tom et al. (1998) developed a typology of consumer orientation toward counterfeit products. There are two groups of people who are likely to purchase counterfeit items. According to Tom et al. (1998), sly shoppers seek out knockoffs with high product parity, while economically concerned people seek out knockoffs with low product parity.

The consensus among researchers who study counterfeit goods is that they negatively impact legitimate businesses. Companies whose goods are counterfeited spend enormous amounts of money researching, developing, and marketing products that are, in turn, manufactured by outside agents and sold without paying any sort of royalty to the company. Take the example of Kate Spade handbags, a high-end consumer item. Bian and Veloutsou (2011) contend that there is a 1:1 relationship between the number of authentic Kate Spade handbags sold and the number of illegal copies sold. Similarly, despite Louis Vuitton having 20 full-time anti-counterfeiting employees, fake Louis Vuitton handbags are readily available (Green and Smith, 2002). Compounding the problem of counterfeiting, only a small percentage of counterfeiters is ever caught; the penalties are fairly minor, and enforcement is very expensive (Higgins and Rubin, 1986; Hilton et al., 2004).

Numerous studies have explored people's motivations for buying counterfeit consumer goods. The consensus among researchers is that people purchase counterfeit items so they can confer the status of a luxury or designer item at a lower cost (see Strizhakova et al., 2008; Globerman, 1988; Higgins and Rubin, 1986; Tom et al., 1998). According to Mason (2000), this is rooted in conspicuous consumption, as many buyers are likely to purchase counterfeit goods for their status-conferring potential than their actual utility. Several studies have also shown that the majority of respondents do not have any substantial ethical concerns with purchasing counterfeit goods (Amendolara, 2005; d'Astous and Legendre, 2009; Penz and Stottinger, 2005; Tom et al. 1998).

A related theme in the literature considers differences in the attitudes of people who purchase counterfeit goods compared to people who do not purchase them. A small number of studies has examined the attitudes of people who purchase counterfeit products. Results show that consumers who knowingly purchase counterfeit goods hold attitudes that are more favorable to counterfeiting (Penz and Stottinger, 2005; Tom et al., 1998). More specifically, purchasers of counterfeit products are likely to have had a previous positive experience purchasing a counterfeit item and a lower potential for embarrassment (Penz and Stottinger, 2005).

In another study, d'Astous and Legendre (2009) found that there is an inverse relationship between respondents' rationalization of purchasing counterfeit goods and their knowledge concerning socially responsible consuming, as well as their involvement in socially responsible consuming. This ties in with Eckhardt's (2010) broader finding that many people use economic rationalization to justify their unethical consumer consumption. One interesting finding is that brand loyalty is inversely related to buying counterfeit products (Cheng San, 2012). Cheng San (2012) found in her study of Malaysian adults that respondents' degrees of attitudinal brand loyalty and behavioral brand loyalty are inversely related to their likelihood of purchasing counterfeit clothing and footwear.

Several studies have also examined if some social groups are more likely to buy counterfeit goods than others. A small number of studies considered the demographic correlates associated with the purchase of counterfeit items. Results show that younger people are more likely to purchase counterfeit items than older people and that gender is sometimes a factor (Bian and Veloutsou, 2011; Penz and Stottinger, 2005; Tom et al., 1998).

364

Most of the research concerning counterfeit goods examines the effectiveness of supply-side strategies such as increasing governmental seizures of counterfeit goods and tougher importation laws. The International Agreement on Trade-Related Aspects of Intellectual Property Rights (known as TRIPS) and the US Trademark Counterfeiting Act have been passed into law to make it more difficult for counterfeit items to be manufactured, shipped internationally, and sold (Green and Smith, 2002; Norum and Cuno, 2011; Phillips, 2006). Nevertheless, counterfeiting costs US businesses $250 billion alone (Norum and Cuno, 2011). Findings show that increased law enforcement and innovative product designs and changes are expenses that raise the price of the goods that are being sold while only having the potential to curb some counterfeiting (Globerman, 1988; Higgins and Rubin, 1986; Hilton et al., 2004; Qian, 2008).

THE RISE OF KNOCKOFFS

Counterfeit jerseys first emerged in the developing world in the 1980s. Soccer fans in Africa and South and Central America were able to purchase inexpensive and low-quality knockoff jerseys at bazaars, markets, and sporting events. Now, with the omnipresence of the Internet, fans in both the developed and developing worlds can purchase counterfeit jerseys online. There are four principal reasons to explain why so many sports fans wear counterfeit jerseys. One is the low price. The second reason is their widespread availability. Third, teams have so many third, throwback, and commemorative jerseys that it is hard for fans to keep up. The fourth reason is that wearing jerseys to games has become normative, and fans want to fit in.

THE LOW PRICE OF COUNTERFEIT JERSEYS

It is not just that knockoff jerseys are affordable—they are much cheaper than authentic and licensed ones. An authentic MLB jersey costs roughly ten times more than a knockoff. Even licensed replica jerseys cost four to five times as much as knockoffs. Without question, MLB teams sell more replica than authentic jerseys. A relatively new development with replica jerseys is that more and more teams are engaging in what I would refer to as cutting corners with them. For example, the only difference that existed traditionally between authentic and replica NHL and MLB jerseys was the weight of the fabric and the tagging. They had the same crests, numbers, and letters. Now, replica jerseys generally have crests that are made out of dyed tackle twill fabric instead of twill that has designs embroidered onto them. For names and numbers, one layer of dyed twill is generally used for teams with outlined designs, rather than sewing different layers of twill on top of each other. In fact, thread lines are often simulated with dye to make numbers look sewn on when they are not. I have to think that this is not lost on many fans who have high expectations regarding the replica jerseys they purchase.

As part of my research, I administered survey questions to 645 university students and asked them if they would rather have one authentic jersey or eight knockoff versions. Not surprisingly, almost half (47.5 percent) of the respondents answered that they would rather have the eight counterfeit jerseys. Only a small number of sports fans have the money to purchase a high number of authentic jerseys. All told, the lure of counterfeit jerseys represents a quality/quantity conundrum for most people. It seems that jersey owners feel that they need to ultimately decide between having a larger number of low-quality reproduction jerseys or a smaller number of authentic jerseys. In this day and age of ever changing jersey styles, commemorative jerseys, All-Star jerseys, etc., it makes sense that fans do not want to invest heavily in a jersey that will be restyled or phased out by the team.

THE WIDESPREAD AVAILABILITY OF COUNTERFEIT JERSEYS

Not only are counterfeit jerseys affordable, they are also widely available. In this age of telecommunication, it is remarkably easy for someone to purchase a knockoff jersey online. A basic Internet search for "cheap MLB jerseys" yields pages upon pages of hits with websites that sell numbered jerseys of NFL, NBA, MLB, NHL, and soccer teams from around the world. Internet shoppers simply browse the images of the hundreds of jerseys for sale, select the jerseys and sizes they wish to purchase, enter their credit card or PayPal information, and in six weeks or so will have the jerseys delivered right to their residence. Virtually all of these jerseys are made in China. Sometimes, they are sold on Chinese websites, while some are sold by entrepreneurs living elsewhere.

Many of these counterfeit jersey–selling websites offer free shipping for purchases over $150 or $200. Moreover, many of these sites are willing to fill very big orders. As such, many people pool their orders with coworkers and/or friends. Similarly, many North American entrepreneurs routinely make big orders and purchase enough jerseys to sell at flea markets, fairs, and sporting events. Thousands of North American sports fans have purchased knockoff jerseys from people selling them out of a backpack in stadium parking lots or from informal stands set up around the outside of North American stadia.

THE HIGH NUMBER OF JERSEYS PER TEAM

Through the early 1990s, most professional sports teams had two jersey styles: a home jersey and an away jersey. Today, many professional sports teams wear third and fourth jerseys, commemorative jerseys, and throwback jerseys. In the case of Major League Baseball, all but two teams wear at least one alternate third jersey. In 2013, every team wore commemorative jerseys for Memorial Day, where camouflage numbers and designs were used. Many MLB teams also had Spanish heritage jerseys (Los Mets, Piratas, Tigres, Gigantes, etc.), St. Patrick's Day jerseys, and throwback jerseys honoring past teams. One team, the Milwaukee Brewers, has a Polish- and Italian-heritage jersey, while the Toronto Blue Jays wear a Canada Day jersey on July 1. Championship teams have also worn special champion jerseys for Opening Day, where the team's regular design motif is surrounded by gold piping. In 2014, the Chicago Cubs wore ten different throwback jerseys to commemorate the 100th anniversary of Wrigley Field.

It appears that fans and players alike enjoy a team wearing multiple jerseys. Multiple jersey, pants, and helmet combinations have been very successful recruiting tools by American universities such as the University of Maryland, Oklahoma State University, and the University of Oregon. Unfortunately, for baseball fans seeking to buy commemorative jerseys, however, most teams only sell authentic versions of them. As such, a Brewers fan seeking a Birrai jersey or a Red Sox fan seeking a World Series Champion jersey will have to pay $250 or so for that item. For fans who wear multiple jerseys and collect what we can call novelty jerseys, this can be very expensive.

A related issue is that many teams across the professional teams in North America and abroad change their jersey styles fairly often. Every year, British soccer teams have different away strips. Moreover, many teams, including Newcastle United, have had multiple sponsors in the last few years. It makes sense that many Manchester United fans would rather not wear last year's jersey sponsored by Aon when the team is planning to change their sponsorship to Chevrolet. Similarly, it makes sense that Houston Astros fans would much rather wear jerseys with the current navy, orange, and yellow color scheme than the maroon jerseys of two years ago. Because so many teams have been rebranded, it puts financial pressure on fans to "keep up," so to speak, with the most current jersey designs and trends.

THE NORMATIVE BASIS OF WEARING JERSEYS TO GAMES

If you look at pictures of World Series games or Super Bowls throughout the 1960s, you will not see any fans wearing team gear in the stands. In fact, most fans dressed formally for sporting events. Men wore jackets, ties, and often fedoras. Women wore dresses, high heels, and fur coats. As society became more casual in the 1970s, stadium patrons were less likely to dress up. During this time, fans would wear T-shirts and hats with their favorite teams' logos and colors to games. In the late 1980s, jerseys began to be marketed and sold to fans. At this point, more and more fans wore jerseys to games.

Now, a very high percentage of fans at professional sporting events wear jerseys of their favorite teams. Fans not wearing jerseys are likely to still wear shirts, hats, hoodies, and jackets connected to the team they root for. In fact, so many fans wear jerseys that it has become normative. I would go as far to say that wearing jerseys to games has become a way for fans to prove their fandom and transmit the message to others that they belong to the community of fans that supports a given team. Because so many Western people exhibit high rates of consumerism and seem to embrace the notion that "more is better," it follows that owning multiple jerseys—even if they are counterfeit—allows fans to prove their respective degrees of fandom to an elevated degree.

STRATEGIES TO CURB COUNTERFEIT JERSEY SALES

Several different strategies have been used to reduce counterfeit jersey sales. Most of them are considered to be supply-side strategies that focus on law enforcement and ways to thwart the abilities of counterfeiters to make sellable items. On the demand-side, few efforts have been made that seek to change people's perceptions of knockoff jerseys.

SUPPLY-SIDE STRATEGIES

In 2003, the US government seized more than 6,500 shipments of counterfeit goods entering the country worth an estimated $94 million (Hilton et al., 2004). Since then, similar amounts of seizures have been made (Zimmerman, 2013). Tougher importation laws, more thorough customs inspections, and more seizures of contraband represent the main law enforcement strategies used to curb counterfeiting.

Relaxed importation laws represent a double-edged sword for American corporations. Historically, tough importation laws and substantial tariffs have made it difficult for jerseys made outside of the United States to be sold within the country. In short, protective economic measures have sheltered American companies from foreign competition. American sporting goods companies also tended to produce their goods domestically. Since the passage of the North American Free Trade Agreement and other international trade treaties in the early 1990s, however, it has become easier for companies to have goods manufactured in countries with low labor costs and have them shipped to marketplaces in the developed world. In other words, importation laws have been relaxed so much in countries like the United States and Canada that it has become commonplace for apparel companies like Nike, Reebok, and Adidas to open factories abroad or outsource production to countries like Mexico, Bangladesh, and China. This saves sports apparel manufacturers millions of dollars in labor costs.

The upside for American sporting goods and apparel companies is that their labor costs have gone down dramatically. The downside, however, is that because so many consumer goods are made in Asia, such huge amounts of cargo enter the United States and other developed countries that it is impossible to inspect it all. Counterfeiters take advantage of this loophole by shipping freight, knowing it will likely reach its destination without being inspected.

Contraband takes a variety of different forms. It is illegal to import ivory, Cuban cigars, and different foods and drugs among other things into the United States. In addition to having to search cargo containers, mail freight, and people's suitcases for counterfeit goods, customs agents must also search for the above-mentioned items. Countries like the United

States engage in so much international trade that it is simply unrealistic to expect that all incoming freight is thoroughly inspected. Yes, it is subject to X-rays and drug-detecting dogs, but to go through all of the boxes looking for counterfeit goods would take too much manpower and time. Simply put, searching for counterfeit jerseys is too time consuming and expensive to truly be considered a law enforcement priority. Of course, it is important, but many might argue that it is a lower priority than seizing drugs, weapons, alcohol, tobacco, and other goods that are sold on the black market.

One strategy recently adopted by many jersey manufacturers is to use complicated design features that are difficult to counterfeit. For example, Nike's design of the 2010 Team Canada hockey logo includes many aboriginal symbols that were sublimated right into the twill. Similarly, numbers used in recent MLB and NHL All-Star games include stars and other designs on the twill that are hard to copy. Another example includes Team USA's 2014 hockey jersey, where Nike sublimated fairly large blue stars around the already blue collar of the jersey. The idea of making jerseys tougher to counterfeit is similar to how countries include watermarks, seals, and other security features in their paper currency to make it more difficult to reproduce. This also ties in with the industry expectation that counterfeit jerseys will be such poor representations of the licensed jerseys that fans would be too embarrassed to wear them.

Another strategy that jersey companies engage in is to regularly redesign to stay one step ahead of the counterfeiters. This strategy has long been used in the apparel industry, where high-end clothiers constantly change their collections to keep things innovative, fresh, and out of the hands of copycats. There is less incentive for a counterfeiter to expend the time, energy, and money that it would take to reproduce a piece of clothing if its window to be sold is fairly small. As such, there are thousands of versions of old jerseys for sale online that will not have the same consumer appeal as jerseys that are worn today. Ultimately, this benefits companies that make legitimate jerseys in that there will always be a greater demand for current jerseys that players are wearing. It is also likely to frustrate many fans who buy a jersey only to have a team restyle their look the next season.

DEMAND-SIDE STRATEGIES

The main demand-side strategy is to come up with ways to change people's perceptions of counterfeit jerseys. One way this could be done is through an aggressive public relations campaign. When people watch movies at home, they are generally reminded that copying the movie is against the law. Similarly, many record companies have sought to change people's views concerning downloading music by investing heavily in radio and print advertising. These ads remind the consumer that illegally downloading music is not a victimless crime and that it funds terrorism around the world. Have these strategies been effective? Can they be used to curb counterfeit jersey sales? My guess is no. My suspicion is that most sports fans see jersey companies as greedy and taking advantage of consumers. As long as this is the case, hundreds of thousands of people will continue to seek out cheaper alternatives to authentic jerseys.

FUTURE PROSPECTS?

The future prospects for knockoff jerseys appear to be pretty clear. As long as there remains a cheaper alternative to licensed jerseys, people will likely still purchase them, regardless of their quality or resemblance to the genuine article. In the next few paragraphs, additional strategies for reducing the presence of counterfeit jerseys are discussed and evaluated.

REDUCING THE PRICE OF LICENSED JERSEYS

One strategy to reduce counterfeit jersey sales is for manufacturers to consider reducing the price for licensed jerseys. Maybe more people will actually buy legitimate ones if they are a little more affordable. The core problem with this suggestion is that many people are likely to assume that jerseys are a much higher-margin consumer good than they really are. Most people know that it does not cost anywhere near $250 to make a white polyester shirt with a team name, player's name, and player's number sewn onto it. What most people do not realize is how expensive it is for companies like Majestic, Nike, Reebok, and others to obtain the licensing rights to legally manufacture these jerseys.

In North America, the major professional leagues all have apparel contracts. Nike pays substantial amounts of money to be the exclusive jersey manufacturer of the National Football League (NFL). Similar arrangements exist between Majestic and Major League Baseball, Reebok and the National Hockey League (NHL), and Adidas and the National Basketball

Association. This ties in with the old business adage that "it takes money to make money." These companies stand to make a lot by selling these jerseys, but have to pay millions of dollars for the rights to do so. Within the last several years, Nike replaced Reebok as the official supplier of NFL jerseys, and Reebok replaced CCM/Koho as the official jersey supplier of the NHL. Obviously, these companies see the benefit in outbidding the other companies for the exclusive rights to manufacture these jerseys.

Even within the North American college ranks, most NCAA Division 1 schools have an apparel contract. The University of Notre Dame is an Adidas school, meaning that all players and coaches must wear Adidas gear while representing the team. Similarly, North Carolina State is among the many other Adidas schools. The University of North Carolina, like the University of Michigan, Pennsylvania State University, and several others is a Nike school. Once again, these companies make huge investments based upon the even higher estimated profits of selling those goods on the open market.

Outside of North America, most high-level professional football, cricket, basketball, and other sports teams have their own apparel contracts. For example, Newcastle United and Italy wear Puma jerseys, while Manchester United, Holland, and Brazil wear Nike jerseys. Similarly, France and Argentina wear Adidas soccer jerseys, whereas Ireland, England, and Canada wear Umbro soccer jerseys. Again, the pattern is simple. Companies pay teams lots of money to be the exclusive manufacturer of their jerseys. This raises the obvious question: Why would companies like Puma, Nike, and Adidas be willing to sell jerseys for less money when they pay so much money in licensing fees? The answer is that it could be because they could possibly make even more money. Of course, that is a big gamble to make.

BETTER REGULATING WEBSITES LIKE EBAY

A second strategy is to push for sites like eBay and Etsy to be better regulated. EBay has, for example, drastically reduced the number of fake autographs and counterfeit sports cards on its site by requiring that at independent third party assess most of these items before they are sold. Counterfeit game-worn jerseys, autographs, and cards have really impacted the legitimate sports memorabilia market. Too many buyers have paid top dollar for items that were wholly misrepresented to them. As such, it has become worth it for consumers to pay more for items that have been inspected by a third party. The main problem with this is that many consumers are okay with counterfeits and prefer buying them because they are so affordable compared to licensed ones. As long as the demand for these jerseys remains high, people are likely to figure out how to obtain them.

WHAT CAN ATHLETES THEMSELVES DO?

Numerous fans seek autographs from their favorite players as they arrive to the venues for games, as they warm up for games, once games are finished, and as players leave the stadium. Perhaps professional athletes could also exercise some control over this issue by not signing knockoff jerseys or posing with fans wearing knockoff jerseys to games. Perhaps the MLB Players' Association could adopt a code of ethics whereby professional athletes only sign licensed gear.

This seems like a plausible solution. There are some concerns, however. One is that some fans might be unwittingly wearing knockoff jerseys that they received as gifts or thought were licensed. Their feelings would likely be hurt if their favorite players snubbed them. Another issue is that some players themselves would surely feel uncomfortable denying someone an autograph. That certainly has the potential for bad public relations and fan appeal. Lastly, players sign things so quickly and have so many items placed in front of them that it is not necessarily reasonable to expect that they would inspect everything before they sign it. High-profile professional athletes usually want to get in and out of those situations fairly quickly.

BANNING FANS WITH KNOCKOFF JERSEYS FROM GAMES

The last and most Draconian strategy would be to consider banning fans wearing knockoff jerseys from games. Just like fans are asked to remove offensive T-shirts by ushers and security, fans with counterfeit jerseys could be asked to remove their jerseys. There are several problems with this suggestion. Again, not everybody can tell the difference between a counterfeit and a licensed jersey. Even after training sessions, busy employees could easily make a mistake and ask a fan to leave who is, indeed, wearing a licensed jersey. If a fan wearing a licensed jersey were asked to leave a sporting event, she or he would have the right to both be upset and expect some sort of compensation from the team.

One thing we really do not know is the number of people who unwittingly wear counterfeit jerseys, thinking they are licensed. Certainly, people receive counterfeit jerseys as gifts. Certainly, others have unknowingly purchased counterfeit jerseys on eBay or in the parking lot of a stadium. Maybe they know the items are counterfeit, maybe they do not. The point remains that there are at least some fans out there who do not know that their jerseys are counterfeit. It would be off-putting to be asked to leave an athletic event when you genuinely believe that the jersey you are wearing is licensed.

CONCLUSIONS

Although counterfeit jerseys have not been around for that long, they have certainly made their presence known. They are affordable, widely available, and, in many cases, close approximations of the jerseys that they are copying. It makes perfect sense that sports fans purchase counterfeit jerseys because they are around 90 percent cheaper than the licensed authentic versions sold by teams. Because so many teams have so many third and commemorative jerseys, counterfeit jerseys can be used to help build a jersey collection in a short period of time and help display a person's high degree of fandom to others.

Most of the studies that look at counterfeiting explore supply-side strategies like increased law enforcement to help limit its scope. Over time, however, law enforcement measures have proven to be very expensive and generally ineffective. Although many jersey manufacturers have tried to foil the efforts of counterfeiters, this appears to be a cat-and-mouse game that the counterfeiters are clearly winning. Although this selection outlines some drastic measures to curb counterfeiting, the reality is that it will continue as long as the consumer demand for cheap jerseys remains high.

REFERENCES

Amendolara, L. D. (2005). "Knocking out knock-offs: Effectuating the criminalization of trafficking in counterfeit goods." *Fordham Intellectual Property, Media and Entertainment Law Journal* 15, 788–836.

Bian, X., and C. Veloutsou. (2011). "Consumers' attitudes regarding non-deceptive counterfeit brands in the UK and China." *Brand Management* 14, 211–222.

Carter, D. (2011). *Money Games: Profiting from the Convergence of Sports and Entertainment*. Palo Alto, CA: Stanford University Press.

Cheng San, A. N. (2012). "Behavioral loyalty and attitudinal loyalty: Malaysian's intention on counterfeit clothing and footwear." *Journal of Public Administration and Governance* 2, 106–122.

Coakley, J. (2009). *Sports in Society: Issues and Controversies*, 10th edition. New York: McGraw-Hill.

d'Astous, A., and A. Legendre. (2009). "Understanding consumers' ethical justifications: A scale for appraising consumers' reasons for not behaving ethically." *Journal of Business Ethics* 87, 255–268.

Eckhardt, G. M., R. Belk, and T. M. Devinney. (2010) "Why don't consumers consume ethically?" *Journal of Consumer Behaviour* 9, 426–436.

Fried, G., T. DeSchriver, and M. Mondello. (2013). *Sport Finance*, 3rd edition. Champaign, IL: Human Kinetics.

Globerman, S. (1988). "Addressing international product piracy." *Journal of International Business Studies* 19, 497–504.

Green, R. T., and T. Smith. (2002). "Countering brand counterfeiters." *Journal of International Marketing* 10, 89–106.

Henderson, W. F. (2012). *Game-Worn MLB Jersey Guide: 1970–2012*. Unpublished manuscript.

Higgins, R. S., and P. H. Rubin. (1986). "Counterfeit goods." *Journal of Law and Economics* 29, 211–230.

Hilton, B., C. J. Choi, and S. Chen. (2004). "The ethics of counterfeiting in the fashion industry: Quality, credence and profit." *Journal of Business Ethics* 55, 345–354.

Mason, R. (2000). "Conspicuous consumption and the positional economy: Policy and prescription since 1970." *Managerial and Decision Economics* 21, 123–132.

Norum, P. S., and A. Cuno. (2011). "Analysis of the demand for counterfeit goods." *Journal of Fashion Marketing and Management* 15, 27–40.

Penz, E., and B. Stottinger. (2005). "Forget the 'real' thing—take the copy! An explanatory model for the volitional purchase of counterfeit products." *Advances in Consumer Research* 32, 568–575.

Phillips, T. (2006). *Knockoff: The Deadly Trade in Counterfeit Goods.* Philadelphia: Kogan Page Limited.

Qian, Y. (2008). "Impacts of entry by counterfeiters." *Quarterly Journal of Economics* 4, 1577–1609.

Strizhakova, Y., R. A. Coulter, and L. L. Price. (2008). "Branded products as a passport to global citizenship: Perspectives from developed and developing countries." *Journal of International Marketing* 16, 57–85.

Tom, G., B. Garibaldi, Y. Zeng, and J. Pilcher. (2000). "Consumer demand for counterfeit goods." *Psychology & Marketing* 15, 405–421.

Zimmerman, A. (2013). "Contending with Chinese counterfeits: Culture, growth, and management responses." *Business Horizons* 56, 141–148.

CHAPTER TWENTY THREE

Conclusion

A Sociological Look at the Current State of Sports in the United States

BY **BRANDON LANG**

As mentioned in the early pages of this book, I am a huge sports fan. I grew up playing sports. I love attending sporting events at all levels. My two favorite teams are the Toronto Maple Leafs and the Toronto Blue Jays. Like many fans, I watch most of the games, attend games when I can, and faithfully buy team merchandise. Sports for me is a year-round endeavor. Baseball season begins when the hockey season ends, and the hockey season begins during the early stages of the baseball playoffs. I play hockey year round and coach my two sons' sports teams.

There is no question that sports have enhanced the quality of my life. They have brought me closer to my kids, provided me with countless hours of joy and excitement, and even helped to keep me fit. The problem is that I, like many others, am growing disillusioned with many aspects of sports. Going to professional games is outrageously expensive, youth sports have changed due to a growing number of overbearing and hypercompetitive parents, and watching games on television often feels more like watching an infomercial compared to an actual game. In this final chapter, two views concerning the current state of sports are out-lined. The optimistic view suggests that the benefits of sports outweigh the problems, whereas the pessimistic view suggests that the concerns many people share outweigh the benefits.

THE OPTIMISTIC VIEW

Clearly, sports have numerous positive qualities. Millions of Americans cherish their weekly tennis game, bowling night, or recreational basketball game. Simply put, for millions of people, playing sports is a fun way to get exercise, socialize with others, and unwind. Similarly, watching sports is just as enjoyable and relaxing for people who enjoy interacting with others and cheering for a given team. Many fans enjoy the drama of sports and the feeling that comes with cheering for a successful team.

Today's athletes are bigger, faster, and stronger than ever before. Athletes in all of the major sports are so superior to their predecessors that it makes watching games that much more enjoyable. Part and parcel of this is record breaking. It is very exciting for fans to see records set in sports like swimming, track, and baseball. A related issue is that many of today's sporting events take place in state-of-the-art stadia. Consider how nice AT&T Stadium is, where the Dallas Cowboys play. Like scores of other newly built stadia, it has more bathrooms, wider concourses, better sightlines, a number of restaurants and bars, a world-class art collection, and more comfortable seats than Texas Stadium ever had. For the most part, newly constructed stadia have perfect sod and well-maintained facilities and offer state-of-the-art in-game entertainment features.

THE PESSIMISTIC VIEW

Unfortunately, there is an increasing number of negative qualities in sports. Consider the elevated pressure placed on youth athletes, for example. Seasons are longer, training is more comprehensive, the travel is more extensive—and the stakes are higher. Many youth athletes are demeaned by intense coaches and parents and arrive at the point where they no longer enjoy the sport that they play. Simply put, the high expectations and pressure placed upon them are often too much for many of them to handle.

Many people are less interested in sports because of the increased expenses associated with playing and watching them. As documented earlier, the costs of playing sports are often very expensive. Equipment, jerseys, travel, and fees are prohibitively expensive for a growing number of people. Watching sports is also more expensive than ever. Tickets, concessions, and parking also add to this cost. Watching televised games is even more expensive than ever. Very few games are aired on regular broadcast channels, meaning that people must have cable in order to watch them. In many cases, people even need a fairly high tier of cable in order to watch all of the games.

Unquestionably, teams at all levels feel such pressure to win that more corruption and cheating seem inevitable. In this day and age of "Deflategate," it's quite apparent that both amateur and professional teams bend—and sometimes break—the rules in order to win. So many of the athletes we revere have used performance-enhancing drugs for one reason or another. Dozens of athletes, including Lance Armstrong, Alex Rodriguez, and Ryan Braun, have used steroids to gain an edge. What kind of message does that send to fans? What about the message this sends to kids? It is unfortunate that we have come to the point where cheating is so rampant that players who have no interest in PEDs or other forms of cheating have had to engage in such in order to stay competitive.

Another concern relates to the rash of injuries in sports. Yes, as fans, we cheer for bigger and faster players. The problem is that more and more players are negatively impacted by concussions and other very serious injuries. Although efforts are made to give athletes baseline tests and to sit injured players, the likelihood of a player getting injured in a contact sport like football appears to be higher than ever. This is especially nerve-wracking for the parents of athletes whose children play contact sports.

CONCLUSIONS

As is the case for millions of others, sports are a very big part of my identity. I regularly attend sporting events, closely follow my favorite teams, and I play hockey once or twice a week. There is no question that I will always be a sports fan. I may not go to as many games as I once did or sit in the same quality of seats, but I will continue to support my favorite teams. Nothing could ever replace for me the feeling of going to a live game. Although I am more disillusioned now than ever before about the state of sports, I am by no means cynical. I have long accepted that sports teams are businesses and that they are oriented toward making people money. We are now at a point that for leagues, team owners, and even players, money often trumps civic pride and loyalty. I may not like that, but I have accepted it. This is the future of sports in America.

About the Editor

Brandon Lang is an associate professor of sociology at Bloomsburg University of Pennsylvania, where he teaches a variety of sociology classes relating to such topics as sports, community, music, environment, medicine, and social problems. Lang's current research examines the challenges faced by physician residents during their training. His recent research looked at issues relating to counterfeit sports jerseys and public perceptions of Native American team names. He obtained his BA from Trent University in Peterborough, Ontario, Canada, in 1994, his MA from Goddard College in Plainfield, Vermont, in 1996, and his PhD in sociology from North Carolina State University in Raleigh in 2002. His wife, Molly, is an assistant teaching professor at Penn State Erie: The Behrend College. They met in graduate school in North Carolina. Together, they have three young children. Adam is 14, Sarah is 12, and Nathan is 9.

CPSIA information can be obtained
at www.ICGtesting.com
Printed in the USA
BVHW011810290822
645772BV00010B/445